PREVENTION MAGAZINE

HANDS-ON
HEALING

PREVENTION MAGAZINE'S
HANDS-ON HEALING

MASSAGE REMEDIES FOR HUNDREDS OF HEALTH PROBLEMS

By the editors of
Prevention® Magazine Health Books

Edited by John Feltman

WINGS BOOKS
New York • Avenel, New Jersey

Copyright © 1989 by Rodale Press, Inc.

The illustration "The Ear" on page 246 is from the book *Body Reflexology* by Mildred Carter © 1983, reprinted by permission of the publisher, Parker Publishing Company, West Nyack, New York.

This 1995 edition is published by Wings Books,
distributed by Random House Value Publishing, Inc.,
40 Engelhard Avenue, Avenel, New Jersey 07001,
by arrangement with Rodale Press, Inc.

Random House
New York • Toronto • London • Sydney • Auckland

Printed and bound in the United States of America

Library of Congress Cataloging-in-Publication Data

Prevention magazine's hands-on healing : massage remedies for hundreds of health problems /
    by the editors of Prevention Magazine Health Books ; edited by John Feltman.
       p.   cm.
    Originally published : Emmaus, Pa. : Rodale Press, 1989.
    Includes index.
    ISBN 0-517-12244-8
    1. Massage–Therapeutic use. I. Feltman, John. II. Prevention
    Magazine Health Books.
  RM721.H18 1995
  615.8'22–dc20
                                         94-31387
                                           CIP

8 7 6 5 4 3 2 1

Editor
John Feltman

Writing Contributions
Don Barone

    Alexander Technique

    Aston-Patterning

    Hellerwork

    Oriental Massage

    Physical Therapy

    Sports Massage

    Tapes That Teach

Martha Capwell

    Physiatry

Deborah Grandinetti

    Aromatherapy

Marcia Holman

    Emergency First-Aid Techniques

Lance Jacobs

    Back Pain

    Craniosacral Therapy

    Foot Pain

    Headache and Jaw Pain

    Leg Pain

    Lomilomi

    Myotherapy

    Neck Pain

    Reichian Therapy

    Rolfing

    Shoulder Pain

William LeGro

    Deep Muscle Therapy

    Dō-In

    Friction Rubs

    Higher Dimensions of Healing

    Mensendieck System

    Osteopathy

    Reflexology

    Therapeutic Touch

Alexis Lieberman

    Naprapathy

Judith Lin

    Applied Kinesiology

    Body Wraps

    Facial Massage

    Massage Oils

    The Massage Setting

    Polarity Therapy

    The Spa Experience

    Swedish Massage

    Trager Approach

Michael McGrath

    Pet Massage

Connie Nesteruk

    Infant Massage

Russell Wild

   Acupressure

   Born to Be Touched

   Chiropractic

   Esalen Massage

   Feldenkrais Method

   Hydrotherapy

   Massage Tools

   Psychic Surgery

   The Sense That Sets Us Right

Book Design
Linda Jacopetti

Illustrator
Stewart Jackson

Research Chief
Ann Gossy

Research Editor
Holly Clemson

Research Associates
Christine Dreisbach, Karen Feridun,
   Staci Hadeed, Dawn Horvath,
   Christine Kraft, Karen Lombardi

Editorial/Production Coordinator
Jane Sherman

Copy Editor
Mary Green

Office Personnel
Roberta Mulliner, Stacy Miller,
   Kelly Trumbauer

**Managing Editor, Prevention Magazine
   Health Books**
Debora Tkac

**Vice President and Editor in Chief,
   Prevention Magazine Health
   Books**
William Gottlieb

Group Vice President, Health
Mark Bricklin

CONTENTS

Part I

THE PRIMAL POWER OF TOUCH

Chapter 1

THE SENSE THAT SETS US RIGHT

All across the nation people are being rubbed the right way. They're being massaged in Muskegon, palmed in Peoria and Rolfed in Rochester. Chiropractors are adjusting their spines, reflexologists are pressing their toes and myotherapists are manipulating their "trigger points."

In the pages that follow, you'll be taking a fascinating, and hopefully rewarding, journey into this world of hands-on healing. You'll learn about restorative and therapeutic techniques developed in China, India, Scandinavia, Japan and right here at home. You'll experience ancient practices that predate civilization. And you'll visit an ultramodern university "touch" laboratory. Along the way, you will meet physicians who consider their hands-on approach a step ahead of the conventional wisdom, and you will meet "Pedro," a self-styled "psychic surgeon" who operates a step ahead of the law.

Many are choosing the hands-on path to deeper relaxation, greater self-awareness and more robust health. Here you will be introduced to a wide sampling of physically stimulating arts, such as Swedish massage, polarity, Tragering and deep muscle therapy. Some of these you may find tantalizing, some not. Some you may think are brilliant, others a bit out of touch.

Which brings us to the point at hand and the all-important common denominator among all these healing alternatives: touch.

It generally feels good to have another human being's skin come into contact with our own. Touching can reassure us, relax us, comfort us or arouse us like nothing else. In a way, the importance of touch is so basic that we tend to take it for granted, just as we do breathing. Or, if we're really forced to think about touch, we may blather something like "it generally feels good. . . ."

But there's much, *much* more to touch than that it generally feels good. We humans *need* to touch and be touched, "just like we need food and water," says Saul Schanberg, M.D., Ph.D., a professor of pharmacology and biological psychiatry at Duke Univer-

2

sity who is currently engaged in some pretty touchy research. His studies, along with those of other prominent researchers, are shedding light on just how powerful and absolutely *primal* touch is.

Touch, the Forgotten Sense

"Think about touch," says Dr. Schanberg. "Often we regard it as an amorphous, nonspecific kind of thing. But it isn't. I can make you roll over with laughter with touch or I can put you to sleep with touch."

In many ways, the other senses come up short when compared to the power of touch, says Dr. Schanberg. "Touch is essentially more varied than are our visual or auditory senses," he says. "Think about how hard it is to make yourself relax using just your eyes or your ears. Yes, you can play your favorite music. Or you can gaze at a relaxing scene. But have someone who's really good give you a massage and in 20 minutes you'll be so relaxed you'll have a hard time getting up off that table."

As for the agony and ecstasy of life, here again, says Dr. Schanberg, touch is the champion of the senses. "In terms of sexual arousal, whatever you might see won't compare to ten seconds of the right touch," he says. "And as for pain, no matter how much you think a shrill sound or shocking image could make you grimace—forget it. There's nothing that'll compare to one stiff jab.

"So is touch important to us? Absolutely. Is it appreciated? Not nearly enough."

For one thing, you need to recognize that your skin, aside from being your gateway to touch and a great place to hang your clothes, is also one of your largest organs. In a grown man, it covers about 19 square feet and weighs about 8 pounds.

And there's much more to skin than meets the eye, or even the hand. "A piece of skin the size of a quarter contains more than 3 million cells, 100 to 340 sweat glands, 50 nerve endings and 3 feet of blood vessels," writes anthropologist Ashley Montagu in *Touching: The Human Significance of the Skin.*

But it's not the physical properties of the epidermis that have modern researchers excited. Their studies are beginning to reveal what has been intuitively sensed for centuries: that the connection between touch and well-being is *far* more than skin deep.

Touchstone Research

Serious research on the importance of touch began only about 30 years ago. But since that time, scientists have shown that the amount of body contact in our lives plays a vital role in our mental and physical development as infants and in our happiness and vigor as adults. Touch influences our ability to deal with stress and pain, to form close relationships with other people ("bonding"), and even to fight off disease.

Touch among the Animals

Birds do it. Bees do it. Even apes in trees do it . . . touch, that is. Especially the apes in trees. In fact, in addition to live births, giving milk and having hair on their bodies, the need for touch is the one thing that all mammals—humans included—seem to share.

There may not be any connection between the hair on our bodies and the need for touch, but giving milk to live newborns? That's another story. "Mammalian systems are designed so that the infant caregiving process involves an enormous amount of contact," says Seymour Levine, Ph.D., a professor of psychology at Stanford University Medical School.

Among our closest relatives, the primates, contact between mother and baby is constant, he points out. "The infant chimpanzee for almost four months never gets off the mother." But for *all* mammals, he says, "touch is clearly important developmentally."

When that thesis was put to the test on both human infants and baby rats, the results were unequivocal. (See chapter 2.) As a result of such studies linking touch to growth, the Australian Department of Agriculture began a program to knead the backs of baby pigs. And no surprise: The Australians reported that the massaged piggies grew faster, 30 percent faster.

Touch loses some of its importance as mammals grow older. But it still quite obviously remains important, and not only to humans. Consider the other mammals that we humans come into contact with most often.

What dog owner cannot say that Fido doesn't revel in having his neck or chin scratched? How many cat owners have never had an arching, purring feline rub against their pajama legs? Is there any doubt that Silver enjoyed having his nose stroked by the Lone Ranger? And what dairy farmer will tell you that cows don't like to be milked?

Even the largest of all mammals seem to enjoy touch. Despite every good reason to fear humans, whales such as the humpbacks (which grow to 62 feet and weigh up to 53 tons) have been known to pop their prodigious heads out of the sea and allow themselves to be petted and scratched, sometimes for hours. Participants in popular whale-watches off the Massachusetts coast have described our sizable floating cousins as positively cuddly.

Here's a sampling from the scientific research:

- Various studies have shown that when a person's wrist is gently held by someone else, heartbeat slows and blood pressure declines.

- Children and adolescents hospitalized for psychiatric problems show remarkable reductions in anxiety levels and positive changes in attitude when they receive a brief daily back rub.
- The arteries of rabbits fed a high-cholesterol diet and petted regularly had 60 percent less blockage than did the arteries of unpetted but similarly fed rabbits.
- Rats that were handled for 15 minutes a day during the first three weeks of their lives showed dramatically less brain cell deterioration and memory loss as they grew old, compared with nonhandled rats.

Despite all these great reasons to *really* reach out and touch someone (not just by telephone), we Americans find it difficult, and we don't do it often. Aside from a brisk handshake or an occasional embrace at the airport gate, touching just isn't a big part of our culture.

A Touch-Starved Culture?

There's a touch of difference between our predominantly Anglo-Saxon culture and some other cultures of the world, to say the least. One study in the 1960s showed this stark contrast by noting the number of touches exchanged by pairs of people sitting in coffee shops around the world: In San Juan, Puerto Rico, people touched 180 times an hour; in Paris, France, 110 times an hour; in Gainesville, Florida, 2 times an hour; and in London, England, they never touched.

What explains these differences? Tiffany Field, Ph.D., a psychologist at the University of Miami, thinks our physical distancing partially reflects our psychological needs for autonomy and independence.

A society's touch habits reflect the way people relate on other levels, explains William E. Whitehead, Ph.D., an associate professor of medical psychology at the Johns Hopkins University School of Medicine. Americans, he says, tend to be a touch "cooler" than, say, the cheek-kissing Italians or Spaniards.

Dr. Whitehead also thinks part of the blame for our society's taboo on touch lies with the chin-scratching father of modern-day psychology, Sigmund Freud. "Freud encouraged austerity in dealing with children. And parents, in an effort to be *good* parents, bought into that behavior," says Dr. Whitehead. People who aren't cuddled a lot as kids, he adds, tend to develop into nontouching adults. The cycle then repeats itself, generation after generation.

But Dr. Whitehead, Dr. Field and others say that things are changing. Americans, particularly as they become more aware of the potential benefits of touch, are starting to do something about it. This change is especially tangible in the healing arts.

Chapter 2

BORN TO
BE TOUCHED

The need for touch, as important as it is throughout our lives, is never more crucial than immediately following and shortly after exit from the womb. Because vision and hearing take time to fully develop, touch becomes "possibly the most critical of all the senses to the newborn," says Duke University's Dr. Saul Schanberg.

There's no question that babies deprived of motherly affection don't fare too well—emotionally or physically. Years of experience with infants raised in public institutions have shown this to be true. Earlier in the century, infants forced to live in such sterile environments often wasted away and died.

Back then, no one could provide any good explanations. Today, scientists like Dr. Schanberg and Dr. Tiffany Field, of the University of Miami, offer fresh insight. Their studies on both human and animal babies have produced convincing evidence that the brain—by releasing or withholding certain chemicals—regulates the physical and emotional development of the infant. And the brain's actions, in turn, are controlled by—you guessed it—touch.

Consider the dramatic results of a study conducted by Dr. Field and Dr. Schanberg involving 40 premature infants. Half of the tiny babies, selected at random, were gently stroked for 45 minutes a day. The other 20 were not. Although all were fed the same amount of calories, after ten days, the touched babies weighed in 47 percent heavier than the unstimulated group.

Not only were those babies bigger, they were happier as well, says Dr. Field. "The stroked kids," she says, "were more active, more alert and more responsive to social stimulation." A miracle? Dr. Field doesn't think so. As astonishing as the effects of stroking seem to be, she says, they also make a lot of sense.

Recent animal studies, in fact, suggest a very plausible scientific explanation for such "miraculous" growth.

The Hormonal Link

In the rat world, the equivalent of maternal stroking, hugging and tickling is licking. But because it's difficult to teach a mother rat to lick or not lick on command, setting up a well-controlled laboratory study proved to be a bit of a problem, says Dr. Schanberg. It took about two years before he and his colleagues discovered that a wet paintbrush makes a fairly good tongue substitute.

Soon white-coated Picassos, brushes in hand, were fooling newborn rats into thinking their mothers were mighty fickle caregivers. As the animals were made to believe that their mothers' affections were being turned on and off, it soon became clear that something else was being turned on and off at the same time: the brain's release of *beta-endorphin*, a chemical that appears to affect many aspects of growth and development.

When an infant rat senses that its mother is absent, it reacts the way you might if you were stuck at sea in a small lifeboat, says Dr. Schanberg. "First it cries, then it immediately quiets down." In a lifeboat, you'd probably do everything to conserve your food and water. And the helpless baby whose mom has disappeared shifts all its energy to support its life functions —neglecting those cellular functions that can make it grow up big and strong. Doing these things, after all, can well wait until Mommy gets home.

Are the same kinds of physical reactions going on in human infants deprived of touch? Dr. Schanberg and Dr. Field are convinced that the processes are very similar.

As a result of these and other recent studies on the extreme importance of touch to newborns, the field of pediatrics will probably never be the same. "There was about a 30-year period where the advice was to keep the baby away from the mother for the first week. But in the last 6 or 7 years there has been a complete turnaround in pediatric practice," says Stephen J. Suomi, Ph.D., of the National Institute of Child Health and Human Development. "Now major efforts are being made to keep babies with their mothers right from the beginning."

"Hug Therapy" for Adults

In other areas of health care, as well, there has been a resurgence of touch. Dr. Kildare and Ben Casey sometimes got personal with their patients on TV, but could you imagine either one prescribing "hug therapy" back in the early 1960s? Today, a small but growing number of psychologists and M.D.'s are handing out verbal prescriptions that "read" something like this: "Rx—for maintenance of your spirit, exchange four to six hugs daily."

Similarly, some doctors are scribbling out advice that reads something like this: "Rx—for indigestion, insomnia or the blues: one fluffy puppy—to be snuggled at meals, at bedtime or when just home from a tough day at the office." Animals are perfectly fine sources of tactile comfort, says Alan M. Beck, Sc.D., director of the Center for the Interaction of Animals and Society at the University of Pennsylvania. Numerous studies, he adds, "definitely show that petting an animal can lower one's blood pressure." The prescription, he adds, needn't read "fluffy puppy" either. For some, "an iguana or a duck can be just as effective." Other doctors suggest that there are health benefits to be had even from cuddling inanimate objects—teddy bears, for instance.

Dr. Suomi sees the pro-touch movement as somewhat akin to the eat-more-fiber movement—a return to the norms and values of preindustrialized society. "Look at primitive cultures—they're all very touch-oriented," he says. "If you want to go back further and look at the higher primates (the closest biological relatives to humans), in every single species contact plays a very powerful role."

In modern times, it may be argued, health care strayed far from those primal roots. For while it might seem powerfully logical to incorporate touch as part of the healing process, you've possibly come away from more than one physician's office having been touched by nothing but a ghastly cold stethoscope. But rest assured, times are changing.

Medicine is changing, as doctors become more aware of the power of touch and as more patients turn to the hands-on skills of osteopathic physicians and physiatrists for a multitude of problems. And the field of alternatives to drug- and scalpel-based medical care is rapidly growing: Witness chiropractic and physical therapy, for instance. As the role of stress in promoting disease becomes better understood, various massage and bodywork therapies are also gaining greater respect. Meanwhile, ancient healing arts such as acupressure are enjoying surprising popularity in this age of computers.

Your ticket to discovery through touch lies in the following pages. Enjoy the journey.

Part II

A DIRECTORY OF HANDS-ON THERAPIES

Chapter 3

ACUPRESSURE

Open your mouth wide and peek into the mirror. You won't see any traffic lights, stop signs or speed posts. Nevertheless, acupressurists say, they're there, because the human body is a network of highways and byways called *meridians*. These meridians weave through every one of the body's vital organs, through the bloodstream, through the bones and through the muscles. Along these roads travel not cars and trucks but *chi*, the body's vital force.

You can't see, smell or hear chi, and modern scientists have found no proof that it exists. But according to the teachings of ancient Chinese medicine, chi is something you can touch. That's what acupressurists do. With the touch of their fingers, they say they can influence the flow of chi and, most important, break up the occasional traffic jams that can rob you of vitality and good health.

Unlike brain surgeons or cardiologists, acupressurists say theirs is a simple art, one you can easily learn to do yourself and *to* yourself. The only thing you need to learn—and the thing you will learn in the following pages—is where on your body to find chi.

To become a competent self-acupressurist, you won't have to memorize every twist and turn of each one of your body's many meridians—that would get too complicated. You'll only need to learn how to find a few points along your highway system of meridians. These are the entrance and exit ramps for chi. You can find them just below the skin. They are the *tsubos*, or acupressure points.

Skeptic with a Sore Throat

Elizabeth Diaz, 51, of El Segundo, California, was suffering from a sore throat, pain in both ears and a generally achy body when she first experienced acupressure. "I was very skeptical," she says. "Why in the world would just pressing a couple of points do anything for me?" Fifteen minutes later, all her pain was gone.

A 40-year-old Pennsylvania woman suffered an acute gallbladder

A Glossary of Acupressure Terms

Many of the terms used when discussing acupressure may be unfamiliar. Here is a brief explanation of some of the more common ones.

Acupressure. An ancient healing art in which finger pressure is applied to specific sensitive points on the body.

Acupuncture. This technique involves the insertion of small needles under the skin to activate the flow of chi. Effective particularly as an anesthetic, acupuncture is not nearly as painful as it looks.

Chi. According to traditional oriental medicine, this is the body's vital life force. Also known as *ki* in Japan and *prana* in India.

Meridians. These are the 14 pathways in the body through which chi is believed to flow. Each meridian passes through many parts of the body.

Moxibustion. Like acupressure and acupuncture, the aim here is directed to the tsubos. Rather than using fingers or needles, the practitioner uses a small dollop of herb, which is ignited and generally allowed to burn down to the skin.

Shiatsu. Developed in Japan, this is a stylized method for manipulating the tsubos, either through pressing with the fingers and hands, or through the use of elbows, knees and feet. There are various forms of shiatsu.

Tsubos. Points along the meridians where the energy flow may become blocked. Also known as acupressure or acupuncture points. Manipulating the body's approximately 360 tsubos is thought to release the flow of chi.

attack in the middle of the night. Having read something about acupressure, she had her husband press the appropriate point. "It was like a miracle. The pain was totally relieved!" she exclaims.

A Philadelphia woman suffered a foot injury while out walking her dog. Shortly thereafter, she started receiving acupressure treatments to alleviate the pain. Not only did the pain in her foot go away, but "I generally feel a whole lot healthier," she says.

And Patrick J. LaRiccia, M.D., a physician at Presbyterian/University of Pennsylvania Medical Center, says he goes once a week to have his points pressed. "I think we will discover a scientific explanation in the future that will validate much of the ancient teachings," he says. In the meantime, he says the treatments relax him and give him "a feeling of balance." He also makes regular referrals of patients suffering from problems like bum backs and stiff necks.

Nobody's Kid Brother

"Acu*pressure?*" you're undoubtedly asking yourself at this point. "Is that anything like acu*puncture?*"

You bet it is. Acupressure points are the same as acupuncture points. The two practices share the same principles, the same theory of chi and meridians and the same roots in ancient Chinese medicine. What's the difference? With one you press; with the other you stick needles under the skin. Aside from that, the main difference is that acupuncture typically receives a lot more attention.

In some ways, acupressure has been relegated to the role of acupuncture's kid brother, says Michael Reed Gach, author of several books on acupressure and founder of the Acupressure Institute in Berkeley, California. In reality, he says, "the Chinese used their hands long before they had needles."

It took a while before acupuncture began to be considered by physicians in this country as anything other than oriental voodoo. Today, although only theories exist as to how it works, M.D.'s from such prestigious places as Stanford, UCLA and the Mayo Clinic are using acupuncture needles to relieve pain and treat a variety of conditions.

But its "kid brother," acupressure,

"is as effective and sometimes more effective than acupuncture" for many of those conditions, says Gach. He emphasizes, however, that individual circumstances will ultimately determine when it's best to apply hands and when it's best to insert needles.

Acupuncture, for instance, is often best for relieving chronic or severe pain, says Gach. "I wouldn't rely on acupressure during surgery," he says, alluding to the use of acupuncture anesthesia by some surgeons in China. For treating diseases of the internal organs, Gach also says acupuncture is usually better than acupressure.

But where there are tension and stress, aches and pains, menstrual cramps, arthritis or asthma, then acupressure is the treatment of choice, according to Gach. The same goes for general preventive health care, fighting colds, improving muscle tone or boosting your energy level. "Acupressure," says Gach, "has the big advantage of using the power and sensitivity of the human hand."

Acupressure is also more aesthetically pleasing than acupuncture. "Give most people a choice between cold needles or warm hands, and guess which one they'll pick," he says. It is also much easier to do to yourself and makes more sense for the elderly and the very young, for whom acupuncture may be too traumatic.

David J. Nickel, a certified acupuncturist and doctor of oriental medicine, uses both acupuncture and acupressure in his Santa Monica, California, practice. He says acupressure is most helpful for back and neck pain and tension, sports injuries, gynecological problems, jet-lag, moodiness, poor appetite, sluggishness and hyperactivity.

Marshall Ho'o, a doctor of oriental medicine at the East–West Clinic in Reseda, California, says he's been practicing acupressure for many of his 78 years. He says sexual problems, such as impotency and frigidity, are amenable to treatment, as are headaches, backaches and tummyaches. And, because there is "a transfer of chi" when one person does acupressure on another, Dr. Ho'o says it's a great tool for relationship building. "Acupressure is a form of communication," he says.

A Matter of Style

Just as Mozart and Liberace both produced music by pressing keys on a piano—but in very different ways—so can the body's acupressure points be manipulated in very different ways.

Dr. Nickel, for example, relishes the simplicity of acupressure and has adapted for himself the simplest of styles. The systemic plotting of the acupressure points came from trial-and-error investigations dating back 5,000 years, he says, but that doesn't mean you can't play around with it. "Let's say you feel uncomfortable but you're not sure where to press. Just start feeling around. Where it's sore, press. If that doesn't work, try somewhere else." (Acupressurists believe that soreness surrounding a point indi-

Measuring the Invisible

Modern scientists aren't certain just how much power is locked into the ancient Chinese system of points and meridians, but many agree that the points—although you can't see them—do exist.

"You can measure acupressure points with sophisticated equipment. There's no question about it," says Daniel Kirsch, Ph.D., dean of the Graduate School of Electromedical Science at City University, Los Angeles and editor of the *American Journal of Electromedicine*. He says the ancient acupressure points are "points of high conductivity," or points where the skin provides the least resistance to electrical inputs. A firm believer in the effectiveness of acupressure as a means of pain relief and more, Dr. Kirsch says the points are "windows into the body."

The ancient Chinese drew lines through these points to form what they called meridians. Whether the meridians are real or imaginary is a subject of debate among modern scientists. But at least one doctor, Robert O. Becker, M.D., makes the claim in his book *The Body Electric* that his sensitive instruments have picked up a flow of electrical current along the ancient meridians.

cates a blockage of chi. Stimulation of the point releases the chi, so the soreness will go away.)

Charts showing the acupressure points are good guides, says Dr. Nickel, but he also emphasizes your own intuition and experimentation. As for how to press a particular point, "you can use your thumb, index finger, any finger. And you can use the fingertip or knuckle; it doesn't much matter. Press till it starts to hurt," he says, generally for five seconds, then rest five seconds. Continue alternating in this manner for a total of about one minute per point. Keep your finger on the point at all times.

Michael Reed Gach suggests pressing a point until you feel "a balance between pleasure and pain." Some people require more pressure than others; those with well-developed muscles generally need the most. Gach says certain points should be pressed for one to two minutes continuously, while your eyes are closed and you breathe deeply into your abdomen.

Various practitioners may differ on how hard and how long to press the points. Whether the pressure need come from a finger at all is also debatable. Gach, for instance, has devised a system called *acu-yoga*, which uses yogic postures to press the acupressure points against the floor.

Shiatsu and Beyond

Many acupressure practitioners in this country subscribe to one form or another of *shiatsu*, the Japanese method of stimulating the flow of chi.

Usually, the points are held for three to ten seconds. The shiatsu practitioner may use a combination of fingers (most often thumbs), elbows, knees or even feet to press the points, usually in a rhythmic pattern. Often there's also some stroking and twisting of the body, somewhat similar to what a massage therapist might do.

One of the best-known shiatsu practitioners in the United States is Wataru Ohashi. He has written several books on shiatsu, operates New York City's Ohashi Institute and is founder of his own particular brand of shiatsu, called *Ohashiatsu*. "I can't be so arrogant as to say I can represent all shiatsu," says Ohashi, "but I can talk about what we do in this school."

Ohashi explains that the hands-on aspect of shiatsu is an integral part of maintaining health, along with meditation, diet and exercise. He says the specific points on the body are really secondary to the meridians, which are best manipulated with the use of two hands. Ohashi says he has used his method to deal with any number of conditions, including insomnia, digestive problems and lower back pain, but he prefers to think of shiatsu's strength as lying in disease prevention, rather than treatment.

Instead of using fingers, hands, elbows or needles, other practitioners prefer to stimulate the points by burning herbs. This is called *moxibustion*. (See the box "Moxibustion—Igniting the Healing Process" on page 15.) A modern method for stimulating the points uses electrical current.

"Some people believe in different forms of pressure. Some people say, 'I'll add heat.' But basically it's all the same," says Dr. Ho'o. He maintains that stimulating the right points is all-important, and precisely how they're stimulated varies from school to school.

Getting Your Points Pressed

Lying on a thin mattress, staring up at the ceiling, awaiting your first shiatsu treatment, you're not sure what to expect. You've heard it may be painful at times and profoundly relaxing at times. Since the usage goes back thousands of years and millions in the Far East swear by it, you figure it probably can't do any harm and may do some good.

Carol Matthews, a Pennsylvania practitioner, asks how you feel. "A little tense today," you say. For the next hour, she presses you at different points along your body, firmly in some places, softly in others. She rubs some spots vigorously. She ripples her hands down both sides of your spine. She bends your arms and legs and jiggles them around a bit. Sure enough, some things she does are slightly painful, but other things are profoundly relaxing.

By the time your session is over, you feel peaceful and a bit dreamy, not unlike how you might feel waking up extremely late on a Sunday morning.

Moxibustion—Igniting the Healing Process

Most Americans have heard of acupuncture, and many have heard of acupressure, but few have heard of the related practice of moxibustion. Yet according to Marshall Ho'o, a doctor of oriental medicine, moxibustion in China is no less important than the other two.

So what is it? Moxibustion involves the burning of an herb on or near the ancient Chinese tsubos, or acupressure points, to activate the flow of chi, the body's energy flow. The herb is typically pinched into a little cone (which is called a *moxa* and is about the size of a rice grain) and ignited right on the skin. Traditionally, this is repeated three times over the same point. For the fainthearted, a thin slice of gingerroot, garlic or onion may be placed between the skin and the burning herb. This allows for heat to pass through without marking the skin or making you wince.

Moxibustion, according to Laila Wah, director of Philadelphia's Gautama Institute for the Oriental Healing Arts, "warms the body, builds chi and builds red and white blood cells."

The best moxa, says Dr. Ho'o, comes from the hills of China. It is the herb *Artemisia vulgaris*, or mugwort. He speculates that moxibustion might be more popular in this country, were it not for the smoldering herb's pungent odor.

THE HEALING POWER OF ACUPRESSURE

Ask an acupressurist about the importance of points and meridians and he may compare it to the importance of the heart and the blood vessels. For just as we need the flow of blood through our bodies, so too, according to ancient Chinese thought, do we require the smooth flow of chi. "If there's an imbalance in our energy flow, this can cause disturbances in our bodies. If unattended, these become sicknesses," says Wataru Ohashi.

Katsusuke Serizawa, M.D., a Japanese expert on oriental healing, draws a distinction between what is best handled by treatment of your points and meridians and what is best handled by your family physician or local hospital. Oriental medicine, he says in his book *Tsubo*, "is powerless" to cure victims of such illnesses as cancer, typhus, dysentery and all sicknesses "clearly caused by bacteria, like acute high fevers and contagious diseases."

But the acupressure or acupuncture approach, says Dr. Serizawa, can offer relief from symptoms including chills, flushing, pain and numbness, headaches, heaviness in the head, dizziness, ringing in the ears, constipation, sluggishness and knee and back pain. Point stimulation is especially good, he adds, for people who are suffering from no definite illness but who are sluggish, lack appetite, tire easily,

have poor facial color or are upset in the stomach or intestines.

Pain on the Wane

In this country, "pain alleviation is the most common use of acupressure and the problem for which it is most effective," says Carol A. Warfield, M.D., assistant professor of anesthesia at Harvard Medical School and director of the Pain Management Center at Boston's Beth Israel Hospital.

For more than ten years, Dr. Warfield and her associates have been using electrical stimulation of the classical Chinese points to alleviate patients' pain. Dr. Warfield, who keeps a large poster displaying the ancient points on her office wall, says electrical stimulation seems about as effective as pressing with the fingers.

How effective is that? "About 30 percent of our patients benefit from the treatments, but it largely depends on the kind of pain we're dealing with," she says. "Pain following trauma or injury seems to respond very well, but cancer pain doesn't seem to respond nearly as well." Why and how acupressure works is still subject to debate, says Dr. Warfield. But studies have shown that manipulating points works to release endorphins and enkephalins, "the body's natural narcotics," she says.

Whatever the explanation, all Ed McMullen, 70, of El Cerrito, California, cares about is that it works. He was out playing golf, stumped his club and wound up with an intense neck pain.

Getting to the Point

There's no way to say for sure how many acupressure practitioners there are in this country, for the profession is generally unregulated. Acupressurist Michael Reed Gach estimates that "several hundred thousand Americans know how to do some form of acupressure, and a few thousand are practicing professionally." He says that the majority of practitioners charge from $30 to $50 per session, usually about an hour and a half long.

The following organizations and schools can offer you some assistance in either finding a professional or learning more about acupressure yourself.

Acupressure Institute
1533 Shattuck Avenue
Berkeley, CA 94709
(415) 845-1059
(The Institute also offers a selection of books and video tapes.)

American Oriental Bodywork
  Therapy Association
50 Maple Place
Manhasset, NY 11030
(516) 365-5025

Gautama Institute for the Oriental
  Healing Arts
1223 Rodman Street
Philadelphia, PA 19147
(215) 985-4466

Ohashi Institute
12 West 27th Street
New York, NY 10001
(212) 684-4190

You might also wish to learn more about acupressure by reading one of the following books.

Acupressure for Athletes by David J. Nickel (Henry Holt).

Do-It-Yourself Shiatsu by Wataru Ohashi (E. P. Dutton).

Greater Energy at Your Fingertips by Michael Reed Gach (Celestial Arts).

Pressure Points: Do-It-Yourself Acupuncture without Needles, by Keith Kenyon, M.D. (Arco Publishing Company).

Tsubo: Vital Points for Oriental Therapy by Katsusuke Serizawa, M.D. (Japan Publications).

That was the first time he saw an acupressurist. His pain went away so fast that he now sees her for all his aches and pains. "I'm active. I play golf and chop wood, and sometimes I get stiff when I overdo," he says. "I go and get worked on and I catch right up again."

Relaxation

Acupressure can be "profoundly relaxing," says Diana Kehlmann, 51, of Berkeley. "The state an acupressurist can put you into is like a form of deep meditation."

Ellen Salvadori, 44, a practicing psychotherapist in Manhattan, says when she herself gets overexcited, acupressure "quiets me down." Impressed with the results she has seen in herself, she now refers patients "when they're feeling stressed out."

Energizing the Body

It may seem strange that something that can calm you down can also perk you up, but not to Karlis Ullis, M.D., assistant clinical professor at the UCLA School of Medicine. "People who are hyperactive can use acupressure to calm down," he says. "On the other hand, athletes can energize themselves before an event by stimulating their points."

Michael Reed Gach, in his book *Greater Energy at Your Fingertips*, explains: "Acupressure releases muscular tension, enabling the blood to flow freely. An increase of circulation also brings more oxygen and other nutrients to affected areas. This increases your overall energy."

Sports Injuries

Dr. Ullis, whose specialty is sports medicine, says, "Acupressure can facilitate healing of sports injuries." In fact, he regularly uses *electro-acutherapy* (electrical stimulation of the points, such as used by Dr. Warfield) on his athlete patients. "What we're really doing is signaling the nervous system to turn on the mechanisms of healing," he says.

Headaches

Missie Bossi, 33, of El Sobrante, California, says she suffered regularly from migraine headaches, until she found acupressure. Her problems reached a peak one year at Christmas, when the stress of holding a job and mothering were just too much. The resultant splitting pain between the ears lasted for seven days. Painkillers were of no help. Then she went to see an acupressurist. "Unbelievable!" she exclaims. "It just relaxed me so much that the headache went away." Since that time, she's run to get a treatment every time the pain starts coming on. "I haven't had a bad headache since," she says.

PRESS HERE FOR RELIEF

Acupressurists say that pressing specific points on the body—such as those shown on the following pages—can have a soothing, uplifting or healing effect on your body and mind. What follows are commonly used acupressure points for a variety of problems. If you can't at first find the exact spot on your body, poke around a bit—acupressure points are generally a bit more tender than the surrounding area. Use the tip of your index finger, your middle finger, or both, side by side. In some spots, it may be easier to use your thumb. A few seconds of pressure, repeated several times, will often be enough. You should push till you feel some discomfort.

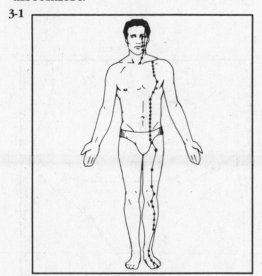

According to acupressure theory, 14 meridians, or major channels of energy run through your body. Each meridian is named for the organ or function connected to its energy flow. The stomach meridian and its points are illustrated here. Stimulating these points can release that blocked energy.

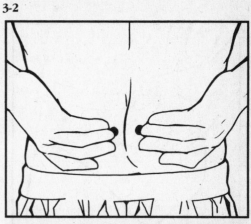

Try pressing on these two points simultaneously the next time your back is feeling at all sore. You can find them on either side of the lower spine, just around the corner from the bottommost rib.

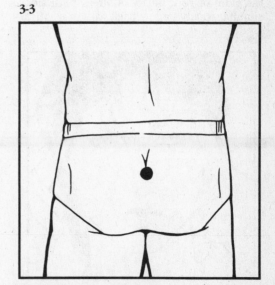

Acupressurists say you can give a lift to an aching back with a little pressure on this point, just beneath the tip of the tail bone.

(continued)

PRESS HERE FOR RELIEF—*Continued*

3-4

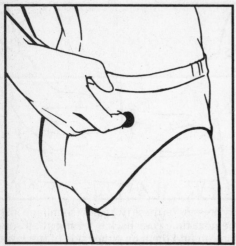

For these points (one on each side), you'll have to press hard. They lie deep below the skin. Look for the center of the depression at the sides of your buttocks. Press both sides simultaneously for low back pain or sciatica.

3-5

Located on both sides of the forehead, lateral to the eyebrows and about a finger's width away, you will find two points for dealing with headaches.

3-6

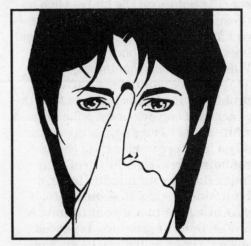

A finger press right between the eyes can bring headache relief, according to ancient Chinese tradition.

3-7

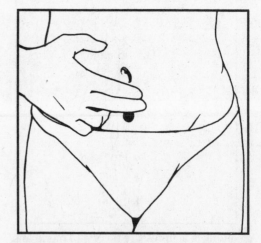

Two finger widths below your belly button you'll find a spot used to treat menstrual pain. Acupressurists suggest you start therapy several days before your period is due and continue for several days after.

3-8

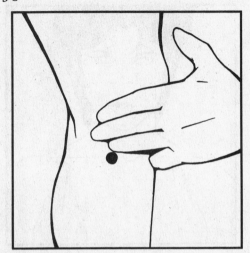

Three finger widths under each kneecap, at the side of your leg, you'll find additional points for combating menstrual difficulties.

3-10

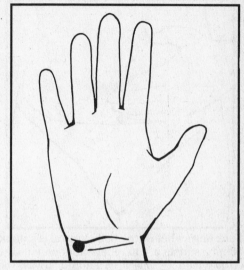

This point, located under the little finger at the first crease of the wrist, is pressed to treat insomnia.

3-9

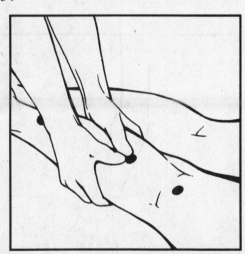

To relieve nocturnal leg cramps, acupressurists apply strong pressure to the points behind the knee, in the center of the calf and where the Achilles tendon joins the calf muscle.

3-11

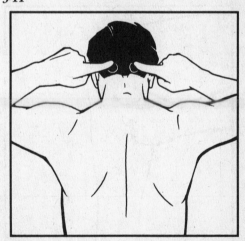

Pressing these two points, right at the natural hairline on either side of the spine, is an additional anti-insomnia measure.

(continued)

PRESS HERE FOR RELIEF—*Continued*

3-12

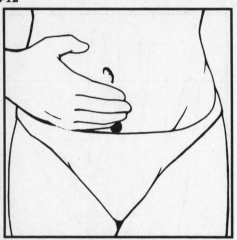

Four fingers below the belly button is a point acupressurists use to relieve abdominal pain. (Note: Pain in this area should always be checked out by a physician.)

3-13

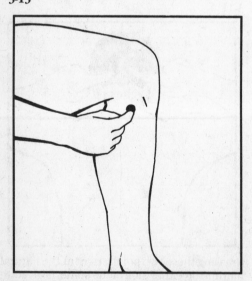

If this spot a little behind and about two finger widths below the lower part of the kneecap is tender to the touch, acupressurists say it could mean gallbladder trouble.

3-14

Pressing these points, just below the collar bone, is said to help quiet coughing. Pressure here is also supposedly helpful in treating asthma. (Note: These conditions may require a doctor's care.)

3-15

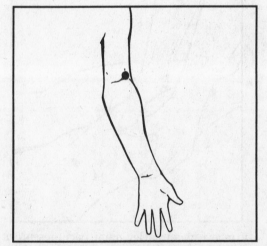

More cough-controlling points are found by bending the elbow part way and finding the bottom of the biceps. The points, one on each arm, are right to the outside of that bulge.

3-16

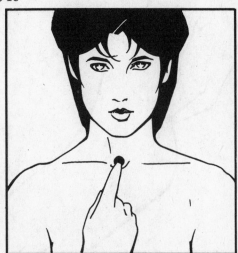

Just above the breastbone you'll find a point to press for nagging hiccups.

3-18

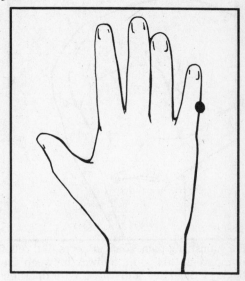

Tennis elbow anyone? If so, a little pressure on the outside of your little finger's knuckle (on the hand *opposite* the injury) may help volley the pain into oblivion.

3-17

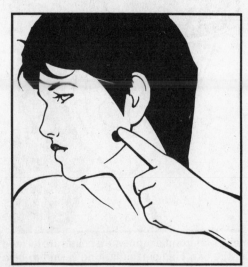

For temporary relief of toothache, acupressurists suggest pressing right above the corner of the jaw on the affected side.

3-19

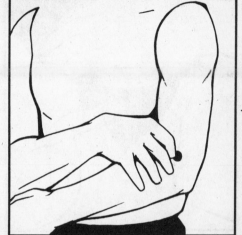

For another approach to tennis elbow pain: Find the exact spot of greatest pain, then press the corresponding point on the *opposite* arm.

(continued)

PRESS HERE FOR RELIEF—*Continued*

3-20

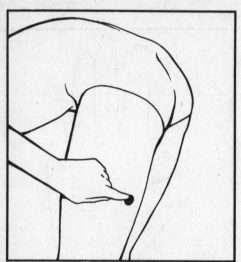

For hamstring pain, some athletes find relief by pressing this point, midway between the back of the knee and the elastic on their underwear. Again, the leg *opposite* the injury is pressed.

3-21

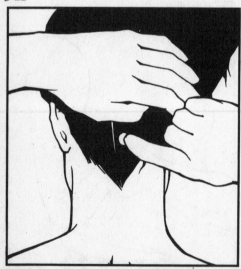

Athletes press this spot just before an athletic event for greater energy. It's right at the nape of the neck. Push hard and quickly against it ten times.

3-22

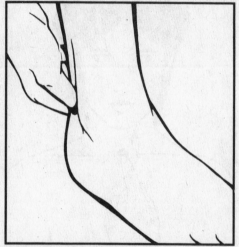

This point, found just behind the ankle, is also worth ten jabs next time you're participating in your favorite sport, acupressurists say. Breathe deeply as you apply pressure.

3-23

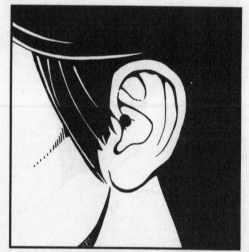

Many important acupressure points are located on the ear. This particular one is said to be a terrific pick-me-up spot. As with all ear points, expect to feel a hot stinging sensation during pressure.

Chapter 4

ALEXANDER TECHNIQUE

Whack.

"Sit up straight."

"Ouch . . . yes, Grandma."

That's how many of us learned about better posture—by way of a light thump on the back of the head from the family matriarch. You better believe you learned to sit up straight at the dinner table. But out of her sight you probably reverted to a slouch that would have made Quasimodo envious.

The Alexander Technique® takes up where Grandma left off. But its instructors eschew the school-of-hard-knocks method of teaching better posture, preferring instead a hands-on approach that gently guides students to a new way of using their bodies. They do give Grandma her due, though. "There's been a folk wisdom throughout the centuries about the importance of good posture," says Ronald Dennis, Ed.D., Executive Director of the American Center for the Alexander Technique, in New York City.

"We work with students to help them improve the use of their body. We help them identify and change bad postural habits which may be causing them undue stress and fatigue."

Theater of the Body

F. M. Alexander had a problem. Sometimes, when reciting on stage, this Australian Shakespearean actor had to wonder "wherefore art thou . . . *voice?*" Macbeth's soliloquy became a whisper. Even those sitting in the front-row seats could barely hear King Lear.

Around the turn of this century, when Alexander sought treatment for his chronic problem of voice loss, he was told to "stop talking and your voice will come back." And it did. But not for long.

Finally, Alexander took matters into his own hands. By using a mirror, he began to study the way he spoke. Eventually he discovered that he had been using his body wrong. "Alexander found that use affects functioning," says Dr. Dennis. "The way you utilize yourself, the way you carry yourself, the way you move is called your *use*. It's your voluntary activity, and it affects the involuntary aspects of your body. If you slouch and compress your chest, for example, then your lungs won't work so well."

Alexander found that a new relationship of head, neck and spine was required to reduce his considerable postural stress, and with steady practice of the new technique, his vocal powers returned. To this day, many of the most enthusiastic students of the Alexander Technique are actors and singers who know all too well the relevance of postural control to effective vocal production.

"The Head Leads, the Spine Follows"

"The technique is based on the principle of allowing your spine to lengthen—to find its optimal length," says Pamela Anderson, director of the teachers' certification program at the American Center for the Alexander Technique.

Anderson, who has been teaching the technique for over 11 years, says that if your goal is to have a better posture, you should realize ahead of time that the world may be working against you. "Most furniture is not built for good use," she says. "Chairs, for example, often have a slight backward slope so that when you sit down you naturally have to lean back. It's an incentive to slouch."

Other factors conspire against good posture as well, according to Alexander's interpretation. Try this, for example. Put this book down for a second, and get up off the chair you're sitting in. Now think about how you got up, and see if Pamela has your number. "Ninety-eight percent of the human population will shorten to stand," she says. "They'll scrunch down and push off. What they're actually doing is working against their more efficient coordination." A better way, Alexander students are told, is to picture your head floating up to the ceiling, leading your body effortlessly upward out of the chair.

If you want to learn to move more efficiently, look to the animal kingdom. Remember all those grainy film documentaries about the Serengeti Plain that you saw on public television during pledge week? Think back to how the lion hung around in the tall grass till a herd of wildebeests wandered by. We should all move so efficiently. "In all movement you want to allow your spine to be as lengthened as possible," says Anderson. "Watch four-legged animals get ready to move. They don't prepare by shortening. There is a sense of poise. Their head leads and their spine follows."

A Lesson in Balance

"That's it ... just let your neck go free ... move your head forward and up. There you go, just relax."

Gently, Pamela's hands cradle your head and neck. Her fingers at the base of your skull smoothly and skillfully move it in the direction she wants it to go. In time, you switch to automatic pilot.

"Let your head balance on top of your spine. Feel it lengthen. Do you feel like you're getting wider? More relaxed?"

You bet. Midway through the les-

"Professors" of Posture

There are more than 300 teachers of the Alexander Technique nationwide. Almost half were trained at the American Center for the Alexander Technique in New York City, which was the first center of its kind in the United States.

Ronald Dennis, the center's executive director, has some advice on what you should look for in an Alexander teacher. "Find a teacher who is affiliated with the national professional society—the North American Society of Teachers of the Alexander Technique. That means the teacher must have had three years and 1,600 hours of training, of which 80 percent is direct hands-on.

"No reputable teacher would talk about *curing* anything," Dennis emphasizes. "What he or she may be able to do is help you acquire improved postural habits. Any other benefits are indirect."

A typical Alexander session will last about 45 minutes and cost roughly $25 to $60, depending on your teacher's experience. Dennis adds that it generally takes about 30 lessons to acquire a basic grounding in the technique.

To find an Alexander teacher near you, contact the North American Society of Teachers of the Alexander Technique (NASTAT), P.O. Box 3992, Champaign, IL 61827–3992 (217) 359-3529.

The following books can tell you more about the Alexander Technique:

Back Trouble: A New Approach to Prevention and Recovery by Deborah Caplan (Triad Publishing Company).

Body Awareness in Action by Frank Pierce Jones (Pantheon Books).

Constructive Conscious Control of the Individual by F. Matthias Alexander (Centerline Press).

F. Matthias Alexander, The Man and His Work by Lulie Westfeldt (Centerline Press).

Man's Supreme Inheritance by F. Matthias Alexander (Centerline Press).

The Universal Constant in Living by F. Matthias Alexander (Centerline Press).

The Use of the Self by F. Matthias Alexander (Centerline Press).

son Pamela asks you to get up on a table and lie down. As she holds your head and neck, she guides you through activities designed to release your back muscles. Soon, you bottom out—feeling more of the table against you as you relax and the arch of your back starts to straighten out.

Speaking softly, Pamela explains that when your back muscles release, your spine drops down into the table. It's a good indication that you are widening and loosening. Soon you begin to wonder, if the table wasn't here, could you just float? Maybe. "Balance is inherent in our structure," says Pamela. "Unfortunately, what we have done is learned to take ourselves out of balance."

Time to get back in balance the Alexander way. "When I give the direction 'neck free, head forward and up,' what happens is that you rid yourself of compression," she says. " 'Neck free' means letting go of that downward pull. 'Head forward and up' allows you to poise your head on top of your spine. The directions are geared toward letting go of that initial compression."

Compression, it seems, is the root of all evil. And it can bother you even while you sit. If you find yourself with rounded or hunched shoulders after you've been sitting a while, Anderson has a trick you can use that makes sitting up straight easy. "Find your 'sit bones,' " she says. "They're the bones on the bottom of your pelvis. They serve the same function when we sit

as our feet do when we stand. Most of us roll back on our buttocks when we sit. But you need to balance on your sit bones because that makes sitting up straight very easy. It gives you a steady base of support."

For Alexander students, being light on your seat is as important as being light on your feet.

THE HEALING POWER OF THE ALEXANDER TECHNIQUE

Watch how toddlers move around. They wobble. They lurch. They make their parents jump. But they rarely fall down. Theirs is a natural balancing act. "Two-year-olds are very open and expansive, but most of us lose that," says Judith C. Trobe, P.T., a physical therapist and teacher of the Alexander Technique. "The body likes to be open and expanded. But we generally walk around pressing our heads back and down. It's an unconscious behavior that eventually causes pain."

As a physical therapist, Judith has to treat that pain. And she's been using the Alexander Technique as part of her treatment for years. She says it's very effective against pain caused by compression, and that its benefits can be seen right away. "People in pain are very easy to teach because the body has an immediate feedback mechanism," she says. "When they are in balance and directing themselves, allowing gravity to be their ally, the pain goes away. So people with pain immediately know when the technique works."

And Trobe has seen it relieve a wide variety of pain—from low back pain to knee pain. "Your knees take an enormous amount of stress," she says, "and if your weight is dumped into them, rather than moving up and off the end of your spine, it adds even more stress. Walking correctly will take a lot of pressure off those joints."

She's seen the Alexander Technique work for arthritis, too. "It doesn't reverse the process, but it can prevent progression," she claims. "Arthritis occurs when boney substances rub up against one another. Because the technique helps expand the space inside the body, what you end up doing is keeping those surfaces away from each other."

And then there was her psychotherapist student. "She had tendinitis of the left hip. Medication didn't relieve the pain, so her physician sent her to me as a last resort," Trobe recalls. "I found that she had a chronic habit of compressing into her left side. When I put my hands on her and led her through a lesson—showing her how to expand her spine, taking the full weight of her torso off of her left leg—her pain disappeared. She came in hurting, and she left pain free.

"The technique isn't magic. It's just a learning process. The brain has an enormous capacity to be reprogrammed, to relearn correct posture."

Better Living through Better Posture

Diane Riley's life was anything but pain free. If she had compressed any more into her body, she would have turned inside out. "Growing up, I had terrible posture. My father was a doctor. When he brought home a posture brace, it did the opposite of what we wanted. It pulled my shoulders back, but everything else still dropped. It didn't do anything but humiliate me."

To make matters worse, she chose a career on the stage as a professional singer. After one of her singing lessons, her instructor told her that her singing was beautiful. But then she asked Diane why her body was so deformed.

No one seeing her sitting at a table today would think this pretty 36-year-old had a deformed body. In fact, it is anything but.

Ten years ago Diane discovered the Alexander Technique. She says it straightened out her life as well as her body. "Within three or four months there were just incredible physical changes in me. My whole body was realigned. My singing became a lot freer. My breath became longer. There was just a tremendous improvement in my singing ability. The Alexander Technique totally changed my life. I feel much more integrated, much more whole, much more in control."

Chapter 5

APPLIED KINESIOLOGY

So here you are, in yet another doctor's office for yet another diagnosis of that vague, icky feeling that's been sitting like a disgruntled Buddha in your stomach for months.

"I've got a few ideas what it might be, but first I'd like to conduct a few tests," the doctor says. Oh no, not more tests! You've had blood tests and urine tests, skin tests and allergy tests. You've been poked and prodded, x-rayed and hooked up and monitored—but nobody's been able to put a finger on what's bugging you.

But here you go again, this time with a chiropractor who specializes in applied kinesiology, something you'd never even heard of until the other night when a friend went on and on about how it helped his migraines. It sounded really good, so here you are in another white medical gown, lying faceup under bright lights on an examination table.

"Raise your arm, please," the doctor says. He lifts your right arm from

your side and guides it to a position perpendicular to the table, your hand stretched above your head.

"Hold it right there," he says. You wince, expecting the worst. He's going to stab you with a big needle. Or hit you in the elbow with a rubber hammer. Or tell you to take a deep breath while he presses some sensitive spot in your groin. But instead, he begins to gently push your arm back down. "Try to hold it up," he says. You try, but your arm sinks back onto the table. "Hmm," the doctor says.

He moves to your left arm. "Raise," he says, guiding it upward. "Hold." Again, he starts to push down. This time your arm doesn't budge. You win. But how? Did he let you? Or is one arm really stronger than the other? Now he guides your left finger to a spot on your chest near your breastbone and tells you to hold it there. He raises and pushes down on your right arm again. But this time something is different. Your arm feels strangely stronger. As hard as he pushes—and you can feel the effort he's making—he can't get it to budge.

The exam continues. He lifts and pushes your legs at various angles. He bends your arms at the elbow, then tries to straighten them out. He positions you as if you were in the midpoint of a sit-up, then tries to push you down on your back. Now he puts a few crystals of sugar onto your tongue or has you inhale assorted fumes, and then retests your muscles to see if these substances made a difference. And when he is finished— within a half hour or so—he gives you an amazingly detailed evaluation of your glands, organs, lymphatic system, nervous system, circulation, muscles and bones —not to mention the problem that brought you to him in the first place.

Muscling In on Disease

Applied kinesiologists believe that specific muscle functions are related to certain body systems and hence can be used to diagnose a wide variety of disorders—an approach introduced in the 1960s by Dr. George Goodheart, founder of applied kinesiology, who made these connections in the course of his chiropractic practice. According to Dr. Goodheart, a person with gastric disease, for instance, will display weakness in a certain pectoral muscle in the top of the chest, while a person with kidney disease will have a weak psoas muscle near the bottom of the spine. Hence, your muscles' inability to stand up to the doctor doesn't mean you're a 95-pound weakling. It's actually viewed as a helpful sign that clues him in on possible trouble spots throughout the body, from malfunctioning organs to unbalanced energy meridians.

"We have the best diagnostic tool right in front of us, and that's the patient," says Alan Weinstein, D.C. "We actually do many of the same kinds of tests as other doctors, but muscle testing enables us to look at exactly how the body is functioning."

Linda Arnold, an administrator with a computer company, is one patient who has been functioning a lot better thanks to applied kinesiology. Before seeing Dr. Weinstein, she had suffered for several months with intense muscle spasms.

"They started at my left shoulder, worked up my neck and into my head. Nothing could help the pain. I was in the hospital twice, where I had traction, physical therapy and painkilling drugs every three or four hours."

On top of that, her car was rear-ended in a traffic accident. "After the accident, drugs couldn't even touch the pain," she says. "I couldn't sleep for two days at a time."

She visited Dr. Weinstein on the recommendation of a friend. "I was so skeptical. Here he was pushing on my leg, putting things in my mouth, and I was thinking, 'What is this person doing?' But he asked me to give him three weeks to help. In only two weeks I noticed major improvements."

Dr. Weinstein found that the causes of Arnold's problem were threefold: vitamin and mineral deficiencies, structural imbalances and a bad attitude. "Halfway through the testing, he said, 'You live on junk food, don't you?' He was right. I was working horrendous hours and living out of a candy machine. I was missing major nutrients," says Arnold, who now takes nutritional supplements and tries to eat better overall.

Her weak neck and shoulder muscles also required attention. Dr. Weinstein balanced them, which improved their strength, and adjusted her spine. He also helped her adjust her attitude. "She'd previously been on medication for so long with no improvement that she believed she would never get better," he says. Today, Arnold's a lot better. "When I'm under severe stress," she says, "the pain will come back and nag me a little, but it never comes on the way it used to."

The Triangle of Health

Applied kinesiologists view human health as a triangle with three equally important sides. Nutrition is encompassed on the triangle's *chemical* side, which also includes the effects of drugs and other substances. The *structural* side takes into account muscles, bones, joints, nerves, organs and their various relationships. And the *mental* side includes things like emotions, moods and attitudes. Research has shown that each of these aspects is closely related to the others.

The body's chemical functioning can affect its physical functioning. "I had a patient who had severe lower back pain every Saturday morning before he went flyfishing," recalls applied kinesiologist William Erbe, D.C. "I would get him straightened out, but the problem kept recurring. Finally I asked him if he made his own flies. He said yes, and I knew what the problem was. We tested his reaction to the glue he used to make them. He could not handle the toxicity."

The structural can affect the chemical. "Adjusting the spine actually results in certain chemical changes," says Dr. Weinstein. In addition to spinal manipulations, applied kinesiologists give other hands-on treatments, including cranial adjustments, acupressure, and stimulation of nerve receptors. "We rub, tap, tug—whatever is necessary to get the patient better in every realm," says Dr. Weinstein.

And the mental can affect the other aspects. "Certain emotions can cause a person to be ill," says Dr. Weinstein. "If you had a trauma in your life or some kind of emotional upheaval, we may be able to pick that up during the testing."

"As chiropractors, we try to correct structure initially," says Dr. Erbe. "But the adjustment might not hold, and if it doesn't, we want to know why."

Charlie Johnson-O'Dowd, president of an independent film company,

To Find Out More

The cost of a typical applied kinesiology session varies widely, depending on the practitioner. Most certified applied kinesiologists—of which there are several hundred in the United States—are chiropractors, though some are M.D.'s, osteopathic physicians, podiatrists and dentists. To be certified, a health professional must possess a license to diagnose and participate in certified training through the International College of Applied Kinesiology (ICAK). For help finding a certified practitioner in your area, contact ICAK, P.O. Box 25276, Shawnee Mission, KS 66225 (913) 648-2828.

Applied Kinesiology by Tom and Carole Valentine (Thorsons Publishers) provides a patient's-eye view of this approach. You may order a copy through Harper & Row; call (800) 638-3030.

Touch for Health, a manual of self-help techniques, by John F. Thie, D.C., and other materials on applied kinesiology are available from TH Enterprises Store, 1200 North Lake Avenue, Pasadena, CA 91104 (818) 798-7893. Ask for a catalog.

ended up in Dr. Erbe's office after suffering muscle spasms that "basically tied up my body in knots. Everything would curl up into a ball. My whole body would just be crippled. A couple of times I was rushed to the emergency room."

Dr. Erbe's diagnosis: Johnson-O'Dowd's problem was a glandular one, which has since been corrected with nutritional therapy. He has also enjoyed other benefits. "I used to have a real swayback, and now I stand much straighter. I'm stronger, even though I don't get much exercise. And I used to suffer from sinus headaches all the time, but I've been free of them for two years."

"Many patients come in with the same symptoms, but they never have the same treatment," notes Dr. Erbe. Susan Johnson, special projects director for a business organization, had neck problems similar to Linda Arnold's. Dr. Weinstein adjusted her neck and treated her for a calcium deficiency. "The pain went away immediately and I haven't had any further problems in months," she says. "As for other benefits, my energy level is up a thousand percent. I used to be one of those people who was shot by 2:00 or 3:00 in the afternoon. Now I can go from 6:00 in the morning till midnight. This whole thing is new and wonderful for me."

THE HEALING POWER OF APPLIED KINESIOLOGY

Among other things, "Applied kinesiology is the only branch of the healing arts that appears to be fully equipped to deal with the general malaise—the 'I just don't feel good' syndrome," say authors and satisfied patients Tom and Carole Valentine in their book *Applied Kinesiology.* "Perhaps you or a family member has a glandular malfunction that isn't critical enough to display serious symptoms yet. Applied kinesiology muscle testing can detect the essence or beginnings of a problem before it becomes acute, with obvious symptoms."

Allergy Relief

Practitioners say allergies can easily be pinpointed during muscle testing. And if you already know you have allergies but find your medication doesn't seem to be helping, you can get that checked, too. "More than half the people we tested one day were allergic to or at least sensitive to their allergy medication," says Dr. Erbe. "It was making them worse."

Lessening Anxiety

Anxiety can be lowered via stimulation of certain reflex points, says Pasadena chiropractor John Thie. By simply holding two of these points on your temples for a few moments, your pulse rate on the right and left sides of your head is synchronized, calling forth the natural calming action of your body, he says.

Back Relief

Back problems can sometimes be alleviated. "I saw one man who used to need two hours to get out of bed, his back was so bad," says Dr. Thie. "A surgeon wanted to operate on him. Following treatment, he's normal, with no surgery."

An Easier Pregnancy

The stresses and strains of pregnancy can be lessened through an ongoing program of muscle testing and treatment, according to Tom and Carole Valentine. Following birth, applied kinesiology can supplement good pediatric care in treating structural imbalances in the muscles and bones of a growing child that might lead to chronic pain in later years.

Help for the Elderly

Problems of aging can often be minimized. "I have an 80-year-old patient who had to give up his weekly golf because his legs gave out on him," says Dr. Thie. "I worked on the reflexes in his legs, to give him more energy. That helped him feel more hopeful, more confident about his own recuperative powers. And the strength in his legs actually returned."

TOUCH FOR HEALTH

When Dr. John Thie first met applied kinesiology's developer Dr. George Goodheart in 1964, he was astounded to learn that rubbing reflex points on the body could change muscle strength and function. He was so excited by this knowledge that he spread word of the technique to his colleagues and became founding chair-person of the International College of Applied Kinesiology.

But he had another plan brewing. "I thought, this is so simple—this push-ing on the arms and legs and rubbing on spots—my patients can do it for themselves. They don't have to come to me." He named his self-help system Touch for Health, wrote a manual for his patients, and began teaching classes to regular folks all over the country. Today, the manual is published in 15 languages, and the system is taught in 50 countries and practiced by at least a million people.

Dr. Thie's manual runs the reader through the paces of basic muscle testing, and describes techniques for balancing energy and strengthening weak muscles.

Touch for Health bases its "bal-ancing" treatment on the body's energy flows. One muscle for each flow is tested, then balanced. The idea is that once your energy is balanced, your body will be better able to heal itself. "It's like closing a cut that's been bleeding, holding it together and trust-ing that God made you in such a manner that it will heal naturally," says Dr. Thie.

An example of testing and treat-ment for one muscle, in this case the latissimus dorsi in the back, is pic-tured here. (You'll benefit most from the entire system if you work with a partner.)

For information on classes, con-tact the Touch for Health Foundation, 1174 North Lake Avenue, Pasadena, CA 91104 (818) 794-1181.

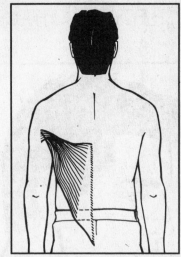

5-1

Applied kinesiologists say the latissimus dorsi muscle (shown here), which holds the shoul-der down and helps keep the back straight, is related to the pancreas, where insulin is pro-duced. Weakness is associated with allergies as well as intolerance for sugar, caffeine or tobacco.

5-2

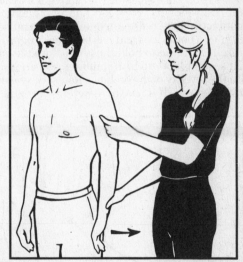

To test, subject holds arm straight down at the side, palm facing away from the body, elbow straight. Tester then tries to pull the arm away from the body, firmly but gently. The arm tests weak if it gives way to the tester's pull. Repeat test on other arm.

(continued)

TOUCH FOR HEALTH—*Continued*

5-3

If the muscle tests weak, place the pads of your fingers on the bone just above and behind the ear on both sides of your partner's head (at point shown). A few seconds after making contact, a slight pulse can be felt. After a pulse is felt on both sides and has become synchronized, continue to hold the points for at least 20 seconds and up to 10 minutes, depending on the severity of the problem. Retest the weak muscle to see if it has increased in strength.

5-4

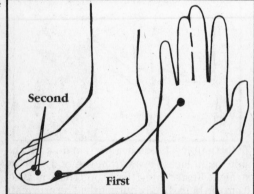

On the same side of the body as the weak muscle, locate the two sets of acupuncture holding points shown here.

5-5

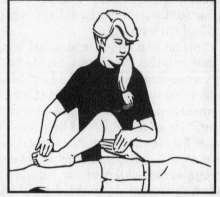

Hold the first hand and foot points simultaneously, one with each hand. Maintain light pressure for about 30 seconds or until you feel a pulse in the leg. Then move to the second two points and hold these until you feel a pulse in the leg. Retest the weak muscle.

5-6

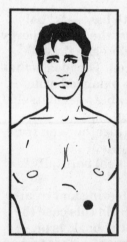
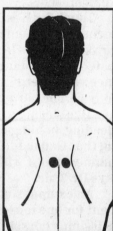

To clear blockages in energy flow, massage the points shown. First, find the point in the front, left side, on the ribs near the cartilage. Move around the point with your fingers using deep massage for 20 to 30 seconds. Then do the same on the two points on the back, one inch to each side of the spine. Retest the weak muscle.

Chapter 6

AROMATHERAPY

A pungent, clean scent—juniper tempered by lavender, rosemary and lemon—lightly perfumes the air, teasing your memory. You close your eyes and you're in a pine forest, the air clean and new.

Actually, you're not. You're lying face down on a massage table in a city apartment, where the wind outside carries exhaust fumes and other not-so-pleasant urban smells. But none of that intrudes here. In this room, with a little help from these natural plant essences, the bustle outside gives way to calm within. You feel nostalgic for this island called Manhattan as you imagine it once was, all woodland, back when the Dutch were still safely in Holland. So much for reverie . . .

A soothing, confident hand brings you back to the present, brushing the hair off your neck and cupping the base of your skull. The other hand presses down gently on the slope between your shoulders.

And there the hands remain for a brief while, allowing rapport to build between you and their owner, Judith Jackson, a prominent aromatherapist

who learned this art in London.

Jackson's right hand moves down below your shoulder blades. Then, folding down the pink terry cloth towel that covers you, she presses that hand on your midback; and, in time, on your bared bottom.

Pass the Vitality, Please

Now the massage begins in earnest. Jackson brings her right hand to the back of your neck. You feel the flesh and muscle mass there being drawn together. Next her fingers gently dig in along the base of the skull, so gently, in fact, you wonder if they're having any effect.

Jackson tells you later that the pressure points in this area "communicate with" the brain, pituitary gland, and the optic and auditory systems. The points she uses correspond to the acupuncture points oriental medicine recognizes.

Next, she sweeps her fingers over the top of your head and through your

A Word about Oils

There are several hundred essential oils produced today. Be aware that there are synthetic products masquerading as the real thing.

Use your nose to help you distinguish. The pure, natural essence will have a lively, characteristic smell—and it may be more expensive. Some botanicals contain precious little essence.

The amount of essential oil in a plant can vary from more than 10 percent to as little as 0.01 percent. An ounce of rose essence, for example, can require up to a ton of rose petals. The oils aren't always in the flowers, however. Sometimes, they're in the roots, sometimes in the bark, sometimes in the rinds of fruit and sometimes in the resin.

Typically, essences are extracted by distillation. The harvested plants are placed in a vat; then steam is passed through them. The essences evaporate along with the water. Later, the distilled product is cooled. Since the essence of the plant is not water soluble, it is easily separated from water. With citrus fruits, the essence is squeezed—by hand—from the peel.

If you're interested in experimenting with essential oils, you can use the essences individually, or mix them to multiply the therapeutic benefits. Check an aromatherapy book to determine which oils have the most suitable properties for your needs. Many of the books will contain recipes to get you started.

Where to find essential oils? Your local health food store may carry them. If not, some firms sell them through mail order.

Judith Jackson sells her product line through Saks Fifth Avenue, and makes some available by mail order. Aveda, a Minneapolis firm that does a multi-million dollar business in aromatherapy products, distributes its line through professional beauty salons throughout the country. For information on their product line call (800) 328-0849.

For more information, contact:

Judith Jackson Inc.
10 Serenity Lane
Cos Cobb, CT 06807

Aveda
321 Lincoln Street NE
Minneapolis, MN 55413

Alexander Avery
Box 68183
Northrop Creek Road
Birkenfeld, OR 97016

Aroma Vera
Box 3609R
Culver City, CA 90231

hair, stimulating your cranial nerves. She's awakening your system so you'll fully appreciate the "aroma" part of the experience that's about to follow. Up to now, her hands have been dry.

That's about to change. Jackson reaches for "Vitality Body Essence," a blend of plant essences in a vegetable oil base she sells commercially. Its juniper scent is the very same one a white china room fragrancer has been dispensing since the massage began. She rubs a teaspoonful of the liquid in her palms to warm it.

Having your skin anointed with fragrant oil is a new experience for you. You feel sort of, well . . . basted . . . even though the consistency is closer to water than say, salad oil.

During the next hour, Jackson works the oil into your skin, using the raking and stroking motions of Swedish massage, and the pressure-point techniques of eastern disciplines. The skin and underlying muscles along your spine and upper back enjoy a particularly vigorous workout.

Even your hands and feet get attention. Your face Jackson strokes with a less potent essence mixed especially for the face. The massage progresses through 47 steps in all.

When she's done, she retreats quietly from the table, leaving you to rise at your leisure. Your feet touch ground and you feel energy streaming through your legs. Your neck and shoulders feel loose, your mind a little clearer than before.

Later, in the bathroom, you pull out the makeup case you brought with you. One look in the mirror and you decide you don't need it. Your hair feels a little oiled at the roots, but it's no big deal. Your eyes are bright and clear; your complexion is glowing with healthy color. On your way out of the city, you notice you're the only motorist smiling as you edge crosstown.

"The Most Complete Treatment"

Each step of the massage Judith Jackson gives is detailed in her primer, *Scentual Touch: A Personal Guide to Aromatherapy.* Jackson learned this distinctive approach from Micheline Arcier, a London salon owner Jackson first encountered back in 1971 when she was a harried businesswoman who needed to unwind.

A subsequent invitation to write on the subject for *Harper's Bazaar* led Jackson to study with Arcier. Eventually, Jackson became a therapist and teacher herself. With the publication of her book in 1986, she joined the first wave of aromatherapy advocates intent on importing this European find to the United States. Now she treats clients, trains students and sells a line of aromatherapy products through Saks Fifth Avenue, and direct mail.

Jackson says she is drawn to this style of massage because it "addresses mind, body and spirit. That's what struck me when I went to my first class at Madame Arcier's. As a non-invasive technique, I thought this had to be the most complete body and face treatment I'd ever experienced.

"It even has a spiritual component to it. Aromatherapy relates to nature and the wellsprings of the inner spirit. It's almost a pantheistic kind of experience. These fragrances really do take you to the heart of plant creation."

How It Works

The particular massage sequence Jackson uses was developed by Arcier, in consultation with a doctor, biochemist and chiropractor. From the West, Arcier borrowed some techniques from Swedish and neuromuscular massage. From the East, she incorporated shiatsu, reflexology and polarity therapy, an American invention that's essentially oriental in its approach.

Swedish massage works the soft tissue and helps stimulate circulation of the blood and lymph. And getting the lymph circulating, so it can be cleansed in the lymph nodes, is a key to making the aromatherapy massage effective, says Jackson.

Shiatsu is a pressure-point whole body massage. Reflexology applies pressure to the feet to diagnose the health of corresponding body organs, and to treat the ailing ones.

Polarity therapy, a synthesis itself, makes strategic use of the positive and negative energy charges in the body to unblock stagnant energy.

In essence, this massage sequence relies on the Western techniques to soothe and the Eastern ones to energize.

As Jackson summarizes in her book, "The massage loosens tight muscles and blocked tissues, zeroing in on central points in the energy system. As the skin responds to the massage, its nerve endings communicate with the internal organs, glands, nerves and circulatory system."

How do the essential oils aid the process? In several ways.

"When you apply pure essential oil, it seems to help in the cleansing process," says Jackson. "Many of them have antibacterial actions.

"Let's look at the properties of the active ingredients in 'Vitality Body Essence'—juniper, lavender and lemon. All are said to work as antiseptics. Juniper, additionally, is valued as a tonic for the nervous system; while lavender is considered 'restorative.'

"The essential oils do penetrate into a few of the deeper layers of the skin," Jackson continues. "So they really help to do things to the tissue that are particular to that essence.

"Juniper, for instance, is a diuretic. So if you use it where you have quite a bit of water in the tissue, it should help to flush that out. Or if you use geranium, which is a natural astringent, it causes a certain amount of contraction."

The actual scent of the oil may also affect the body, by altering brain activity. Clinical studies suggest that certain essences are valuable as antidepressants, others as natural relaxants. The nose, in fact, is directly connected to the brain's emotion-regulating limbic system. "Smell definitely turns on glandular response and it definitely turns on nerve center response," asserts Jackson.

Studies at Yale University and at the University of Warwick in England have shown that inhaling the aroma of spiced apple pie, or the seashore, can be as relaxing as some stress reduction techniques.

Robert B. Tisserand, author of *The Art Of Aromatherapy,* speculates that because the essence "is the most ethe-

So You Want to Try It

If you're determined to experience an aromatherapy massage for yourself, it might be challenging—though not impossible—to find someone competent to give you one.

The art is relatively new in the United States. There is no national association overseeing training standards. Techniques vary from practitioner to practitioner, although students of Judith Jackson and Micheline Arcier are likely to conform to the sequence Arcier developed.

Most of Jackson's students are employed by spas in larger cities or resort areas like Palm Desert and Fort Lauderdale. If you live elsewhere, seek someone who is a licensed, certified massage practitioner, and who can show you proof of training in the use of essential oils. Don't be afraid to ask the practitioner for the name of some regular clients you can call.

Your other option is to pick up Jackson's *Scentual Touch: A Personal Guide to Aromatherapy* (Ballantine Books). The book contains diagrams for giving a full body massage to a partner, a self-massage and special massages for couples or children. It also includes recipes for creating your own essential blends.

Another informative book is *The Art of Aromatherapy: The Healing and Beautifying Properties of the Essential Oils of Flowers and Herbs,* by Robert B. Tisserand (Inner Traditions International). In addition to exploring the history and philosophy of aromatherapy, this book lists the properties of 29 different essences. It also contains a separate alphabetical listing of conditions, and the essences considered helpful in treating them.

Rejuvenation: A Wellness Guide for Women and Men, written by Horst Rechelbacher (Inner Traditions International) is another helpful source. The author is founder and chairman of Aveda, the largest aromatherapy products distributor in the United States. The book details the properties of various plants and flowers and discusses how to use aromatherapy principals in your own environment.

real and subtle part of a plant, its therapeutic action takes place on a more subtle level than that of the whole plant or its extract." Consequently, he believes that the essence generally seems to have a much more pronounced effect on the mind and emotions than herbal medicines in general.

Revived in Paris

Although aromatic oils were used therapeutically in ancient Egypt and Babylon, and later in Greece, the specialized knowledge of how various essences affect the body and psyche was gradually lost over the years.

Rene-Maurice Gattefosse, a French chemist, helped revive that knowledge. He is credited with coining the word "aromatherapy" and with pioneering its modern-day branch.

Early in this century, he founded an essential oil house and began to explore the properties of the oils. One day, after he burned his hand in a small laboratory explosion, he immediately plunged the hand into a vat of pure lavender essence. As the story goes, his hand healed with remarkable speed.

Gattefosse inspired Dr. Jean Valnet, a Parisian physician who used essential oils, mostly internally, to treat soldiers injured during World War I. He also influenced Marguerite Maury, a biochemist who developed a special way to apply the penetrating oils with massage. Micheline Arcier, Judith Jackson's teacher, studied under both Valnet and Maury.

THE HEALING POWER OF AROMATHERAPY

Aromatherapy massage has been used to treat conditions ranging from acne to varicose veins. If you've got a problem, chances are there's an essence supposedly good for it.

If you have allergies, aromatherapists suggest you try chamomile or melissa. If you have laryngitis, benzoin, frankincense, lavender and sandalwood are recommended. The list goes on and on.

Judith Jackson says she's most enthusiastic about the benefits aromatherapy massage brings to the range of circulatory problems. In her practice, Jackson has seen it reduce swelling in the ankles and legs, improve poor circulation, minimize sensitivity to bruising and—as a side benefit—send the blues on their way.

The swelling responded to juniper. The poor circulation responded to sandalwood and patchouli. The person who bruised easily was treated with rosemary, and counseled to increase her vitamin C intake, Jackson says.

As for depression, "You can really give yourself a lift by doing a neck and shoulder massage, using something uplifting like basil or prairie sage," she adds.

Jackson finds that many of her clients visit her to relieve stress. "I have a number of working women whom I treat. They call me up and they say, 'I need to be balanced again' with that certain edge in their voice."

And Jackson believes that the massage can heal in emotional ways, too. In her book, she adapts the technique for couples and children.

"I think that we too often grow apart physically even in quite close families," she says. "There isn't the physical touching, especially in America where we're all in such a hurry. And that's a shame. That misses a lot of what people should be to each other."

THE ESSENCE OF AROMATHERAPY MASSAGE

Aromatherapists seek to restore body and mind with a hands-on approach that's as fragrant as it is soothing. Here are some of the highlights.

6-1

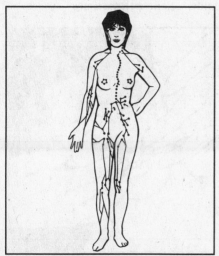

Stimulating the lymph system is the key to an effective aromatherapy massage, practitioners say. Made up of water and waste products, lymph drains from the tissues through tiny, thread-like capillaries that cover the body. Major lymph pathways and nodes are shown here.

6-2

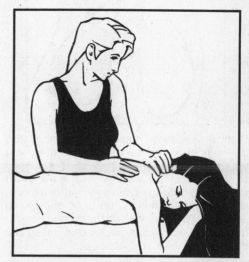

It takes trust to surrender to another's touch. Help your partner develop trust in you by establishing contact. Cup your left hand around the base of the skull and hold it there, as you rest your flat right hand horizontally between the shoulders. Hold for 20 seconds.

(continued)

THE ESSENCE OF AROMATHERAPY MASSAGE—*Continued*

6-3

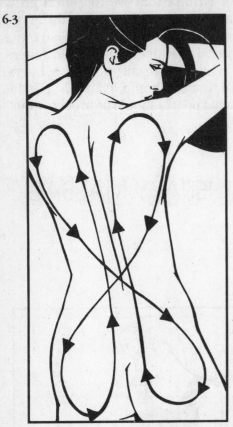

Pour a massage oil containing essences into the palm of your hand to warm it before you apply it to your partner's back. Use both hands to stroke from the tailbone to the neck and over the shoulders. Then sweep down again, crossing your hands at mid-back, and sweep around each buttock. Keep the motion continuous and your hands flat as they make the curves.

6-4

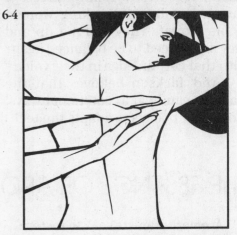

Break up tightness and congestion in the back tissue by scooping up the skin between your two hands. As you scoop, roll your fingers in together and touch, as you turn your hands inward. Begin just above the buttocks and keep going until you reach the top of the shoulders. Repeat three times.

6-5

Taking care not to get oil in your partner's eyes, spread four fingers of each hand on either side of the face. Put two fingers on the chin, two over the upper lip. Then rake outward to the ears. Practitioners say this coaxes the lymph to flow into the mandibular lymph nodes at either side of the lower jaw, helping to cleanse the face internally.

Chapter 7

ASTON-PATTERNING

The feather doesn't fall. It descends. Gently. Slowly, it spirals its way down. An invisible current of air momentarily stops it. The feather arcs upward, and then, taking a slightly different flight path, it continues its controlled descent.

Twelve sets of eyes are glued on the flight of this lonely feather. A silver-haired woman shifts on her stool as the feather heads her way. The brown and white glider suddenly pauses in midair, turns, and floats in another direction, toward another observer. The women sitting around in a large circle hold their breath for fear of disturbing this thing that so obviously was meant to fly.

To make the final point that it really does ride the wind, the feather completes one last spiral, and then, as if it knew all along where it was going to come to rest, it makes a perfect landing at Judith Aston's feet.

The students, sitting in a large classroom in Mill Valley, California, have just seen with their own eyes, the theory that is the basis of the Aston-Patterning® approach. "Your body wants to move like a feather," Judith says as she sits on a stool and preens the just-landed feather.

"The body wants to move in an asymmetrical spiral. The concept of asymmetry is an important part of our work. Often movement is taught in straight lines: Feet must face straight ahead, legs must move perpendicularly. But straight line movement increases tension."

Joanna Witt knows there's even tension in paradise, so she left her home in Honolulu, Hawaii, and enrolled in this Aston-Patterning class. After incorporating the three-dimensional spiral concept into her movement, she noticed that "my body control improved and I could be more relaxed."

What Judith Aston is trying to accomplish is "to educate people about how they can live optimally in their bodies. This process involves movement education, fitness training, environmental modification and bodywork." It's a process that took a long time to develop.

How to Throw Your Weight Around

Eighty-two-year-old Martha Procter of Mill Valley has got rhythm. A gardener, she had a specific goal in mind when she went to see Judith Aston. She wanted to be able to use her body more efficiently and effectively while she pruned her shrubs and trees, and Aston-Patterning helped her reach that goal. "When I prune, instead of just reaching with my arm, I now throw my whole body into it."

"I get a rhythm going and there is no stress or strain," she says. "Now I do it much more easily."

What Judith Aston taught Martha was a weight transfer system that's well within your reach. "Transfer your weight to your right foot by leaning to the side, and lift your left foot up," Aston explains. "Now transfer your weight back to the middle, where you balance on both feet. Now do the same sequence to the left.

"As you do this, notice if from the point of middle balance you have to go further in one direction than the other. The side that goes further may be the side that's overworked.

"Now put one foot forward, and transfer your weight over the forward foot by leaning from your ankle. Now reach forward. Contrast that with putting both feet on the same line and reaching forward. Notice the twisting that goes on in the body as you do that. That twisting can cause overwork and strain."

Weight transfer can even help you bend. "If you're sitting on a chair and you want to pick something up off the floor, slide to the front of the chair," says Aston. "Sit on your pelvis, not your legs. Use your hip hinge, where your legs meet the pelvis, to lean forward and transfer your weight toward your feet. Your trunk will move forward.

"Now as you move forward, flex your hip more deeply, then round your spine and pick up the object. Contrast that with rounding the spine and then reaching. It strains the body. By keeping your body long and using your joints instead of your midback to flex, simple tasks such as bending and reaching become effortless."

An Eye for Movement

For some, people watching is a pleasant way to pass time. For Judith Aston, though, people watching is a full-time avocation. It began at an early age. As a child, she began to notice that some people moved differently than others. "I remember saying I saw Mrs. What's-her-name the other day. People would say 'Who?' and I'd say, 'You know, she walks like this,' then I'd imitate her walk and they'd say, 'Oh, you mean Mrs. Brown.'"

Movement became Judith's life. She took up dancing and graduated from UCLA with degrees in dance and fine arts. Just as her career started to really move, it came to a screeching halt in 1967 when she was involved in two separate car accidents.

Doctors told her she should learn to type, because she would never be able to dance again. But when movement is your life you can't take a diagnosis like that sitting down. So Judith traveled far and wide for therapy for her injured back. "Finally, one doctor told me he knew of this 'white witch' named Dr. Ida Rolf, and that maybe I should see her. So I camped out on her doorstep."

Luckily Ida Rolf invited Judith inside. After one session of Rolfing her pain wasn't gone, "but there was a significant change in my body. I could feel the improvement."

A collaboration between the two soon took place, with Judith developing a movement program incorporating Rolfing techniques. But her eye for human movement began to notice something. Many of the Rolfed bodies tended to look alike. "I began to disagree that bodies should be perfectly symmetrical and rigidly straight. That's when I needed to develop my own program." That program is Aston-Patterning.

Poised for Patterning?

Maybe Aston-Patterning sounds like it could be fun for you, but you're not quite sure. If that's the case, Judith Aston has developed a checklist that may help you answer that question.

1. Stop and consider how you feel about your appearance. Are you looking vital? Is your posture good or does it show signs of aging or injury? Is your movement graceful and fluid or is it stiff and jerky?

2. Is your range of motion full or is it limited? Are your muscles in good tone? All over? Or are they too tight or too loose, or a combination of the two?

3. Do you have strength in your body? Is it available as you need it? Has it lessened in certain areas?

4. How do you measure your endurance? Is your stamina still there? Can you perform tasks without fatigue, or do you find yourself exhausted and out of breath?

5. Do you feel balanced? How do your body parts feel in relation to each other? How do they relate to the whole body? How does your body feel when performing the tasks you do? Do your arms feel like they're doing all the work, for instance, or do they feel like they're receiving the cooperation of the rest of your body? Are everyday activities getting harder?

If your responses suggest a number of problem areas, you might want to give Aston-Patterning a try.

A Personalized Program

"We don't believe that one program fits all. We design a program specifically for each individual," Aston says.

To do that, Aston-Patterners ask clients for a personal history because

"daily habits formulate a pattern in your body. As people move within that pattern, it can lead to limitation when the use pattern becomes a misuse pattern that becomes an abuse pattern."

"Our bodies are so elastic, they will adjust to environmental designs," Aston continues. "They adjust to curved seats, for example, where your front is too loose and your back is bent and stretched. We literally mold ourselves to our world."

Aston-Patterners want to break that mold and to do that they map out a plan of action. As you lie down on a table their hands effortlessly glide over your body searching for areas of tension. Once the areas of tension are located and mapped on a body chart, you are asked to stand up, and the camera begins to roll.

"We often use videotape to document a person's changes—the before-and-after approach. It begins to educate them about themselves, showing them how they walk, stand, or perform a task." Once the taping stops, the healing begins.

Finding the Pattern

There are about 50 certified Aston-Patterners located across the United States, and their ranks are growing.

Sessions last between one and two hours. The first session is the longest, because you will be asked to fill out a detailed history.

Costs vary, but you should expect to pay somewhere between $35 and $75 an hour. As for how frequently you may need to see the practitioner, it can vary from four to six times a year, to an hour a week for several months, depending on your needs. Short-range goals may include increased ease or decreased discomfort. A long-range goal might be improvement of athletic performance.

As Judith Aston puts it, "Basically you're done at any time that you feel more balanced in a way that fits your need."

For more information about the technique and practitioners in your area, write to Judith Aston, Aston Patterning Center, P.O. Box 3568, Incline Village, NV 89450.

THE HEALING POWER OF ASTON-PATTERNING

"I felt like I was being sculpted," says Charles Seltzer, a professional musician based in San Francisco. "I felt like a clay sculpture that was being very slightly remolded. The hands-on work doesn't seem to touch you very deep, but it affects you very deeply."

Pressure often means pain. But in an Aston-Patterner's hands, deep connective tissue massage really doesn't bring pain. "It all has a lot to do with the angle of the practitioner's hands on the person," says Aston. "Tissue runs in a certain direction. Massaging in that direction is smoother and less painful than going opposite the grain."

Strokes are soft and smooth as both hands work in concert with each other. "We glide and develop a tempo," she explains. "The second hand is used to move the tissue in an asymmetrical spiral. It creates slack in the tissue which puts us very deep. But to the client it doesn't feel deep because we gently spiral in, we don't just compress tissue. We go where the tissue directs us to go. We try to match each person's particular configuration."

That matching ability is what Sam Cardenas, R.P.T., likes best about Aston-Patterning. Cardenas owns a physical therapy clinic in San Francisco where some of the therapists are also certified Aston-Patterners. "The technique fits very well with physical therapy," he says. "If someone comes in with an injury, we work to treat the whole person, not just that person's ankle or knee. A case in point: A runner had a chronic ankle problem. The physical therapist trained in Aston-Patterning worked with her until she became aware of how she walked, how she ran, and how she could change those activities so that she wouldn't keep hurting her ankle. We got rid of the pain, but we also changed the underlying mechanics. Hopefully that will eliminate the problem in the future."

Low Back Pain

Aston-Patterners have been trained to become keen observers of the human body, and Edith Murphy, a physical therapist who works in Cardenas's clinic has noticed that people with low back pain often have similar body patterns. "Often, the person has a flattened low back, the pelvis is tucked under, and looking from the side the chest cavity appears to be leaning back instead of being directly over the pelvis."

As an Aston-Patterner, Murphy's goal is to find areas of tightness, and then relieve that tension with deep, spiralling massage. Now, you might think that if you have low back pain, the last thing you'd want someone to do is spiral down into it, but those with the problem who've felt the Aston-Patterning touch swear by it. "The hands-on part is a painless encouragement for healing," is how David Gamble describes the massage aspect of Aston-Patterning.

For close to 20 years, Gamble lived with low back pain. Then one day he discovered Aston-Patterning. "They showed me that the way I was moving was actually hurting me. Almost overnight I ended the back problem." Just one session left him "feeling lighter and taller. My movement became effortless. It's the state I like to live in."

To become a permanent resident of that state, Gamble learned a few tricks to keep his back pain at bay. "Now I picture my body as a tube with circles of energy. In my normal reaction to daily life those circles get off center, so the energy gets choked off in the tube. The circles, like cross-sections of the joints, are at my ankles, knees, hips and neck. So I just try to relax in those areas, and the circles naturally start to line up."

A Skiing Accident

Not lining up correctly is what caused all the problems for Christy Seidel, a two-time winner of the Governor's Cup in bicycling races in Colorado. Her problems began on a ski slope. During a downhill race in Aspen, one of Christy's ski tips caught a gate and she "really twisted and tore up the knee."

After two reconstructive surgeries, and two years of rehabilitation, Christy found that just trying to walk was a challenge. "A year ago when I started Aston-Patterning it was difficult to walk several blocks," she says. "I was in pretty sorry shape. Almost immediately after having the massage, I could tell that things in my knee were a little looser. It was easier to walk to the corner store, and things kept get-

ting better. Now I bike and swim three times a week, and I'm an avid athlete again."

A Clearer Voice

For Clara Howard of Mill Valley, just voicing her satisfaction with Aston-Patterning is a victory. Because of a mishap in surgery, she almost completely lost her ability to speak.

Fortunately her gasps for help were heard by Judith Aston. "I found that the position in which she held her chest reduced the volume of breath she could take," says Aston.

"By working with her to more fully exhale, her inhalation became more natural also, and as she exhaled she reduced some of the tension around her throat, allowing it to open more. Her alignment also improved as her chest relaxed and her head moved back, creating a straighter air passage."

There's no communication problem now, as Clara demonstrated in an interview for this book. "In the past I dreaded hearing the telephone ring because I knew that when I answered it, the person on the other end would not be able to hear me. But the breathing concepts that Judith taught me have helped significantly," Clara says as she looks down, and with a smile on her face, watches the tape recorder capture her new-found voice.

Chapter 8

BODY WRAPS

It's like a scene from "The Creature that Crawled Out from the Slime." But The Creature is *you*.

Moments ago, you stood in the sunny doorway fresh and bright in a white robe. Now you're flat on your back in the dim room, disappearing inch by inch beneath a layer of dark-green ooze. Inga, the lab-coated attendant, scoops the stuff with bare hands from an aluminum mixing bowl. Seaweed, she tells you, slathering it on thick. You're up to your neck in the gooey paste of algae and sea water. Something smells fishy. You do.

Smoothing on the last handful of deep-sea goop, Inga rinses her hands under a faucet and quickly proceeds to enfold you in a warm cocoon of sheets and towels and blankets. Your hair wrapped in a towel, you've changed character. Now you're The Mummy.

But mummies don't sweat, and that's what you're here for. Inga settles into a chair behind you. Her fingertips rest assuringly on your temples. You wait. A few minutes pass. It starts slowly. Your face grows moist, then your neck. Salty beads tickle as they roll down your cheeks one by one.

Inga wipes your forehead with a cool, damp cloth. You sense a radiant heat emanating from beneath your wraps. It builds up slowly but has a sharp edge, like the hot flush that crawls through you when you when you eat too-spicy food. Toxins, Inga explains. Poisons being pulled out from all the dank corners of your cells. Whatever it is, it feels good. Wet and sticky but good.

Twenty minutes after the initial wrap-up, Inga undoes the blankets and leads you slip-sliding to a shower. You feel weak and wasted. Torrents of dirty green water spin down the drain, taking with them any last traces of tension you might have had.

Thalassotherapy—the proper term for this seaweed slathering—is one of several types of body wraps, treatments in which your body is "wrapped" in a variety of materials or substances believed to be therapeutic. Their reputed benefits vary, from removing toxins to relieving chronic aches and pains. Many such treatments are available at spas, but you might also find a practitioner closer to home. This sampling of body wrap techniques will show you what to look for.

51

"Cooking" with Herbs

More readily available than thalassotherapy, *herbal wraps* actually promise quite similar benefits.

The essential ingredients of herbal wraps—mixes of dried herbs—come in three basic formulas, explains Lane Tietgen, director of The Cliff Spa in Utah. One formula has a stimulating effect, another is calming, and the third is cleansing.

To get cooking for an herbal wrap at The Cliff, an attendant tosses a folded bedsheet, two or three towels and a cheesecloth bag full of herbs into a large vat of steaming hot water. When you arrive for your treatment 24 hours later, the liquid has attained a consistency "four or five shades darker than Chinese restaurant tea," says Tietgen. The sheet and towels are thoroughly steeped in it.

A massage therapist draws the sheet out of the brew, drains off excess liquid and drapes it on a massage table. You climb onto the table nude or in your bathing suit and lie down. She folds the still-warm sheet over you, tops it with steaming herb-soaked towels, a wool blanket and a foil-and-plastic "space blanket" to help retain heat. After 20 sweaty minutes or so—during which, again, you are said to be excreting toxins—you head for the shower. When you get back, you can opt for a head-to-toe massage. Then, if not sooner, you enter another world.

"You'll feel spaced-out," says Tietgen. "It's obvious an herbal wrap does something in the way of relaxing and cleansing." How does it work? "From a scientific point of view, I don't know. I don't think anybody else knows, either. It just does."

Mud and More Mud

Healers in early civilizations unearthed the healing powers of mud, and their counterparts still use it today. It's a dirty job, but somebody's got to do it.

"Mud is one of the most effective ways in the world to apply heat to the body," says John Wilkinson, D.C., a chiropractor and longtime owner of Doctor Wilkinson's Hot Springs in Calistoga, California. "Penetrating very deeply, heat stimulates perspiration that draws toxins out of your body."

Calistoga has been a hotspot since the late 1800s, when visitors took note of its plentiful supplies of natural volcanic ash and hot mineral water. The treatments at Doc Wilkinson's spa help maintain the town's reputation as the *mud bath* capital of the country.

If you're ready to be reduced to a quivering mud-covered mass, check in for "the works" at Doc's. Your private bathtub of black, oozing mud is prepared at the proper temperature (about 103°F) and the proper consistency ("You don't sink to the bottom and you don't float to the top"). You lower yourself in slowly. Up to your neck in the hot stew, you're sweating away before you know it. About 15 minutes later you emerge and take a shower. Then you climb into a whirl-pool, sweating again while hot mineral water swirls around you. A quarter-hour later, you crawl out, are wrapped in dry blankets and led to a quiet room where you collapse. Then you get a massage. Then you get up, get dressed, and get going. Or try to, anyway.

A variation on the mud bath is the *mud wrap.* "I import mud from the Dead Sea," says Dolores Schneider, director of Sharon Springs Spa in New York State. "The Dead Sea is the lowest place on the planet. Its bottom has the richest sediment, loaded with minerals." These minerals, she claims, are absorbed through the skin during a treatment, immediately benefiting those with nutritional deficiencies.

Instead of lowering you into a tub of mud, the folks at Sharon Springs will coat you with a nice even layer of the stuff, then swaddle you in plastic wrap and a blanket, in which you'll stay sweatily snuggled for a half hour.

As if cleaning out toxins and replenishing minerals weren't benefit enough, "a mud wrap is a beauty treatment, too," says Schneider. "Your skin will be smoother."

And then there are *mud packs,* which are applied to specific parts of your body—particularly arthritic joints or sore muscles—to ease pain. At Sharon Springs, your stiff knee will be wrapped in a mud-soaked cloth pack held in place with plastic wrap and blankets. When all that comes off 30 minutes later, says Schneider, you may feel remarkably relieved of pain.

The last word on mud is something called *parafango,* which combines muddy volcanic ash (*fango* means "mud" in Italian) with paraffin. The treatment is common in Europe and is growing in popularity in this country, says Lane Tietgen, whose spa specializes in it.

When you show up for a parafango session, don't be surprised to see an industrial piece of equipment that resembles a Dairy Queen machine, as Tietgen describes it. "Except it's hot instead of cold, and instead of ice cream, you get this thick, brown mixture."

Armed with a steel tray of this therapeutic brownie batter, your therapist smooths it onto an ailing part of your body, then wraps it with a piece of cloth. The paraffin quickly solidifies, sealing the hot mud in place. About 20 minutes later, your pain may be peeling off at the same time the therapist removes the parafango.

"When it comes right down to the nitty-gritty, mud is a good way of relaxing all the systems of the body," says Dr. Wilkinson. "There's no magic formula or special chemicals. It just seems to work and people get a lot of good from it."

Enzyme Energy

To enjoy the benefits of mud without the mess, consider an *enzyme bath* instead. Enzymes, a type of protein, are normally found in the cells of plants and animals where they foster various chemical reactions. More recently, they can also be found in a little spa in northern California.

There, at a place called Osmosis, enzyme powder taken from organically grown vegetables and other plants is mixed with powdered cedar wood, rice bran and warm water in a hot tub. Within 24 hours the fermenting reddish batter has heated itself up and is ready for guests.

"It's pleasantly moist and fragrant," says Amie Hill, an attendant who will march into the steaming tub with a pitchfork, clear out a person-size space and help you crawl in, covering you up to the chin with the substance like a beachgoer buried in warm sand. A quarter-hour later she'll lead you out onto the porch and fluff your skin off with a natural bristle brush. After a shower and a rest under warm blankets, you can go. If you want to.

"It's very rejuvenating. People seem to feel energized as well as relaxed, not wiped out as in some other heat treatments," says Michael Stusser, who came upon the treatment during travels in Japan and established Osmosis to share it with others in this country. "It's a biologically generated heat source. An electrochemical field is created, which I think must be affecting those kinds of energies within the body."

Specialized Packs

Far from the spa scene, some physicians—particularly the naturo-pathic sort—have been giving their patients body wraps for years. One common type is the *poultice,* a cloth pack of herbs, mashed vegetables or similar organic substances applied to the body.

"A wide range of plants help relieve symptoms of illness and pain, and actually heal some infections," says Dr. Jan Gagnon, a naturopathic physician in Seattle. "Carrot packs placed over a person's throat, for example, can help with sore throat. Comfrey roots or basil leaves help bee stings heal. A hot castor oil pack kept on your chest overnight while you sleep is wonderful for everything from tension to respiratory infections."

Following a basic recipe, you can apply poultices to yourself, she says. For starters, cut and mash plant leaves with a small amount of warm water, or put them in a food processor, until they become a kind of paste. Spread this paste onto a layer of cheesecloth (or thick flannel for a castor oil pack) and cover it with a second layer of cloth. Place the pack on your chest or tie it loosely around your aching body part. Leave it on for about an hour while you lie or sit still, then rest or engage in low activity afterward. (For a castor oil pack, apply a heating pad with a towel over it.)

"In many cases, you benefit from the plant constituents being absorbed through your skin," claims Dr. Gagnon. "Some poultices increase your circulation and help your white blood cells get where they need to go to help you heal." Others can relieve pain and congestion, she says.

The immune system is especially enhanced by *wet sheet treatments,* according to Dr. Gagnon. The one- to two-hour process takes you through a complicated series of steps, wrapping you mummy-style in a cold, wet sheet covered with wool blankets. Your body responds at first by shivering, then by relaxing, then by heating up, and finally by perspiring profusely for up to an hour while it supposedly pours out toxins. This intense treatment is best given by a professional, says Dr. Gagnon.

habits can be countered, too. "We do herbal wraps for people who've had too much to drink during the holiday season," says Tietgen. "It really helps get rid of that miserable feeling." Wet sheet treatments have been known to have a pronounced effect among cigarette smokers: During the perspiration stage, the sheet turns yellow, notes Dr. Gagnon.

Arthritis, rheumatism and sore muscles are said to benefit from the close application of heat in the various treatments. "The knees, the shoulders, wherever there's pain—a mud bath can help," says Schneider. Parafango has been helpful providing temporary re-

THE HEALING POWER OF BODY WRAPS

One thing right off: Body wraps won't help you lose weight, though some practitioners might make that claim. It's just not so, say spa directors Lane Tietgen and Dolores Schneider. "Sure, you can lose a pound of water perspiring, but drink a glass of water and you gain it right back," Schneider says.

The main benefit of most body wraps, they claim, is detoxification through perspiration. "Herbal wraps are good for overexercised muscles," says Tietgen. "They help clear out the lactic acid that accumulates in painful deposits during exercise." The aftereffects of overindulgence or poor health

Wrap Resources

For information on mud baths contact Doctor Wilkinson's Hot Springs, 1507 Lincoln Avenue, Calistoga, CA 94515 (707) 942-4102.

For more information on enzyme baths, contact Osmosis, P.O. Box 1713, Sebastopol, CA 95473 (707) 823-8231.

For help in locating a naturopathic physician trained in poultices, wet sheet treatments and other natural healing treatments, contact the American Association of Naturopathic Physicians, P.O. Box 33046, Portland, OR 97233 (503) 255-4863.

For addresses and phone numbers of other spas mentioned, see chapter 50.

lief from chronic back pain and muscle spasms, among other things, says Tietgen.

Enzyme baths reportedly have similar results. A number of chiropractors have even referred their patients to Osmosis as a treatment for problems like sciatica.

Poultices promise relief from a wide range of conditions, including sunburn, bee stings, bruises and minor infections. Perhaps most significant are the effects of body wraps upon stress.

"In the old days, people came to mud baths for aches and pains, but now most of them come for stress relief," says Dr. Wilkinson. "Removed from a stress-filled world, for a short time you're in a state of suspended animation, with no pressure on your bones, your muscles or your mind."

"People leave here so relaxed," says Amie Hill of Osmosis. "They have this sort of rosy-cheeked innocence. I almost wish I could keep them from going back out there into the big world."

Chapter 9

CHIROPRACTIC

In a peaceful little town called Palmerton, tucked into the foothills of Pennsylvania's Pocono Mountains, 52-year-old Shirley Kopfer lies face-down on a padded table. A medium-built, middle-aged man walks up behind her. He greets Kopfer warmly, then proceeds to press his thumbs into her waist, twist her arms, turn her head from side to side and thrust his palms into her back.

Standing by Kopfer's side, you can't help feeling a bit concerned. Yet it's obvious that she relishes the treatment. After all, she's been coming to see Louis Sportelli, D.C., a chiropractor, regularly for over ten years. "This isn't exactly your afternoon tea party, but in my case I know it's necessary," she says. Standing, she removes all doubt as to whether she liked the treatment: "I have three men in my life," she says, "God, my husband and Dr. Lou."

More gushing testimony to the effectiveness of chiropractic comes from Dr. Sportelli's patients up and down the hall, some of whom talk while hooked up to strange-looking back-and-neck-stretching contraptions.

"I feel so much better," says one patient, unbuckling her head from a sling hung from the ceiling. "I never thought I'd come to a chiropractor, but it really has helped me," says another. "I probably wouldn't be walking anymore if it weren't for this guy here," says a third, an elderly gentleman, as he motions to Dr. Sportelli.

If there were a hallway you could walk from Boston to Miami to Seattle, you undoubtedly would hear many more comments like these from the approximately 15 million Americans who regularly see chiropractors. They come for many reasons, but mostly for back and neck pain. The plenitude of chiropractors must say something for the popularity of their services: there are now an estimated 40,000 in America, and 2,500 are joining the ranks each year.

With these impressive numbers, chiropractic is without question the big daddy of the hands-on healing arts. Chiropractors like to point out that they form the second largest group of primary-care health providers in the United States (after M.D.'s). But, what is it exactly that these 40,000 chiropractors do? Let's pop back in on Dr. Sportelli.

Hands Meet Spine

"Hi, I'm Louis Sportelli!" says the man in the white coat, shaking your hand vigorously. He looks the part, all right, but he's not *stuffy* enough to be a doctor, you think. He is a doctor, though, as are all chiropractors, otherwise known as doctors of chiropractic, or D.C.'s. They're licensed in all 50 states and Canada, and in order to obtain the license they must first complete at least two years of college followed by four years of chiropractic school.

During those formative years, budding chiropractors have it drummed into them that good health and good anatomy are as inseparable as good wine and good grapes. They are taught that any misalignment of bones, especially the little bones that make up your spine and encase your central nervous system, can lead not only to aches and pains but also to a variety of ailments, from headaches to arm pain to an upset stomach.

And chiropractors are taught that often the key to treating such problems is to carefully manipulate these spine bones, the vertebrae, back into shape. Sometimes they use traction devices like the ones in Dr. Sportelli's office, but mostly they use their hands.

Chiropractors don't really work on your spine to play with bones, though. "They work on the spine to get to the nervous system," says Lawrence DeMann, Jr., D.C., director of New York's Manhattan Chiropractic Center. The nervous system, he says, "is the central computer system for the body"—so a problem in your main terminal can manifest itself just about anywhere in the body.

Shirley Kopfer has serious back problems, involving arthritis, so her hands-on treatment is sometimes painful. Perhaps more representative of the chiropractic experience is that of Tracy Kovaleski, a 26-year-old who's been coming to Dr. Sportelli a year and a half now for her tension headaches. "It was scary at first, but it doesn't hurt a bit," she says.

A Typical Visit

What should *you* expect when you see a chiropractor? Let's start at the top . . . no, the back, assuming that's what's hurting you. A visit to the chiropractor will likely incorporate several standard procedures.

First thing he'll do is examine you. (We'll say *he* for convenience, but 16 percent of all chiropractors are women.) He'll take your pulse. He'll hit you with a little hammer on the knee to test your reflexes. He'll ask you about your personal habits. Do you smoke or drink? What illnesses run in your family? He'll ask you to describe your symptoms. So far, it's just like going to any doctor's office, perhaps somewhat more personal, less rushed. But soon he does some things to you that no doctor has ever done before.

As chiropractors look first to your skeleton, the next step in your examination is a little test of how well your bones, and the muscles that push and pull them, work or don't work. So, if you're ready ... Please lean over and touch your toes. Good. Now lean back, as far as you can go. Tilt your head to the left. Good. Tilt it to the right, all the way. Now lift each knee as high as you can.

And so on ... until the chiropractor gets a pretty good idea of how well your joints are joined. He carries a large plastic protractor to actually measure the number of degrees you can bend your various body parts.

Next comes the spinal exam. The chiropractor runs his fingers over every inch of your spine, pushing a bit here, and pinching a bit there. It doesn't hurt; it just feels ... well, it makes you feel somewhat vulnerable.

After this point in the examination, most chiropractors will want to do a spinal x-ray, says Dr. Sportelli. This, he says, is one of the methods by which your chiropractor can really know what's going on. But you may be inclined to balk, knowing that x-ray radiation carries some risk. Dr. Sportelli maintains that the benefits overshadow any risk.

"You may not see any connection between a fall 25 years ago, an accident as a child, or some other seemingly unrelated item and your present illness, but all these factors will be significant to your chiropractor, and may be present on your x-ray," says Dr. Sportelli, who is a member of the Governing Board of the American Chiropractic Association. Whether an x-ray is part of your initial visit or not, if you proceed with treatment, your chiropractor will wish to *adjust* you.

The "Adjustment"

Now it's your turn to join the millions of others who have experienced a chiropractic *adjustment*. Keep in mind that adjustments—the hands-on part of chiropractic—are not the only things chiropractors do, but, as Dr. DeMann says, "they are central to everything else."

Hop up on the table.

Not all adjustments, sometimes called *manipulations*, are the same. The chiropractor will concentrate on that area of your spine which seems to be out of alignment, based either on your physical examination or what is seen on your x-rays. The specifics of the adjustment will also vary depending on your symptoms.

Chiropractors believe that different segments of your spine connect to various parts of your nervous system. So a problem with your left hand, for example, might indicate that a specific vertebra—the one where the hand's nerves originate—is out of alignment.

The manner in which you're adjusted will also depend on the individual style of your chiropractor. Dr. DeMann likens chiropractic to ballet. "We can all have the same choreography, but each dancer, or chiropractor, will look different in practice."

You're a bit nervous to have your chiropractor practicing his two-step on your back as you lie facedown on his padded table. But it's too late to get up and leave. He rubs you a bit, just to "soften things up," he says. He leans you to one side, pulling the higher leg up toward your chest. He places his knee on your upper thigh, and starts to push down. His one hand reaches across your shoulder, and he starts to push in the opposite direction. You feel yourself being twisted. The last thing you hear is "O.K, now." He pushes down harder on your leg and against your shoulder and . . . *Crack!*

The startling sound of your spine cracking is a new sensation for your body. He rolls you over onto the other side. You're too dumbstruck to speak. Once again you hear "Okay, relax," and . . . *Crack!*

The doctor has just applied a common technique for relieving back pain. He smiles and asks if there's any pain. Amazingly, the answer is no.

First-time adjustments are scary for many, but the fear is unfounded, says Dr. Sportelli. And Dr. DeMann says that the cracking sounds you often hear during an adjustment are no different from what you hear when you crack your knuckles.

But you can't help thinking that cracked knuckles are one thing, backs are another. You're now on your back, however, and the chiropractor circles around so that his tummy is pressed against your head. He gently cradles you, the sides of your head in the palms of his hands. Ahh, you think, he's about to do something nice like before when he rubbed your back, when all of a sudden . . . *Crack!*

Just a second ago you were looking at that nice plant by the window. Now you're looking at the wall on the other side of the room, and now—*Crack!*

You're looking at that plant by the window again. The doctor has just given you a common adjustment for neck stiffness.

When it's all over, you stand and tentatively take your first step. You dress. You thank the chiropractor. You head home. You think it's all over. Until that night.

Round about your usual bedtime, you set the alarm, fluff the pillow under your head, and lie back for a good night's sleep. When all of a sudden . . . *Crack!*

There's some settling going on in your skeleton, somewhere. You're not sure if it's good or bad, or whether it will eventually take care of your back problems. You do feel that, somehow, you'll never be exactly the same.

When will you have to return for another adjustment? "The number of treatments required by any particular patient varies enormously," says Dr. Sportelli. "Sometimes we can never correct a situation. We can only make the patient's life more livable."

Part of making a patient's life more livable, he says, involves a "holistic approach" to medicine. The chiropractor, aside from adjusting you, may also advise you on matters of nutrition and exercise, posture, and general lifestyle.

The Road to Respect

The first reportedly successful application of chiropractic was in a small town in Iowa on September 18, 1895. A self-educated healer named D. D. Palmer is said to have cured an acquaintance of deafness by manipulating his spine back into alignment. Palmer became the world's first chiropractor, as well as the first in a long line to be jailed for practicing medicine without a license.

Most states were licensing chiropractors by the late 1950s, but "prejudice and hostility" against them continued for years, particularly among physicians who saw them as competition, says Russell Gibbons, editor of the journal *Chiropractic History*. In fact, from the day D. D. Palmer first claimed that he cured deafness, medical doctors have sneered at chiropractic. But starting in the early 1970s, a number of studies brought the profession new respect.

The Oregon Workmen's Compensation Board, for example, found that chiropractors got workers with back injuries back on the job faster than physicians did. Of those chiropractic patients studied, 82 percent returned to work within one week of their injury; of those patients who sought a physician's care, only 41 percent returned within a week.

Another study at the University of Utah looked at 232 persons who had been treated for back problems, some by physicians, some by chiropractors. The researchers concluded that "the intervention of a chiropractor in problems [related to] neck and spine injuries was at least as effective as that of a physician."

And finally, an exhaustive study ordered by the New Zealand government in 1979 concluded: "Modern chiropractic is far from being an 'unscientific cult.'" The report added that spinal manipulation in the hands of an educated chiropractor is safe and "effective in relieving musculoskeletal symptoms such as back pain, and other symptoms known to respond to such therapy, such as migraine."

Summing up other studies, Scott Haldeman, M.D., D.C., Ph.D., a teacher of medicine at the University of California and of chiropractic at the Los Angeles Chiropractic College, says, "Most of the things we know about chiropractic circle around the management of back and neck pain." And for these problems, he says, "If the patient wishes quicker relief he very

Shopping for a Chiropractor

With 40,000 chiropractors in the United States, and their numbers growing rapidly, chances are you have a choice of at least several in your community. But where do you start? "Finding a good chiropractor is like finding a good physician, or a good plumber—start with their reputation," says Scott Haldeman, M.D., D.C., who considers himself both a pretty good chiropractor *and* physician. He recommends you begin your search by asking friends, family and neighbors.

Should you not be acquainted with anyone seeing a chiropractor (once you ask around, you may be surprised), there are other avenues. Dr. Louis Sportelli suggests you ask for a referral from your local chiropractic association.

If you have other questions about this form of therapy, you can contact one of the two largest national chiropractic groups, the American Chiropractic Association (ACA) and the International Chiropractors Association (ICA). Once distinguished by their widely varying philosophies and politics, the difference between the ACA and ICA these days, says Dr. Sportelli, "is so slim it's ridiculous."

In fact, according to officials at both groups, they may have merged by the time you're reading this book. You may also want to be aware of a third group, smaller than the other two, the Federation of Straight Chiropractors. Members of the Federation believe in "superstraight" chiropractic. That is, they adjust spines only. No nutritional advice or other nonskeletal services are provided.

The ACA also offers the following tips for evaluating a chiropractor:

• Does his conduct indicate that he is concerned about you as an individual?

• Is his office neat and clean?

• Will he offer you emergency care if you need it?

• When away from the office, does he provide another chiropractor to take calls?

• Does he explain the necessity for all examinations and therapy and justify the need for treatment?

In addition, the ACA suggests that any chiropractor who treats you should first tell you everything he plans to do, and then get your permission to do it. He should explain alternative treatments. And he should explain the financial aspects of treatment. (According to the ACA, the average chiropractic patient comes into the office about once every three

---

well may get quicker relief from the chiropractor than from the medical physician."

Medicare, Medicaid, vocational rehabilitation programs and workers' compensation programs across the country now recognize chiropractic. Just as important, most commercial

weeks. The average cost per visit is about $30.)

Lastly, says Dr. Haldeman, don't keep going back to the same chiropractor for treatment after treatment unless it's working for you. "If a treatment is going to help," he says, "it will generally work within four to six weeks."

For more information on chiropractic:

The American Chiropractic
  Association
1701 Clarendon Boulevard
Arlington, VA 22209
(703) 276-8800

The Federation of Straight
  Chiropractors
642 Broad Street
Clifton, NJ 07013
(201) 777-1197

The International Chiropractors
  Association
1901 L Street NW
Suite 800
Washington, DC 20036
(202) 659-6476

health insurance policies today cover chiropractic care. Even hospitals are now starting to grant privileges to, and even hire, chiropractors.

THE HEALING POWER OF CHIROPRACTIC

Many personal testimonies attest not just to the effectiveness of chiropractic, but to its wonders. Talk to Budd Coates, for example. He's a world-class marathon runner who ran to a chiropractor's office after he fell on some leaves and started to have hip problems. "It was like magic," says Coates. "He put me on his table, did this thing to me and the problem disappeared."

You could also talk to Deborah Grandinetti. In college she started to experience a mysterious, painful neck cramp. "It got stuck so bad," she says, "I couldn't even move it." Grandinetti went to see a chiropractor, and after only two consecutive days of treatment, she says, "I got better."

Or you could ask Brian Hernon about his experience. Running circles around indoor tracks in high school and college set the stage for some painful knee problems that began in his early thirties. So he went to a chiropractor. After only one treatment, he says, "I got immediate relief."

One of Dr. DeMann's patients is Peter Martins, director of the New York City Ballet. About eight years ago, while he was still dancing, Martins developed a back problem that kept him off his feet for six months. The performer visited numerous doctors and tried various treatments—all unsuccessful

—before considering chiropractic. "I did a few very light adjustments on his spine," says Dr. DeMann, and in a few months Martins was back on stage.

Once, recalls Dr. DeMann, he was called to see Imelda Marcos, wife of the former Philippine leader, who was experiencing acute pain in her arm during a visit to New York. "I traced the problem right to her fifth and sixth cervical vertebrae," he says, and after a few simple adjustments she was cured.

With such diverse success stories, one may wonder—what are the limitations of chiropractic? To Dr. Sportelli, the sky's the limit. For orthopedic conditions (those involving muscles and bones), there's no question: one should try chiropractic first, he says. But for many other health problems, he asserts, a chiropractor just may be able to help.

John D. Vilardo, D.C., an associate with Atlanta's Sparlin Chiropractic Clinic, agrees. He says chiropractic has the ability to "turn on the power of the body's healing capacity." Yet the public still perceives chiropractors as primarily back and neck specialists. In fact, nearly nine out of every ten people who walk into a chiropractor's office come for aching muscles or creaky bones, and of these, 85 percent point to their lower back or neck, according to the American Chiropractic Association.

A nationwide poll taken by two *New York Times* health writers found that chiropractors are seen three times more often for back-related ills than all other types of medical doctors combined. The poll also found that sore-back sufferers say they find relief with chiropractors 56 percent of the time.

A Knack for Backs

What do chiropractors do to help all those sore backs? It really depends, says Dr. Vilardo. "Low back pain can be caused by anything from a strained muscle to a kidney infection to a trauma," he says. The first step is to find out what's causing your pain, and there are various tests to determine this.

If it's a simple muscle strain, that usually can be fixed up with a little rest, says Dr. Vilardo. A kidney infection may require antibiotics, for which the chiropractor will refer the patient to an M.D. But if the problem is a pinched nerve, then "the bone obviously needs to be put back in its original position," and this, he says, is when a hands-on adjustment can help.

A common adjustment for low back pain is the *side posture adjustment*, described earlier. "It will usually take care of the problem," says Dr. Vilardo.

After back problems, chiropractors are most often consulted for the ailments listed below.

Spinal Disk Problems

Think of your spinal disks as jelly doughnuts, says Dr. Vilardo. Some slipped disks are so serious that the jellylike cartilage squeezes out completely from between the doughnut-shaped vertebrae. In these cases, "chiropractors usually can't help," he says. Surgery is often required. But less serious slipped disks (where the "jelly" protrudes but hasn't popped out) often can be helped.

For working on disk problems, the chiropractor may use a table somewhat like the rack of medieval days. The patient lies face down on the "rack," holding a bar over and above the head with both hands. The table can slide backwards, down, or side to side, allowing the chiropractor to stretch the spine while his index fingers work to reset the misaligned bones and cartilage. "Usually a patient will respond after two to three weeks of treatment," says Dr. Vilardo.

Headaches

"One patient of mine had headaches for 35 years—ever since she fell out of a tree when she was ten," says Dr. Vilardo. "She'd tried every medication known, nothing worked. She came to me in desperation." After several adjustments, he adds, her headaches became a thing of the past. "All she had was a pinched nerve."

Whether it's a pinched nerve or simply "nerves," chiropractors claim frequent success with headaches. One common technique, says Dr. Vilardo, is for the chiropractor to stand behind the seated patient, and gently (using the sides of the index fingers) push into place the bones in the upper neck.

Whiplash

Sudden jolts to the body can cause a whiplash injury anywhere on your spine, but most often in the neck. Dr. Vilardo says that a chiropractic adjustment is ill-advised until the swelling goes down, usually within 2 weeks. After that, he says, an adjustment can usually help. Here's one technique: with the patient lying face down, the chiropractor cradles the head to one side, and (again using the index finger) tries to slide the neck bones into their proper places.

Arm and Shoulder Pain

These can be caused by a pinched nerve in the neck, or injury to the arm or shoulder itself, says Dr. Vilardo. The chiropractor may decide to use a common adjustment for the neck. Or, he may decide to go directly to the shoulder. In that case, the patient sits with his arm bent over his chest. The doctor then reaches over the patient from behind and pulls up and back on the bent elbow.

Chiropractors do not recommend that you try any of these adjustments at home.

Chapter 10

CRANIOSACRAL THERAPY

You may not know it, but your head is expanding right now. In another few seconds it will start shrinking. If it's already shrinking, then it will start expanding again in just a moment.

You won't see such change in the mirror, and chances are good you could go the rest of your life without noticing it and never lose a good night's sleep. Maybe.

But, if you've ever suffered from such things as migraine headaches, temporomandibular joint (TMJ) dysfunction, ringing in the ears, dyslexia, depression or any number of chronic aches and pains throughout your body, then the fact that your head expands and contracts at a rate of 8 to 12 times a minute could become quite important to you.

In fact, this knowledge, combined with the skilled touch of someone practicing a hands-on healing technique known as craniosacral therapy, might help provide relief from many such disorders. And that could be worth a good night's sleep.

Cranial Respiration

Craniosacral therapists lightly manipulate the bones of the skull. In so doing they also manipulate the membranes beneath the skull that support the brain, as well as the cerebrospinal fluid that cushions and bathes the brain and spinal cord from cranium to sacrum.

In much the same way that contracting your calf muscles helps move blood in the lower legs back to the heart, craniosacral therapists believe that the motion of the skull helps move cerebrospinal fluid around your brain and down your spine to the sacrum, which gently rocks in rhythm with the motions of the skull.

But these therapists also believe that all the bumps, bruises and sharp blows to the head you've received since the day you were born have probably knocked some of those bones out of alignment, causing them to freeze up or move improperly.

By gently manipulating the skull bones at the sutures (those fibrous joints that hold bones together in the skull), craniosacral therapists seek to realign the bones so that they move in sync with one another, allowing the cerebrospinal fluid to circulate freely. During the manipulation process, therapists also remove the stresses that accumulate in the membranes supporting and surrounding the brain and spinal column.

As Jim Asher of the Colorado Cranial Institute in Boulder, explains: "We're moving fluid, rebalancing fluid, stretching membranes and sometimes balancing bones."

Exactly why this stretching and balancing produces the results it does is still a matter of some speculation. "I can't answer questions with the word 'exactly' in them," says John Upledger, D.O., a craniosacral instructor and director of the Upledger Institute in Palm Beach Gardens, Florida.

"In some cases manipulation might increase the circulation of the cerebrospinal fluid," he says, "but the primary goal is to mobilize the system. What we want is to see that system moving symmetrically and without a lot of resistance to its activity. The benefit of that can be as far reaching as taking away a chronic pain in your left leg."

Meant for Motion

Though craniosacral therapy started out as a branch of osteopathy, the inability of its practitioners to explain exactly how the technique works hurt its popularity. But even more than the mysterious nature of its healing powers, there's another, more basic reason why you've probably never heard of craniosacral therapy before.

As noted above, craniosacral therapists believe the bones in your skull were meant for motion, and they use their gentle, hands-on technique to help increase and synchronize that motion. But *Gray's Anatomy* (the bible of anatomical reference books), along with most other anatomy texts, says the bones of the skull are immobile. Many doctors agree, implying that any therapy based on movable skull bones must clearly be nonsense.

But the massage therapists, osteopathic physicians and physicians who do practice craniosacral therapy disagree with the accepted view of cranial immobility. They point instead to the teachings of William G. Sutherland, a turn-of-the-century osteopathic physician whose ideas about flexible sutures and cranial movement have only recently been subjected to serious, scientific scrutiny.

Dr. Sutherland believed that the skull moved in response to the body's production of cerebrospinal fluid deep inside the ventricles of the brain. He theorized that the ventricles pulse as they release cerebrospinal fluid, increasing the hydraulic pressure inside the skull and causing it to expand.

Dr. Sutherland wondered what would happen if the skull bones were prevented from moving, and wrapped his head with bandages in order to find out. The result was "an immediate change of the movement of the diaphragmatic respiratory mechanism," he wrote. This sudden change that Dr. Sutherland noted in his breathing pattern helped convince him that the cranial respiratory system was "the primary respiratory mechanism" of the body, and that breathing was, in his words, "secondary thereto."

The idea that the skull was designed to expand and contract and that the craniosacral system was the primary respiratory system of the body did little to endear Dr. Sutherland to mainstream medical practitioners.

He did, however, obtain some fairly remarkable results with his cranial work, and detailed the technique in a small book called *The Cranial Bowl*, which he filled with case histories. Recently, an interdisciplinary team of osteopathic physicians, anatomists, biophysicists and others at the Department of Biomechanics at Michigan State University's College of Osteopathic Medicine launched a scientific investigation of Dr. Sutherland's work, determined to put his theories to the test once and for all.

Dr. Upledger was a member of the Michigan State investigating team.

"The department said we're either going to prove it true or prove it false," he says, "so we started looking." The result: "We found that it had a pretty good scientific base."

An Uphill Battle

Indeed, just about everyone who has seriously examined Dr. Sutherland's theories has concluded that he was correct, and that restrictions in the craniosacral rhythm may be implicated in such things as migraines, depression, cerebral palsy and more.

Does that mean you'll be able to walk into an osteopathic physician's office and request a session of craniosacral therapy? Hardly.

Notes Stephen Blood, D.O., president of the Cranial Academy in Meridian, Idaho, an organization dedicated to furthering the cause of craniosacral therapy among osteopathic physicians: "It is still practiced in our profession, but it is practiced by a small minority of the 24,000 osteopathic physicians in the country."

Small minority is right. The Cranial Academy has fewer than 300 members. And, as Dr. Blood points out, it wages an uphill battle in trying to popularize the technique with the many osteopathic physicians who've never tried craniosacral therapy.

"For one, it takes a level of palpatory skill that's not there for everyone," he explains. "Also, it's very time consuming and it's not cost-effective for the osteopathic physician. You could normally see two or three patients in the time that it takes to do a single session of cranial work."

Dr. Upledger agrees. "I book patients at 45-minute intervals when I'm doing cranial work. Most osteopathic physicians aren't going to spend 45 minutes with a patient."

As a result, craniosacral work is now practiced mostly by physical therapists, massage professionals and other bodywork specialists, many of whom routinely spend an hour or more with individual clients and think nothing of it.

Many of Asher's students at the Colorado Cranial Institute are massage professionals who have experienced craniosacral therapy as clients and simply want to add it to their repertoire. "Basically," Asher explains, "the students come in and study for about four days, then they go out and practice for three to six months."

Students eventually progress from the basic level to intermediate and advanced. The total time involved can vary from a year to 18 months, depending on the student's progress and the amount of time spent in practice between levels. The school has been in existence since 1980.

Dr. Upledger's school utilizes the same basic format as Asher's, with some minor variations. "We have four levels," he says. "People take an introductory seminar, then go out and practice a few months. They come back and we give them an intermediate seminar. They practice that, and then

there are two more levels they go through. It's about 20 days of training over a year or year and a half."

Dr. Upledger says his students are primarily physical therapists, chiropractors, M.D.'s or D.O.'s. The Upledger Institute has been in existence for about four years, and Upledger estimates that more than 2,000 people have attended his training seminars to date.

Both Dr. Upledger and Asher agree that the most important skill any craniosacral student can possess, regardless of background, is "very good palpatory ability, or the ability to develop it."

A Keen Sense of Touch

Dan Matarazzo has been practicing craniosacral therapy for the past four years in Tucson, Arizona. He developed his "palpatory ability" at the Colorado Cranial Institute, and like many of its graduates, he mixes cranial work with other techniques. In Matarazzo's case it's Rolfing, a deep tissue technique that, while effective, can be uncomfortable for some people.

Matarazzo says that craniosacral therapy can be a very beneficial technique for patients who suffer from shyness and who are unable to relax in typical massage settings.

"Cranial work can be done on people who are fully clothed," he explains. "On the other hand, something like

Rolfing is a much more direct intervention in the body and it's usually done in your underwear. There are some people who are just not ready for that. So, where it's applicable, I use cranial work instead and find it really effective."

One of craniosacral therapy's most effective applications, Matarazzo says, is with TMJ-related jaw pain: "I see a lot of occipital and temporal problems, with the temporals leading to TMJ problems." (The temporal bones are located on the side of the skull, around the ears. The occipital bone is located in the lower back part of the skull, where it wraps around to join the temporals.)

Like most craniosacral practitioners, Matarazzo uses his keen sense of touch to detect problems throughout the body, even though his hands never leave the skull. "I see a lot of people with occipital problems that tell me they have some pelvic problems as well. There's a real relationship between the occiput and the sacrum. You can tell what's going on in the pelvis by the way the occiput is sitting."

Not surprising, perhaps, Matarazzo finds headaches the easiest malady for cranial work to treat. "The hardest things tend to be old head injuries that the patient may have internalized and may not even be aware of," he says.

Like Matarazzo, Theresa Pearce is trained in both craniosacral therapy and Rolfing. Unlike Matarazzo, however, this Grand Rapids, Michigan,

practitioner never combines the two therapies for use on the same patient.

"Most of those who come to me for cranial work come because of stress, chronic headaches or neck pain," she says. "They are the type of people who can't seem to let go and relax."

Pearce also finds that craniosacral therapy is effective on TMJ pain. She believes most TMJ problems can be traced back to birth trauma. "I'm 33, and a lot of people from my generation have gone through forceps deliveries," she says. "You can see that in people, the way their skulls are pressed in on the sides, and the way a lot of them have TMJ symptoms now."

Craniosacral and Kids

The trauma placed on the human skull during birth has been a subject of natural fascination for craniosacral therapists. One of the first osteopathic physicians to explore and apply cranial work to young children was Dr. Beryl F. Arbuckle, a pediatrician who studied with Dr. Sutherland and soon became one of craniosacral therapy's most vocal proponents.

Dr. Arbuckle applied Dr. Sutherland's techniques to the management of cerebral palsy cases, and with great success. As her fame grew, she began treating patients from all over the world and was eventually awarded osteopathic medicine's highest honor, the Andrew Taylor Still Medallion. Even so, her method of treatment—

craniosacral therapy—languished in obscurity.

The use of this technique for treating children has not been completely forgotten or abandoned, however. "Cranial manipulation and pediatrics just go hand-in-hand," says the Cranial Academy's Dr. Blood. "I can't imagine being able to work on children and not taking advantage of it."

And neither, it seems, can pediatrician Paul Dunn, one of the few M.D.'s in the nation who uses craniosacral therapy in his practice. "The first time I heard of it was in 1969," recalls the Oak Park, Illinois, physician. "A family came in with a severely brain damaged child and said that an osteopathic physician was manipulating the child's skull bones. They asked me what I thought of it. I told them I really didn't think it could be done, but if they thought it was helping, go ahead."

Several years later, in 1974, Dr. Dunn attended a medical meeting where he met an osteopathic physician who was using the technique in his practice. His interest was piqued. After visiting extensively with one of the osteopathic physicians, Dr. Dunn decided to learn the technique himself. "It's been 14 years now and I'm quite pleased with it," he says.

Dr. Dunn incorporates craniosacral work into the holistic approach he takes when treating children. "We use it as part of the picture," he explains. "But the kids we use it on are those who have brain injuries, developmental delays, hyperactivity and so on. In itself it is not a cure-all, but it is a very useful adjunct to the other types of treatment we do."

For the last eight years, Dr. Dunn has also been using craniosacral therapy as part of his approach to help adult patients suffering from long-standing fatigue, depression, headaches, gastrointestinal problems and other problems.

Despite such stories of positive results, there's little chance of craniosacral therapy gaining widespread

Craniosacral Resources

For more information on craniosacral therapy:

Colorado Cranial Institute
466 Marine Street
Boulder, CO 80302
(303) 447-2760

Executive Director
The Cranial Academy
1140 West Eighth Street
Meridian, ID 83642
(208) 888-1201

The Upledger Institute
11211 Prosperity Farms Road
Palm Beach Gardens, FL 33410
(407) 622-4334

The following books can provide additional background:

The Cranial Bowl by William G. Sutherland (Free Press Co.).

Craniosacral Therapy by John Upledger and Jon Vredevoogd (Eastland).

popularity in the medical community any time soon.

Dr. Dunn estimates that the number of M.D.'s who use craniosacral therapy "are relatively few."

THE HEALING POWER OF CRANIOSACRAL THERAPY

The lights are dim, the padded bench soft. You close your eyes as the craniosacral therapist seated behind you grasps your head and begins manipulating the eight bones of your skull. The grip, strengthened by years of practice, is firm, but the touch is incredibly light.

"This can't possibly be doing anything," you think to yourself. A minute later you hear yourself snoring and realize that somehow, somewhere, some part of you is asleep. That realization makes whatever part of your brain that was dozing snap back to consciousness.

The hands have moved from the back of your skull to the sides, pulling at the large parietal bones near the top of your head. You feel completely calm and serene, though you realize you only met the person tugging on your head an hour ago. By the time that thought starts to sink in you're sleeping again, one part of your brain snoring away while the other part listens and feels almost embarrassed, never having heard itself snore before.

The rest of the session is more of the same. Lapses of consciousness followed by dreams.

"It was like I was there but I wasn't there," recalls Margaret Long, a Grand Rapids patient of Theresa Pearce. "It was almost as though I had been drugged. I was aware of what was going on in the room, but I wasn't there.

"I must sound like some kind of space cadet," Long laughs. "I'm the type of person who always has to be in control, but going through something like that was really nice for me."

Also nice was the way craniosacral therapy relieved Long's pain: "I have always had a lot of headaches," she says. "Whenever Theresa's done work on me, it's always been for neck or head pain and it's always been very effective. All the tension that builds up in my face and jaw and the back of my head is released, and the relief lasts about a week or so—which is pretty long-term relief when compared with taking painkillers every day."

Patricia Merkle has been visiting Dan Matarazzo for the past two years. "He alternates Rolfing and craniosacral work with me, depending on what he feels needs to be done," she says.

"It's really pleasant, really relaxing," Merkle says of the craniosacral work she has had. "Sometimes I drift off and I'm not there at all. Other times my mind sticks around and I can feel what he's doing and know what is going on." Merkle says she prefers the craniosacral work for its relaxing properties, relying on the deep tissue work of Rolfing for relief from physical maladies.

Even so, she says cranial work has also brought about some fairly surprising physical results. "I've felt a hip release and a leg release after having the joint freeze or stiffen up," Merkle says. "It's the type of thing you might treat with a heating pad, but with the craniosacral work it's an instantaneous release—you don't have to wait for it to happen."

Merkle and Long both realize that relatively few others have ever experienced the subtle powers of this gentle healing art. "Cranial work comes to people when they are ready for it," says Long. "If someone came to me and said he had some headaches, I might try to explain craniosacral to him, but if I got a puzzled look or any negative feedback, I'd just stop talking about it." Unfortunately, that seems to be the way it's gone with craniosacral therapy all along.

HANDS-ON TECHNIQUES

The following illustrations depict procedures used by trained craniosacral therapists. They are not intended for do-it-yourself applications.

10-1

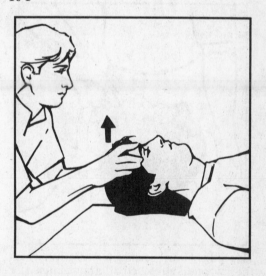

The craniosacral therapist places his hands near the temples and lifts upward, decompressing the frontal bone and stretching the membrane beneath. This move, a frontal lift, is used to help relieve eye strain and sinus pressure.

(continued)

HANDS-ON TECHNIQUES—*Continued*

10-2

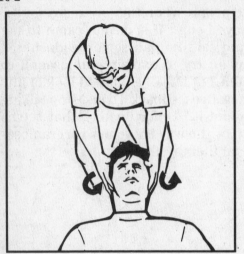

Here, the therapist places his hands on the temporal bones and, through manipulation, helps bring them back into balance. This move is used to help alleviate ringing in the ears.

10-4

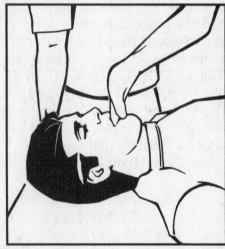

The therapist applies pressure to the bones in the roof of the mouth, balancing the upper jaw and bringing relief to the maxillary sinuses.

10-3

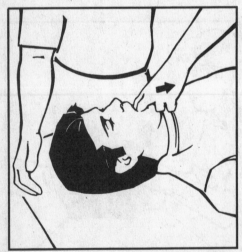

This rather bizarre-looking technique, in which the jawbone is stretched to its limit, is used for relieving temporomandibular joint (TMJ) pain.

10-5

The parietal lift helps balance the large parietal bones on either side of the skull and stretches the membrane beneath, to help relieve headache pain and stress.

Chapter 11

DEEP MUSCLE THERAPY

1950: At age three, little Otto is attacked by a wicked rooster and is knocked into a gulley full of wicked red ants.

1954: Little Otto falls out of a tree onto his little red wagon and breaks his left arm.

1956: Little Otto descends a steep, long flight of wooden stairs on his tailbone. From then on, his mother scolds him, "Don't go around with your fanny sticking out. Stand up straight!"

1959: A cruel neighbor child named Max pokes a stick in front of Otto's speeding roller skates. The tumble to the sidewalk breaks Otto's right wrist.

Somehow, despite college and motorcycles, Otto makes it through most of the 1960s relatively unscathed. From the late 1960s through the mid-1980s, however, the now big Otto surfs and bicycles. When he paddles a surfboard he must arch his back and neck up so he can see a monster wave about to crash down on him. When he bikes,

he must arch his neck up to see where he's going.

After 18 years of this—along with a whiplash-causing auto accident (he wasn't watching where he was going), a blow between the eyes from the point of a surfboard, bad form in weight lifting (remember, he never stood up straight), and a career spent hunched over a desk—Otto hurts. Otto feels old.

Unsticking Stuck Muscles

Old aching Otto lies on Victoria Ross's massage table in her office outside Philadelphia. Ross is a leading instructor in Pfrimmer deep muscle therapy and heads one of only two Pfrimmer schools in the country.

She's found dried-up, stuck-together muscles in Otto's right forearm (from the break), his left shoulder (he tore it swinging a baseball bat for the first time in 30 years), his left hip (she says it probably contributed to the shoulder injury) and the intercostals (the muscles between his ribs). Dried up and stuck together. Just how Otto feels.

Dried-out muscles? "Yes," Ross replies. "A damaged muscle actually feels dried out and stringy, as if the fibers within the muscle bundle are stuck together. The fibers of a healthy muscle will glide smoothly along one another. They're supposed to be bathed in lymphatic fluid, but when they're damaged and stuck together the fluid can't get in there, and they literally get dried out."

With her fingers Ross rubs back and forth across the edge of Otto's forearm. "Can you feel how that kind of pops around?"

"Ouch! Yes!" Otto says hastily. "Do you have to fix that? Can't I just get new muscles?"

Ross can feel the damage mainly through palpation, a touching art learned in the intensive two-week Pfrimmer course that follows at least 500 hours of instruction in anatomy, physiology and other preparatory curricula. There are, after all, about 900 muscles in the body. "You have to have good schooling in anatomy to know exactly where the muscles are and how the fibers are running, so you can evaluate their health," Ross says. "And sometimes you can make an accurate guess just from the symptoms people describe. If they say their chiropractic treatments don't last, for instance, it's usually because damaged muscles pull the bones out of place."

What makes Pfrimmer deep muscle therapy unique is that the therapist works across the muscle fiber in both directions, back and forth, with her fingers and thumbs to literally unstick and separate the muscles. This back-and-forth motion is also what distinguishes Pfrimmer from several other cross-fiber techniques. (See the box "What's in a Name?" on page 77.)

Another Pfrimmer advantage, Ross says, is that "it's very broad in its scope. It deals with all the body systems, so even though the main goal is to correct damaged muscles, it also clears the tissues and organs of toxins."

You don't need to be attacked by a wicked rooster or break an arm to get muscle damage, Ross says. "Much more often damage comes from structural imbalances, poor diet, mental and emotional stress, and job-related physical stress."

Pfrimmer therapists work with both severe and simple muscle ailments. "Every problem is legitimate," Ross says. "Everybody should be able to feel the best they can, based on their constitution and circumstances. There are lots of elusive aches and pains that we can help, and there's always at least some improvement." (For the name of a Pfrimmer therapist near you, write the International Association of Pfrimmer Deep Muscle Therapists, P.O. Box 807, Smithfield, NC 27577.)

Till It Hurts Good

So Otto aches, but he doesn't want anyone to touch his sore shoulder. "It

Deep Muscle Massage: What's in a Name?

In the field of massage devoted to deep tissue work, you're going to hear a lot of similar-sounding names that will make you wonder what's what. There's Deep This and Muscle That and So-and-So Connective Massage. How do you tell the difference or even know if there *is* a difference?

Massage Magazine editor and publisher Robert Calvert offers the following capsule definitions for the utterly bewildered.

Deep muscle massage. A generic term that applies to any massage technique that uses deep muscle massage. Anatomically oriented, it can be corrective or therapeutic. "Deep muscle massage doesn't denote any particular therapy that's practiced or taught in schools throughout the country," says Calvert. "But it can mean a different thing to a different therapist."

Deep muscle therapy. Synonomous with deep muscle massage; also a broad term connoting work on the deeper layers of muscle.

Deep tissue therapy. A deep muscle massage. Technically, this is probably the appropriate term for deep muscle therapy. The difference is semantic.

Pfrimmer deep muscle therapy. A method of working across muscle fibers in both directions, back and forth. To the chagrin of Pfrimmer therapists, many non-Pfrimmer therapists use the term deep muscle therapy without using the Pfrimmer technique.

Connective tissue massage. A very technical work that requires a lot of anatomical knowledge. It has strong European medical roots and was developed by Elisabeth Dicke. It works only on the fascia, the membrane sheaths enveloping the muscles and organs. Tissue integrity is the primary goal. This is one of the major themes of all so-called bodywork techniques.

Rolfing. This therapy has its roots in connective tissue massage. It involves particularly deep bodywork whose primary goal is structural integrity.

Myotherapy. This deep muscle massage is a distinct therapy popularized by Bonnie Prudden. Although its goal is, like connective tissue massage, tissue integrity, its techniques are much different.

hurts," he whines.

Ross reassures him that she won't go deeper than he can tolerate. "People in great pain can be touched," she says. "The correction takes place on the discomfort level. If the person has bursitis, for example, it's going to hurt just touching them feather light. Then

Therese Pfrimmer's Insight: Rare but Well Done

People can find inspiration in the common and the singular. In 1947 Therese Pfrimmer found it in a side of beef. A side of beef with freezer burn.

"She'd been paralyzed from the waist down by severe muscle strain," Pfrimmer therapist Victoria Ross explains. "She didn't accept the doctors' prognosis that she would never walk again. While sitting in a wheelchair, she began working on her legs. When she dug into the muscles in this particular way they felt like an old matted mattress, with the stuffing all wadded up. When she worked the muscles in this way, she found that strange sensation disappeared."

In three months Pfrimmer, an Ontario massage therapist, was up and walking around. But it wasn't until she met and palpated the side of beef that she understood how her massage method worked.

"She was working in a restaurant where she had to cut whole sides of beef," Ross says. "She noticed that this one piece with freezer burn felt just the way her legs had felt. And when she applied her massage method to it, the fibers were rearranged and straightened themselves out."

Pfrimmer said, "Eureka!" Pfrimmer Deep Muscle Therapy was born.

you know that's the level you have to work on for correction. While it's not deep, you can eventually work your way down. If, on the other hand, you have to go so deep you can't see your knuckle anymore before it starts to hurt, then that's the level at which you work.

"It's like rubbing a child's skinned knee: You rub it so the child can feel you're doing something good. It may hurt, but it hurts good. We have a lot of people who are hurting, and we have to talk them through it. They're very protective of their injury. We tell them we're going to work feather light. And if they let us do that, they'll see how after a few strokes we can go deeper and deeper without it hurting more."

But doesn't massaging a damaged muscle damage it even more? "We don't work deeply on a torn muscle," Ross says. "If we're not sure it's torn, we recommend the person get an x-ray. And we have to rule out serious conditions. If the symptoms the person describes make it appear there could be a blood clot or a herniated disk, it's not wise to work on him. We recommend he have a medical evaluation."

The only real pain Otto had was in his shoulder, and it didn't hurt more when Ross worked on it. And two weeks later Otto notices that his shoulder feels almost normal. "The next time you come in, I'll work a little deeper," Ross promises. "And that left hip imbalance needs to be corrected. It sets you up for shoulder injuries."

Otto also learns that if his intercostals were corrected, he'd have greater chest expansion, and, Ross says, "it would make you look trimmer."

"Forget my shoulder, forget my hip," an eager Otto replies. "Do my intercostals."

THE HEALiNG POWER OF DEEP MUSCLE THERAPY

Whiplash is at the top of a list of injuries deep muscle therapy is said to help. Ailments involving damaged but noninjured muscles include low back pain, neck pain and sciatica. The three most common digestive problems a practitioner sees are hiatal hernia, constipation and colitis. Deep muscle therapy is also used for circulatory problems, including varicose veins.

But the conditions can be more serious. "Our practice sees a very large percentage of degenerative muscle diseases," Ross says. "A lot of our clients come in on wheelchairs and stretchers. We work hand-in-hand with neurologists and rehabilitation hospitals who treat diseases like multiple sclerosis, amyotrophic lateral sclerosis, muscular dystrophy and Parkinson's disease. We can't cure them, but there is a healing effect. With such degenerative conditions, our goal is to see the person frequently in the beginning to reverse some of the symptoms, and then to go to a maintenance program to retard the progression of the disease. Deep muscle therapy is great for keeping a step ahead."

She describes one 35-year-old woman who had had hypercalcemia from the ages of three to six. This disfiguring, brain-damaging condition left the woman "wrenched around so the top half of her body was facing in a different direction than the bottom half," Ross says. "She couldn't close her eyes or her mouth. But since the disease ended long ago and is not progressive, when we work on her there's a constant improvement. Even though she's never going to be perfect, both halves of her body are now going in the same direction. She can sit in a chair, she can close her eyes and mouth, and she can say a few words. We're working on her limbs now."

With lesser problems, results sometimes come much more quickly. "One woman had broken two bones in the arch of her foot years ago, and it was getting worse," Ross says. "She was otherwise healthy, but there were damaged muscles and tendons that had gotten stuck together, and the arch bones were stuck in the wrong place. One treatment cleared it completely."

Chapter 12

DŌ-IN

Macrobiotics (literally, "great life") is usually seen as a diet balancing the two forces of the universe, *yin* (female, negative, spiritual, expanding) and *yang* (male, positive, material, contracting). Yin foods, such as sweets, fruits, and vegetables, are kept in proper balance with yang foods, like salt, meat, fish and fowl, by emphasizing the more neutral grains. But diet is not the only way to a new awareness of your place in the natural world, says macrobiotics proponent Michio Kushi.

There's also Dō-In (pronounced dough-in), an ancient macrobiotic exercise practice that Kushi introduced into the United States in 1968. Dō-In has existed as long as human life, Kushi says, as a natural adaptation of man to environment. It became a more formally structured system more than 10,000 years ago, he says. In rediscovering the precepts of Dō-In, Kushi acknowledges his debt to an enlightening experience during meditation, and to the wisdom found in texts and teachings from around the world. These teachings had a common source, Kushi believes, and the unifying thread is the need and the means for humans to adapt to the natural world around them.

"In recent times we've lost this common ground," Kushi says. Modern Western society makes people "limit their environment to their occupations, or friends, or nation. This limitation is a delusion. There are no limitations, there is no borderline between a person and the environment. A human being is a manifestation of infinity; we are humanized infinity. Unless we realize the totality of our environment, ultimate freedom, happiness, health, and longevity cannot be achieved."

The Dō-In exercises were developed over centuries in the oriental religions of Shintoism, Hinduism, Taoism, and Buddhism. So although they are physical practices and their purpose is to produce physical health, spiritual harmony with the universe is the ultimate goal.

But you're a Westerner, raised with Western attitudes. Do you have to abandon your heritage to benefit from Dō-In? "No," Kushi says. "You can begin with just the exercises. You can keep your traditions. But the exercises will naturally make you want to change your diet. And by changing your diet you start changing your outlook. You automatically begin having a wider view of the world. You start seeing the planet as a living whole, not divided into nations. People are already connected by trade, communications and transportation. A new orientation is beginning, and modern civilized society is ending. There's a new way of thinking coming about, and the physical exercises of Dō-In are the first step."

The Dō-In Exercises

The Dō-In exercises are self-help techniques that often resemble yoga postures. They're designed to work on the body's so-called energy merid-ians as delineated in the practice of acupuncture and shiatsu. Here are just a few examples:

Massage of the Feet and Toes

This is actually foots-on healing. Kushi says it helps the circulation in the feet and legs, and works the meridians related to the stomach, intestines, liver, spleen, bladder, and kidneys.

Lie on your back with your knees bent and about three feet apart. Raise your feet off the floor and rub them with each other's first and second toes. Do the soles, the tops and the toes rapidly more than 100 times until both feet are very warm.

Abdominal Massage

This is said to relax your abdominal muscles and stimulate the organs they surround, helping digestion and relieving constipation.

Lying on your back with your knees bent and stomach muscles relaxed, hold your right wrist in your left hand. With the four fingertips of your right hand, push slowly and deeply first on the left side of the abdomen from bottom to top. Exhale each time you press in. After each press-down, lift your hand up quickly. Next do the upper part of the abdomen from right to left, the right side from top to bottom, the lower abdomen from left to right, and the center from top to bottom. Repeat the cycle three times. Then, holding your right hand on top of your left, massage the navel area with the palm of your left hand in a circular motion 16 times.

Neck Extension

This exercise is said to stimulate the thyroid and parathyroid glands and increase circulation in the head, neck and shoulders.

Hold your chin with your left palm, and put your right palm on the upper left side of your head, with your right wrist curving over the top of your head. While exhaling through your mouth, pull down to the right with your right (top) hand and push up to the left with your left (bottom) hand. Repeat three times, then switch hands and repeat three times, moving your head in the opposite direction.

Nose Work

Your nose is good for more than sneezing. By trying these nose squeezes, you'll be helping the functioning of your stomach, lungs and pancreas, as well as your thought processes, according to Kushi.

Rapidly rub the sides of your nose in an up-and-down direction with your thumb and forefinger. Then, using your thumb, index and middle fingers, start at the top of the bridge of your nose and squeeze along the bridge down to the tip. Immediately release your fingers after each squeeze. Finally, close one nostril by pressing your thumb along the side of your nose. Slowly exhale and inhale five to ten times, then repeat with the other nostril.

Ear Work

This exercise is said to improve circulation and stimulate your kidneys. Simply pull and stretch your ears up, out like Dumbo, and down. Do this five times in each direction. Then apply both palms to the kidneys and hold them there for three to five minutes.

THE HEALING POWER OF DŌ-IN

Dō-In's healing power is not limited to the physical realm, Kushi says, although the physical is a good start. Given the relationship between meridians and health, there is no illness or affliction the Dō-In exercises won't benefit, proponents claim.

DŌ-IN FOR THE EYES

The exercises in this series are said to improve eyesight and help eye ailments like myopia, far-sightedness, astigmatism and glaucoma. Proponents say they also improve circulation and help control blood pressure and heart rate.

12-1

Hold both palms over your eyes and breathe in and out several times. Then with the index, middle and ring fingers of each hand press firmly on the top bone of your eye socket. Move from the area nearest the nose to the outer area. Do the same on the bottom bone of the eye socket. Repeat the exercise three times.

12-2

Again with your index, middle and ring fingers, carefully press in between the top of the eyeball and the socket, lightly vibrating your fingers. Then release the pressure quickly.

12-3

Repeat for the bottom of the eyeball and socket.

(continued)

DŌ-IN FOR THE EYES—*Continued*

12-4

Close your eyes and press slowly and gently on your eyes with the tips of your index, middle and ring fingers, and release quickly. Repeat ten times.

12-6

Use your thumb and index finger to pinch the bridge of your nose at the corners of your eyes, pushing in deeply for ten seconds and releasing suddenly.

12-5

Grasp your upper eyelids between thumbs and index fingers and vibrate them 50 to 100 times.

DŌ-IN FOR DIGESTION

Practitioners say this series helps the digestion where it begins, in the mouth's salivary glands. It is also said to promote physical strength and ease excretion.

12-7

To improve circulation in the mouth area, use a circular motion with the four fingers of each hand to press in deeply all around the mouth and the sides of the jaw from chin to ears. Do this five to ten times.

12-8

In addition to strengthening the digestion, this one supposedly clears tension caused by nasal mucus buildup. With one finger on either side of your face push in with a circular motion beneath your cheekbone about one finger width from your nose.

12-9

This exercise is designed to help stimulate the salivary glands. Use your thumbs to push up hard under your lower jawbone from chin to ears, as if you were seeing what you'd look like with a chin lift. Repeat this five times.

Chapter 13

EMERGENCY FIRST-AID TECHNIQUES

An eight-year-old boy saves his little brother from fatally choking on a piece of candy.

A trainer eases an endurance swimmer's cramps and prevents her from drowning in the open sea.

A man stops his neighbor from bleeding to death from a power saw accident.

A wife starts her husband's heart again.

There are thousands of daily situations in which the difference between life and death is only a matter of minutes. When someone is choking, drowning or having a heart attack, brain damage can occur quickly unless effective action is taken. In such cases, you may not have time to dial 911 or to stand by helplessly waiting for the paramedics to arrive on the scene.

So what do you do? Fortunately, you can do what the people in the above examples did—use your hands.

Not only are your hands often the best lifesaving equipment available, they also serve as a form of soothing communication in traumatic situations. "By touching an injured person," explains Richard A. Parker, D.O., staff physician, San Diego Sports Medicine Center, "you put them at ease and break down their fears. A caring touch assures them that you will not hurt them and you are there to help. That's important in getting people calm and ready for treatment."

It only takes a little know-how to use your hands for emergencies. At the most, a few hours of special training is all that is required to save someone's life.

Here are a few ways that you can use your hands in "code blue" situations, besides simply dialing the emergency number or waving for help.

Give the Hug of Life

It's hard to believe that something as simple as a behind-the-back bear hug could save the life of a movie star (Cher), a Mayor of New York (Ed Koch), a President of the United States

(Ronald Reagan) and as many as 15,000 other people who would have otherwise choked to death—typically while eating—over the last 15 years.

Yet, the Heimlich maneuver—named for the man who invented the procedure—is perhaps one of the most dramatic examples of hands-on life-saving techniques. It's even been endorsed by the Surgeon General, who describes the procedure as "safe, effective and easily mastered by the average person."

So simple is the maneuver, in fact, says Henry Heimlich, M.D., professor of advanced clinical sciences at Xavier University in Cincinnati, and president of the Heimlich Institute, that a little boy used it to save his brother from choking after seeing the procedure performed on a TV sitcom.

What's more, the Heimlich maneuver is so effective for clearing obstructed airways that it has won the approval of the American Heart Association (AHA) and the American Red Cross (ARC). Both organizations now recommend it for all but infants under one year of age. (For the very young, a back blow administered while the child is held with head lower than the body is still the treatment of choice.)

"We found that the Heimlich maneuver is easy. And studies show it is as effective, and possibly more effective than back blows for clearing obstruction," says Joseph Ornato, M.D., professor of internal medicine (cardiology division) at the Medical College of Virginia and chairman of the Advanced Cardiac Life Support Committee of the AHA.

Just what's the difference between the two procedures? According to the U.S. Surgeon General, slapping on someone's back can drive a foreign object even deeper into the throat.

The Heimlich maneuver does just the opposite. Even if you are choking and can't breathe, he says, there's still air in your lungs. Properly compressing the lungs drives the air out and forces the obstruction to pop out of the throat and mouth.

Know the Signs of Choking

How do you know when to do the Heimlich maneuver? If someone grasps his or her throat, can't breathe, can't speak, turns blue, falls, or is unconscious, choking should be suspected. Another clue, says Dr. Heimlich, is if the person is near an eating area. "Ninety percent of choking victims are eating when choking occurs." If these conditions are present, don't waste any time—give the "hug of life."

THE HEIMLICH MANEUVER

Here are simple, fast steps to follow in an emergency choking situation.

13-1

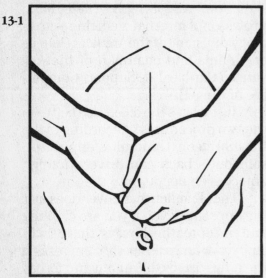

Stand behind the choking person and reach around with your arms. Make a fist with one hand, placing the thumb side against the abdomen above the belly button, and below the rib cage. Grasp the fist with the other hand.

13-2

Push inward and upward with one motion.

13-3

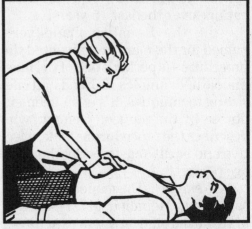

If the victim is much larger than you or is lying down, turn him faceup and straddle him. Place your fist in between the belly button and rib cage and thrust upward.

13-4

If the choking victim is a child (at least a year old), seat her on your lap. Reach around and place your index and middle fingers above the navel, below the ribcage. Press inward with a rapid thrust.

Learn to Jump-Start a Heart

Since 1960, over 40 million individuals worldwide have learned how to head off "sudden death" simply by using their hands. How? They've taken a course in CPR, which stands for cardiopulmonary resuscitation, a life-saving technique that restarts the lungs breathing and the heart pumping.

These are the people you want to have nearby in life-threatening emergencies. CPR can often prevent people from dying from electric shock, drowning, drug overdoses, highway accidents, suffocation, even severe allergic reactions. It can also serve as a first line of defense against this country's most common killer: heart disease.

"We tend to associate life-threatening emergencies with anonymous highway mishaps, complete with sirens blaring and lights flashing," notes Brian Ruberry, spokesperson for the American Red Cross national headquarters in Washington, D.C. "Yet, in 75 percent of the cases, it's a family member at home, the neighbor next door or the co-worker in the office who suddenly keels over for no apparent reason."

In fact, an estimated six million Americans carry a clinical diagnosis of coronary heart disease. And when heart attacks strike, two-thirds of all sudden deaths occur *before* the victim can even get to a hospital.

The good news is that promptly initiated CPR may save the victim's life."It would behoove anyone with a family member at high risk for heart disease to learn CPR," says Ruberry.

CPR training is also a good idea for parents and caretakers of infants and children. There's a high incidence of kids who suffocate on plastic bags, wander into swimming pools or choke on marbles and other small objects. CPR could help prevent those mishaps, too, from becoming tragedies.

The ABCs of CPR

How do you learn CPR? You take a course, sponsored by your local American Red Cross or American Heart Association. In a few short hours, you learn to recognize the warning signals of a heart attack, stroke, choking and other respiratory and cardiac emergencies. And you're taught how to perform immediate emergency techniques to keep the victim breathing and his heart pumping until a rescue unit takes over.

Instructors emphasize the following ABCs of CPR:

A is for Airway. It's dangerous to perform CPR on people who are still breathing, such as fainters or sleepers. One of the first things you'll learn in CPR class is how to determine if a victim is breathing. If he's not, you'll be shown how to open his airways and how to prepare yourself to breathe for him.

B is for Breathing. Next, CPR instructors explain how to place your mouth over the victim's and breathe air into him until he can once again breathe on his own.

C is for Circulation. The third part of the coursework involves learning how to locate the carotid pulse on the victim's neck and check for a heartbeat. For the most important hands-on portion, you'll be taught exactly how to take over for the victim's heart and pump blood through his body until a rescue squad can take over.

You'll learn a quick way to locate where to place your hands on the victim's chest and how to press downward. Then, you'll practice how to coordinate the chest compressions with rescue breathing and periodically recheck the pulse.

The Only Way to Learn

We've illustrated some of the basic steps involved in CPR. But you won't really be qualified to perform the procedure until you've completed the coursework.

"Reading about CPR is like an athlete reading an article about how to play basketball," Ruberry says. "You really can't acquire the skill until you've had the hands-on practice."

In addition to practicing your skills on mannequins, a CPR course will give you the confidence to act quickly and appropriately. "The training helps you become a better responder so you won't become paralyzed in an emergency," says Ruberry. Someone's life could depend on your cool head and quick, trained hands.

CPR: A COURSE THAT SAVES LIVES

The following views of cardiopulmonary resuscitation are for illustration purposes only. CPR can be learned only from a qualified instructor.

13-5

After calling for help, the rescuer first opens the victim's airways. She places the victim on his back, lifts his chin up and tilts his forehead back.

13-6

To begin rescue breathing, she pinches the victim's nostrils while keeping her hand on the forehead.

13-7

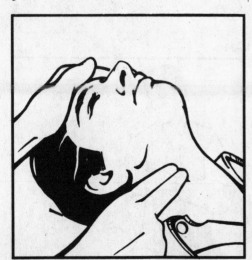

The rescuer feels for the carotid pulse in the groove between the Adam's apple and neck muscle, while maintaining head tilt with the other hand.

13-8

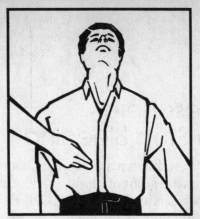

Finding the proper hand position for chest compression. The first two fingers follow the lowest rib up to the notch where the rib meets the sternum.

13-9

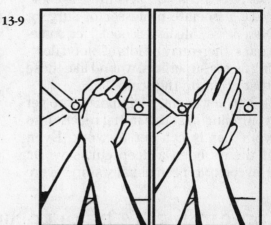

The heel of one hand is placed on the sternum. Then the other hand is placed on top of the first.

13-10

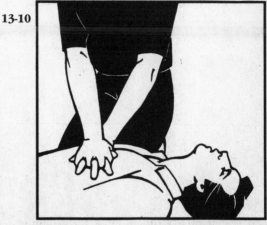

With elbows locked, and shoulders directly over hands, the rescuer presses downward about two inches at a rate of 80 to 100 compressions per minute. After every 15 compressions, two more rescue breaths are delivered.

Press Here to Stop Bleeding

Few things make people as squeamish as the sight of blood. It's alarming to see a steady stream of dark red oozing from a vein, even worse to witness bright red spurting from an artery.

"People associate loss of blood with death," says Christine Haycock, M.D., associate professor of surgery, New Jersey Medical School. "Yet, sometimes, there may be lots of blood flowing from a superficial wound like those that occur on the scalp."

In any event, it's important to get your mind past this initial reaction so your hands can get to work. Even if there's been a deep cut, says Dr. Haycock, you can usually stop severe bleeding in minutes just by applying pressure to the wound. By using your hands to stop bleeding, you may prevent shock, unconsciousness, even death.

The purpose of pressing directly at the sight of bleeding is simple: You seal off the ruptured blood vessels and allow natural clots to form. If this fails to stop the flow, you may also need to press certain arteries that supply the blood to the affected area.

A final note. Avoid doing what the cowboys in old Westerns did. Don't wind a bandana or other tourniquet above the injured limb and twist it until the bleeding stops. Why? You could damage the blood vessels, nerves and other tissue—perhaps necessitating amputation.

TO STOP SEVERE BLEEDING

Hands-on pressure can often stop severe bleeding and help prevent shock.

13-11

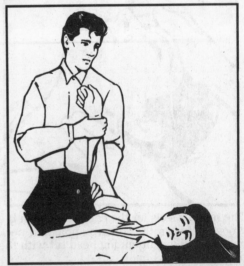

With the victim lying down, raise the bleeding part if no fracture is suspected. Pick out any easily removable objects, like glass.

13-12

Use a piece of clean cloth (a T-shirt, necktie, or sock), and press hard on the wound. Tie the cloth pad in place just loose enough to allow circulation. Continue to apply pressure until the bleeding stops.

13-13

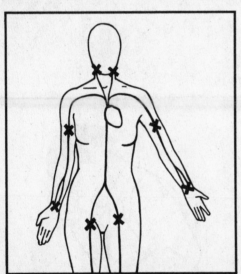

If pressing on the wound does not stop the blood flow, apply pressure at points located between the wound and the heart where the artery can be pressed against the bone.

13-14

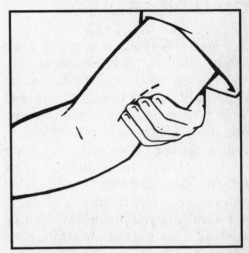

For a bleeding arm, press the brachial artery, which is midway between the elbow and armpit, in the groove between the front and back muscles of the upper arm.

13-15

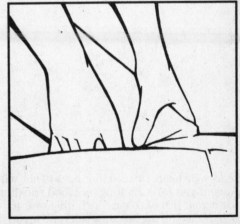

For a leg injury, press the heel of your hand against the femoral artery, located on the inner thigh, just below the groin.

Putting the Pinch on a Nosebleed

Remember your classmate in grade school who was always marching to the nurse's office, head tilted back, because he suddenly got a nosebleed? Well, nosebleeds can happen to anyone at any time, because of an infection, injury, dry air or a number of other reasons. They are a nuisance, but they're often fairly easy to stop—all you need is a free hand.

Basically, you pinch the bleeding nostril for several minutes until clots can form and block off the blood flow. A cold compress on the bridge of your nose could speed up this process.

If that doesn't do the trick and your nose continues to bleed bright red, it could mean you are bleeding from an artery. In that case, says Dr. Haycock, you'll need to increase pressure. Pack your nose with a wet paper towel and get to a doctor immediately.

NOSEBLEED RELIEF

The idea here is to pinch the nostrils until clots form and block the flow.

13-16

Lean your head forward, not back. That will prevent you from choking on blood trickling down your throat. Then pinch the lower part of your nose on the bleeding side, and breathe through your mouth. Hold for several minutes, then release slowly.

How to Soothe a Strain

It's the second day of your hiking trip. As you're trekking down a steep trail, you hear a sharp cry of pain. You turn around to discover your companion doubled over, clutching her lower leg.

Sure enough, she's suffered a strain, a common injury to the muscles or tendons, which often results from overexertion. Her leg feels tender and will soon begin to swell. Probably by morning it will feel painfully stiff.

Is that the end of your vacation? Perhaps not, *if* you act fast. "What you want to do is reduce the swelling, which cuts off blood circulation," suggests Dr. Parker. "Just remember the four-letter word RICE." That stands for *r*est, applying an *i*ce pack, wrapping the injury with a *c*ompress like an ace bandage, and *e*levating the injured limb. "All these things help reduce swelling so healing can take place."

What if a strained muscle occurs when you're stuck somewhere—like a road race—without access to ice or an ace bandage? You can reduce swelling by gently moving the injured part with your hands, says Dr. Parker. "If your running mate has strained his calf muscle, for example, you can gently tip his toes up and back toward his body. This kind of contract-relax action can help him get back on his feet faster."

First-Aid Resources

To enroll in a CPR course, contact your local chapter of the American Red Cross or American Heart Association. You can sign up for brief three- or four-hour courses or a more detailed nine-hour course. Completed coursework certifies you to perform CPR for one or two years.

The following reference works may also be useful in preparing for emergency situations.

The AMA Family Medical Guide, edited by Jeffrey R. M. Kunz, M.D., and Asher J. Finkel, M.D. (Random House). Easy-to-read sections tell how to stop bleeding, treat strains and perform other hands-on first-aid procedures.

Heartsaver Manual, A Student Handbook for Cardiopulmonary Resuscitation and First Aid for Choking, 1987. Reviews the up-to-date techniques taught in CPR courses. For a copy, contact the American Heart Association, 7320 Greenville Avenue, Dallas, TX 75231.

The Medical Emergency Video, with Henry J. Heimlich, M.D. A step-by-step visual guide to the Heimlich maneuver and other first-aid techniques. Available from London-Hill Productions, 56 Hanover Court, Langhorne, PA 19047.

Standard First Aid and Personal Safety, prepared by the American Red Cross for first-aid classes. Includes CPR, Heimlich, bleeding control and other how-to procedures for all kinds of emergency situations. Contact your local Red Cross chapter.

Chapter 14

ESALEN MASSAGE

A wave crawls in from the sea. Stiffening and swelling, like a giant cobra on the attack, it swoops down upon the coastline, crashing with the sound of thunder against the jagged rocks. Where there was tranquillity, there is now a savage barrage of foam, spray, seaweed, and a thousand ripples that gush through the sand and stones.

You clasp the wooden guardrail as you watch the drama unfold from 80 feet above. A cool breeze ruffles your hair and provides much-needed relief from the broiling sun beating down on your bare shoulders. The sky is blue. The mountains behind you are green. The ocean is their perfect offspring.

You've just been lying on your back for over an hour. Over you, a pair of soft hands soaked in warm oil stroked, rubbed and gently twisted and tugged you from foot to head. You're still in a dreamlike reverie.

This is California's Esalen Institute, founded 25 years ago as a mecca for seekers of universal truths and searchers of the soul. Here, off Route 1 about a third of the way from San Francisco to Los Angeles, one can attend seminars on the newest in New Age philosophy. Esalen is a place for you to expand your consciousness, magnify your awareness, and engulf yourself in internal peace and harmony.

It's also a place to get a darn good massage.

A Hybrid Style

The institute itself is a California-accredited massage school. About 20 of the school's star graduates remain to teach others and work their art. They are the torchbearers of a form of massage they call, naturally enough, *Esalen massage.* What makes it different from other forms of massage?

For starters, when an Esalen massage is given at the institute (and some feel that a true Esalen massage can *only* be given at the institute), the setting alone makes it special—11 outdoor massage tables crown a huge cliff, overlooking the Pacific Ocean. The air

96

is clear and fresh. The sounds, of splashing water and wind through the pines, are more tranquilizing than if Mozart himself were playing you a sonata. The smells of salt and of the minerals from the nearby hot springs make you feel as if you're sampling the very best that Mother Earth has to offer.

The massage technique also promises something different, although what this something is eludes you at first. "Esalen massage is a process of unraveling toward a feeling of real peace and acceptance in the individual, of organic wholeness, of balance," says Brita Ostrom, a practitioner of Esalen massage for more than 20 years.

In simpler terms, Esalen is a hybrid style, blending Swedish massage with aspects of other bodywork techniques such as Aston-Patterning, craniosacral balancing, deep tissue massage, Feldenkrais, Rolfing and the Trager approach. (See chapters 7, 10, 11, 16, 35 and 39, respectively, for more information on these methods.) "It's like a smorgasbord," says Esalen massage practitioner Attila Vaas. "It's a style so flexible and adaptive that we can really meet the needs of the individual."

The guests at Esalen may not be aware that many of the massage practitioners have learned from such venerable masters of whole-body healing as Ida Rolf (founder of Rolfing), Moshe Feldenkrais (founder of the Feldenkrais Method), and Judith Aston (of Aston-Patterning fame); all of whom have given seminars at the Institute.

What matters to guests is that they get an enjoyable massage. This they most assuredly do.

"I had great expectations when I came here, and it lived up to all of them," says Ron Reams, 37, of Tampa, Florida, as he leaves the massage area. "I'm in grace here," says another happy customer who lives nearby and comes in for a massage at least once a month. "This is about as good as a massage can get," says a third.

Long, Smooth Strokes

From a distance, Esalen massage looks like an improvised ballet, without tutus. The well-tanned practitioners, typically sporting dark sunglasses and little else, stand, sit or kneel alongside their clients. With hands, elbows, sometimes knees, they stroke or manipulate their paler, prone clients with a smoothness of motion and an intensity in their eyes that 19-year Esalen veteran Peggy Horan calls an altered state.

"It's very trancelike for us. Giving a massage for us is more than a job, it's yoga and meditation, in which we communicate with the client not only with our hands, eyes and speech, but with our whole being," she says.

If there's anything that would make Esalen massage recognizable to the casual bystander, it is the long, flowing strokes, often starting at the bottom of the feet and continuing up to the top of the head (at which point the hair may be gently pulled). The absence of clothes helps in this regard. "We try to work with the body as a whole, not breaking it up into segments," says Ostrom.

When it comes time for your turn, you pay your $50 for about an hour-and-15-minute massage. Picking a practitioner at Esalen isn't easy; there's a two-page menu to choose from, handed to you at the front office: "ANNA has an approach which is tender and nourishing, while working with a gentle yet deep pressure . . . DEAN uses gentle movement, stretches, and subtle pressure to encourage release of tension and open up the body's energetic field . . . LIONESS combines opening the energy meridians, acupressure and deep massage . . . She works with body, mind, and breath."

As the menu makes clear, there may be a big difference in the way any two practitioners perform Esalen massage. You choose Peggy Horan, because she has 19 years of experience and because her style promises to be "gentle, yet firm and flowing." Sounds good. It is.

On the table, under the heat of the intense California sun, a brisk wind flurrying across your body, absorbing the sounds and smells of the sea, you sense Horan's hands melting into the environment, an environment which seems to exist solely for *your* relaxation.

Horan asks you to turn over a couple of times, and you comply, placidly. You slip in and out of consciousness, as if you're catnapping on a plane or

A Place to Explore Your Potential

You'll find no calculus classes at the Esalen Institute, no English literature, and no American History 101. But Esalen is unarguably an institute of higher education.

Founded in the 1960s, the beautiful campus/resort initially attracted as instructors the likes of Aldous Huxley, Abraham Maslow and Fritz Perls—some of the most avant-garde thinkers of the day. George Harrison and Ringo Starr came to study here under Ravi Shankar. Joan Baez, Joni Mitchell and Arlo Guthrie came to sing about peace and love. It was the dawning of the Age of Aquarius, and Esalen was at its heart.

Today, that heart's still beating. Recent workshop offerings have included: "Singing Gestalt," "Vipassana Meditation," "The Further Reaches of Human Energy," "Awakening Inner Power," and "The Body and Zen."

Aside from the various workshops at Esalen (which generally cost about $600 for a five-day session and $300 for a weekend workshop), you can also enjoy bathing in spring-fed hot tubs, massages overlooking the ocean, and the most awe-inspiring scenery imaginable. Accommodations are clean and functional, but don't expect a television or telephone in your room—and there's no room service, either.

train. Horan's long strokes seem to keep perfect cadence with the waves below. Your shoulders are rolled, your legs gently pulled and pushed this way and that, your head tenderly rocked from side to side. Your hair is softly pulled and twisted.

An indeterminate number of minutes later, you walk over to the railing and gaze out into the vast expanse of the Pacific Ocean. There, standing on the edge of a continent, you feel as if you're on the edge of the universe. You stretch out your gaze as far as it will go. Staring out across countless miles of ocean, it seems as if taxes, mortgages, bosses, bills, honking cars and alarm clocks are all as far away as whatever may lie on the other side.

THE HEALING POWER OF ESALEN MASSAGE

"There's healing when a person releases after holding on for many years," says Esalen massage practitioner Peggy Horan. Getting people to release, to open up, to relax, is what Esalen massage is all about.

"Some people come here and relax for the first time in their lives," says Horan. She's seen some fairly tense individuals, including army officers and corporate executives, frolicking in the hot tubs after an afternoon massage. "If they get here, they'll relax—it's getting them here that's not always easy," she says.

Just about any form of massage

The Essence of Esalen

Anyone can claim to do Esalen massage, but to make sure you've found the real McCoy, ask to see a certificate from the Esalen Institute, says the massage school's Brita Ostrom. Or contact the Institute, and you will be provided with a list of graduates around the country.

"But if you want the total experience—waves, salt spray, sunlight—you've got to come here," says practitioner Peggy Horan.

You will find the Esalen Institute about a three-hour drive south of San Francisco. For a catalog listing upcoming seminars and events, or for directions and reservations, write to the Esalen Institute, Big Sur, CA 93920. Or call (408) 667-3000.

can foster relaxation and have healing powers, but Esalen massage is special, say its advocates. "Other massages may be just mechanical," says Horan. "Esalen massage caters to the whole person with warm and caring hands."

One woman who lives not far from Esalen says the massages offer her "an opportunity to bring my attention into my body, to get harmony in my body, to bring my body together."

Another visitor adds, "I think the eclectic approach at Esalen makes the massage here really valuable. Throw in the waves and the breeze, and nothing could be more soothing."

Chapter 15

FACIAL MASSAGE

Express yourself! Pull up to a mirror and smile. Frown. Squint. Pout. Pucker up. While you're at it, notice the crinkles and wrinkles, perfectly normal, that accompany each action. What's behind them? If you could look beneath your skin's surface, you'd see an intricate network of hundreds of tiny muscles. Pushing and pulling the skin like soft putty this way and that across your forehead, around your eyes, along the sides of your mouth, these "muscles of facial expression" do a beautiful job of helping you communicate to others what you're thinking and feeling. But their revelations can clue the world in to things that perhaps you'd rather keep to yourself—like your age.

"Everybody gets wrinkles sooner or later, and there's not much you can do to prevent this," says Henry Zackin,

M.D., a New York City plastic surgeon. "As you go through your normal daily activity—talking, smiling, eating, whatever—you're moving the skin around because it's attached to the muscle."

This continual movement, along with the effects of heredity, sun damage, smoking and other poor health habits, eventually results in a breakdown of the elastic fibers in the skin, says Dr. Zackin.

Still, many of us will go to great lengths to try to avoid the unavoidable. Some engage in camouflage with expensive face creams. Others practice daily exercises that are supposed to help keep our chins up. Or get facial massages with the same hope.

Can any massage actually give you an eternally youthful look? "They're really worthless in the long run," Dr. Zacken says. "They might smooth the skin a little or bring extra blood flow to the skin, but they won't do anything spectacular in terms of preventing aging. They're not harmful, but their effects are only temporary." Temporary or not, many massage enthusiasts are more than happy with the results.

Saving Face

Actress Lindsay Wagner hasn't played the role of television's Bionic Woman for more than a decade, but she still claims super looks—thanks, she says, to *facial acupressure,* or *acupressure facelift.* Wagner came upon these techniques through Robert Klein, a homeopath and acupuncturist. Quickly convinced of their face value to anyone with 20 minutes a day and a little discipline, she coauthored a do-it-yourself book with Klein on the subject. (See the box "Facial Follow-Up" on page 104.) She also produced a videotape.

Facial acupressure, claim Wagner and Klein, liberates blocked energy in your face, which in turn can smooth out existing wrinkles, restore your complexion and make you feel better overall. Not to mention actually slow down facial aging.

"I've noticed a big difference in my appearance," says Roxi Lamb, a Washington, D.C., actress and reflexologist who has been using the technique on herself for a couple of years. She has also added acupressure facelifts to her repertoire with clients.

The system entails gently massaging a series of 16 acupressure points—13 of them on the face, one on the neck, one on the hand and one on the arm. These "master points," related to energy flowing through the head and face, are often blocked by things such as stress, illness and poor diets, explains Lamb. She says that massaging these points unblocks them, increases the flow of oxygen and reduces stress and tension, which leads to the partial disappearance of facial lines. "The lines are actually still there," says Lamb, "but they don't look nearly as deep." You might even get rid of a headache or improve your digestion while you're at it, she adds, because the points run along energy meridians that flow through and affect the entire body.

"It's simple and very helpful," says Irving Beyda, a realtor and client of Lamb's. He and his entire family learned the routine by watching the Lindsay Wagner videotape together for several evenings. "Actually, what I had in mind when I started was just feeling good. But I look in the mirror in the morning when I shave and notice my face is a lot softer, more relaxed. I show less tension, and this makes me look younger."

"I've noticed a big difference around my eyes in just a few months," says Lori Bahnam, a California homemaker who gives herself a daily session.

"I used to have lots of crow's feet, but they're disappearing. Other lines on my face seem to be lessening, too."

If you're interested in trying it, get a copy of Wagner's book or video. Have patience, says Lamb, when it comes to finding your acupressure points, which will present themselves as sensitive spots or tiny indentations on your face. Once you've found them, massage each one in small circles for up to a minute. Noticeable results should be yours, Wagner promises, within a month.

"You will never need a surgical facelift if you do an acupressure facelift every day," claims Lamb. "You must be diligent about this. Aging's deteriorating effect is something we let ourselves think exists, but it doesn't have to happen."

Almost identical to acupressure facelift, with the addition of a couple of acupressure points, is *Dō-In facelift*, says Jacqueline Wurn. A yoga teacher who specializes in oriental techniques, Wurn likes to "charge" her hands before giving a client a session by rubbing her palms and fingers together vigorously until they tingle. This charge, she claims, adds magnetic energy to the work.

"I know my face looks better when I do Dō-In facelift," Wurn says. "I have gotten compliments on how good my skin looks. But the benefits are even greater than that. We all tend to hold tension patterns, to get facial blocks. This facelift helps these muscles learn a new, relaxed way of being."

A Lifting Experience

For something a little different, try *facial rejuvenation*, developed by massage therapists Eva Graf and Linda Burnham of The Center of the Light in Massachusetts. According to Graf, details of the system along with its name were given to her by spiritual guides more than 20 years ago. Burnham has since helped her refine the technique and teach it to others. (There is, by the way, at least one other technique called facial rejuvenation. Unrelated to this one, it involves chemical applications to the facial skin that cause it to peel.)

The Graf system involves a series of 12 "nerve pressure points," not the same as acupressure points but possibly overlapping them to some extent. As with acupressure facelift, these points are gently massaged, body energy is realigned and tension is released. But there's more: Tissues of the face can actually be rejuvenated, claims Graf.

"There are people who say that's not possible, but some of my clients actually retain youthfulness," she says. "I have seen actual rekindling of cells, cases where cheeks were sagging and then over a period of time were rebuilt, until it looked like a totally different face. It depends on what the person is willing to let go of and rejuvenate."

Graf spent time in Hollywood working on people who needed to "put their best face forward" for their work in the movie industry. Scott Truel, a

A Wrinkle in Time

If the passing years naturally bring wrinkles, chronically tense facial muscles can make time fly.

"The muscles of the face can get as tight as any others in the body," says Gene Arbetter, massage therapist and national information director for the American Massage Therapy Association. "When they are, they can create more wrinkles or make the ones you already have appear more prominent. If you're constantly gritting your teeth or feeling stressed out, your face is going to wrinkle. It's inevitable."

A relaxing face massage can help bring your muscles back toward a normal, healthy, neutral state, he says. Look for a rosier complexion, too, since massage draws fresh blood to the area, delivering nutrients and drawing out wastes.

"I have a client who carries a lot of work-related stress in her face," he says. "Recently I followed up her basic full-body massage with a little extra massage on her face. When she stood up, there was such a difference in the muscle tone of her face that it was startling. She couldn't believe the difference."

Visit a pro for a face massage or help yourself to simple techniques you can do anywhere, from standing in your shower to sitting at your desk. Try this: Placing your fingertips lightly on your face, in small circles gently move your skin over your muscles under and over your cheekbones, on your temples and jaw hinge, and any place else that feels good.

Or this: Gently pinch and release the brow ridges above and below your eyes. Use your fingertips on the upper ridges and the pads of your upturned thumbs on the lower ridges. For best results, "think your way through your skin to the muscles below," Arbetter advises. Focus in on the muscle layers and how they feel. And be sure you do all the movements in an upward direction or you'll be dragging your skin further down.

"Nothing says that your wrinkles are going to go away," says Arbetter. "But instead of having your face scrunched up in one way or another, you can soften your muscles and help them do what they need to do."

trained practitioner of facial rejuvenation, uses it in Cambridge, Massachusetts on people from all walks of life.

"Most people don't get touched on their head and face very much unless they are intimately involved with someone," he says, "so they tend to hold a lot of tension in their muscles. They'll have mental tension and old emotional stuff left over from their childhood."

A facial rejuvenation session with Truel probably won't seem much different from an ordinary Swedish massage, except that "the whole focus of this facial is spiritual," he explains. "Other techniques focus solely on the skin. I move to deeper levels where the person can reach a space of complete quiet and clarity."

So you lie on Truel's massage table. He briefly steams your face with a warm herb-soaked washcloth, then applies herbal oil specially formulated "to release negative energy." He massages your face, scalp, neck and shoulders for an hour, focusing on sending energy into the nerve contact points to lead negative energy up and out.

"It feels so good," says Naomi Bauer, a client of Truel's. "The first thing I noticed was that it relaxed my jaw. That changed a muscular pattern and really affected how my face looked. Then my skin became more firm. I have less puffiness under my eyes. It refines my complexion, clears my pores and smooths out my skin. It relaxes all the muscles in my face so that I appear younger. But the oddest thing is that it also made my stomach muscles tighter because, as I understand it, the reflexes on my face are related to my stomach muscles."

"I tend to think of it as a reversal of gravity," Graf says. "Things that were being pulled down are lifted—spirit,

Facial Follow-Up

For step-by-step instructions on acupressure facelift, see the book *Lindsay Wagner's New Beauty: The Acupressure Facelift,* by Lindsay Wagner and Robert Klein (Prentice-Hall Press). Or check your video store for the videotape of the same name.

Further information on the Graf system of facial rejuvenation plus a periodic newsletter are available through The Center of the Light, P.O. Box 540, Great Barrington, MA 01230 (413) 229-2396.

heart, mind and body."

"I notice that people's skin changes under my hands," says Truel. "You're not going to come for a treatment and leave with a brand-new face. But after the third or fourth week, I'll notice that this face is not the same as it was when we started."

THE HEALING POWER OF FACIAL MASSAGE

Relaxing tense muscles in your face can help decrease wrinkles and improve your complexion, says massage therapist Gene Arbetter. Acupressure facelift practitioner Roxi Lamb says her technique will make your wrinkles seem to disappear and leave you looking fresh, bright-eyed and rosy-cheeked.

Acupressure facelift might help you sleep, too. "I have back problems and used to have to take aspirin to sleep," says Lori Bahnam. "But when I do facial acupressure before bed, I get so relaxed I fall right to sleep."

It might help you wake up, too. "Sometimes when I'm exhausted, I sit down at my desk at the office and run through the pressure points. It really relaxes me," says realtor Irving Beyda.

Facial rejuvenation promises all these things and more, says Scott Truel. It's great for releasing tension in the neck and shoulders and for clearing up the across-the-forehead lines of people who "mentalize" (worry) a lot, he says. It can have an emotional impact as well. "Sometimes people will cry," says Truel. "They suddenly become very clear about something painful that happened in their lives. It can be quite a release."

From clearing up long-term facial stress patterns to preventing and even reversing the effects of aging, these techniques promise a lot. Truth be told, none of us will be young forever —but a little massage here and a little acupressure there might actually help us put on a happier, more courageous face as the years pass by.

Chapter 16

FELDENKRAIS METHOD

Imagine John Wayne walking like Charlie Chaplin. Picture Fred Astaire moving about like Groucho Marx. Think of Elvis Presley striding across a stage like Kareem Abdul-Jabbar.

Having a hard time with those images? That's because the way we move is a part of who we are. The way we walk, sit, hold our head, balance our shoulders, sing "Love Me Tender" or dribble a basketball is all part of what Dr. Moshe Feldenkrais called our "integrated whole."

Unfortunately, for many of us, awkwardness, clumsiness, cricks, cramps, fatigue and low self-esteem are also part of this same integrated whole. But it doesn't have to be so, said Dr. Feldenkrais, developer of a process that might be described as a kind of marriage counseling for the body and the mind.

As is the case with many rocky marriages, the body and the mind often fall into some dull, and eventually harmful, patterns. Dr. Feldenkrais, an Israeli nuclear physicist-turned body guru (who died in 1984), insisted that just as the atom can be split, so can these patterns be broken.

In North America, about 300 carry on the teachings of Dr. Feldenkrais. (Accredited practitioners generally study at least 3½ years, part-time.) Although no medical evidence exists to support their practice, they say they have helped many. This help may come in the form of relief from back pain, teeth-grinding, or whiplash. It may allow someone to walk without a cane, dance more gracefully, play the violin better, run more swiftly, or enjoy increased confidence.

How? It's all done through special group movements or one-on-one hands-on manipulation of the body. Feldenkrais practitioners call their more physical work Functional Integration®.

New Ways of Moving

In Feldenkrais, unlike chiropractic, there are no *Ca-a-a-a-racks!* Unlike Rolfing, there are no *O-o-o-o-O-o-o-ws!* And unlike typical massage, there are few *A-a-a-ahs*. Feldenkrais, even its advocates admit, moves slowly.

"Feldenkrais is about patience, not rushing," practitioner Larry Goldfarb says, midway through a Functional Integration session with 45-year-old Beverly Burns. She had spine surgery last year, walks with a cane and suffers from limited motion.

In their session together, Burns, lying mostly on her side, has every conceivable part of her nervous, muscular and skeletal systems either rubbed a little, twisted a little or bent a little. Never a lot. Always very slowly. Unlike physical therapy, the idea is not to take her to the limit of any individual movement, says Goldfarb. He seeks instead to teach her that there are no limits to the number of movements her body can make.

"Feel that movement?" he asks as he slowly rotates her left arm. "Feel that?" he asks as he gently squeezes her shoulder blade. But mostly the time is spent in seemingly unrelated chitchat. Goldfarb says he is all the while nonverbally "suggesting movements, then waiting to see if the person's nervous system puts it together."

"We're all locked into habitual movements," he says. To prove it, he asks you to clasp your hands together. Go ahead. Lock your knuckles. Now take them apart. Clasp them. Take them apart. Clasp. "Notice," says Goldfarb, "you always interlock your fingers the same way." Try moving one hand's fingers differently between the others. It feels odd.

Witness another pattern: Clap your hands. Either your right hand will stay motionless and your left hand will move, or your right hand will travel to your left hand. Or both may move, but the fingers of one will always meet the palm of the other. Try it any other way, and it feels strange.

So what? So, in cases such as Burns's, where the body suddenly (because of her spinal operation) has new limitations, old movements, like reaching for a can of soup off the top shelf in a supermarket, can create problems. You can force movement in the habitual fashion (often meaning pain and possibly added injury), *or* you can learn other ways of reaching for that same can.

In essence, this is what the Feldenkrais Method aims to do—introduce new ways of moving. Or, as Dr. Feldenkrais said, to "freely choose new habit patterns which are more appropriate and fitting to one's unique person."

Exploring New Horizons

Feldenkrais practitioner David Zemach-Bersin of Berkeley makes this analogy: "In psychotherapy, the goal is to move unconscious feelings and thought patterns into awareness; in Feldenkrais, we're trying to bring unconscious movements and body patterns into awareness."

To accomplish this, "teacher and student work together slowly—because the nervous system can only make distinctions slowly," he says. (Feldenkrais practitioners call themselves "teachers" and their clients "students." They insist that they simply educate —each person must heal himself.)

According to Allison Rapp, a Washington, D.C., practitioner, Feldenkrais's real power is in "breaking up old patterns and creating new possibilities."

Rapp says she can create at least a few new possibilities for you in seconds. Try this: Stand up and reach behind you to the right as far as you can, arm straight out, without straining. Look to see where your hand is. Do it several times. Now, instead of moving your eyes to the right as you move your head in that same direction, break the pattern: Move your eyes *left*. Repeat several times. Notice how much farther you can twist.

Rapp says that as babies we had a ball exploring what our bodies could do. But that stopped at a young age.

As for the few talented folks who can imitate others' voices, or make machinegun or popcorn sounds with their mouths, "these people kept exploring after most of us were content to say 'ma-ma' and 'da-da.' They show us there is a range of possibility far beyond what most of us realize."

Rapp says that rather than help people to make unusual sound effects, she works with those looking to improve their golf swing, reach the right notes on their violas, or, in the case of a five-year-old boy with cerebral palsy, simply stand without braces.

"Anyone can benefit," says Rapp. "Feldenkrais is about exploring new horizons."

Breaking Bad Habits

In the Kentfield, California, office of Larry Goldfarb, you are about to explore new horizons and learn a new way of moving. What's wrong with the old? It could have something to do with the stiff neck you feel from time to time, says Goldfarb.

He has you lie on your back, then asks you to lift your head. You do it, just like you've done it several thousand times in your lifetime: Wrong. "We," says Goldfarb, diplomatically, "have this silly notion that our head and neck move without the rest of our spine." He points out that your head rises without movement of your chest or upper back as you begin to get up.

She's Not Just Horsing Around

She would have blown 'em away on "What's My Line?" Linda Tellington-Jones uses a Feldenkrais-inspired training method with animals, including snakes and octopuses. But her specialty is working with horses.

Already an ace horse trainer and rider, Tellington-Jones in 1975 enrolled in a four-year training program with Dr. Moshe Feldenkrais in the hope of learning new ways to help riders. "But the second day it dawned on me," she says. "What's so special about human beings?"

She started to apply Feldenkrais's theories to horses—rotating their ears, twirling their lips, spinning their tails, and picking up their legs. She found that she could train green horses in record time, or quickly improve the performance of seasoned ones, be they runners, jumpers or pleasure horses.

She has since used Feldenkrais's theories to develop her own hands-on techniques for training or simply calming wild beasts and cuddly pets. She has worked with cats, dogs, llamas, pythons, cockatoos and, at least once, an octopus. "You can take an octopus that's really nervous and by doing these little circular motions, you can get it to relax," she says.

For more information on Tellington-Jones's methods, a copy of her book *An Introduction to the Tellington-Jones Equine Awareness Method* or a subscription to her newsletter, write: T-E-A-M News International, Box 5, Site 9, R.R. 8, Edmonton, Alberta T5L 4H8.

How to get the rest of the spine to move with your head? Goldfarb presses your stomach, instructing you to gently pull your pelvis and chest while pressing your lower back toward the table. As part of the movement sequence, he asks you to move your eyes down, let your tongue stick out and relax your jaw. He gently lifts your head several times.

After this movement, Goldfarb's hands softly move your legs, arms, hands, feet, chest and head around for about a half hour ("suggesting movements," as he earlier explained). You feel nimble and light as you get up and start to walk about.

"That's a feeling of freedom," says Goldfarb. "A chronic habitual pattern was broken."

THE HEALING POWER OF THE FELDENKRAIS METHOD

"Because Feldenkrais work looks at human function, there is no limit to the kinds of problems we see," says practitioner David Zemach-Bersin. Here is a sampling.

Back Pain

"People always ask me how I hurt my back—but it wasn't one incident. It had been building up over time," says John Catalina, 37, of the San Francisco area. As a yacht skipper, he does a lot of bending over, lifting, and pulling. "Using Feldenkrais techniques, I'm learning how to do everything more efficiently now."

TMJ Syndrome

Tension and jaw pain are often connected. "You can't help the problem unless the tension is de-anchored," says Zemach-Bersin. In other words, the problem is not only in the jaw, "but in the head, the neck, the back, and the pelvis." Solution? He uses Functional Integration and movement to teach the body to move more smoothly.

Whiplash

In a videotape made of Dr. Feldenkrais, he works with a young woman suffering from whiplash. He rolls her shoulders and gently rocks her head. Within minutes, she is able to move her previously frozen neck in any direction she likes.

Lack of Coordination

Practitioner Allison Rapp coached a five-year-old boy suffering from cere-

---

Beginning Your Feldenkrais Education

Dr. Moshe Feldenkrais left several books explaining his theories about the body and the brain. *Awareness through Movement* (Harper & Row) offers a number of practical exercises. Other books include *The Potent Self* (Harper & Row), *The Case of Nora* (Harper & Row) and *Body and Mature Behavior* (International Universities Press).

These volumes, as well as other information on Feldenkrais, are available through The Feldenkrais Guild, 706 Ellsworth Street, P.O. Box 489, Albany, OR 97321 (800) 775-2118. Another source for information is The Feldenkrais Foundation, P.O. Box 70157, Washington, DC 20088 (301) 656-1548. Either group can put you in touch with a Feldenkrais practitioner in your area.

Private sessions typically cost between $30 and $80 and run from 30 to 75 minutes, sometimes longer for specific problems.

bral palsy to stand without a walker. "I noticed that he always fell in my direction," says Rapp. "So I asked him, 'If you can control which way you're going to fall, why do you have to fall at all?'" The boy broke into laughter, and stood without the walker. "No miracle," says Rapp, "I just made him aware of the control he had."

Rapp also works with musicians and athletes looking to improve their performance. A young viola player, she says, was putting too much body weight on his left leg. Once he was taught how to balance his body effortlessly, he had more energy to apply to playing his instrument. One professional woman golfer was taught to relax better, and her game improved markedly.

Chapter 17

FRICTION RUBS

Deep in the Black Forest of Germany, a stream cascades over a sheer cliff, falling 30 feet to a boardwalk. Along the wooden planks walk half a dozen men and women, dressed in bathing suits, drenched by the crystalline spray. After a few minutes in the bracing waterfall, they return to a platform where spa attendants await, bath brushes bristling.

The attendants attack the bathers' wet skin with Teutonic vigor, brushing from toes and fingers towards the heart. Then they rub their charges dry with rough towels. What was grayish, lifeless-appearing skin is now smooth and glowing pink as a baby's cheeks.

"And when that's done, you're ready to march to Moscow," quips Bernell Baldwin, Ph.D., physiologist at Wildwood Lifestyle Center and Hospital in Wildwood, Georgia. Friction rubs are venerable Northern European treatments, he says, "whereas in America we're more aspirin-oriented." The Germans, he notes, are especially dedicated to the more stringent, martial type of rub. You may think it's too Spartan for you, but the medical benefits are widely known, it's invigorating as all get out, and will indeed make you feel like marching on Moscow, or at least into your daily fray.

Science Friction

At Gurney's Inn Resort and Spa in Montauk, New York, spa director Baroness von Mengersen specializes in "educating" her clients' skin with a dry bristle brush, salt rubs and loofas. Why? "To slough off the dead skin and get the circulation going," she says. "It's very invigorating."

That's not just spa talk. It's easy to see how rubbing can get rid of dead skin, but how does it boost blood circulation?

"The bottom line is convergence," Dr. Baldwin says. Convergence is a principle of the nervous system that is exploited in friction rubs. It's a formula: Touch + temperature + friction = vasoconstriction. "When you produce this friction on various parts of the body in a methodical manner," he says, "you constrict the blood vessels.

As a reaction, the nervous system reflexes cause the blood vessels to rebound, expand and create increased circulation."

An added attraction of increased circulation is that "you increase what is called nutritive blood flow to the cells, not just blood flow through the larger arteries," Dr. Baldwin says. "The net of little capillaries opens up and so the cells get extra oxygen. It's called the Pasteur effect. When oxygen is increased at the cellular level, by-products are reduced, which decreases lactic acid formation [a by-product of muscle exertion that is said to cause fatigue]."

The increased circulation that is produced by friction rubs in turn enhances your immune system, Dr. Baldwin says. "As you improve the logistical deployment of oxygen, the resources of the average cell improve, so the cells become healthier. White blood cell activity and antibody production are increased." Friction rubs are also very good at increasing what Dr. Baldwin calls "lymphatic microcirculation," where lymph fluid rich in white blood cells circulates in its own heart-powered plumbing system.

You can train your body to respond to friction rubs. "With a dry brush you can really educate your skin," Baronness von Mengersen says.

While putting it more scientifically, Dr. Baldwin says the same thing. "Friction rubs are a vasomotor tonic," he says. "The vasomotor system controls the quantity and quality of blood throughout the body. The valves inside the blood vessels have to be controlled very minutely and thoroughly or else there would be too much blood in one part of the body and not enough in another.

"The vasomotor system can be trained, something like muscles in an athlete, so you can get the body to deliver very good circulation over space and time. Vasomotor training is so efficient that despite hot or cold weather or high stress—in almost all situations—the oxygen delivery to the cells is optimum."

Rub-a-Dub-Dub

You don't need a tub. To get a good rub, just try one of these common friction methods. You can friction-rub yourself, or make it mutual. A few precautions: Avoid sensitive areas, like underarms, genitals and women's breasts, or areas affected by skin ailments like rashes, eczema or psoriasis. Never do your face, even with a washcloth, the baronness says, "because you're rubbing and pulling your facial skin in all directions. If I started pulling my facial skin around I'd soon look like a bag."

When you first start your friction program, Baronness von Mengersen says, use a light touch. "After you've educated your skin, you can be more vigorous." Always use circling movements, beginning at your feet and working your way up your legs. Next do your arms from the hands up, then your torso.

Dry Brush

Widely used in Scandinavia, the dry brush is no more than it seems. Spas use nylon bristles because they can be sterilized, the baroness says. "We have a special brush that's a kind of rubber glove with bristles." At home you can use a brush with natural bristles (which are also less likely to scratch). Use one with a detachable handle, like a bath brush.

The dry brush, she says, is the best way to remove dead skin, and can be used every day. Be sure to "tune" your brush to your skin, Dr. Baldwin says: "Fragile skin needs a mild brush."

Wet Friction

This can be as simple as taking a bath or shower and using a brush, but here are some other methods.

Be-bop-a-loofa. The loofa fibrous pad comes in various forms, but overall "is the softest of all the friction rubs we use," the baroness says. She recommends a loofa with peppermint Castile soap as "a nice summer treatment." Like the dry brush, you can do this every day. Follow with a tepid rinse.

Salt rub. "You can't do this more than once a week," the baroness says. "And it's not recommended for someone with very sensitive skin." She uses a paste made of water, almond oil and sea salt. The paste is applied with the hands in the same manner as other rubs. Follow with a tepid rinse.

Dr. Baldwin calls this the "salt glow." In addition to the rubbing, he says, "the salt itself heightens the effect by its granular nature. And sodium chloride chemically assists in activating nerve receptors in the skin."

This is a heavy-duty rub, and precautions beyond the normal ones listed above must be taken. "Take care over bony prominences," he warns. "Rapid movements are more irritating than stimulating." To avoid chilling, drape the body except the area being worked on.

Cold-mitten friction. Called CMF by old hands, this is the champion of friction rubs, the epitome of the convergence formula, and, Dr. Baldwin says, a fine substitute for caffeine. "You get all the benefits of caffeine without the drug," he says. "It revs up the part of the brain that serves as an alarm clock. It doesn't last as long as caffeine, but if you're on a good program of CMF, nutrition, exercise and rest, you don't need more than that."

The mittens are imported from Scandinavia, and "have a nice weave to them calculated to give you friction without trauma," Dr. Baldwin says. "But you can get many of the benefits with just a rough washcloth." You can also make your own mittens by sewing older but still serviceable toweling into mitten shapes.

Before you begin, dip the mittens in cold water, or cold apple cider vinegar water. "You have to match the water temperature and the room temperature to the person's vitality," Dr. Baldwin cautions. "A very aged or ill person needs milder temperatures, while a younger or healthier person can handle the cooler temperatures." Some people even prefer ice water.

Common sense is also needed for the degree of vigor applied: Rub as vigorously as the person can stand, and no more. "It doesn't really have to be Spartan to do the job," he says. Be sure to keep the body covered and expose one area at a time for rubbing, drying it before going on to the next area.

After dipping the mittens in water, squeeze out the excess so there's no dripping. If you're giving CMF to another, hold one of his or her arms up, and place a mitten on each side of the arm. Rub in an oscillating manner, from hand to underarm. Then rotate the mittens' position 90 degrees to make sure you cover the entire arm, and repeat the process. Do this three times, dry the arm with a towel, and drape it. Repeat for the other limbs, always rubbing toward the heart. Finally rub the abdomen and chest, then the back, continuing the bottom to top motions.

"The skin will commonly turn light colored because of the vasoconstriction," Dr. Baldwin says. "Then in a few seconds it will turn a youthful pinkish color, which is the rebound effect of increased circulation."

Frictioning yourself. You can use cold-mitten friction on yourself, but it's time-consuming and it's hard to do justice to your back. Luckily, there's another easy way to get the same benefits. "It can be done very quickly and efficiently," Dr. Baldwin says. "My wife and I do it most every day of the year. Take a conventional hot shower with mild soap. In the summer, end with a short burst of cool water. As the weather gets colder, so should that final burst, until in the middle of winter it's straight cold. Then just take a rough towel and rub vigorously to dry yourself."

It takes only seven or eight minutes, and it's better than coffee, he says. "It will wake you up, ready for the boss and all of his team."

THE HEALING POWER OF FRICTION RUBS

Friction rubs in general are used to improve skin tone and circulation, and anything that improves circulation may help your health. Proponents say cold-mitten friction is good for people who suffer an inordinate number of colds, for those lacking energy, and people who are kicking the caffeine and nicotine habits. Anything that stimulates your immune system is going to increase your ability to fight infections. And remember, your skin is your first line of immune defense.

But the greatest value of friction rubs, Dr. Baldwin says, lies in their "blend of psychology and physiology. Healing is not all just physics and chemistry. With these rubs people have the vivid experience that someone else cares about their well-being. With one-on-one, personal interaction in healing, the effects are maximized."

BRUSH YOUR HEADACHE AWAY

The cause of most headaches, says biophysicist Harry Ehrmantraut, Ph.D., is poor blood circulation in the arteries, veins and muscles of the scalp. When circulation is poor, the oxygen supply isn't what it should be; greater amounts of metabolic wastes form, and they aren't washed away in the blood. By boosting circulation, this friction treatment may brush away the headache you have now, Dr. Ehrmantraut says. And regular use may prevent future headaches from ever getting started in the first place.

It's simple and quick enough to do every day, and this consistency is crucial to making the system work. Use a brush like the one pictured. Start at the temples, just above the eyebrows, and brush in circles, gradually moving toward the back of your head.

"Be sure to pay attention with careful brushing to the uppermost point in front of the ear," Dr. Ehrmantraut says. "The main artery supplying the scalp runs through this area."

After you've finished with the sides of your head, start at the top, just left of center. Again brush in small circles, moving toward the rear and then down the back of your head. Repeat, beginning at the right of center.

17-1

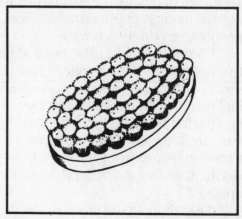

The brush should be a good hairbrush or bath brush with fairly stiff, rounded-tip, natural bristles.

17-2

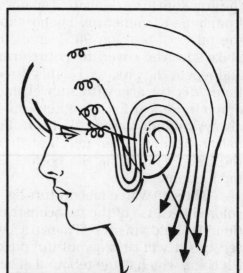

As you brush away your headache, move the brush in half-inch diameter circles, moving up-back-down-forward.

FRICTIONING WITH MITTENS

Cold, wet mittens are good for something better than just throwing snowballs. A special kind of mitten can boost blood circulation and rev up the brain.

17-3

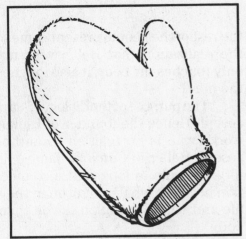

The mitten used for cold-mitten friction is simply rough Turkish toweling or a washcloth sewn into the shape of a mitten. Make a pair of them, put them on, and start rubbing.

17-4

Start the cold-mitten friction rub at the fingers and work your way down to the underarms. Then move on to the legs and work them from toes to thighs. Always keep a bowl of water nearby to dip the mittens in and wring out the excess water.

17-5

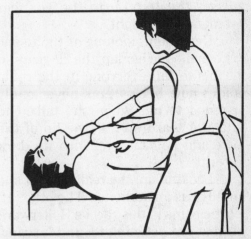

Finally, put your cold mittens on the torso and rub in a circular motion, beginning at the abdomen and working up to the chest. Repeat the motions on the back, working from lower to upper back.

Chapter 18

HELLERWORK

Thirteen people are crying. Over the sobs you can hear seagulls squawking as the birds complain about the waves crashing onto a Martha's Vineyard beach.

Slowly, a well-worn tissue box is being passed around a circle of people sitting Indian-style on the bare cottage floor. A trembling hand reaches in and pulls out a light blue sheet, the bright red nails clashing with the box's paisley print. The middle-aged woman passes the box on to the younger woman on her right.

Head bent, looking at the tissue box cradled in her lap, the 20-year-old begins to tell everyone in the room about how her parents never really listened to her when she talked to them. A teardrop hits the lip of the box and splashes off into its dark interior.

Looking up, she realizes that she finally has an audience. The other 12 participants in this special Hellerwork retreat are listening to, and hearing, every word she says. And they respond.

She breaks into a smile, licking a tear as it rolls by her upturned lips. Her sobs turn to giggles as she and the rest of the people present come to the realization that Hellerwork not only touches the body, it also touches the mind.

"The purpose of the dialogue," says Joseph Heller, the founder of Hellerwork (who is no relation to author Joseph Heller of *Catch 22* fame), "is to get people to look at the connection between what's going on in their life and what's going on inside their body."

Inside the circle, Diane Pescatore of New York City feels the link. "It's a very intimate connection. I was surprised by a lot of the things about myself that I confronted here."

Soon the tissue box comes to rest. The awakening is complete. Outside, the tall grass of the sand dunes sways in the afternoon breeze. You can taste the ocean salt in the air. Chirping replaces squawks as the gray clouds are blown away. And the sun comes out.

Heller Highlights

"Hellerwork is a composite of three elements," says Joseph Heller. "It's deep connective tissue massage focusing

118

on the fascia [plasticlike tissue that wraps around all the muscles], combined with movement education and then dialogue."

What it really is, is one man's personal evolution. Born in 1940 ("a bad time to be born Jewish in Poland"), Heller escaped with his family to Russia, then went on to Paris, where he spent most of his youth until his parents emigrated to Los Angeles in 1957.

He came to Hellerwork, though, by way of the stars. After getting a degree in mathematics at Cal Tech, he spent the next ten years as an aerospace engineer at the Jet Propulsion Lab in Pasadena, California. It was there that he decided that he "preferred people to machines," and he began to attend encounter groups and weekend workshops where he eventually studied Rolfing with Dr. Ida Rolf.

In the early seventies, Heller resigned his position at the J.P.L. and in 1972 he officially became a Rolfer. In 1975 he was selected as the first president of the Rolf Institute.

With Dr. Rolf, he learned how to move tissue in the body, but he was also studying what was later called Aston-Patterning with Judith Aston and learning about how the body moved. In time, this education would be the basis for the second tenet of Hellerwork.

But the evolution continued, until finally the third piece fell into place. "Over time I noticed that people started talking about certain subjects when I worked on certain parts of the body.

That's when I realized that our bodies store emotions and attitudes. I've come to believe that these psychological aspects really do shape our bodies."

Massage, movement and the mind —the three M's—came together and crystallized into the Hellerwork system in 1978.

Getting to Know Gravity

Hellerwork consists of a series of 11 sessions, each lasting 90 minutes (see the box "Eleven Steps to Realignment"). Each focuses on a different part of the body in a prearranged sequence.

The hands-on work is a deep tissue massage that "manipulates the connective tissue, mostly to reduce tension and help realign the parts," Heller explains. "It's where my engineering background comes into play. I look to see if the parts are stacked vertically on top of each other, and if the joints are horizontal.

"What I want to do is align the body with gravity. And that involves more than just how you stand in the earth's gravitational field. It's also becoming aware that you belong here, that you're a part of an ecology. Your alignment with gravity is your most basic form of planetary consciousness."

Your reintroduction to the forces of gravity begins with a series of questions. "I ask people why they want Hellerwork," says Fae Kontje-Gibbs, a Massachusetts Hellerwork practitioner. "Then I ask them what result they

Eleven Steps to Realignment

Hellerwork is based on a series of 11 sessions, each with a different focus. Joseph Heller suggests that you have one session a week, but some people schedule one session a month, while others do the whole program in just a few weeks. However you approach it, this is how your Hellerwork series will progress.

Session 1: Inspiration

With its theme "draw in spirit," this session focuses on your ribcage and the muscles that attach to it. The aim is to open up the breathing and align the ribcage over the pelvis.

Session 2: Standing on Your Own Feet

The theme is self-support and sufficiency. The session focuses on the leg muscles and their alignment.

Session 3: Reaching Out

The theme is giving and receiving, assertion and aggression. The session focuses on your arms, shoulders and the muscles on your side. The purpose is to release tension in those areas and to bring vertical alignment to the sides of the torso.

Session 4: Control and Surrender

This session works to help you release what you're holding inside. The practitioner focuses on the muscles on the bottom of your core (your core being your inner torso from the shoulders to the pelvic floor) and the muscles of your inner thighs.

Session 5: The Guts

The theme is your gut feelings, and the session focuses on the muscles of your stomach area.

Session 6: Holding Back

The session investigates how you hold tension in your back, focusing on your spine and back muscles.

Session 7: Losing Your Head

This session shows how closely your mind and body are connected, by focusing on the muscles of your face, head, and neck. The aim is to release muscle tension and help align your head over your torso.

Session 8: The Feminine

Equally important for both women and men, this session focuses

want to see. That's followed up with a questionnaire in which I ask them to rate themselves on a scale of zero to ten. They rate their health, tension level, stability, energy, sexual enjoyment, looks and so on."

Once you hand back the answer sheet, "we start looking for a trend," says Shirley Norwood, a Hellerwork practitioner based in Houston, Texas. "Sometimes a person will rate herself an eight in almost everything, but a

out the sessions. "We have clients stand against a grid with a plumb line running down their front," says Kontje-Gibbs.

on the entire lower half of the body, including the legs, feet and pelvis.

Session 9: The Masculine

The theme is how we express masculine energy. Both men and women can benefit from the session's focus on the upper half of the body, including the arms, shoulders, ribcage, and neck.

Session 10: Integration

This session reveals the integrity that is already present in your body, by focusing on the major joints including ankles, knees, hips, shoulders, elbows, wrists and spine.

Session 11: Coming Out

Here you learn to take what you've learned in Hellerwork with you, and how to allow full self-expression to radiate through the vehicle of your body.

"Using the grid, we can show them very precisely what changes are occurring in their posture through the series. When the shoulders are released in session three, for example, they drop back and down in a more natural state. You can see it by comparing the before and after shots. People can see how they line up differently on the grid."

The dialogue that takes place in the third session may help lift some burdens off your shoulders, too. "We talk about how hard or easy is it for you to reach out and make contact with people," says Heller.

"We also talk about your assertiveness. Is it hard for you to ask for what you want in life? Is it hard for you to give or receive? Also, how do you deal with anger, and how do you express it? The arms, in general, have to do with aggression. We call our weapons 'arms' because these were the first weapons that we had."

Hopefully, the dialogue part of the session will go a long way in disarming any underlying battle raging inside. "If a person comes to me all stooped over in an attitude I call burdened, I could work on the shoulders, even teach him how to move his head correctly," says Heller. "But if I haven't addressed the attitude that's underneath all that, then sooner or later the person will fall back into that attitude, and the previous body pos-

two in just one category. If that happens, then that's the area we focus on."

Before you come into focus, though, the practitioner will take your picture with the intention of using it to show you how you develop through-

Heller on Hellerwork

Minutes before our interview with Joseph Heller, originator of Hellerwork, the gray Cape Cod sky gave way to bright sunshine. It was during a lunch break, and Joseph pulled up a picnic table bench. His students brought their lunches outside and sat on the ground within earshot. Even a passing rabbit stopped as if curious to hear what this slightly-built man had to say. Talking softly, with a light Polish accent, his voice barely rose over the sound of the waves breaking on a beach not 20 yards away.

Question: If you had to briefly explain to someone what Hellerwork is, how would you do it?

Heller: I often use the automobile as a metaphor. Hellerwork is taking care of your body in the same way you take care of your car. Rather than waiting for the car to break down, you take it in for regular preventive maintenance. Hellerwork is like preventive maintenance for your body.

Question: Do you think of yourself then as a mechanic?

Heller: Sort of, but I really prefer to think of myself as a gardener. I like to think that I grow people, or help people to grow. Grow in the sense of develop more fully, become more of who they are.

Question: How do you help people to grow?

Heller: I work with what I call their channel for life energy. Most people think of their channel of energy as diminishing with age, running out or drying up as they get older. I have a suspicion it doesn't have to be like that. We have this notion that as the body ages, it can only get worse. But I'm not ready to accept that.

I believe that it's possible to develop your body in such a way that as you grow older your experience of living can be enriched. You can be more vibrant and feel more of the depth and breadth and passion of life.

Question: Why is the dialogue process such an important part of the Hellerwork series?

Heller: Because as much as I like to change a person's body, I like even more to change his *mind* about his body. Attitudes shape the body, so changing a person's attitude ultimately affects structure.

ture will come back."

Okay, it's one thing to be asked to bare your body for a massage. But it's a whole other story to be asked to bare your soul at the same time.

Shirley Norwood, who became a Hellerwork practitioner because she "loves to touch and loves to talk," says

Question: You say that the body is the hologram of the being. What do you mean by that?

Heller: The body is a representation of us. It's how we present ourselves in life. With a hologram if you take any part of it and project it, you will still see the whole picture. It's the same thing with the body; any part of it gives you a view into the whole thing.

Question: Hellerwork has evolved out of Rolfing and movement education exercises. Has the evolution stopped or is it still continuing?

Heller: Yes, I hope it will continue to develop. Hellerwork is like the human body. It's a live entity that keeps growing. We're only in the infancy of this work; we're just beginning. I'm sure 100 years from now, Hellerwork practitioners will look back on us and say 'How primitive!' And that's what I want to leave to them, a bodywork system that will grow along with the people it serves.

Finding a Practitioner

There are about 130 trained Hellerwork practitioners. Most are found in the United States, but a few practice in Europe, Canada, New Zealand and Australia.

When looking for a practitioner, look for one who has been certified by the Hellerwork school located in Mt. Shasta, California. To gain certification, practitioners must graduate from a 1,250-hour curriculum of study, and take continuing education courses.

Most sessions for individuals last from an hour to an hour and a half, but expect your first session to run a bit longer. The rates charged for the 11 sessions vary, but the normal range is between $60 and $110 depending on your location and need.

For more information about Hellerwork and how you can find a practitioner near you, write to Joseph Heller, c/o The Body of Knowledge, 415 N. Mt. Shasta Boulevard, #4, Mt. Shasta, CA 96067.

a session will only go as far as you let it. "The magic word is *stop*. If it's too painful, either the bodywork or the dialogue, all you have to do is say stop, and we stop instantly. You are actually in control of the session all the time."

And those who haven't said stop during the session find themselves saying the other magic words, thank you. For when the session ends, the healing part of Hellerwork begins.

THE HEALING POWER OF HELLERWORK

"It was exhilarating," says Sharon Langston of Woodland, California. Wearing nothing but goose bumps, Sharon has just finished the second session which deals with the knees and legs. And she's feeling an immediate before-and-after difference.

"I can stand up straight on my legs again. I feel more centered, my feet are flat on the ground. Before I tended to walk on the outside of my feet, but now my whole foot hits the ground."

With a history of knee problems, including arthroscopic surgery, Sharon was looking forward to this session. And she hasn't been disappointed. "I don't hear that popping sound anymore, and I don't feel the tightness and pain on the outside of my knee now."

But it wasn't only the massage that brought about this healing. "I had been storing up a lot of emotions in my body," Sharon says. "Talking about them during the dialogue helped release the muscle tension in my knee."

For Judy Harlan of Cleveland, the leg session and dialogue helped jog some old memories, but it also helped her jogging. "Joseph watched how I ran, and told me how to use my legs correctly. And that, combined with the hands-on session, really helped my running. After the session I've been able to run farther and faster with less exertion than I did before."

Margaret Hyer of Grapevine, Texas, says the session worked on her thighs. "My legs were always rubbing together when I stood or walked. Now I have space between my legs which I haven't had in years. I'd been holding lots of tension in my thighs, and that just totally pulled my legs in. Until Hellerwork, I thought they were permanently stuck together."

It might unstick your limbs, but will the benefits of Hellerwork stick with you? Joseph Heller thinks so. "We educate you to be more aware of your body—how movement and emotions affect it. If you learn the techniques and keep using them, then you should be able to make Hellerwork's benefits last indefinitely."

Chapter 19

HIGHER DIMENSIONS OF HEALING

There's more to the body than meets the eye. At least that's what Christian preachers and Buddhist monks and Hindu gurus and Moslem ayatollahs—not to mention faith healers and aura balancers and psychic surgeons and witch doctors—would have us believe.

That "more" is the human spirit. Despite their theological differences, these professionals in the art of faith tell us we each have an ethereal body that surrounds and permeates our physical body. It's not a gas like oxygen, it's not made of cells. Some say you can see it—in portraits of Jesus and Buddha it's the halos about their heads. A technique called Kirlian photography supposedly captures its alleged electromagnetic luminescence on film.

Some call it the astral body, some call it energy, some a force. Russians call it bioplasma. Many say it is love, that it comes from God. Or gods.

Most agree on the term spirit. They say spirit is the source of life. Faith makes spirit real for us, lack of faith doesn't disprove spirit. Through prayer, meditation, contemplation, even thought, we can call upon spirit and be healed.

This is what faith healers claim to do. When they call upon spirit, it flows through them (often via the hands) into us. "When God created everything there is, He also created all forms of energy," says Methodist healer Fred H. Ohrenschall of the New Life Clinic at Mt. Washington United Methodist Church in Baltimore. "One kind of energy can be used by the body to re-create itself. When healing takes place, the body does it. The doctor doesn't heal you, the healer doesn't heal you. This energy that we're talking about is simply that energy which is around us all the time. But it can be focused into a person to give the mind and body an extra shot to heal itself."

California psychic healer Greg Schelkun believes "everyone has their own god, and that god is really beyond

125

all words and form. If we can touch that essence and be touched by it, it can do wonders." These wonders, some say, are miracles.

Not all faith healing demands unquenchable, unquestioning faith from the healee. But all faith healing does involve a close bond between healer, healee and spirit, even if the bond is temporary.

Laying On of Hands

When your mother's caress soothed your childhood hurts, you were experiencing laying-on-of-hands healing. The Bible cites other, more dramatic examples, including healing miracles at the hands of Jesus and the apostles.

Why the hands? Why not just prayer? "The common methodology throughout all denominational expressions is prayer," says Robert Cooley, Ph.D., president of Gordon-Conwell Theological Seminary in South Hamilton, Massachusetts.

But some think the actual touch is important in healing. "People are becoming more aware of the importance of touching," says Margaret Rose, lay missioner for prayer and healing for the Episcopal Diocese of Pennsylvania. "It's a sacramental act, but some people regard it as a kind of spiritual first aid because it can be administered spontaneously."

Clinical psychologist and medical educator Jules Older, Ph.D., author of *Touching Is Healing*, denies the importance of faith and prayer but agrees touch is valuable. "I know from my own clinical experience and that of others, as well as some studies, that touching is an enhancer of healing," Dr. Older says. "How this is mediated, I don't know. I strongly suspect it's a combination of the tactility of touch, working in some way we don't understand, and the fact that touch is a form of close relationship. Monkeys go for it too, though they don't believe in any god we know of, and it seems to help them through troubled times."

A more lyrical view of laying on of hands is offered by the Rev. Daryl Burdick, assistant pastor of the Visitation Ministry of Victory Christian Center on the campus of Oral Roberts University in Tulsa. Burdick sees the hands as "a tool of the body. Hands represent authority, power, work. God has given us hands so unique and so beautiful, so tremendously made, so full of compassion and tenderness. Hands represent what is directed by the heart of man. And the heart represents the love of God. The laying on of hands is a demonstration of the power of God that God allows to flow through us."

And what better to touch with than hands? Hands are, well, handy. Besides, Burdick adds, "It would be hard to lay on heads or lay on elbows."

Who Can Heal?

We all have spirit, and most of us have hands. So we can heal by laying on hands, right?

The answer depends on the theological authority. The Roman Catholics say laying on of hands "has to be performed by priests or bishops because it's part of the anointing of the sick," says the Rev. Monsignor Alan Detcher, associate director of the Bishop's Committee on the Liturgy in the National Catholic Office for Information.

But the charismatic movement of the Catholic Church is not so restrictive. Nor are most other religious practitioners. "We have priests, religious sisters and brothers, and lay people involved in healing," says Walter Matthews, associate director of the National Service Committee of the Catholic Charismatic Renewal Council. "At big Charismatic conferences someone leads a prayer for healing and people may spontaneously lay hands on others around them. Prayer for healing in small groups almost always includes laying on of hands."

Although Episcopalians believe that laying on of hands is a sacramental act, it isn't confined to the ordained ministry, Rose says, "because it can be administered spontaneously and need not be preceded by a long preparation. It's often used by lay workers, doctors and nurses, and great things happen as a result."

The United Methodist Church is also deeply involved in laying on of hands, and also doesn't restrict it to the ordained, though its practice is predictably more methodical. Methodism founder John Wesley was a psychic and a healer, says retired Mount Washington Methodist Church pastor Robert Cartwright. The New Life Clinic there is actually a Thursday morning service capped by a healing, where lay member Ohrenschall, Cartwright, three other Methodist ministers and a physician lay on hands.

Schelkun thinks "we all have the ability to heal. As with any talent, some people are better at healing than others." Schelkun believes people who love and care for each other can heal each other, especially husbands and wives, parents and children.

"The primary factor is intent," Schelkun says. "In families that intent is innate. If people can just allow themselves to feel it and use it, that's enough to get it started."

Where Should You Touch?

"Ordinarily we lay hands on the head," Burdick says, "because that's where the mind is. In a hospital we'll also lay hands on the part of the body that needs specific healing." Modesty is valued: When hands are to be laid on places other than the head, men treat men, women treat women.

At large healing services there isn't time to touch any place but the head, neck and shoulders. At the New Life Clinic, for example, dozens may come to kneel at the altar to receive the laying on of hands.

Many healers let their intuition tell them where to place their hands. "I usually put my hands where the symptoms are and/or where I feel other places in the body are affected," Schelkun says.

Ohrenschall says he touches people the way he is "impressed to touch them. You don't have to touch the part of the body that's ailing. This energy has an intelligence all its own. It's like your white blood cells. When you have a cut, you don't have to think, 'I'm going to dispatch 500 of these corpuscles'—they go automatically, they don't have to be coached. The energy acts the same way—it goes to the right place."

No matter where they put their hands, healers are trying to heal the entire person. "I perceive a body as an energy form," Schelkun says. "It's not just biochemistry and molecules so much as the energy that binds the molecules together. The emotional body, the physical body, the mental body all fit in the same realm. I treat the whole person."

The Role of Faith

"Don't worry about it, kid," the late psychic Olga Worrall used to tell unbelievers. "I've got enough faith for the both of us." (Worrall and her husband, Ambrose, also a psychic healer, founded the New Life Clinic in 1958.)

Some people have faith in spirit and healing, some are open-minded, some are questioning, some hostile. Most healers say your faith, or lack thereof, doesn't really matter.

"I've had men come up to the altar rail, stand there and look at me like they could spit in my face," Cartwright says. "They say, 'The only reason I'm here is because my wife made me, and the sooner I get this blankety-blank stuff out of the way the better.' But still they receive healing."

Schelkun asks, "What *is* faith anyway? What we believe isn't important. We believe enough to walk in the door. My favorite people are healthy skeptics, or rather, unhealthy skeptics. We're all born in Missouri, you know. We have got to be shown."

But Dr. Older says faith "isn't involved in the least." Having strong doubts about faith healers or even the existence of spirit, Dr. Older says a temporary healing of a chronic nosebleed was the only effect he ever experienced in several such encounters. "I don't know how to account for that," he says. "But you're working with someone who's identified as a healer; there's a physical contact; there's a need for something; and somewhere in there is an expectation that this thing just might work. Something in that combination seems to have a temporary—though by no means magical—effect."

Perhaps Worrall put it best: "Faith is the lack of resistance to that which you hope to receive."

Do Miracles Exist?

Faith or not, most healers say healing miracles do indeed happen. It all depends on your definition of miracle.

Schelkun's favorite doubter was a man whose wife came for healing.

The wife had multiple sclerosis, "and he didn't believe in any of this stuff," Schelkun says. "He told me about the asthma he'd had since childhood, and I talked him into getting up on my healing table. His wife came back the next day by herself. He wouldn't come. He was in fear, he'd locked himself in the hotel room and he was crying. When I went to see him he told me he didn't believe in God or in healing. To him God was something you made up to make yourself feel better when you were in a lifeboat adrift at sea. And he was crying because despite his disbelief he was breathing normally for the first time in 30 years. The healing had put him in touch with this power."

Healers warn against looking for an instant miracle, although most can cite cases. "People who come to the New Life Clinic for six months and learn how to reprogram their thinking," Ohrenschall says, "seem to have tremendous improvement in their physical health as well. But to have a person come in and get one zap and be healed is rare."

In other words, psychic healing is usually a gradual process. "I have never seen an instantaneous miracle," Dr. Cooley says, "but I have seen the miraculous process, against all doctors' predictions."

Be it instant or gradual, healing by spirit is a miracle, Dr. Cooley says. "The miraculous stems from the fact that the normal processes of disease are reversed: If there is an infection, then that process is reversed. If there is diminished production of blood cells,

that is reversed."

Episcopalian Lay Missioner Rose says "people have had tremendous healing" at Episcopal seminars of 500 people with 40 clergy participating. One example is a man whose doctors had told him he had terminal cancer. "He had an instantaneous healing, not in the service but as he was walking to his car afterwards," Rose says. The diocesan office didn't accept the man's word for it until before and after x-rays verified the healing.

The most eye-opening healings seem to occur at Pentecostal churches. Pastor Burdick tells of a woman with a glass eye who received laying on of hands at such a church. "As she was going up the aisle of this church, the healer's son saw something hit the floor and roll. And all of a sudden this lady started to scream. She had a new eye. What rolled down there was the glass eye."

That's too farfetched a miracle for Dr. Older. "You may have a broken arm healed at Lourdes," he says, "but no amputee there has ever grown a new one."

The kind of healing Dr. Older feels is truly substantial and available to many is a healing of attitudes and feelings. "A real disorder remains," he says, "but the feelings and attitudes that surround it change."

He cites the case of a woman who had lost 90 percent of her vision and cursed God for that. But at a revival meeting she received laying on of hands. She's still 90 percent blind, but now she thanks God for her 10 percent vision. "Now she's active in her church, does volunteer work at the hospital, attends plays," Dr. Older says. "There's been no change in her physical condition, but a tremendous change in her emotional condition. I accept that as a healing." In other words, healing is not necessarily synonymous with cure.

Doing It Yourself

"I think there are some people who have the healing gift and go through their lives not realizing it," Ohrenschall says. "If you want to heal, you've got to develop your own method. You've got to let your spirit teach you. If you're going to be the instrument, you've got to be a tuned instrument. Some people are prodigals. They're wired for it. Most people have to practice, like in anything else."

To heal, healers first make contact with the spirit, however they conceive it to be. Greg Schelkun has a down-to-earth approach. "I use a gas pump analogy," he says. "First you have to find the nozzle. Then you have to find the patient's filler cap—and that means becoming one with the patient. Then you go back and turn the pump on.

"That process happens at deep levels with me now. I've practiced my prayer, meditation and contemplation for 15 years so it's almost second nature to me. It used to take me an hour of prayer to get ready to see my first patients, an hour to do the session,

and an hour and a half to come down from it all. Now I make contact instantly and the patient is on the table only 15 to 20 minutes."

Organized religions are more formal, employing regular church services to create a setting for laying on of hands. Yet Ohrenschall is also refreshingly simple in his approach. When he's garbed in a black robe, standing before the altar at Mt. Washington Methodist Church with the other healers, he sees himself "as a garden hose, just shipping water. I just go into the silence and let the water flow."

If you're interested in trying the laying on of hands approach yourself, here's what healers we've talked to suggest.

1. Choose a location that is quiet, soothing, relaxing, with soft lighting. No disagreeable sights, sounds or smells should intrude.
2. Both you and the healee should try to find a deep sense of peace and calm. The healee can be lying down. You should sit comfortably, but with no slouching and without crossed legs and arms.
3. Assume an attitude of faith in a power greater than you, that you have a spiritual nature, that this power resides in you and all life. Have the unselfish desire to help.
4. Ask for this power to manifest itself. The prayer—or thought or meditation or contemplation—can be silent or spoken. Simple is best. It must be heartfelt, not mindless repetition.

This example is used by the New Life Clinic:

My body is a manifestation of the living spirit. It is created and sustained by the one presence and the one power. That power is flowing in and through me now, animating every organ, every action and every function of my physical body. I am one with the infinite rhythm of life, which flows through me in love, harmony and peace.

5. Maintaining a sense of oneness with spirit and healee, lay hands on the person, being sensitive about pain and modesty. The head is the most natural place, but you may feel drawn to other sites. Follow your intuition.
6. Feel the power flowing through you into the person you're touching.
7. Accept what healing there is. Don't expect instant miracles. Give thanks.
8. Tell the healee to try to maintain after the healing the spiritually poised and receptive attitude achieved during the session.
9. Repeat when the need arises.

How to Find a Healer

If you're the one who needs healing, take precautions. Healing by laying on of hands is scientifically unproven. Just accepting its possible existence takes an act of faith, no matter how small. Faith also begets fakes. Fake healers are the main reason faith healers are so often held in disrepute.

If the "real thing" exists, here are a few guidelines for finding it.

- If you participate in organized religion, this is probably your best bet. Avoid those who make blatant appeals for your money. Regular church services will only include a regular offering. The New Life Clinic will not accept any donation whatsoever.
- "Use your own common sense," New York City psychic healer Rock Kenyon says. "Don't leave your mind at the doorstep." If someone says, "Cross my palm with money and I can heal you," or advertises "Blindness cured for $29.95," keep your hands in your pockets.
- Fulltime healers normally charge $50 to $100 per session. "A healer has to pay the rent, but money's got nothing to do with whether he can heal," Schelkun says. "All the money in the world won't buy a healing. I ask a fee, but I have yet to turn away a person because he can't pay it. Most of the genuine healers I know will make accommodations."
- Don't believe a healer who claims the healing comes from him, or that healing depletes him. Says Schelkun, "I tell my patients that if it were up to *my* energy I would have burnt out years ago."
- "The healer shouldn't depend on externals or theatrics," Kenyon

says. Beware of crystals and potions and special herbs and oils. Spirit needs none of these things.

- Don't trust a healer who says, "Don't trust anybody but me." "Don't abandon your doctor for faith healing," Dr. Cooley says. "I believe that God gifts doctors and nurses with skills and understanding, and that these healing arts and sciences do minister to the human body. The combination of faith *and* medicine is the proper Christian response."

Reiki: Healing with Energy

Reiki (pronounced ray-key) is a Japanese word meaning "universal life energy." It is an allegedly ancient healing art "rediscovered" in the mid-19th century in the visions of a man named Mikao Usui.

Today there's a trademarked version, a more amorphous version, a secret Japanese version, and several freelance types. All the versions aim to relieve the body of physical, emotional and spiritual "blockages."

All lay hands on in certain positions to transmit this universal life energy. (It's the energy, not the person, that heals.) All claim to heal illness and injury by working on the emotional, mental and spiritual levels, not just the physical. None require faith. All have degrees of adeptness.

Western reiki costs hundreds of dollars to attain, a fact that hasn't stopped thousands of people. You can't learn it from a book, proponents say. You have to be initiated by a master to be able to harness and direct the life energy. "Reiki is not something we learn," says Virginia reiki master Thalia Kafatou, Ph.D. "Reiki is something we become." Using the hand positions and hoping for the best doesn't cut it. It takes a master's touch.

The version promoted by Barbara Weber Ray, Ph.D., is trademarked under the name The Radiance Technique®. Dr. Ray founded the American-International Reiki Association, of Santa Monica, California, which publishes *The Radiance Technique Journal* and promotes seminars all over the country. It's by far the most practiced, and most marketed, reiki technique.

Although to become a certified reiki master can cost thousands of dollars in training fees, you can learn enough to treat yourself and family and friends for life by taking just the "first-degree" course, at a cost of $300 or less. (There are seven degrees in the Radiance Technique.) Then, proponents say, you can treat yourself while you're driving or watching television, or even while you're asleep, merely by sleeping with your hands in the right positions. But you don't have to learn reiki to benefit from it. A practitioner will treat you for about $35 to $50 an hour.

An Hour-Long "Attunement"

There is virtually no condition or illness reiki won't tackle, from wrinkles to bad habits to a world in over-whelming need of change. Since everything is made of the same energy, pets and potted plants are just as reiki-izable as people. Nor does the energy have to be specifically directed: It goes where it's needed.

The method is simple. Fully clothed, you lie on a table, like the one in Cara Aisha Lumen's Manhattan apartment. Lumen is a fourth-degree reiki practitioner who looks about two decades younger than her 55 years.

As you lie on your back, Lumen gently places her hands together on six points on your body: the crown of your head, forehead, throat, heart, solar plexus, and genital area. You turn over, and she repeats the process, laying her hands on the backsides of these points, adding the base of the spine and subtracting the crown.

The treatment lasts an hour. Many people feel heat or tingling from her hands; some feel nothing. Most feel stress seeping out of their bodies. Most feel better for having been reiki-ed.

All this constitutes an "attunement," in Radiance parlance. "The attunement process amplifies and directs the life energy. "That amplification will last for awhile. But it ultimately wears off," which is why reiki should become a regular part of your life, Lumen says.

Radiance Technique practitioners of second-degree proficiency and higher also use reiki to send universal life energy through time and space, according to Lumen. "When my son was in a coma after a motorcycle acci-dent in Mexico, I sent energy like you wouldn't believe."

Other benefits of reiki, Lumen says, are "increased tolerance, and growth toward unconditional love and compassion. I like the personal growth aspect the best. Since I've been practicing reiki, people look at me and say, 'Your edges have softened.' "

Mahikari: Giving the Light

Mahikari is yet another Japanese original, the product of a revelation delivered to Tokyo businessman Kotama Okada in 1959. Mahikari has a number of similarities to Dr. Ray's reiki technique:

- Okada was a good businessman and trademarked his revelation.
- Although his revelation was free, you have to pay for it—$80 for a three-day course.
- The healing aspect of mahikari (divine true light) draws on the same universal energy as reiki and other spiritual healing methods.
- Faith is not required.

But in mahikari, healing plays the same role as in organized religion: "A souvenir of the trip," Okada said. Sometimes the souvenir is a miracle.

Followers claim mahikari both spiritually awakens and tunes the soul to its divine purpose. The movement contains the "fundamental principles and universal truth found in the original teachings of all major religions," says Masahiro Kawasaki, who heads up Mahikari Miami and serves as a spokesman for the eastern United States.

Mahikari has its own idiosyncrasies: A three-day study session, termed Kenshu, introduces you to the divine law, the divine plan, and the method of giving the divine true light.

At the end of Kenshu, you get an Omitama, or divine locket. The Omitama supposedly gives you the power to emanate divine true light from your palms and acts as a spiritual lens to focus the light energy. The Omitama comes in real handy. More than 80 percent of human illness and unhappiness, you're taught, is caused by spirits we or our ancestors have wronged. They reside in us, causing untold misery. "When you receive the light, it spreads to all parts and purifies and enlightens these spirits," Kawasaki says. "They then leave voluntarily— sometimes over a period of years."

After learning the purification techniques, you literally "avoid pain by saving others," he says, "instead of thinking about yourself first." In fact, the three basic rules of mahikari, Kawasaki says, are "Give light. Give light. And give light.

But you have to receive the light before you can give it. You kneel with Kawasaki (or another initiate at any mahikari center), facing one another. You each bow twice, clap three times, and bow again. Kawasaki gives thanks to the creator for being allowed to give light, you give thanks for receiving.

For ten minutes Kawasaki holds his hand about a foot in front of you, aiming divine true light from his palm toward your forehead. You then lie on your stomach, while Kawasaki holds his palms (alternating when his arms tire) one foot above each of 27 vital points on your body, from head to toe.

The 27 points done, you struggle back to your knees from a state of deep relaxation. Kawasaki repeats the hand-at-forehead position. As you keep your eyes closed, he then holds both hands above your head, and sweeps each down to the floor, one on each side of your body, still a foot away. As he does this, he shouts, "Oshizumari! Oshizumari! Oshizumari!" He does this several times.

You and Kawasaki then bow twice more, clap three times, bow again, and it's over. Sometimes, Kawasaki cautions, this purification is followed by headaches and diarrhea as your body works out the physical manifestations of departing spirits waving goodbye as they follow the Bekins van into the void.

Aura Balancing

On the 11th floor of an office building across the street from George Washington University in Washington, D.C., Christine Tranka, a practitioner of alternative healing arts, is balancing your aura.

You're lying on her table, she's standing at its head, not making a sound as she moves her hands back and forth several inches away.

"What are you doing?"

"I feel a cold spot here on the left side of your head."

"The window's open."

"It's not that kind of cold. It's heavy and dark. The energy is partially blocked."

You start giggling inanely: In the streets far below, lobbyists and politicians and aides and dealmakers scurry about deciding the fate of the free world and free enterprise, while you float in the twilight zone getting your aura balanced.

Tranka completes the balancing, going from head to toe in 20 minutes, with no further interruptions from you. You felt nothing. Something else you don't feel is the headache you had at the beginning.

The Energy Matrix

Perhaps the best definitions of New Age buzzwords like "aura" and "energy" are offered by Barbara Ann Brennan of East Hampton, New York. Her background is in atmospheric physics, and she worked as a research scientist for NASA, but she's also written a book called *Hands of Light: A Guide to Healing through the Human Energy Field.*

The "energy" is the same life force that comprises everything in the universe. "The energy field is intimately connected with all the functions of being human," Brennan says. "The auric field serves as an energy matrix structure in which the physical body

grows." In other words, the aura is the framework the physical body uses to take shape.

"If something's wrong in the auric field," she says, "it will eventually precipitate down into the physical body and become a disease," a process akin to trickle-down economics. "The reason for aura balancing is to maintain and re-create health in the physical body by creating health and balance and charge in the auric body."

Crucial to the concept of the aura are the chakras. Chakra is a Sanskrit word describing seven different energy centers in the aura corresponding to different areas of the body. "The chakras swirl like whirlpools, drawing energy into the body from the universal energy field all around us," Brennan explains.

Healers use different methods to balance an aura. Brennan's way is to draw energy in through her chakras and send it out her hands. A healer can learn to sense—by touch, sound or sight—where the patient's aura may be "imbalanced, or torn open and leaking energy, or undercharged," she says.

"Where the patient is undercharged, I charge. Where their energy is blocked, I wash it out. Where the auric field is torn, I repair it with energy. Aura balancing is charging and restructuring."

Brennan spends less time healing now, concentrating on teaching people to perceive the aura. "Everybody can learn how to do it," she says. Although some people will be innately better at it than others, she agrees with psychic Greg Schelkun that intent has much to do with healing. You can balance your own aura and those of your family and friends just by studying a book. "Everybody seems to be learning on their own. Never be afraid to put your hands in love on someone," she says. "But don't read a book and try to become a professional. It takes a great deal of training to become a healer and it's a tremendous responsibility."

Josephing

Is there anyone who doesn't feel better after an hour-long massage? Tight muscles loosen, kinks unkink, stagnated blood flows, your mind releases whatever bone of contention it's been gnawing.

Imagine, then, what a 3- to 4-hour massage can do. Massage may be too limiting a word. Try to describe, then, the three-stage, up to *13-hour* and beyond experience the husband and wife team of Spencer Burke and Dawn Brunet offer at their New York City studio.

Burke has named it Josephing: The Art of Freeing the Human Body. Free is an apt word. The goal is to make your body feel free of the earth and your mind feel free of your body.

Josephing's Genesis

In some ways, Josephing resembles typical massage. Burke and Brunet cleanse your body and dry you with hot towels. You then lie on a comfortable pad, your mind drifting along on a stream of soft, soothing music. They rub hot olive oil into your thirsty skin and work your muscles and joints from head to toe. But that's where the similarities between massage and Josephing end.

Consider the name: Josephing. A proper name has become a verb. The term comes from a series of seven dreams Burke had in 1982, and his subsequent reading about Nez Percé Chief Joseph, the brave and eloquent leader whose words and deeds touched the heart of the nation. "The dreams revealed my life's purpose: health, healing and well-being," Burke says. "I open my work to manifest Chief Joseph's consciousness of love. Our bodies do the work of our spirits. If the body's in pain, it can't do God's work."

Burke's attitude toward healing is as unique as Josephing. "We're partners in your health," he says. "Josephing is designed to keep you well for long periods of time. We focus on individual parts of the body until the immune system is fully mobilized. The key is, you have to take responsibility for yourself. The main staple of good health is lifestyle. We don't want you coming back to us week after week or month after month. We work to be rid of you forever."

The Sessions

Another unique aspect of Josephing is its breakdown into three sessions.

In the first session, which runs three to four hours, Brunet concentrates on your feet, ankles, legs, and hips. Attuning herself to the individual needs of each client, her strong-handed therapy combines elements of reflexology, acupressure and deep tissue work.

What Brunet calls "the urban foot" needs "more attention, respect and care than most people realize," she says. "Plus I work on aligning the muscles of the lower body to release tension and fatigue. It also helps sports injuries heal, eliminates waste products, improves circulation and revitalizes the whole body."

You leave floating on air, returning in a few days for the second session, when Burke Josephs your neck, shoulders, arms, chest and back. Again, the session runs three to four hours, "but I spend the time needed, according to what my intuition tells me as I work the muscles," Burke says. "There's no hurry, no planned technique."

Burke uses his hands only part of the time; often he's stroking deeply with his forearms. As with the legs and feet, your upper body muscles are worked over and over again. Sometimes the pressure is deep and intense, other times it's light and soothing.

The final session is what Burke calls the sacrament, the pièce de résistance of Josephing. Burke and Brunet simultaneously work on you until your body radiates fulfillment, and they don't watch the clock. They begin with Brunet doing your feet and legs, Burke your upper body. Soon you don't know whose hands are whose, as the hands harmonize and blend together. "Our clients tell us, after a short while, it feels like one giant hand moving gently and intently over the body," says Brunet. They make sure you're their only client that day, and all their energy is focused on you.

"The best way to describe this session is a finely tuned listening with our hands to the music of your body, a dialogue," Burke explains. "Every muscle is Josephed until we sense completion, culminating in a flow of ecstasy."

Ecstasy really is an accurate word, what with the flickering candles illuminating the room, space-age music appropriate for a journey between galaxies, an electronic device that produces the sound of waves gently crashing on a beach, and your entire body being freed from end to end.

"At some point, an atmosphere of intense peace envelopes us. We share in the experience of wonder as the client seems to drift away, and then—sometimes hours later—merges back into his body looking and feeling years younger.

"The sacrament aims for this out-of-body experience," Burke says, "and 70 to 80 percent of our clients reach this unconditional bliss state. And it happens for me and Dawn at the same time."

Somehow you can feel, as if every muscle and ligament and pore had emotions, through the devotion Burke and Brunet pay to you and your body. Your body feels light and airy, no longer

Healing Resources

For a Radiance Technique practitioner near you, write American-International Reiki Association, Inc., 2210 Wilshire Boulevard, Suite 831, Santa Monica, CA 90403. Another group, Reiki Alliance, can be contacted at P.O. Box 41, Cataldo, ID 83810.

Mahikari headquarters for North America are at 6470 Foothill Boulevard, Tujunga, CA 91042. The rapidly growing movement has centers from coast to coast.

Barbara Ann Brennan teaches a four-year course in aura balancing that meets four days every other month at the Barbara Brennan School of Healing, P.O. Box 2005, East Hampton, NY 11937. Her book, *Hands of Light: A Guide to Healing through the Human Energy Field,* is published by Bantam. Also try *Your Hands Can Heal,* by Eric Weinman,

published by E. P. Dutton. The Southwestern College of Life Sciences, Box 4711, Santa Fe, NM 87502, teaches aura balancing and offers it as a service ($75 to $100 per session). Healing classes and services including aura balancing are also available at The Healing Light Center Church, 204 East Wilson Avenue, Glendale, CA 91206. The center published the book *Wheels of Light,* by the Rev. Rosalyn Bruyere.

Spencer Burke has been teaching Josephing to others. "We are committed to creating a school of natural healing," he says, but at present he and his wife are the only Josephers. The price is normally $100 an hour, but it can be adapted to the client's ability to pay. For information write: Spencer Burke, 418 East 83rd Street, Apartment 3D, New York, NY 10028.

an earthly prison for your spirit. You become a sacrament, a vital part of an almost religious rite celebrating life and the universe and humanity's place in the cosmos.

Burke says Josephing is a freeing and healing beyond therapeutic massage that will help maintain your health, prompt your body's own self-healing power, and release stress. The process reduces tension in muscles, which helps keep your body in its proper alignment, reducing chronic back, neck and leg pain, eliminating fatigue and improving your personal appearance.

Finding a Path

In this chapter we've tried to demystify the mysterious to get across the concept that at the atomic level and below we're all made of energy and that we can make practical use of it. The assertion by most of these spiritual-healing practitioners that faith isn't necessary is reassuring. As one told us, "You don't have to believe in water, but if you jump in the river, you'll still get wet."

Overall, we found the healers to be sincere, well-meaning, hard-work-ing, giving people who want to help people help themselves. It's doubtful another person can empower you with this energy. They can teach you how to use it, however.

Whether you need to dance among the ruins on a Milky Way midnight to feel the spirit, or just switch it on as you would your TV, the goal is to find a person and a method you feel comfortable with, and take it from there.

Chapter 20

HYDROTHERAPY

Why would 20 burly men be standing waist high in plastic garbage cans filled with icy water? Because they're Bears. Not polar bears, but Chicago Bears. After five hours daily of grueling football practice, their severely overworked legs need all the help they can get.

Why icy water? "It helps reduce inflammation of muscle tissues, ligaments and tendons," says Bears trainer Brian McCaskey, so those poor calves and thighs recover faster and don't get so sore.

McCaskey is one of many sports trainers who finds great therapeutic value in one of Earth's most plentiful substances. So too do many M.D.'s and physical therapists. Hefty guys with helmets and shoulder pads are far from the only ones getting soaked—and fatigued legs are far from the only body parts getting dunked.

In fact, hydrotherapy, a very popular healing method around the turn of the century, seems to once again be making a big splash. And when you consider the power of water—hot or cold, bubbly or still—to soothe, invigorate, or stimulate, it's really very much like a massage. Only wetter.

Relief in Many Forms

Water is water. But hydrotherapy comes in many forms. You can heal with cold water, or ice. You can heal with hot water, or steam. You can stand outside a locker room in a water-filled trash can, or sit under a starry sky in a 16-jet, redwood-trimmed whirlpool bath. You can mummify yourself in towels soaked in water. Or you can pummel yourself with a massaging shower head.

At a few places, such as the Weimar Institute, you can experience a little of everything. Visitors to the retreat come for healthy food, clean air, Christian prayer, and lots of long walks up and down the rocky foothills of northern California's Sierra Nevada mountains. Largely to ensure that all this hiking doesn't result in muscular burnout, participants in the Institute's NEWSTART lifestyle program are soaked, steamed, and sprayed for up to half an hour a day.

Cold or Hot?

Quiz: While you're out for a morning jog, your right foot slips into a pothole the size of Luxembourg. You limp home, roll down your sock, and find your ankle starting to swell. You immediately: (*a*) stick your foot in a pot of warm water; (*b*) apply ice to the swollen area; (*c*) have a cup of tea; (*d*) call the embassy of Luxembourg.

Answer: Anything but (*a*).

"Many people would probably say that heat is the way to go—that's not true. For acute injuries you want to go with cold," says Brian McCaskey, trainer for the Chicago Bears football team.

David Webb, M.D., a sports physician whose patients include dancers from the San Francisco and Oakland ballets, says that if you apply heat to a torn muscle or pulled ligament, you'll only make things worse for yourself.

After all the swelling and throbbing is gone, however (usually within 48 to 72 hours), you might consider joining your suffering ankle or knee for a few minutes in the hot tub, says Dr. Webb. "Even then," he adds, "it's best to couple the heat with ice for a kind of 'flushing' effect." This, he says, will help clean up the injury site by carrying away dead cells.

For muscle tightness that is not acute, however, such as a chronically tight neck or set of shoulders attributable to stress or too many hours of bird-watching, then warmth is the way to go. "A hot shower or bath for these kinds of tightness will probably loosen things up a bit," says Dr. Webb.

Much of it is supervised by Peter de Vries, registered nurse and experienced hydrotherapist. He's the tall young man with the beard and the red suspenders . . . you know, the one standing several feet away from you . . . the one with the fire hose spraying you with frigid water, making you jump up and down like a rabbit on a pogo stick, making your teeth chatter so hard you're afraid they're going to crack, and making goose bumps pop up even on the palms of your hands.

Welcome to hydrotherapy station number one: the *contrast shower*. "Dance," suggests de Vries, directing the powerful hose up and down your shivering body and controlling the water temperature of all 16—count 'em—16 shower heads that spit cold water at you from every direction. "Slap your chest," he says, "it'll make it easier." You dance. You slap. You go ah ah ah . . . Ooo Ooo Ooo . . . tap, tap, tap . . . slap, slap, slap . . . you mutter a word you wish you hadn't. "We'll just lower it a few more degrees," says de Vries.

The idea of the contrast shower is to spray you first with hot water (about as hot as you can take it) for approximately three minutes, and then spray you with cold water (about as cold as you can take it) for approximately 30 seconds, then repeat the process three times. Why, you may ask, might anyone in his right mind want to do such a thing?

According to Tom Mullen, M.D., one of several staff physicians at Weimar, the contrast shower may be a way for you to beef up your immune system. He explains that your blood will respond to alternating skin temperatures by racing away from the body's exterior (upon the first sensation of cold) and then back out again. With the application of warm water, the process repeats itself. This "circulatory jogging," says Dr. Mullen, can increase (at least temporarily) your white blood cell count.

Don't think you need 16 shower heads and a fire hose to give yourself a contrast shower, says de Vries. Your home shower will do just fine. Aside from any possible benefits to your body's disease-fighting abilities, a little hot and cold variation is a great way to perk up and really get your juices flowing. The important thing, he says, is to end each session with the cold shower. And, of course—don't forget to dance.

Feeling the Heat

At the other end of de Vries's hydrotherapy suite, one finds the *Russian steam bath*. It's a fiberglass closet, with a pot of steaming water on the floor, a seat, a door, and a hole on the top. The door is the way in. The hole is where your head goes. The white towel next to the bath is what gets wrapped around your neck so that no steam escapes. The little latch on the door is what makes sure *you* don't escape.

Okay, okay, you probably could escape if you really had to—and as the temperature reaches 130°F you're thinking seriously about it. Sweat is pouring off your brow, drip-dripping down your nose, and cascading down your chest. You've been in about 10 minutes, and de Vries says the typical stay is 15 to 20. He gingerly slips a straw in your mouth and lets you sip cool water from a foam cup. He's a nice guy; you wonder if he might let you out early.

But no. You stay a full 20 minutes. Time up, de Vries unlatches the door and directs you into a cold shower for 30 seconds of welcome relief. The Russian steam bath is said to be an excellent way to rid the body of toxins and to beat any nasty vices, such as smoking. Heavy cigarette and cigar puffers, says de Vries, leave dark stains on the seat behind them where tar has escaped the body through their sweating pores.

At home, says de Vries, you can make a fairly good Russian steam bath yourself with a simple wooden chair, a thick woolen blanket (to throw over yourself like a tent) and a pot of steaming water (to slide under you).

Likewise, woolen blankets are about the only thing you need to re-create at home your next hydrotherapy experience at Weimar: *fomentations*, or hot wet packs. The fomentation is made by wrapping a woolen blanket around a swatch of cotton padding steamed to perfection.

Fomentations may cover the entire body, or just a single area. They are used in some hospitals, particularly Adventist hospitals, for a variety of conditions. Dr. Mullen says they offer relief from muscular and skeletal pains, induce sweating to purify the body, and soothe the nerves. They may also help fight disease. "As you raise the body temperature you inhibit the growth of viruses and bacteria," he says. "It's only reasonable to say fomentations can help you to get over a sickness more quickly."

As you lie flat on your back with one large fomentation under your back, another one over your chest and a bowl of hot water at your feet, you feel more than just hot. "Hot" is how you feel on an August day in a supermarket parking lot. This goes beyond that. This is more like "sizzling." Your armpits are sizzling. The backs of your knees are sizzling. Your *eyeballs* (which you can't ever remember even feeling hot before) are sizzling. This is what de Vries calls a "general" fomentation.

Not to worry. After what seems like an eternity but is really only a few

A Note of Caution

Frolicking around in hot water can raise your body temperature and speed up your heartbeat. Especially if you're elderly or pregnant or have a history of high blood pressure, stroke or heart disease, you want to exercise caution by consulting your doctor prior to any hydrotherapy. But even if you're as healthy as Tarzan, it's a good idea to exit a hot whirlpool or steam bath early if you feel dizzy, faint or light-headed.

minutes, de Vries comes to your rescue. This time, a cold shower won't do. This time, wearing rough mittens soaked in ice water, he rubs you from head to feet. Those same feet are meanwhile having ice water poured over them by one of de Vries's assistants. Then the cycle is repeated twice more.

At Weimar a closet-sized metal steamer is used to heat the fomentations, but de Vries says you can get the job done nicely at home by steaming them just as you would vegetables —in a large kettle with a drop-in rack.

Soothing, Swirling Bubbles

So what if the average whirlpool jet releases 789,607 bubbles per second? (A figure somehow derived by experts at the Jacuzzi company, a manufacturer of whirlpool products.) The real question is what can all that bubbling, swirling, foaming water do for you? It obviously does something, as the whirlpool bath is the centerpiece of practically every sports training room in the country, such as the previously mentioned one in Chicago filled with Bears.

Whirlpools combine the best of both hydrotherapy and massage. Maybe that's why whirlpool therapy is sometimes called *hydromassage*. Whether your aim is to relax (and few things in life are as relaxing as a dip in a hot whirlpool bath), to soothe aching muscles, or help heal a sports injury, whirlpools have lots to offer.

These relaxation wonders come in many shapes and sizes. When they're big enough for two or more, made of wood, and filled with hot water and big bubbles, they're often called hot tubs. However, in most sports training rooms, they're metal, spacious enough for only one person, or sometimes just a leg or arm. They're filled with hot water or cold, and generally have one jet producing champagnesized bubbles that whip across your skin at lightning speed.

At Weimar you are invited to stick your leg into a whirlpool made specifically for the legs. Actually, there are two almost identical whirlpools, one filled with hot water (104°F) and the other with cold (74°F). You alternate between the two. This contrast, in addition to the frothing action of the bub-

Getting Your Feet Wet

You can do a fair amount of hydrotherapy right at home—in the bathtub, in the shower, under the garden hose, or in your very own whirlpool bath. For professional attention, you will find hydrotherapy used by virtually all sports trainers and physical therapists. Some hospitals employ various techniques. And the Weimar Institute in Weimar, California, is one of many spas and health resorts nationwide offering various forms of hydrotherapy in conjunction with exercise and diet programs.

The bible of hydrotherapy is *Rational Hydrotherapy*, written at the turn of the century by John H. Kellogg, M.D., (brother of the breakfast cereal magnate). The 1,135-page tome may be difficult to find, but it's well worth the search. You'll find colorful language, quaint illustrations, and anything and *everything* you ever wanted to know about healing with water.

A much more recent book, *Home Remedies* by Agatha Thrash, M.D., and Calvin Thrash, M.D., provides a more modern look at hydrotherapy. It's available from New Lifestyle Books, Rt. 1, Box 441, Seale, AL 36875.

bles, is what really helps those sore muscles, says de Vries.

The forceful jets of water feel like a billion pinpricks. If it's possible for a leg to be dreamy, your leg is dreamy. A little numb and relaxed.

Whirlpools are available for the home through Jacuzzi and other companies—check your yellow pages. If you'd rather not go to the expense of buying equipment, de Vries says that a few minutes in the tub rubbing vigorously with a thick washcloth is the next best thing.

THE HEALING POWER OF HYDROTHERAPY

What's water power good for? Much more than you might imagine, according to hydrotherapy enthusiasts:

Muscle Soreness

Standing around in trash cans filled with cold water, the Chicago Bears "aren't exactly laughing and yukking it up," says team trainer McCaskey. Why do they do it? Because five to ten minutes in cold water after a workout helps tired muscles recover. "The new guys are always reluctant to try it," says the trainer, "but after they do, they're sold."

Athletic Injuries

From Olympic marathoner to sidewalk hop-scotcher, most athletes occasionally suffer from a pulled something-or-other. The proper use of hydrotherapy can make the difference between a mild inconvenience and a major lay-up, says David Webb, M.D., associate clinical director of the Center for Sports Medicine at St. Francis Memorial Hospital in San Francisco. The key to proper treatment of injuries such as ankle sprains, he says, is to apply ice for about 20 minutes every couple of hours until all swelling has stabilized. Ice will reduce the swelling and help control the pain.

Arthritis

There are many kinds of arthritis, and what is helpful in one case may not be helpful in another, but "warm water in most cases will make a person with arthritis feel better," says Bob McDaniel, a representative of the Arthritis Foundation. Some arthritis patients find that ice packs offer the most relief of pain and stiffness.

Calming the Body and Mind

Getting wrapped in sheets soaked in ice water may not sound very calming. But according to Harinder Singh Ghuman, M.D., a psychiatrist at Baltimore's Sheppard and Enoch Pratt Hospital, it can have a profoundly calming effect. So calming is it, that Dr. Ghuman uses the technique on some of his most severely disturbed psychiatric patients. "Cold water has an effect on the nervous system that creates a feeling of warmth and relaxation," he says. Next time you're feeling uptight, try a cold shower, suggests the doctor.

Headaches

Next time your head pounds, try a pot of hot water for your feet and an ice pack for your head. "You'll be drawing congestion toward the feet, and away from the head," says hydrotherapist de Vries. "It sounds hocus-pocus, but I've seen it work many times."

Invigoration

What can possibly get you going in the morning as much as a cold shower? "I use it in place of coffee," says de Vries.

QUICK 'N' EASY HYDROTHERAPY

Unless you're in the middle of the Sahara Desert, the only essential ingredient for hydrotherapy should be readily available to you: water. All the other elements—including whirlpools, massaging shower heads and steam cabinets—are optional. Here are two very simple techniques.

20-2

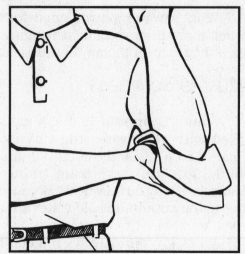

For aching joints—at the elbows or elsewhere—soak a washcloth in hot water and apply to the appropriate spot for about three minutes. (The cloth will have to be reheated intermittently.) Follow up by applying a cold washcloth for about 30 seconds. Repeat until you feel relief.

20-1

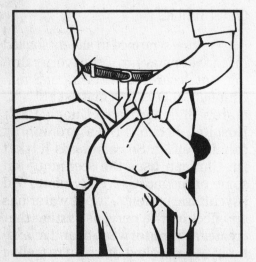

For athletic injuries, such as a sprained ankle, apply ice for about 20 minutes every couple of hours until all swelling has stabilized.

Chapter 21

INFANT MASSAGE

You've created a miracle, all right. One that wails, wees and has you wishing you knew what buttons to push to make parenthood a little less taxing.

You toss another soiled diaper into the bin and sigh. Absently you rub your aching temples and stare at your red-faced, fist-waving bundle of joy.

As your shoulders begin to droop, you notice baby looking at you. You smile. Baby smiles back. His sobs trickle into hiccups. You move your fingers from your temples to baby's, gently circling his forehead. He gurgles, eyes never leaving your face. Softly you stroke his cheeks, tracing his nose and lips with one fingertip.

How incredibly soft his skin is, you marvel. How perfect his ears are, you think as you outline the lobes with your thumbs. You press on his chin, in the dimple, making him laugh. You laugh back, then scoop his now-pliant body into your arms. Diapers you can worry about later.

This moment is special.

Instinctively, you've discovered the glorious good feeling that is infant massage.

Rubbing Baby the Right Way

Just as music hath charms to soothe the savage breast, massage hath charms to soothe the sobbing—and soggy—baby.

While strokes arrived at by happenstance are fine, therapists have developed a relaxing regimen of massage just for infants. Here are some of their suggestions:

Begin a massage with both of you in a quiet but focused state. Baby should be rested and alert. You should be totally *there* for him.

Breathe deeply and slowly, letting the cares of the day drain away. As you relax, so will baby. Go ahead, mug and sing a few snatches of those silly songs that make him laugh. No one's listening or watching.

"I tune everything out when I'm getting ready to massage Lia," says Paula Woods, a Pennsylvania mother. With her first child, Amanda, Woods got so caught up in the drudgery of baby care that the days and months went by in a blur. With three-month-old Lia, she's learning to slow down.

"I try to make complete contact. Massage for me means total devotion to my baby," she says.

You show your devotion with a wet, blubbery kiss on baby's bare stomach. His skin is sweet-smelling from the warm bath of a little while ago. You carry him from the changing table to the floor and ease down, your back against the wall for support.

Legs out in front of you, you spread a thick soft towel across your lap. Baby squirms for a minute, but as you continue to hum and croon, he quiets.

"When the mother is relaxed and ready to enjoy the massage, the baby will, too," says Marge Nocton. "It's incredible how they pick up on the messages you send."

You scrunch up your knees and bring baby's face close to yours. "I would like to massage you now," you say softly, looking into his eyes. You cradle his head with your hands and slowly circle his scalp with your fingers. Tiny circles, all over his wispy hair and around his ears.

By asking your baby permission to touch, you show respect. Your infant can't very well say, "Cut it out, Mom, I'm not in the mood." But he can tell you, in subtle and not-so-subtle ways, when a massage is best left for another time.

His body language speaks volumes to a tuned-in observer. If, as you're beginning the massage, he crosses his arms across his chest, or turns away, breaking eye contact, start over. Ask him to relax again. If he stiffens or even cries, respect his need for privacy.

This day, baby blinks and smiles. You pat his tummy and reach for the bottle of massage oil. A little bit, just a nickel-sized pool, is all you need.

You rub your palms together, warming the oil and coating your hands. You tickle his tummy again and wonder aloud which leg he'd like you to do first. Ah, the left one. He kicks at you, chortling, and you grasp the leg at the ankle with one hand.

"Okay, Bossie, it's milking time," you say with mock sternness, making a face. Infant massage uses two "milking" strokes that likely won't be seen in any dairy.

Indian milking, from the Indian theory of massage, moves from top to bottom on the extremities. Picture your hands pushing tension down your baby's leg and out through his toes. Indian milking is a releasing, relaxing stroke.

Swedish milking, on the other hand, is a stimulating, toning stroke that's done toward the heart (from ankle to baby's thigh, in this case). You'll save that as a wrap-up for the legs later. You chant to baby as you do first one leg, then the other. "Out with the bad," you say, Indian milking from baby's crotch to toes.

A Few Cautions

Therapist Mary Gengler Fuhr urges parents of physically challenged babies to check with their doctors before beginning massage. Contraindications might include seizure medication, brittle bones, heart defects or range of motion limitations. Consult a therapist, Fuhr says, to talk about positions that might be best for an impaired baby during a massage.

Other parents, too, should know there are a few times when massage is inappropriate. Do not massage:

• When the baby has just eaten.
• When the baby has an open cut or a swollen area.
• When the baby has a fever.
• When the baby is under four weeks of age.

This last caution refers to the full body massage. Very young babies will benefit from a loving back rub, however. Hold baby against your chest as if nursing and massage with one hand. Or support baby in a burping position and gently caress the back.

Just take care to use a very, very light touch. Any pressure will be felt as an assault to a newborn's jangled senses.

C'mon Baby, Let's Do the Twist

He likes this next part, you know. You wrap your hands around his leg like it's a Louisville Slugger. "Batter's up," you command, and he kicks. Working up the leg, you squeeze and twist in opposite directions. Every time you change strokes, you repeat the motion several times.

Then it's time for footsies. "I'm gonna get personal with you now," you inform baby. "Gimme that foot." First, a little more oil to help your hands slide over his skin. You push the sole of his foot from heel to toes with your thumbs, again and again.

Next you squeeze each toe. Then, crooking your forefinger, you pull back on the ball of each foot, and press your thumbs all over the sole again.

You finish his feet by pushing the top of his foot with your thumbs, toward his ankle. Then you circle the ankle with your thumbs. Baby's feet feel floppy as pancakes when you're done.

Swedish milking is a pleasant way to move on. "In with the good," you chant again, milking the leg from ankle to hip. A gentle rolling of the leg between your palms sets baby up for the rest of the massage.

Toning the Tummy

When you massage baby's stomach, think "clockwise." Your hands always move in this direction, or from left to right, following the natural course of baby's digestive system. Occasionally after a few minutes of massage you can feel gas bubbling under your fingertips.

You smooth the towel beneath baby and straighten his legs. You'll use the routine developed by infant massage pioneer Vimala McClure to tone baby's elimination system.

The "Water Wheel" has you paddling across the tummy with the edges of each hand, as if you were scooping sand toward yourself. Then you hold baby's legs up at the ankle with one hand and scoop with the other hand. Baby drops his legs. You join thumbs at the middle of his tummy; with thumbs flat, you push out to the sides.

Then you use McClure's "Sun Moon." With your right palm you shape a half-moon, from your left to right on baby's stomach. Your left palm, meanwhile, circles all the way around clockwise. As the right hand glides off the skin, the left comes around to complete its circle.

You walk your fingers from left to right across baby's stomach, then it's on to the chest.

Palms joined at the center of baby's chest, you push out to the shoulders, then move down over the ribs. You glide back up to the chest in a heart-shaped motion. Baby thinks this is great fun. You plant a smooch on his navel and move on to the cross-your-heart.

Dads Have Hands, Too

Sad but true: "Father and child" doesn't sound as natural as "mother and child." But why should Mom have all the intimate time with baby? Dad can't breast-feed, but he surely can massage. That's why infant massage instructors open their classes to today's sensitive guys.

California instructor Jan Benlein recalls a class that brought two grandfathers in with twins. "The parents had to work, but these gentlemen were game, so in they came," she says, laughing. "They were shy and stayed in the back at first. I thought twice they were going to leave, especially when a few mothers started nursing."

Benlein broke the ice by rolling up her sleeves and helping the men tidy up the bottoms of the, uh, productive twins. "By the end of the class, the grandfathers were the stars," she reports. "Men can give a very good massage."

Palms at baby's hips, you slide your hands in a criss-cross to baby's shoulders, one at a time, making an X.

Arms Need Love, Too

Baby's not as crazy about having his arms done, but today he's amenable. You raise one arm and massage the lymph nodes in the armpit. Then just

Learning the Moves

The International Association of Infant Massage Instructors offers five-week courses for parents. Classes, which last for an hour or more, cover the theory and practice of infant massage.

While some mothers take the course before they deliver, most bring their babies to class for hands-on sessions. Instructors include nurses, midwives, certified massage therapists and childbirth educators. Typical of the association's roster is Marge Nocton of Doylestown, Pennsylvania.

"I was a nurse's aide in high school. I loved giving back rubs to patients; they enjoyed it so much," she says. "Years later I listened to that voice inside of me and studied to become certified in several types of massage."

Like other massage instructors, Nocton believes in what she teaches. Her son Shawn, 3, is a happy, loving little boy who gets a rubdown whenever he's in need of a time-out.

Nocton charges $45, which includes a bottle of oil and literature. In New York, instructor Laurie Evans charges from $30 to $60, depending on what she has to pay for the use of meeting facilities.

For information on how to find an instructor in your area, write to the International Association of Infant Massage Instructors at P.O. Box 16103, Portland, OR 97216-0103.

The association's warehouse, called Gentle Touch, provides a free catalog. Write to 4302 20th Avenue, Moline, IL 61265.

Available through the warehouse are:

Infant Massage: A Handbook for Loving Parents by association founder Vimala McClure.

Keeping in Touch, a one-hour video demonstration of infant massage.

Other recommended materials:

Massaging Baby, a cassette tape by Catherine Osterbye. Perinatal Massage Program, The New Age School, P.O. Box 958, Sebastopol, CA 95472-0958 (707) 823-1212.

Tender Touch: The 'How-To' Infant Massage Video, a 28-minute color video with techniques and suggestions for parents. Available from Healthy Alternatives, Inc., P.O. Box 3234, Reston, VA 22090 (703) 430-6650.

And from your public library:

Baby Massage: Parent-Child Bonding through Touching by Amelia D. Auckett (Newmarket Press).

The Complete Baby Exercise Program by Diana Simkin, (New American Library). It includes a special section on infant massage.

Loving Hands: The Traditional Indian Art of Baby Massaging by Frederick Leboyer, the advocate of nonviolent birth (Alfred A. Knopf).

as you did with his legs, you Indian milk the arm from shoulder to hand. Next you squeeze and twist, as if you were wringing a wet towel—only gently.

Fingers get attention, too, with a gentle roll between your finger and thumb for each one.

A little massage for the wrist and top of the hand, then on to Swedish milking. Remember, hand to shoulder this time.

You sense you're losing his attention, so you lean close to his face and whisper, "Your personal masseuse would like to remind you that we're not finished."

Baby smiles as you move to his forehead. Palms across his face, you glide to the sides, by his ears. You press your thumbs gently over his eyes and brows, across the bridge of his nose, then down his cheeks. You trace his upper and lower lips with your thumbs, pushing lightly to the sides.

Working around a yawn, you massage the joints of his jaw with tiny circles. You open up the motion by circling his ears and under his chin.

The Flip Side

Most babies love having their backs massaged, and yours is no exception. You turn him over on your lap across your legs.

With your palms, you glide back and forth across his back. You work from neck to buttocks, up and down the back, at right angles to baby's spine.

Then you cup his buttocks with one hand and glide from the base of the neck to buttock bottom with the other. Next, you hold his legs with one hand and stroke all the way down to his ankles with your free hand.

As the session comes to a close, you lightly trace circles all over the back with your fingers. Baby is *sooo* relaxed now; your humming gets softer and softer. You spread your fingers on one hand and comb his back from top to bottom lightly, very lightly, completing with the words, "relax, relax." Then you scoop him into your arms for a kiss.

THE HEALING POWER OF INFANT MASSAGE

Nearly every baby has a run-in with painful gas or colic. Others cry when constipation puts them out of kilter. Maritta Lord suffered for six weeks along with her baby Jennifer before she learned about infant massage.

"She was very colicky. The crying was just terrible. It tore me apart," says Lord. "Then I began using the stomach strokes every time I changed her diaper. I'd massage her and pump her legs in a bicycling motion until she had a bowel movement.

"Just like that, the crying would stop. And I certainly felt much better!"

Relief is generally so immediate, says California massage instructor Jan

Benlein, that she warns parents to be sure they're covered with a towel.

How else can massage help the helpless? Therapist Annette Bray worked with an Amish mother whose infant had trouble nursing. "We massaged the baby's face and saw a big improvement in sucking ability," says Bray. "Babies can have a great deal of tension accumulate in their muscles, and massage relieves that stress."

Touch amid Trauma

Perhaps the most stressed of all babies is the one born prematurely. Eva Smith's son Gordon arrived much too soon, into a world of tubes, needles and trauma. Gordon spent the first 11 months of his life in hospital nurseries.

"I couldn't actually hold him until he was over three months old," says his mother. "But from the beginning we touched him. Just one arm or leg at a time, since we couldn't do a full massage around all the tubes.

"What amazed me was how he loved to have his feet done. Even after all those heel sticks (for blood), he'd still respond."

Smith says massage was a vital element in helping Gordon identify his parents, the good guys. "When babies are very sick, massage is the only contact they get that doesn't hurt them," she says. "I felt bonded to him right away, though not in the traditional way of holding and nursing, because I was able to touch and help him."

Mary Gengler Fuhr, an occupational therapist in Auburn, Washington, has seen dramatic improvements in physically handicapped babies after massage.

Spastic infants often relax enough to make full sounds for the first time, she says. "Their muscles may be so tight across the chest it's difficult for them to vocalize. After massage, they may be able to coo or gurgle."

Massage also helps "floppy" babies, those with little tone. She says the strokes stimulate and prepare the infant for therapy sessions.

MASSAGING BABY FROM HEAD TO TOE

Touch is an infant's first sense. Here's how to use it to bring the two of you even closer.

21-1

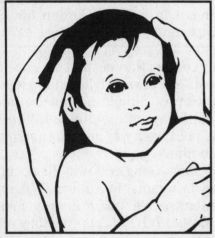

Before oiling your hands, smile, make eye contact with your baby and relax him by gently circling the scalp with your fingertips. If baby enjoys this, continue with the massage.

21-3

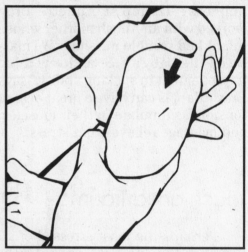

The Indian technique of massage relaxes the long muscles of the leg. Hold the foot in one hand and grasp high at the thigh with the other. Firmly "milk" the leg from top to bottom, thigh to ankle.

21-2

Relieve tension caused by nursing, teething and crying with the soothing strokes of a facial massage. Cover the face with your palms (left) and glide to the cheeks, as if flattening the pages of a book (right). Pay special attention to the tight joints at the jaw, making tiny circles with your fingertips. Press lightly.

21-4

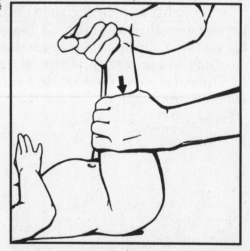

A complementary stroke is Swedish milking. Stroke the leg from ankle to thigh with firm pressure. (Think "to the extremities" in Indian milking and "to the heart" in Swedish milking.)

21-5

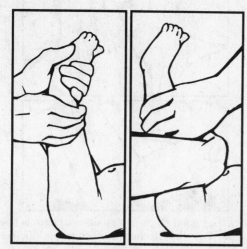

Rev up circulation with the squeeze and twist. Hold the leg as if it were a baseball bat, both hands in a firm grip (left). Work your grip down the leg, turning and gently squeezing in opposite directions toward the toes (right).

21-6

If you have time for nothing else, concentrate your massage on baby's feet. Push the sole from heel to toe with your thumbs and squeeze each toe gently. Using thumbs again, press all over the sole to stimulate nerve endings.

21-7

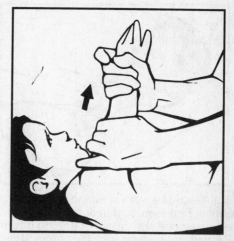

This motion pulls tension from the body. Hold baby's wrist with one hand and grasp the arm at the shoulder with your other. Milk the arm to the baby's hand. Alternate your left and right hands for continuous milking.

21-8

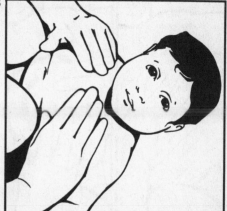

Massage the chest to help tone lungs and heart. Follow the natural curve of the ribcage as you join hands at the center of baby's chest. Then stroke toward the back. A variation of the fingertip stroke is to use the flat palms; as you did on the face, imagine you are flattening the pages of a book.

(continued)

MASSAGING BABY FROM HEAD TO TOE—*Continued*

21-9

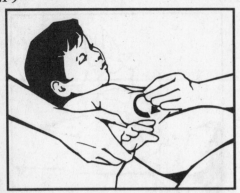

All abdominal strokes are done in a clockwise fashion. End each motion at baby's lower left belly, to guide the digestive process toward elimination. Never massage the umbilical cord.

21-10

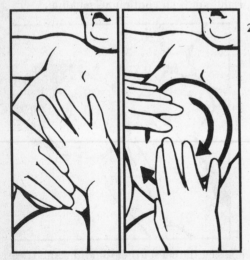

Relieve your baby's pain from gas or constipation with this stroke, called the "Sun Moon." Move your right hand in a semi-circle from top to bottom, left to right, finishing with a glide off the skin. Your left hand, meanwhile, circles the belly completely, never losing touch with the skin. Continue stroking and circling.

21-11

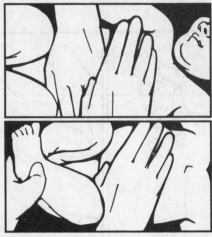

Another good stroke for easing gas pain is the Water Wheel. With hands on edge, paddle like a steam wheeler. Go from top to bottom on baby's belly, scooping with each hand. Avoid pushing on baby's rib cage. Finish by grasping and raising both legs with one hand while paddling with the other.

21-12

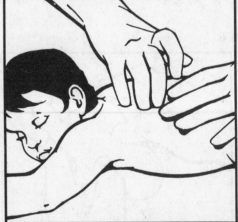

To massage baby's back, lay him facedown across your lap. Spread your fingers to cover the width of his back and stroke from neck to buttocks. Next, with your fingertips, work the muscles on left and right sides of the spine with small circles, moving down to and over the buttocks.

Chapter 22

LOMILOMI (HAWAIIAN MASSAGE)

The waves crash with a muffled roar upon the sand as the soft, salty breeze caresses your face. You stroll over to the edge of the hotel's patio, where groups of coconut palms gently arc toward the sky, their gold-green fronds rustling in the wind. You listen closely and hear their trunks creaking as they sway back and forth with the breeze.

A padded massage table waits beneath a secluded palm on the left, ringed by waist-high bushes of a type that never grow back home. Funny, you thought you'd miss it more, but home seems like a distant memory as you stretch yourself full-length across the padded bench and lay your head on its pillow, waiting. The masseuse will be with you in a moment. Unlike home, there's just no hurrying here.

Somewhere in the distance, you're not sure quite how far, the lilting twang of a steel guitar drifts upon the wind, bringing with it a sweet bit of Hawaiian history in song. The sound of laughter from the hotel pool mixes with the tune. The two sounds join and form a third melody all their own. You sigh once again, the hundredth time today.

The masseuse approaches from your right and lays her hands on your shoulders. The breeze lifts her dark hair and blows a few strands across her face. You close your eyes and see no more, concentrating instead on the feeling of her hands. They are strong and yet softly wise, able to communicate warmth and search out pain. They seem to know where they are going and what to do without being told.

The masseuse picks up a rhythm as she works the area below your neck. Her strokes are broad and flat and you can almost count them out—one, two, three . . . one, two, three . . . . You acknowledge the steady rhythm down in your soul and go with it, drifting off once again.

You knew Hawaii would be good. You knew a massage on the beach would be nice. But this is a Hawaiian

157

massage on a Hawaiian beach, and this is great. This is lomilomi.

"Keepers of the Secret"

Lomilomi. The Hawaiian Islands know how to bring a visitor pleasure, and lomilomi is like that. It is distinctly Hawaiian and belongs to the Hawaiian people in a mysterious way that permits mainlanders to know about it without knowing of it. Snippets of lomilomi lore appear in magazines or occupy a few pages in books now and then, but there seems to be no definitive, authoritative work on the subject. It's as though hard facts about lomilomi lose strength and fade as they travel east across the water.

A decades-old book written by Max Freedom Long is one of the few works on the subject. In *The Secret Science behind Miracles*, Long explains that lomilomi is the type of spiritual massage practiced by kahunas. *Kahu* is Hawaiian for "keeper," while *huna* means "secret," making kahunas the "keepers of the secret"—not a bunch of guys on surfboards in 1960s' beach party movies. The kahunas seem to have lived up to their titles, managing to keep lomilomi a secret far longer than most of Hawaii's other charms.

But Long was a curious man, and he did his best to discover what lomilomi was all about and explain it to the rest of the world. What fascinated him most was the diversity and breadth of this native massage. "If we modern people would combine Swedish massage, the various baths, chiropractic, osteopathy, the use of suggestion and the ancient practice of 'the laying on of hands' (to heal), we should approach the scope of lomilomi as a skilled kahuna might practice it," he writes.

Long offers a detailed account of a lomilomi session witnessed by a friend of his in "the early days." The session was performed on a man who overexerted himself on a trip to Kilauea volcano and returned home tired out, feeling ill and aching in various joints. The man "was especially pained by what seemed to be lumbago," Long says. The kahuna began her treatment by sponging off the patient with an herbal tea, all the while chanting and telling of the benefits that would be brought about through the touch of her hands and the warm stones she would rake from the fire and use to massage his muscles and joints.

"When the patient's aches and pains had been much relieved," Long continues, "the kahuna became more vigorous in her manipulations, twisting and pressing joints, starting with cracking the finger joints and knuckles, and ending by cracking all possible joints in the neck and spine, especially where there was the greatest soreness or pain."

Near the end of the treatment, "the woman placed her hands on the hands of the man and told him to rest and let the healing power run from her hands into his to make him well and free of pain." The healing trance lasted for several minutes. Long says that when the man was later asked about the outcome of the treatment, he said he had no more pain and felt very well.

Looking for Lomilomi

Only a handful of people practice lomilomi in the continental United States. Most of those who do have learned it from a Hawaiian named Margaret Machado at her school on Ke'ei Beach. Though Machado, called Aunty Margaret by her students, emphasizes the spiritual aspects of this ancient healing technique, some of her students downplay that part of it, viewing lomilomi as simply another type of massage for therapists to add to their repertoire.

Sherri Williamson of Golden, Colorado, studied lomilomi with Aunty Margaret. "I was 19, living in Hawaii in 1978, and I had always been interested in massage," she explains. "Aunty Margaret started teaching and I took her first class. She was only going to teach a few people, but it caught on."

Indeed, most of the islands' major hotels now have at least one lomilomi practitioner on their massage staff. After learning lomilomi and spending several years operating her own shop, Williamson moved to Golden, where she now dedicates her time to establishing a nationwide trade association for massage professionals, the Associated Professional Massage Therapists and Allied Health Practitioners International.

"In the past," Williamson says, "the kahunas would dress up in robes and set an atmosphere that would put the patient in a healing frame of mind. In terms of what they did, the healing part, it was almost mind over matter. The person on the table had to be open to the fact that the person doing the massage could channel a higher energy.

"But that doesn't happen anymore," she says. "Today you hardly see that type of treatment at all. The primary difference between today's lomilomi and any other massage is in the type of hands-on application, with the use of the forearms and the broad hand strokes. Today's practitioner simply incorporates some lomilomi strokes into his usual routine."

Williamson's view probably reflects the way lomilomi is most often practiced in the continental United States today. But it's apparently not the only way.

Jan Benlein, a Newport Beach, California, practitioner, says lomilomi is the most spiritual massage. "I use a healing stone," she says. "This is heated before it's applied. In some cases, I've had people ask me to take the stone off them because they are burning, yet the stone has already been removed! I tell them, 'I don't have the stone right now. What you feel is my hand.' There is that much energy between the two of us that they feel a deep burning."

Lisa Griffi, 27, is a client of Benlein's who has experienced this burning. "The first time she did it I noticed a lot of energy flowing. I don't know if it's just the type of massage or if it's Jan herself. The heat was something real new, really bizarre. You think it's really spooky when it happens to you, but if you think more about it, it's just a release of energy."

More Mystery

Robert Calvert, publisher and editor of *Massage Magazine*, seems a logical expert to shed some light on lomilomi. His magazine is located in Kailua-Kona, Hawaii, giving him a unique, close-up perspective on this particular massage.

Calvert is well versed in the technical aspects of lomilomi and bases his observations on years of first-hand experience: "There are similarities to Swedish massage," he says, "but lomilomi practitioners use the elbows and forearms, and those are not used in Swedish at all. Swedish does not have any deep tissue techniques, lomilomi does.

"Lomilomi is often vigorous and deep," he continues, "though I'm not saying Swedish can't be. But it is very distinct in the way the practitioner moves about the body. In many places, in the Orient and South America, there's a belief that you need to massage away from the heart and move energy toward the extremities. The American and European approach is

> ### Lomilomi Resources
>
> For more information about lomilomi, *The Secret Science behind Miracles* by Max Freedom Long is available from De Vorss and Company, Marina del Rey, California.
>
> For help in finding a lomilomi practitioner, write to Mary Golden, P.O. Box 271223, Escondido, CA 92027.

the exact opposite. Lomilomi is somewhere in between. Lomilomi practitioners believe that you should move things out and away from the body, while at the same time they have some techniques that move blood toward the heart."

Calvert says there is—or rather was—a very definite spiritual component to lomilomi as it was originally practiced. "Lomilomi takes a special kind of person to do because of the spiritual part," he says. "But I think you have hardly anyone today who is practicing lomilomi in its true form. Maybe two or three people."

Back to the Beach

The masseuse has almost finished her work. Only the light pressure of her hands upon your face brings your mind back to the present. You wonder how long you've been drifting in the ozone. Her warm palms gently touch your eyes. Your head feels too heavy to lift, so you just lie there like a rag. She begins to speak.

"When someone here greets you with the word *aloha*," she says, "do you know what they mean?" You shake your head no, unwilling to break the grip she has on your eyes.

"*Alo* means you are in the presence of the divine," she says. "*Ha* is the breath the divine gave you when you became a living person. Alo, you behold your creator, who gave you ha, the breath of life." She lays her hand upon your forehead and smiles. It feels warm. "Aloha," she says, and walks away.

THE HEALING POWER OF LOMILOMI

"There is some inner healing work going on," lomilomi practitioner Mary Golden of Escondido, California, says of her massage. "But if you're talking about some other entity coming in, then no. If you mean being in touch with a higher source and having your hands automatically go to the right part of the body and know where to work, yes. But you know that through the touch."

Marion Ceruti, a research physicist and one of Golden's clients, counts on lomilomi for stress reduction and headache relief. "The whole thing is very spiritual," she says. "It's very uplifting to be in the presence of someone doing lomilomi correctly."

Roger O'Brien, another Golden client, says that lomilomi has brought him tremendous relief. "I've been seeing Mary for a year and a half," he says. "I had some connective tissue problems, lot of chest pain, shallow breathing. I remember one time when she worked on my back it opened up my entire breathing apparatus. I could breathe deep once again. It was wonderful the way she worked that out. I've also had problems with a pinched nerve in my arm and neck, and she helped with that as well."

Mary Lou Sampley was a client of Sherri Williamson's who found that lomilomi was the only type of massage capable of relieving the backaches and migraines she suffered after a car crash several years ago.

"I was able to tolerate lomilomi when I had the neck and back injury," she says. "Occasionally I would go somewhere else when I couldn't get to Sherri, and I couldn't take the style of massage the others would give. I needed something thorough, but gentle.

"Lomilomi was the only thing that allowed me to move my neck," Sampley says. "It is deep, but gentle. I know that's a contradiction, but I could not have survived without it. It allowed me to throw painkillers away."

LOMILOMI TECHNIQUES

With a hands-on approach that's as Hawaiian as Oahu and nearly as old, here are some lomilomi techniques in action.

22-1

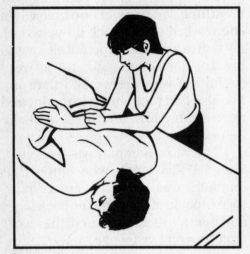

The distinctive forearm movements of a lomilomi practitioner at work. These are typically applied to the long muscles of the back, across the muscle grain.

22-2

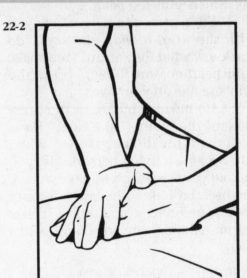

22-3

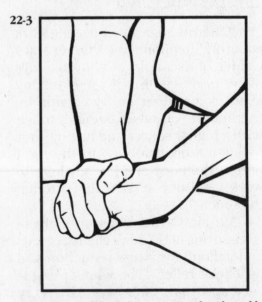

The "Wiggly-Wiggly" movement developed by Aunty Margaret Machado at her lomilomi school in Hawaii. The fingers of the bottom hand are moved in and out as pressure and vibration are applied along the spine.

Chapter 23

MENSENDIECK SYSTEM

"Stand like you always stand," Inge Leenstra commands. So Binky stands in his tight swimming trunks in all his sagging physical glory, brutally exposed on all sides to the harshly acute reflective power of four merciless full-length mirrors surrounding him. Leenstra circles him, frowning, chin in hand, deep in thoughtful appraisal of what Binky's body has become over the years. Binky has never before noticed how much gravity and cookies have altered his once lithe frame. Would Muffy have married him if he had looked like this? Surreptitiously (he fools himself, because Leenstra sees all) he sucks in his gut.

At last Leenstra speaks. "How do you see yourself? What's wrong?"

Binky's ego groans, but his conscience says, "Be honest, now." And he is. "My belly's sticking out, but I'm not pregnant. My lower back curves in, but it's not from giving little Biff and Buffy horsey rides. My butt's protruding, but at least it makes it easier to sit down in a dark theater. My neck stretches forward, but if my head was as far back as my behind I'd fall over backward."

There. The confession hurt, mainly from saying out loud what he's been thinking. But Leenstra doesn't laugh at the sad shapes of Binky in the flesh and four mirrors. She's seen it all, including the pain that comes from poor posture.

What Is It?

Inge Leenstra is one of only five certified practitioners of the Mensendieck System in the United States. Mensendieck (pronounced MEN-sendeek), is named for its creator, American physician Bess Mensendieck, who in 1905 devised this posture-correcting system almost unknown here but still widely practiced in northern Europe, including Leenstra's home country, Holland.

In fact, insurance coverage there

163

pays for Mensendieck therapy. Practitioners study for three years at a Mensendieck Institute, with daily intensive individual instruction for the first two years to virtually reeducate their own muscles. Anatomy and physiology are also important parts of the curriculum, along with neurology, pathology, orthopedics, and obstetrics.

From the third year on, Mensendieck students serve three internships at various teaching hospitals and rehabilitation centers. Study ends with an oath similar to the Hippocratic oath.

Such educational requirements are probably the major reason Mensendieck is such a rare healing commodity in the United States. There are no opportunities to train as a therapist in this country—all teachers and practitioners come from Europe, where they often work in close concert with physicians.

"Mensendieck is both preventive and corrective," according to Leenstra. "Most people come to me when they have pain," she says. "But some come because they have a job that demands a lot of them physically, and they want preventive instruction in how to sit and stand and carry things without pain. A big part of our work is with adolescent children, because by age 18 all the bones are set. So we try to get them in the right posture before it's too late, when their bones are still growing. We also see people with scoliosis [curvature of the spine]. We can't cure it, but we can keep it from getting worse."

Posture Is Personal

The most important attribute of Mensendieck instruction, Leenstra says, is that it's individualized. "There's no one way to correct everybody's posture. So we don't try to make everybody stand the same way. It all depends on the person, their build, age, health, sex. We try to help every person reach the point of the normal, natural curve of their spine. So we custom-design a program for the patient."

The great advantage of Mensendieck is that despite some guidance from the practitioner, you really have to do it yourself. "I can teach you the correct posture, but I also give you homework," Leenstra says. "It's really self-help. Nobody can do it for you."

And she says Mensendieck works on the entire body, not just the part that's giving you problems. "Your back is curved so far forward," Leenstra tells Binky, "no wonder you have trouble with your knees."

"Well, maybe I was born this way," Binky argues. "How can you tell if the way I stand is natural or just bad posture?" (A naturally lazy person, Binky's looking for an easy way out.)

"By seeing how you do specific exercises and movements," Leenstra says. "If your spine curves the wrong way, I'll have you do an exercise to get that curve out. If you can do the exercise, then the problem is posture, not the way your bones are formed. If formation is the problem, then the goal is to get as close to the ideal as possible."

Binky thinks of himself as being "a young 40" but still wonders if he's too old to change his posture. "I've taught people 60 and 70 years old," Leenstra replies. So how fast he relearns normal posture is up to him. "One person may be physically intelligent, while another is physically unintelligent," she says. "Then, too, it depends on how severe your problem is, how much you exercise at home, how motivated you are. Pain is a great motivator." Standing there in pain, Binky feels highly motivated.

Children are notoriously difficult to motivate, but Mensendieck handles this challenge well: "We tell children with scoliosis they either have to do the exercises or wear a corset," Leenstra says. "They become very motivated very quickly."

But doesn't Mensendieck make people constantly aware of their posture, never at ease? "When you first get lessons and see yourself in a mirror, you become conscious of your own body," Leenstra says. "Because there are many things they don't realize about their posture, many people are shocked when they see themselves." She looks at Binky. Binky looks shocked.

But the shock and self-consciousness wear off. "We correct you and teach you, and you see and feel how it can be better," Leenstra says. "Then this conscious awareness has to become unconscious. The more you exercise, the more you feel what to do. It's a process: First you become conscious, then the correct posture becomes automatic."

Mensendieck is a combination of seeing, hearing and feeling, Leenstra says: "We use mirrors so you can see your mistakes; you feel your mistakes by doing the exercises and feeling what is the correct posture; and you hear your mistakes because the therapist is right there telling you what they are." Binky has seen and heard. Now it's time for him to feel.

Mensendiecking Your Body

Binky's particular problem is a sway back, so his exercises aren't for everybody. But they're just what Binky needs.

"Put your feet closer together," Leenstra instructs. Binky narrows his wide stance to the point where his thighs interfere.

"When correcting your posture always start with the feet and work your way up," she explains. "Rest on the balls of your feet, not on your heels." Binky tilts forward slightly.

"Unlock your knees. That's too much. Less. Less. That's right." Binky's knees are a fraction of an inch from being locked.

"Now pull your buttocks together and bring your rear under. More. More.

Posture and Movement Tips

"Each of us has a posture pattern and also a movement pattern," says Mensendieck practitioner Inge Leenstra. "We begin with posture, but it evolves into movement. Often pain comes from wrong movement." Leenstra can teach Binky (and you) how to walk, write, sit, drive, garden, walk the dog, sleep, jog, work at a computer terminal, talk on the phone.

Keeping in mind that one person's problem may not be yours, you may find some of her tips and exercises helpful in your daily life.

Balance

"Your weight should be balanced over all your joints," Leenstra says. "All joints should carry their proper proportion of weight. Many people stand with too much weight on one leg. Your weight should be divided between both legs." The correct posture is a balanced one. No more sexy stances, no more sashaying down the beach at Ipanema.

Slowly but Surely

"Do the exercises very slowly," Leenstra says. "When you do them fast you don't train the muscles as well. Four times slowly is better than 40 times fast. In the beginning the posture is tiring, so do it for just a few minutes several times a day, whenever you think of it."

How to Walk

You have to learn all over again, but at least you don't have to crawl first. Assume the proper stance, and squeeze your buttocks together and under. This will help you shift your weight forward and naturally make you take a step forward. As you walk, keep your center of gravity ahead of your feet, and keep your body tall, your chin parallel to the floor, and your breastbone slightly forward and diagonal.

How to Sit

In a straightbacked chair, sit on your "sitting bones"—the bottom of your pelvis—not leaning forward or back. Your spine should be in its correct standing position, with neck and lower back slightly forward (or concave), and your middle back slightly backward (or convex). *No slouching, Binky!* Feet should be flat on the floor and lower legs at a 90 degree angle to the thighs, which should be parallel to the floor.

How to Sleep

The most relaxed sleeping position is to lie on one side. Bring your

That's it." Binky thinks, she doesn't know what she's asking. This is like pulling together the *Titanic*. But his backache is beginning to disappear.

"Contract your abdominal muscles, the ones that run vertically from

top leg up in a crooked position, and bring your top arm up near your head. Your bottom leg should be straight and your bottom arm down along your side. "How about pillows?" Binky asks. "Pillow*s?*" Leenstra says. "One pillow. One *thin* pillow. Otherwise your neck is pushed out of its proper position."

How to Pick Something Up

Put one foot slightly ahead of the other, bend at your knees and hips while keeping your body as erect as possible, then lift yourself forward and up with your thigh and buttock muscles.

The Trapezius Exercise

These broad muscles run from the spine to the shoulder blades (the lower and middle trapezius) and from the shoulders to the base of the skull (the upper trapezius). When strained, they're notorious for causing headaches. The upper muscles are usually overdeveloped and the middle and lower muscles are usually underdeveloped.

This exercise is a shoulder shrug. It will strengthen the lower "traps" so you can naturally hold your shoulders in the correct position, which is down and back. Sit straight up with hands resting on legs just above the knees, to anchor your arms and keep them from moving. Slowly bring the shoulders forward and up while inhaling. Then move them back, bringing shoulder blades together slightly and down while exhaling. Move only your shoulders, not arms or neck. Do this five times, very slowly, and repeat five times a day.

The Pelvic Rock

If you have a swayback, this exercise will strengthen your abdominal muscles so you can hold your pelvis in the correct position. Stand correctly. While breathing in, relax the abdominal and buttock muscles and let the buttocks move up and back. Then push them further back but only to the point where your lower back begins to hurt. While exhaling, pull the buttocks together and under and pull up with the abdominal muscles, assuming the correct posture again. Always move only the pelvis, keeping the knees, legs and upper body in proper posture. Do five repetitions five times daily.

your pelvis to your breastbone. Pull them up. Don't hold your stomach in, but up. And hold your breastbone high." Binky does.

"Now pull your shoulder blades together and down a bit in back. Lower,

More on Mensendieck

Ellen Lagerwerff and Karen Perlroth, certified Mensendieck therapists, have written a very practical, self-help volume with detailed instructions and drawings. Entitled *Mensendieck Your Posture—Encountering Gravity the Correct and Beautiful Way*, it was published by Aries Press. The co-authors are in private practice in Palo Alto and in Portola Valley, California, respectively. For information on other Mensendieck practitioners, send a legal size, self-addressed stamped envelope to the Academy of Mensendieck Specialists, P.O. Box 9450, Stanford, CA 94305.

lower. Hold your chin parallel to the floor. Put your hands on your lower abdomen and lean just a bit forward. Now look in the side mirror. It's better already."

Binky looks. He does look better. But he feels as stiff as a ramrod. He thinks, is this the Army all over again? Leenstra reads his mind. "Military posture is wrong—too much chest out, stomach in, chin up. Imagine a vertical line from your ear, through the middle of your shoulder joint, the center of your hip, the center of your knee, and ending slightly in front of your ankle. That's where the line should be. In a military posture the line is far behind these points."

Binky notices that his chronic lower back pain is absent as long as he maintains the correct posture. And Leenstra reassures him that as he strengthens his muscles through exercising, the correct posture will become more and more natural.

Binky likes his new stance. Now if he can just figure out how to move.

THE HEALING POWER OF MENSENDIECK

Most ailments helped by Mensendieck involve the muscles surrounding the spine, pelvis, knees, ankles, and shoulders. But breathing problems can also be alleviated, says Inge Leenstra. "Asthma patients are often hunched over, and have to learn correct posture so they can breathe more easily."

Depressed people also often have that hunched-over posture, Leenstra says. "Their muscles are all tightened in that position, looking at the ground, and we teach them how to relax."

Mensendieck practitioners can help prepare a pregnant woman for childbirth, and then help her regain her normal shape after months of added weight. Mensendieck is also used in conjunction with physical therapy for a wide variety of neurological and orthopedic disorders.

Chapter 24

MYOTHERAPY

"To my humble mind," says Robert Dillashaw, victim of a painful whiplash condition that stiffened his neck and left shoulder, "it seemed as if something wonderful had just happened. The therapist applied this pressure with her elbow for a few seconds, and there was some initial pain, but after that my shoulder just didn't hurt as much any more." And now, Dillashaw says, it just doesn't hurt at all.

The mysterious but effective treatment Dillashaw received for his injury is called trigger-point myotherapy. And the 39-year-old office worker isn't the only one who doesn't understand just how it works or why. All he knows is that it does work, "and I'm willing to accept relief from pain no matter how it's done."

Many victims of chronic muscle pain will readily agree with that sentiment, and a growing number have joined the ranks of myotherapy converts in the 30 or so states where practitioners are found. An increasing number of doctors and dentists have joined as well, drawn by myotherapy's power to bring relief where other remedies have failed.

"Prior to myotherapy I would have sent my patients for physical therapy," says Dejan Dordevich, M.D., a West Coast rheumatologist. "But I believe myotherapy is much more effective. My patients have responded very well to it. In many of the musculoskeletal problems that we treat, myotherapy is now the treatment of choice."

Robert Echenberg, M.D., a Pennsylvania obstetrician, has been sending patients to a nearby myotherapist for the past two years. "There's a lot of back pain involved in pregnancy," he says. "And from what I've learned about myotherapy, the goal is to alleviate muscle spasm, and it *does* seem to work."

Before learning about myotherapy, Dr. Echenberg says, "we would tell people to try some relaxation techniques, heat and rest, tub baths, whirlpools and that type of thing." Unfortunately, he notes, that type of thing wasn't terribly effective. "I'm happy that myotherapy's there for me to use," he says.

Few disciplines, however, seem to have embraced this approach quite as happily as dentistry, which has

Is It for You?

Those physicians and laymen who remain wary of myotherapy often cite a single, important reason for their skepticism—one that practitioners must grudgingly concede.

"We don't know *why* it works," says Pennsylvania myotherapist Nancy Bleam. "There have been two medical opinions on the subject. One says that endorphins (natural pain-relieving substances produced by the body) are involved. The other theory points to an electrical effect. But most of us are so busy fixing people that we don't have the time to do research."

How can you know if myotherapy is right for you? There are no guidelines, but here are some factors that may make you a good myotherapy candidate:

• The pain in your head, neck, torso or limb does not seem to have a direct structural origin.

• Your structural problems, such as arthritis, have been controlled physically (by medication, for example), but you continue to have pain for reasons that may be functional.

• You have probable structural problems, such as suspected lumbar disk prolapse (slipping) that may be treatable by surgery. But either you or your doctor is reluctant to proceed.

That, admittedly, covers a fairly large field of musculoskeletal pain sufferers. But what it often boils down to is the person other methods have failed to help. As Bonnie Prudden says, "The patient is usually somebody the doctor can't get well anyway, so they're glad to refer him to us."

Bob Dillashaw would agree with that. "I used to believe this type of stuff was all humbug," he says. "Now I'm starting to believe that maybe there's something better than always going to a doctor and having muscle relaxants prescribed."

found in myotherapy a possible solution to the nagging problem of TMJ (temporomandibular joint) disorder. This painful condition, which affects the joints of the jaw, plagues an estimated ten million Americans.

TMJ's symptoms are so wide-ranging that physical therapists, neurologists, psychiatrists, chiropractors and even surgeons, have been called on to provide treatment—all with varying degrees of success. Myotherapy, it seems, is providing a solution for large numbers of TMJ victims searching for alternative procedures.

Myotherapy's TMJ proponents have nothing but praise for this non-invasive, relatively inexpensive technique. Says Samuel Higdon, a Portland, Oregon, dentist: "My practice is limited to TMJ problems, and the people I started referring initially for myotherapy were the people who had not responded to physical therapy. They started getting good results."

The Pressure's On

So what do myotherapists do that brings about such impressive results for everything from bad backs to bad bites? Actually, what they do appears surprisingly simple and easy, and in many ways it is. Myotherapists routinely teach the technique to the family members of their patients, permitting them to continue therapy at home.

A visit to one of the 150 or more certified myotherapists across the nation puts one in touch with a practitioner who, armed with nothing more than fingers, knuckles and elbows, searches for sensitive "trigger points" buried in the muscles of the back, neck, chest, buttocks, arms, legs, face and feet.

Once a trigger point is found, the myotherapist applies pressure—generally for about seven seconds—to the area directly above it, using her fingers and knuckles in the tender areas around the face and extremities, bearing down with the elbow on larger areas in the back and legs.

Though the amount of pressure exerted may vary, the sensation produced by a myotherapist at work is invariably one of pain and then relief, in roughly equal proportions. As trigger points, for reasons still largely unknown, release their grip on afflicted muscles, years of tension and pain melt away—often after a single session. Strength and mobility are restored to a stiff shoulder, neck or back.

A slight soreness remains for a day or two afterward, as does the sensation of muscles trying to retighten themselves into their old, knotted formations. The myotherapist usually prescribes a regimen of stretching motions and exercises to help keep the muscles loose and limber.

Thousands of ordinary folks have learned to do myotherapy at home, thanks largely to the work of its best-known practitioner, Bonnie Prudden, whose 1979 book, *Pain Erasure: The Bonnie Prudden Way,* helped spread knowledge of the techniques. A more recent version, *Myotherapy: Bonnie Prudden's Complete Guide to Pain-Free Living,* includes some updated techniques and a "Quick Fix" chapter designed to relieve those everyday aches and pains that have many of us relying on aspirin.

Prudden, now in her seventies, still tours the country giving public seminars on the benefits of myotherapy. When not on tour, she can be found teaching certified myotherapists at her Stockbridge, Massachusetts, school. The students she instructs are put through a rigorous 1,400 hours of hands-on training before being awarded the title "Bonnie Prudden Certified Myotherapist."

In addition to Prudden's school, the Academy for Myotherapy and Physical Fitness (AMPF) in Lenox, Massachusetts, and the Shaw Myotherapy Institute in Springfield, Virginia, also train and certify myotherapists.

The AMPF runs a nine-month program consisting of approximately 800 hours of instruction. About 35 to 40 hours of that is "business basics," says AMPF President Art Schmalbach, but the rest is spent in anatomy, physiology, kinesiology, myotherapy theory, myotherapy technique, corrective exercise and so on. Graduates are awarded a certificate upon completing the coursework and passing a final exam. Nancy Shaw puts her students through a similar curriculum at the Shaw Myotherapy Institute, and she also awards a certificate upon graduation.

That means three different types of certified myotherapists are practicing today, but not to worry. While each of the schools varies slightly in its philosophical approach to myotherapy, the hands-on techniques they teach are remarkably similar. This is probably due as much to Bonnie Prudden's strong impact on the field as it is to the basic, pragmatic nature of myotherapy itself. Shaw, for example, was one of Prudden's earliest graduates, and the AMPF was formerly the Bonnie Prudden School of Physical Fitness and Myotherapy.

The National Association for Trigger Point Myotherapy (NATPM) in Portland, Oregon, also helps ensure the good conduct and safe practices of more than half of the nation's certified myotherapists, while the International Myotherapy Association regulates the activities of many others. As a result, one finds a certain "commonality of practice" among certified myotherapists, regardless of the school issuing their certification.

Though the first may cost about $100, myotherapists typically charge between $35 and $65 for subsequent sessions. Most sessions average 90 minutes in length, and most myotherapists say that no more than five to eight sessions are needed to bring a patient relief.

Triggers of Pain

Ask a myotherapist what causes pain and you'll get a ready response: trigger points. These small, hypersensitive spots in the muscle tissue are capable of causing pain anywhere in the body, myotherapists believe, and it's this view of muscles as the cause of pain—rather than the victims of pain—that helps set myotherapy apart from other forms of therapy.

Though there is some debate as to the exact nature of trigger points, medical literature from as far back as the 1840s documents the appearance of "painful hard places" in the muscle tissue of certain patients. Later researchers, the distant forebearers of modern myotherapists, noticed that pressure applied to these "muscle calluses" brought relief from stiffness and pain.

Continued research has led to the belief that these self-sustaining trigger points form in response to the twists, turns, stresses and strains each of us place on our muscles during the course of a full, active life. Once activated, trigger points force the muscle to shorten and remain that way, often for decades, protecting itself from more harm by limiting its range of motion.

That tensed-up position is the one the muscle's comfortable with. It doesn't make *us* comfortable, but it makes the muscle feel safe to be all tied up in knots, and it'll fight to go back into that spasm. Which is why myotherapists place so much emphasis on stretching and exercise.

Trigger points also have the ability to "refer" pain to other parts of the body, sometimes quite distant from the trigger point itself. Thankfully, this referred pain occurs in predictable patterns specific for each muscle. By knowing anatomy and being able to read these patterns, myotherapists are able to erase many of those mysterious aches and pains we sometimes suffer for no apparent reason at all.

Severe trauma—such as the auto accident that jerked and twisted Bob Dillashaw's head and neck—can create "active" trigger points accompanied by acute, ongoing pain in the damaged muscles, as well as referred pain in more distant areas. A myotherapist would expect to find acute pain near the active trigger points in Dillashaw's neck and shoulders, but would also look for referred pain in his jaw, temple and arms.

Less severe trauma, which can include everything from the strain placed on a newborn's body during birth to the degenerative effects of arthritis, creates "latent" trigger points, according to myotherapists. These do not cause pain, but can hinder mobility and cause weakness in the affected muscles. Like a fuse waiting for a match, most latent trigger points lie dormant for years after the initial trauma, ready for stress, either physical or emotional, to set them off.

Referred Pain, Referred Treatment

Chances are you already know exactly what an activated trigger point feels like. Maybe it's that stiff neck, backache, soreness, cramp or other form of muscular torture that grabbed you one day and never really let go. You've probably tried heat, rest or liniment to relieve the discomfort, and those old standbys may have helped for a while. But don't be fooled, myotherapists warn, the problem is by no means solved. The trigger point has simply backed off for a time, waiting for another day.

That day arrived recently for Ken Heaton, a 35-year-old design engineer and recreational runner who discovered, the hard way, that getting to see a trigger-point myotherapist can be tougher than you think.

For one thing, trigger-point myotherapists will see you *only if you are referred by a physician.* In no case will you be able to walk in off the

Myotherapist, M.D.

Because of its insistence on physician referrals, myotherapy has always needed to maintain a good working relationship with mainstream medical practitioners. Yet, muscle pain and myotherapy have received little attention from modern medicine. As noted trigger-point researcher Janet Travell, M.D., notes: "It is the bones, joints, bursae and nerves on which physicians usually concentrate their attention."

So it was that myotherapists received a pleasant surprise and tremendous shot in the arm when Kitty Spivak, M.D., joined their ranks after graduating from Bonnie Prudden's school in 1983. She is currently the only physician in the nation who is also a certified myotherapist.

Before becoming a myotherapist, she says, "I simply gave patients with headaches and low back pain the medication I was taught to prescribe and told them to go to bed for a week." Then Prudden came to town and did a workshop. "I tried some of her techniques," Dr. Spivak says. "They worked so well that I ended up going to her school."

About half of Dr. Spivak's patients are her own. The other half are referred to her from physicians in and around Greensboro, North Carolina, where she practices. "My overall success rate is about 85 percent," she says. "Most pain clinics are between 50 and 70 percent—which is considered very good."

Other physicians are beginning to open up, she says. "I'm getting more referrals because of the success I've had with patients." Still, some think her practices are a bit strange: "Physicians typically don't like to spend 60 or 90 minutes with a single patient. They are surprised when they find out that's what I'm doing.

"I only see four patients a day because it does take time," Dr. Spivak says. "Most physicians don't want to do that."

street and make an appointment with a true, trigger-point myotherapist. If you have seen a myotherapist without a physician's referral, then you have not seen a *certified* trigger-point myotherapist, and it's hard to say exactly what type of therapy you received. "Myotherapy" is a generic term ("myo" is simply the Latin for "muscle") and any massage therapist can claim to be a myotherapist without fear of prosecution.

"We don't own the term," says NATPM President Cecelia Tuskes, who notes that a number of massage therapists have taken to using the term generically. "The only way you can be sure is if a doctor refers you."

Dependency on referrals places a great deal of pressure on myotherapy to appeal to mainstream physicians, which it sometimes fails to do. Such was the case for Heaton, who was nursing a tender shoulder beset with trigger points when myotherapy entered his life.

Heaton's problem was the direct result of a trapezius muscle he'd torn three years earlier. "I'd been in therapy ever since to relieve the pain," he says, "but with no results. Then the running club I belong to brought in this myotherapist for a demonstration. She worked on five or six people with different problems and it worked for them and for me. I had almost immediate relief."

Heaton was sure he'd found the answer to his problem. When told he would need a doctor's referral to see the myotherapist as a regular patient, Heaton paid a visit to his physician, but found the doctor's attitude about alternative care far from sympathetic. "He wouldn't approve of it," Heaton says. "He didn't think it would do any good."

Undeterred, Heaton visited another doctor and finally received the referral he needed. "Hey, you have to get *your* way in *your* treatment," he says, but his temporary predicament points out a dilemma that seems unique to myotherapy—namely, it depends on doctor referrals while threatening to take the doctor out of the healing loop. That it is able to do so is perhaps myotherapy's best referral of all.

Myotherapy Resources

These schools teach myotherapy techniques:

Academy for Myotherapy and Physical Fitness
9 School Street
Lenox, MA 01240

Bonnie Prudden, Inc.
P.O. Box 59
Stockbridge, MA 01262
(800) 221-4634

Shaw Myotherapy Institute
6417 Loisdale Road, Suite 309
Springfield, VA 22150

You can also consult the following books:

Myotherapy: Bonnie Prudden's Complete Guide to Pain-Free Living by Bonnie Prudden (Ballantine Books).

Pain Erasure: The Bonnie Prudden Way by Bonnie Prudden (Ballantine Books).

THE HEALING POWER OF MYOTHERAPY

Myotherapists say their technique has the power to bring relief from the aches and pains caused by accidents, sports, occupational stresses, and certain diseases. Here's a rundown of those conditions myotherapists feel respond best to treatment.

Back Pain

Back pain, primarily lower back pain, is the number one complaint of myotherapy patients. It is also, thankfully, one of the easiest conditions for a myotherapist to treat.

"I just smile when a back patient comes in," says Nancy Shaw, who operates a flourishing myotherapy practice at her Virginia school. "Usually just a very few sessions bring quick results." Other myotherapists agree, claiming an average success rate of about 80 to 90 percent.

Neck and Upper Back Pain

"I went to see a myotherapist for neck pains caused by a degenerative vertebrae condition," says Dianne Plum. She gave me three treatments and showed my husband how to do it. I was doing very well, then I got in a car accident and got whiplash."

Needless to say, Dianne Plum's neck has been through a lot of pain. Fortunately, neck pain is another complaint that myotherapists find rather easy to relieve. As Plum notes: "The myotherapist worked on me about four times and got rid of the pain. Now I'm able to do the exercises at my physical therapy sessions and I'm doing much, much better. It's really helped."

Headache

Therapists say the pain of headache can strike in any of five separate regions of the head and face, involving trigger points in more than 15 muscles ranging from the shoulders to the eyes.

Myotherapists are called on quite often to relieve the pain of headaches, and they in turn must call on their fingers, elbows and knuckles to work the many trigger points that contribute to this elusive pain. "Migraine headaches are very difficult," concedes Massachusetts myotherapist Helen Loehr. "So many factors may come into play: food, genes . . . . I can provide relief, but if I'm not careful I can also turn a beginning migraine into a full-blown migraine."

Then, there's the experience of myotherapist Cecelia Tuskes, who says, "My migraine headaches were cured because my husband picked up Bonnie Prudden's book, turned to the section on migraines and did what the book said. We were so impressed we ended up in myotherapy school."

Shoulder Pain

This one always ranks in the top five, and it's one of the toughest challenges for myotherapists. "The shoulder has big muscles, small muscles, deep ones, shallow ones, some that lift it, others that turn it—it's complicated and difficult to treat," says Shaw.

Just don't tell that to shoulder pain sufferer Ken Heaton. "Myotherapy gave me more relief in four treatments than I had with years of physical therapy and six physical therapists," he says. Perhaps relief is a relative thing.

Jaw (TMJ) Pain

This is another prevalent complaint, but one in which myotherapy seems to work very well. The myotherapist may begin searching for trigger points in the hands and arms and finish with her fingers inside your mouth, clearing out trigger points in the gums. That may seem a bit strange, but myotherapist Christine Ford reports an 80 to 90 percent success rate. Nancy Shaw boasts 98 percent.

TRIGGER-POINT TACTICS

Here are some basic myotherapy techniques you can try on a partner or yourself. Most people tend to press harder than necessary at first, so take it easy and start slowly.

24-1

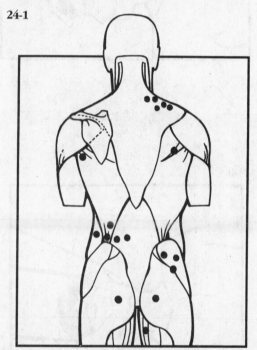

Some of the more prominent (read painful) trigger points of the back. By applying pressure to these, a myotherapist can often relieve pain in areas ranging from head to knees. In general, pressure should be sustained for five to seven seconds.

24-2

To find out just what a trigger point feels like, ask your partner to sit next to a table. Have him lay his arm out flat, palm down. Place your elbow on top of the forearm just below his elbow, as shown, and press down slowly—he'll let you know if you've found it. Now switch places.

(continued)

TRIGGER-POINT TACTICS—*Continued*

Myotherapy is used frequently to treat temporomandibular joint (jaw) pain. Some fairly sensitive trigger points can be found (from top) in
the platysma muscle behind the jaw bone, the
orbicularis oris circling the mouth and in the
masseter muscle covering the jaw joint itself,
as shown in the final two illustrations. Keep
the pressure light and hold for about seven
seconds.

24-5

24-3

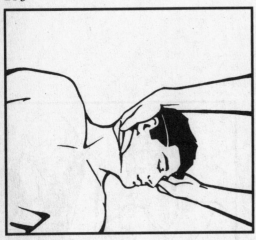

24-6

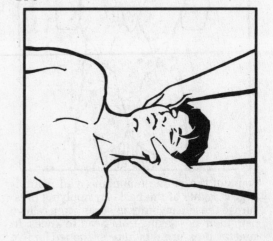

24-4

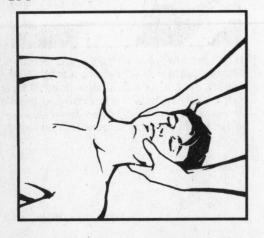

Short wooden shafts known as "bolos" help myotherapists reach trigger points in tight spots. You can make something similar yourself (from a broomstick handle) to reach trigger points in the shoulder and neck. Hold the pressure for about seven seconds.

24-7

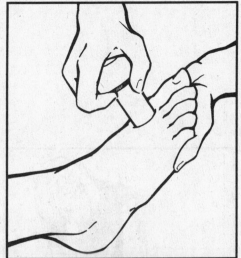

24-8

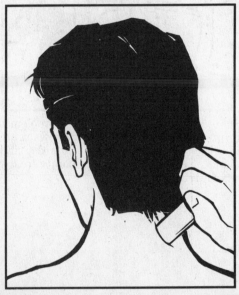

24-9

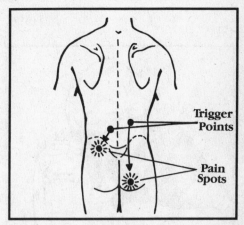

Trigger points in the lower back can refer pain to the upper hip and lower buttocks. Because such pain usually follows specific patterns, myotherapists can sometimes relieve aches that seem to come from nowhere.

24-10

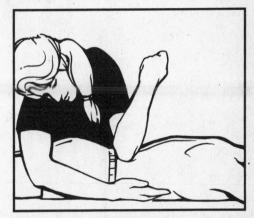

Lower back pain is the leading complaint among myotherapy patients. Here, pressure is being applied to a common trigger point near the kidney.

(continued)

TRIGGER-POINT TACTICS—*Continued*

24-11

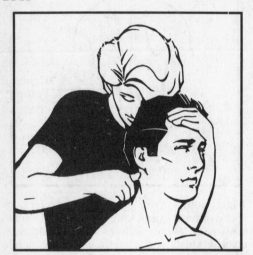

Two sensitive trigger points on the back of the neck can be found just below the hairline and 2½ inches to either side of the spine. Pressure applied to them for about five seconds, then slowly released, can sometimes help relieve headache pain.

24-12

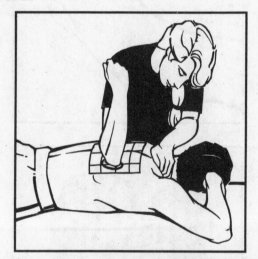

Shoulder pain can be a very tough problem for myotherapists to treat. The grid shows an area to search for trigger points, while the circle marks a spot where sensitive points are usually found.

Chapter 25

NAPRAPATHY

After the long car drive, the slight, dull pain that's almost always present in your back is feeling particularly troublesome. You sit stiffly on the chair in Doctor of Naprapathy Robert Burg's office. He asks a series of pointed questions. Many are similar to those you'd b asked in any doctor's office, but others seem to be much more to the point. "Exactly where is the pain?" "When did the pain first start?" "Does your mother remember you having it when you were very young?" "What kind of pain is it: Does it ache or radiate? Is it sore or sharp?"

Next, he asks you to bend in all directions as he watches your spine and your hips. How flexible are you? Does each vertebra move on its own, or do a few move as a unit? Are your legs the same length? He gathers more data.

There's no sense of hurry or judgment as Dr. Burg, who asks you to call him Bob, questions you. Moments later,

however, you are lying face down on a massage table wearing a green cotton robe that's open in back.

Hands That See, Hands That Heal

As he begins to touch your back, encouraging you to relax completely and let him move your body, you realize that this is not to be your typical massage. He's still gathering data.

You provide the feedback as he asks, "Does it hurt when I touch here?" "Tell me if anything feels particularly good or relieving." "Try to pull your arm down toward the table while I hold it back."

"I see with my hands," says Dr. Burg, explaining his technique. "I start working the tissues with my hands and when I feel limitations, I try to increase the range of motion in those areas."

181

Dr. Burg watches your muscles as you pull against his hold, and tests each of your joints with his hands. He reaches under your leg and lifts it back. He pulls back on your right arm and shoulder until you are nearly lying on your back. Whenever he finds a joint that isn't as flexible in one direction as the other, or is less flexible than the same joint on your other side, he gently stretches it, coaxing it to relax and release its tension.

"Stretching is the most important thing you can do structurally," he comments. "Building up muscle mass is less important. Very few people need a whole lot of muscle in their lives, but they do need structural integrity."

Nothing he does is really painful—every stretch, push and pull is gentle. The only discomfort is at places where your muscles or tissues are already sensitive or sore. Once you stop worrying about *how* he's going to touch you, you begin to become concerned about *where* he's going to touch. But soon you relax, realizing that his treatment will be confined to your back and shoulders, legs, arms and hands, and neck and face.

He touches all the vertebrae on your back, pausing to massage the ones that hurt. It's sore under your shoulder blade, and so he spends a long time working there.

The data gathering, the massage of sore points and what naprapaths call "stretchment" of inflexible areas, extends down your arms and legs and on to your hands and feet.

A Balanced Body Is a Healthy Body

Naprapaths believe that tensions in the connective tissues of the body, triggered by stress or trauma, cause the tissues to contract and move out of balance. This imbalance gets in the way of good circulation, nerve conduction and lymphatic drainage, explains Dr. Burg, who is a former member of the board of trustees and former naprapathic department chairman at the Chicago National College of Naprapathy, the only school of naprapathy in the United States.

"Connective tissue is everywhere, and if it is out of balance, you'll have sickness," he says. "If, on the other hand, the body is structurally healthy, it will be able to take care of itself."

Later, you lie on your back, while Dr. Burg checks how flexible your neck is, lifts your arms, and massages your shoulders. After two hours, the session is over. "I always spend an hour and a half or two hours the first time someone visits me," he explains. "After that, sessions cost $50 instead of the first-visit charge of $60, and they tend to be shorter." Other naprapaths often charge about half what he does, and spend about half the time with each client, he points out.

Once you're dressed again, Dr. Burg returns to the small, plant-decorated office, and explains what went on. "Your right shoulder is pulled forward for some reason. That's why I worked your right shoulder back so far; I was trying to stretch the connective tissue holding your shoulder blade.

"Also, your right side needs stretching in comparison with left. The left side is more flexible and stretched out." You feel a sudden flash of recognition and intuitive agreement. Had he said your left side needed stretching you know you would have disagreed.

Dr. Burg recommends some stretching exercises, especially tailored to your body, and explains that he doesn't know how much effect one treatment will have. Most people feel relief from back or neck pain with three or four treatments, he says. Others prefer to maintain their health by seeing a naprapath regularly—once a month or less frequently—over a period of years.

What Is Naprapathy?

The word *naprapathy* (nuh-PRAH-pathy) comes from the Czechoslovakian word *napravit*, which means "to correct or fix," combined with the Greek word *pathos*, which means "suffering." So naprapathy means to "correct suffering." Practitioners of this hands-on healing system manipulate the muscles, tendons, and ligaments of the body in order to alleviate tension and promote fluidity of motion, according to Dr. Burg. Many naprapaths also make dietary recommendations because they believe that the chemistry of the body must, like its connective tissues, be in balance.

Developed by a chiropractor named Oakley Smith in 1905, naprapathy bears a great resemblance to chiropractic. But chiropractors do *bone* alignment, explains Chicago naprapath Jacquelin S. McCord. "The advantage of naprapathy is that we do connective tissue manipulation. So while chiropractors just promote nerve conduction, we promote nerve conduction *and* improved circulation."

In 1905, Smith founded the Chicago College of Naprapathy. The school has since separated into two schools, reunited itself back into one school called the Chicago National College of Naprapathy, and is now approved by the Illinois Board of Higher Education to grant a Doctor of Naprapathy degree.

All naprapaths are trained in Chicago, at the School of Naprapathy in Sweden where the field is widely accepted and popular, or at a new college in Spain. During the four-year academic program, students learn naprapathic theory and technique, a full range of biological sciences, and nutrition. The final year they work in a supervised clinic.

Because the field is relatively small, the practice of naprapathy is still flexible. In fact, it has changed considerably over the past 50 years. About 40 years ago dietary recommendations were added to the practice, and neuromuscular methods picked up from other types of body therapists followed in recent years. As a result, each naprapath you visit could have a slightly different focus or way of treating you.

Some naprapaths do "mono treatments," focusing on just one part of the body or a particular problem. Others, like Dr. Burg, do whole-body treatments, either to correct problems, or for prevention. It's important to ask a naprapath which approach he or she follows before making an appointment.

"I do a whole-body treatment," Dr. Burg explains, "because I've never found where a particular problem ends. If you have a cervical problem, for example, I could just treat your neck. But if I don't also change the balance in the rest of your body, the connective tissues in your neck will just go back to the way they were before."

The large majority of naprapaths work in the Chicago area. But to find a naprapath in your area, you can call or write the Chicago National College of Naprapathy, 3330 North Milwaukee Avenue, Chicago, IL 60641 (312) 282-2686.

THE HEALING POWER OF NAPRAPATHY

Most naprapaths maintain that their method of healing may be helpful for all physical problems. The theory is that a body with unobstructed nerve conduction, lymphatic drainage and blood circulation will be healthier. If you aren't healthy, then the physical structure will also reflect this. Just as obstructions and tension in the connective tissues could cause back or neck pain, they could also contribute to liver disorders or a weak heart, say naprapaths.

"You could have an infected kidney, for instance," says Dr. Burg. "An M.D. would kill the germ in the kidney that is infecting it. We ask, 'Why did the germ get in there in the first place?' If the kidney tissues were truly healthy, the germ couldn't infect it.

"Or maybe you have an ulcer," he continues. "You could take medicine to coat the ulcerated lining of your stomach. But we think that you'll be better off if you correct the problem that led to the stomach lining losing its natural protection. To do that, we determine if contracted muscles and ligaments are irritating nerves that lead to the area, or are blocking good circulation somehow. When we reduce the structural pressure and get the body back into balance, it will often heal itself."

Most people see naprapaths to alleviate body pain—usually back or neck pain, and Dr. Burg says he is most successful treating those problems. But sometimes there are happy surprises, as well. "I get lots of patients with sports injuries, or knee or neck pain, and I help them, usually quickly and easily," he says. "Some of them, though, find that the treatments have relieved their allergies or asthma, too."

Chapter 26

ORIENTAL MASSAGE

Before Ming, there was massage in China. It was around before Genghis Khan, back in the days when the Great Wall was just a fence. "Massage has been practiced in China for four or five thousand years," says David Palmer, an oriental massage practitioner and director of the Amma Institute in San Francisco.

Amma is the Chinese word for massage. According to Palmer, "the Chinese characters that spell out the word have many different translations, one of which is 'to calm with the hand.'"

And who better to calm with the hand than those who *see* with their hands. "Prior to World War II, amma was primarily a massage given by blind people. It was the profession reserved for the blind," says Palmer. Even today, almost half of all amma practitioners are blind.

From its origin in China, amma migrated through the Korean Penin-sula, where it took a sharp left turn, landing in Japan over 1,500 years ago. Today, centuries after its origin, the word amma has become synonymous with what's commonly referred to as Japanese massage.

The Japanese Touch

In Japan, amma got the Toyota treatment. It was streamlined and im-proved, taking on a uniquely Japanese flair.

When Western massage methods washed ashore on Japan around 1880, some of those techniques were incor-porated into traditional amma. But for the most part, the two massage practices remained worlds apart. "Jap-anese massage doesn't use oils the way Swedish massage does, and it can be done through clothing," says Palmer.

There are other significant differ-ences. Amma massage tends to move outward away from the heart. Western massage stresses movement inward toward the heart.

Though going in different directions, the two techniques end up achieving similar results. In his book, *Tsubo, Vital Points for Oriental Therapy,* Katsusuke Serizawa, M.D., a world-renowned authority on oriental massage and its benefits, states that "Amma relieves weariness, sluggishness, stiff shoulders, heaviness in the head, insomnia, pains in the hips and back, chills of the hands and feet and swelling."

"Theoretically," says Palmer, "Western massage is based on Western cellular, biological principles. Oriental massage is based on principles that involve channels of energy flowing through the body. But the outcome is often the same."

Opening the Channels

In Japan today you'll find two different types of traditional massage: amma and shiatsu. (See chapter 3 for more information on shiatsu.) "Amma is the traditional Japanese massage, with 50 to 60 licensed schools teaching it there," says Palmer. "There is only one licensed school teaching shiatsu."

Enrollments aside, the differences between the two massage techniques are considerable. "Shiatsu involves direct pressure and lifting off. Amma includes a shiatsu technique, but it also includes lots of stroking, kneading, stretching and percussive movements with the thumbs, fingers, elbows, knees and feet on acupressure points."

Like acupressure, amma is based on the theory of meridians and points called tsubos (pronounced *sue-boes*). According to Chinese anatomy, there are more than 360 main tsubos in your body. (The technique taught at the Amma Institute covers 140 of these points.)

It's in these channels where the stuff of life, known as either yin (located in the front of your body) or yang (located in the back of the body) energy, flows "like streams, and we can access those streams through wells called tsubos," explains Palmer.

"Sometimes these streams of energy get dammed up, congested. Oriental massage is a way of breaking up the congestion and opening the channels so that the energy can run freely through all parts of your body." Rebalancing a person's energy in turn promotes the natural self-healing ability of the body, says Palmer.

Think of the amma practitioner as a hands-on scuba diver. First he finds the well, which points him toward the stream. Then he plunges in, sinking to a predetermined depth. "Down to the muddy bottom," says Palmer.

"The pressure we exert doesn't go all the way to the rock bottom, because that would hurt, and massage should be pleasurable. We go for the layer just above, the place where all the silt collects and dams up the channel of energy. When we press we stir up the muddy bottom and break it up."

A New Kind of Pressure on the Job

Instead of a coffee break, you can now take a massage break. Oriental massage is expanding far beyond the confines of Chinatown and moving into the workplace. "We've done it in companies like Apple Computer and Pacific Bell," says David Palmer, the father of what's being called on-site massage.

Palmer, and scores of students he's trained, want to make oriental massage accessible to as many people as possible. In fact, they're already looking *beyond* the workplace. "We can do the massage just about anywhere," he says, "whether you're at a mall, an airport, a nursing home—or even at the beach."

A special portable chair developed by Palmer and manufactured by Living Earth Crafts in Santa Rosa, California, makes it easier for practitioners to get at those tense muscles. On-site massage is convenient because it's done in the seated position. The person keeps his clothes on. No oils are used, and it generally takes about 15 minutes.

This specialized massage works on specific points of your body that can be reached even while you sit at your desk. "Generally it's done on only the upper body. We massage the shoulders, neck, back, arms, hands and scalp," Palmer says.

Currently there are about 600 people throughout the country who have been specially trained in on-site massage. But co-workers can be taught to do it to one another. Some typical directions: "Take your forearms and, starting next to the neck, press down on the tops of the shoulders of your co-worker. Hold for one breath, then lift up. Repeat the process, working your way out to the corners of the shoulders. Press on just the muscles; stop when you come to the shoulder bone."

Typically, on-site massage practitioners come to an office and schedule individual massage breaks throughout the day. A 15-minute session ranges in price from $10 to $20, with $12 being about average.

For more information on how you can bring this mini-massage to your workplace, write to On-Site Massage Association, 1596 Post Street, San Francisco, CA 94109 (800) 678-6762.

Pressing with Precision

"Primarily the work is done with the thumbs," explains Palmer. "In oriental massage there is no gliding motion because there is no lubrication. The work is done on specific points. It emphasizes precision."

Practitioners use six different massage techniques, according to Dr. Serizawa.

Light pressure. This improves circulation and provides stimulation to the nerves, muscles and internal organs.

Rubbing and kneading. Used mostly on the muscles, this boosts the circulation and metabolism. It also helps muscles recover from fatigue, while strengthening them, and improving their resilience.

Pressing. This technique calms nerves and muscles. It's good for treating neuralgia and muscular aches and tensions.

Vibration. The stimulation from this treatment improves the functioning of finely branched nerves and small muscles.

Tapping. This technique improves blood circulation and the motor nerves in skin and muscles. It relieves fatigue and stimulates metabolism.

Circular pressure. Practitioners use this method to break up and stimulate the absorption of deposits in joints.

Now that you know the techniques, let the amma session begin.

A Unique Experience

You cross San Francisco's Powell Street and enter another world. It's a world of fortune-tellers, caged Pekin ducks and chopsticks. You pop your quarter into the parking meter, and strain to read the instructions that are printed in Chinese characters. You wonder which centuries-old character could possibly be used to denote "tow-away zone."

You've entered Chinatown, and it's not so much a place as it is a feeling. Here songbirds chirp merrily, while just two blocks away in a different part of town, pigeons are content to sit on statues in silence. Opening the door with the "Amma Massage" sign on it, you trip over other people's shoes that have been left in the hallway.

In your head you flash back to all those old movies in which oriental ladies with white painted faces were always telling Gregory Peck to lie on his stomach while they walked across his back. Is that what's about to happen to you?

"The idea that most people have about the China Doll-like lady tiptoeing across somebody's back is wrong. That's not a primary technique of oriental massage," says Palmer. Feel better? So push back the sliding screen door and enter.

Most likely, your practitioner *will* begin your massage by having you lie on your stomach. But he won't be standing on you.

"Typically we start working the person's back, usually the upper body area," says Palmer. "That's because all the yang energy channels run through the shoulder area. So we begin with the shoulders, then work our way down the arms."

If you've ever had Swedish massage, you will notice a difference right away. "In traditional amma, you will always have a towel or clothing over the body part that is being worked on. There's no skin-to-skin contact like with Western massage."

The amma practitioner's goal is to massage all of the 12 meridian lines in your body, and he'll do that in a uniquely oriental way. "There is no sliding along the body part," Palmer explains. "Oriental massage strokes work by grabbing and moving your skin around, utilizing a rolling motion of the practitioner's wrist. Unlike shiatsu, which is just straight pressure, we use subtle movements of our wrists over each tsubo."

Whether they're rolling with their wrists or pressing down with their thumbs, amma practitioners say they focus their mind at the exact point of contact, so their consciousness can connect with yours, and with your tsubos.

"Every tsubo has unique characteristics, like a person," says Palmer. "Every one feels different, and has its own personality. They have very poetic names like Bamboo Garden, or Tip of the Dove's Tail, or Bubbling Spring." (That last one is located on the bottom of your foot.)

An oriental massage is never quite over until you hear these words: "Thank you very much." Sometimes you may even hear the words twice as the practitioner thanks your body, and then you, for allowing him to perform his art on you. Once the artwork is complete, you begin to see the total picture of oriental massage and its benefits.

Going to the Source

A typical oriental massage session lasts 30 to 60 minutes and costs between $20 and $50. Currently there are approximately 3,000 amma practitioners in the United States. They've all had to go through extensive instruction in oriental massage techniques. In fact, David Palmer, who has taught many of them, says, "We are very conservative about what it takes to make a good practitioner. We say that the first thousand massages are practice massages." For information on how to find a certified amma practitioner near you, write to: The Amma Institute, 1596 Post Street, San Francisco, CA 94109.

While you're waiting for a reply you might want to check these books for more about oriental massage in general, and amma in particular:

Chinese Massage, A Handbook of Therapeutic Massage from the Anhui Medical School, China (Hartley and Marks). This book is a direct translation of a health manual used in China today.

Massage, The Oriental Method by Katsusuke Serizawa, M.D. (Japan Publications).

Tsubo, Vital Points for Oriental Therapy by Katsusuke Serizawa, M.D. (Japan Publications).

The Web That Has No Weaver by Ted Kaptchuk, O.M.D. (Congdon & Weed).

THE HEALING POWER OF ORIENTAL MASSAGE

Because oriental massage has its roots in traditional Chinese medicine, David Palmer calls amma "the healing art of the people."

Unlike most medicine for the masses, though, amma leaves everyone feeling different. "When you rebalance energy," he says, "it has a different effect on each person. Generally though, it's not like Swedish massage, which has a very sedating effect. Oriental massage makes people feel revitalized."

Kathy Cronin, a San Francisco secretary, says oriental massage puts her more in touch with her own body. "I enjoyed the Swedish massage that I had, but this seems to go deeper. It feels like more than just moving muscles around. Oriental massage puts you into contact with parts of your body that you are not used to thinking about."

Others, too, have felt that oriental massage helped give them a new perspective. "It makes me feel light and springy. All my body parts seem to move better," says Gracia Alkema, an editor for a West Coast scientific book publisher.

Most of her adult life, Gracia had low back pain. But after turning to amma, her back problems disappeared.

Every other week, Gracia and her husband have a one-hour massage session. Afterward, she says, she "feels totally relaxed. It just works all the tension right out of me."

And tension is something that Kate Sweeney has a lot of stock in. As a representative for a San Francisco stockbrokerage house, Sweeney says she "could have really used oriental massage on the afternoon of the October 19th market crash in 1987." But she was too busy.

Even in more settled times, as the market moves up and down, "the stress builds up in a constant pattern," she says. So every month, sometimes every week, Sweeney goes for an amma session. "It works wonders. The tension in my body really gets worked out. It flows to the pressure points, and then just seems to flow out."

While amma seems to work well healing simple stress and tension, another related type of oriental massage is used to treat a wide range of specific health problems, from stiff joints to internal disorders. Called *tui na*, this method has a 2,000-year history in China. Traditionally, it was passed down from generation to generation as a valuable form of self-doctoring. Today, it is taught at all traditional medical schools in China, and all major hospitals in that country have tui na departments.

The technique is also taught at many oriental medical schools in the United States, among them the Pacific College of Oriental Medicine in San Diego. "Tui na is much more problem-oriented than other forms of massage," says Bill Helm, dean of the tui na department at the school. "As far as I'm concerned, it's one of the best medical treatments available."

Tui na is similar to amma in its absence of the long, flowing strokes of Western massage. Instead, practitioners gently but vigorously press, push, grasp, rub, vibrate, push, drag, squeeze, twist and tap, among other things. A major technique is the "rolling method," heavy on wrist action, in which the backside of the working hand is rolled side to side in hundreds of rapid repetitions over ailing areas. A flowing motion is created as the practitioner moves his rhythmically rolling hand along a limb or torso "like a wave path," as Helm puts it, stimulating energy at acupressure points and moving it along in a continuous stream.

A typical tui na treatment consists of a series of techniques and is performed very rapidly, usually in 20 or 30 minutes. In that time, a wide range of problems can be addressed.

Injuries

The rolling method is said to be very effective for bruises, sprains and breaks. "Say somebody takes a fall and bangs his elbow," says Helm. "It swells up. What happens is that the chi stagnates, the blood doesn't move, and this creates pain. What we do is work the acupressure points, to get the chi moving again."

Low Back Pain; Slipped Disks

The painful aftereffects of strains, sprains and chronic stress are treated with a combination of rolling, grasping, pulling and pressing along the back and in related areas such as the legs.

Headaches

"Indicative of internal disharmony," according to a tui na textbook, headaches are treated in such a way that blood circulation is activated to help relieve pain. A woman with a migraine headache might be given a ten-part treatment that combines rolling of the hand along her neck, shoulder and cervical area, grasping along her neck and shoulders, pulling in parts of her chest and flexing her knees while she lies on her back.

High Blood Pressure

A tui na textbook describes a man with high blood pressure as easily angered and frustrated, with "heart and kidney disharmony with an excess of liver fire." His 24-part, half-hour treatment consisted of—among other techniques—kneading his forehead, fingering acupressure points along his spine, pressing the back of his neck, and grasping, rolling and rubbing down one of his legs. After six months his blood pressure had decreased.

Pediatric Problems

Tui na is unique in that it has a completely separate pediatric system for treating children. Quite different from tui na for adults, it is gentler and treats acupressure points that are located at different places than in adults. It is said to be effective in many diseases common to children, among them infantile diarrhea, constipation, asthma, and bed-wetting.

ORIENTAL MASSAGE—THE BASICS AND BEYOND

Oriental massage practitioners use six basic techniques that focus on the acupressure points in the body. These techniques are illustrated here, along with some more advanced procedures for treating specific problems.

26-2

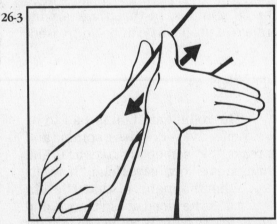

Use your four fingers lightly for massaging the neck area.

26-1

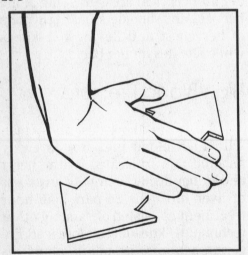

Light pressure is the most widely used technique. It involves stroking and rubbing with the hands while exerting a small degree of pressure. The pressure should be even throughout the massage, and very light. Just enough to move the needle on a bathroom scale is good.

26-3

Rubbing and kneading is used mainly on the muscles. For large muscles in the arms (as well as the back, chest and abdomen), use the palms of both hands to rub and knead. Hold the muscle firmly but lightly.

26-4

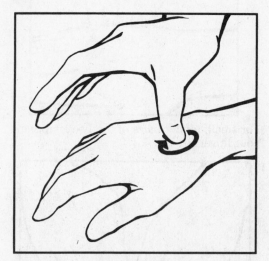

For muscles in the more restricted zones, such as the backs of the hands, press with your thumb as you rotate it.

26-5

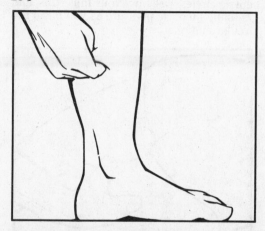

For the long, thick muscles of the legs, use your thumb and index fingers in a pinching and kneading fashion.

26-6

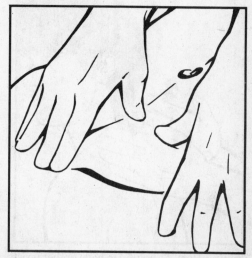

This pressing technique uses the thumbs. Pressure can also be applied with the palms or all four fingers. This technique is used most often on the muscles and joints of the arms and legs and in the abdominal region, shown here. The pressure should be light, and last from three to five seconds.

26-7

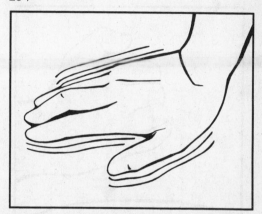

Vibration. You can use your palm and fingertips to hold a muscle and shake it lightly. Strive to maintain a rhythmic motion.

(continued)

26-8

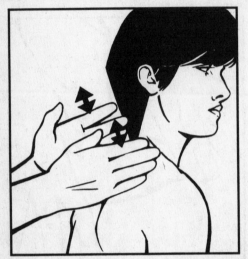

Tapping. Here it's helpful to have limber wrists. You can use one hand or both and tap lightly and rapidly. A skilled practitioner can tap about 13 or 14 times a second.

26-9

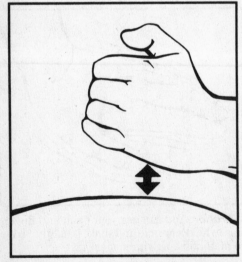

For large areas or parts of the body with hard muscles, use your fists but don't pound.

26-10

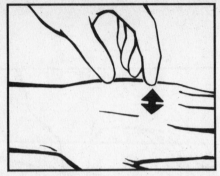

For small, tender parts of the body, tap with your fingertips.

26-11

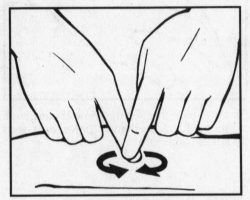

Circular pressure. This rubbing and kneading method applies pressure in decreasing concentric circles. Use only your fingertips, and gradually increase pressure as you make the circular motions.

26-12

For sciatica, practitioners massage down the center of the back of the thigh, using the palm of the hand.

26-13

To treat backaches, the back and buttocks are massaged using small circular motions with the fingers or palms of the hands.

26-15

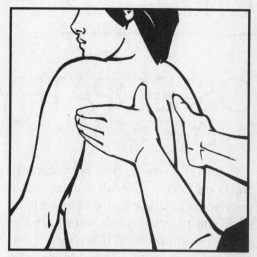

Part of traditional treatment for asthma involves massaging the inner edges of the shoulder blades. The practitioner presses with the thumbs while making small circular motions with the fingertips.

26-14

To treat gastritis, practitioners begin by working with the balls of their thumbs on the muscles located just under the shoulder blades.

26-16

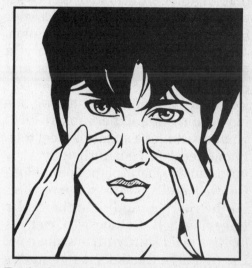

Toothaches in the upper jaw are treated by massaging points just below the eyes and near the nostrils.

Chapter 27

OSTEOPATHY

It's only when you drag your aching body into his examining room that you begin to think Robert Luber is no ordinary physician. Oh, there are the typical stainless steel trays, jars of cotton swabs, bottles of medicines, and you suspect (but would rather not see) that syringes and hypodermic needles are lurking in a drawer ready to poke holes in you.

But there's also a table you're accustomed to seeing only in a chiropractor's office, the kind of table with rollers that mechanically massage your back to loosen you up for manipulation. Affixed to the wall next to it is a machine with knobs and dials and cables leading to a pair of pads. It looks like it could deliver a few volts in your direction. Other cables lead to what resembles a stainless steel telephone receiver (but turns out to be ultrasound). Charts of the spine adorn the wall, and a plastic spine reclines on the counter. And then there's Dr. Luber himself. He doesn't cover his madras plaid shirt with a white coat. His friendly, casual demeanor makes him seem human and approachable.

You're right. Dr. Luber *isn't* an ordinary doctor. He's an osteopathic physician. Osteopathy and ordinary are mutually exclusive terms. Only 5 percent of American doctors are osteopathic. The initials after their names are D.O., not M.D. And although osteopathy was founded only in 1874, its extraordinariness dates back 2,400 years to Hippocrates.

Taking the Oath

Osteopathy (pronounced os-tee-AH-path-ee) is one of two schools of Western medical thought. The traditional (M.D.) school is called allopathic. All medical students, whether allopathic or osteopathic, take the Hippocratic oath upon graduation. And the importance of Hippocrates to osteopathic medicine can't be understated. In the fourth century B.C. he was teaching that it is "our natures that are the physicians of our diseases." Doctors, he said, should study the entire patient and his environment.

But it was a rival school of thought that gained the upper hand. While

Hippocrates focused on individual health, the Cnidian school focused on individual diseases and symptoms.

The Hippocratic approach found a new hero in Andrew Still, M.D. He was a frontier doctor practicing in the 1860s, at a time when most doctors "were using leeches and poisons and potions," Dr. Luber says. Doctors bled and purged their patients, fed them heavy metals, and operated on them with dirty hands.

Dr. Still's three children died in the meningitis epidemic of 1864, and he blamed their deaths on the "gross ignorance" of the medical profession. Casting about for a better way, "he felt that with attention to the structure of the human body he could release some of the healing power within the body itself," says David Heilig, D.O., professor and vice chairman of the Department of Osteopathic Principles and Practice at the Philadelphia College of Osteopathic Medicine. "This was before anyone knew about such things as phagocytes or antibodies."

By 1874, Dr. Still had founded osteopathy. He based his new system on the Hippocratic notions that the body can cure itself, and that one studies health to understand disease. To this underpinning Dr. Still added the theory that the structures and the functions of the body mutually depend on and affect each other. Optimum function depends on unimpeded flow of blood and nerve impulses. So a disorder of the musculoskeletal structure can affect the functioning of other body systems, he said. And a mechanical disorder can be mechanically corrected by manipulation. He emphasized preventive medicine, nutrition and fitness.

Dr. Still's methods gained popularity quickly, and people weary of leeches and mercury came from around the world seeking his treatments. Dr. Still saw himself as a mechanic of the body, helping the body to heal itself. By the time he died in 1917, there were 5,000 such "mechanics" and osteopathy had made the same strides as mainstream medicine. But osteopathy retained the principles that made it different in very important ways.

Similar but Different

You can't tell a D.O.'s waiting room from an M.D.'s. A D.O. is likely to make you wait just as long in that waiting room. A D.O.'s handwriting is liable to be just as messy as an M.D.'s—"somewhere back at the elementary school level," Dr. Luber quips.

Those who know little about osteopathy will be reassured to find out that "the training of an osteopathic physician is essentially identical to that of an allopathic physician," says Joseph W. Stella, D.O., president of the American Osteopathic Association.

So you can find an osteopathic physician who's a family doctor or a gynecologist or an oncologist or a radiologist or a pediatrician or a psychiatrist or a surgeon, or any other specialist found in mainstream medicine.

But in some of his training and practice, and especially in outlook, a D.O. is fundamentally different from an M.D. Because osteopathy is still a holistic discipline, more than half of all D.O.'s become family doctors. Most M.D. students "are specialty oriented from the second or third year on," Dr. Luber says, "so they come out unprepared to treat people. They have to take specialty training residencies at hospitals to further their knowledge in a limited area." But osteopathic colleges train students to treat the whole person, so "every osteopathic surgeon or specialist graduates as a general practitioner first and then goes into specialties," he says. "Today there are osteopathic residents in internal medicine, obstetrics, family practice, osteopathic manipulation and many other specialties.

"We still look at the entire patient instead of just the disease," Dr. Stella says. "No matter what we do for the patient or how we do it, the entire body must still function as a whole. We can't just treat a part."

Osteopathy's holistic philosophy is evident also in the emphasis on preventive medicine, Dr. Heilig says. "I draw an imaginary line between two types of care," he says. "On one side is preventive care. That takes into account everything from a person's heredity to his structure to his psychological, family and even economic environment. Attention to these factors may help prevent disease or maintain health. When you have some of those factors going bad, they become noxious influences. The patient experiences lowered resistance, and crosses over the line to crisis care.

"Crisis care is needed when those noxious stimuli are allowed to continue and cause illness. But crisis care is not synonymous with health care."

The Touch

Doctors of osteopathy are the physicians who most often practice hands-on healing. Touch is an important assist. "There is a kind of cybernetic loop established between patient and physician," Dr. Heilig says. "Not only is the patient getting a response from the doctor's hands, but the doctor is picking up messages through his hands. The D.O. is interested in examining the parts of the body the patient is talking about, not just in listening to symptoms. He asks where it hurts and then he checks it out."

The patient sees it as touching, but the D.O. sees it as palpation, a tool to help diagnosis. When palpating you, the doctor is feeling for changes in the muscles that may indicate disease as well as structural problems. For example, a Philadelphia College of Osteopathic Medicine study, reported in the *British Medical Journal* in 1987, reported on changes found in the upper part of the back related to myocardial infarction and other heart diseases.

"Or say I found a lot of tension and muscular changes in the middle of the back opposite the solar plexus,"

Dr. Heilig says. "I know that area contains the nerve supply to the stomach and some neighboring organs, so then I'd ask the patient if he's been having stomach problems. If the answer is yes, I'd go on to other studies to confirm it. The palpation raises your index of suspicion."

Observation and palpation are an osteopathic ART. Literally. Here's what Dr. Heilig and other doctors look for:

- *A* stands for asymmetry. "I may observe, for instance, that one side of the chest is different from the other," Dr. Heilig says. Or that a person stands lopsided.
- *R* is restriction of motion. This is discovered partly "by moving a person through an active range of motions, and partly by having him make the motions himself. I look not only at the range of motion but the quality, and I palpate an area as it's going through the motion."
- *T* is tissue texture change. "It may include redness or blanching, roughness or smoothness, dryness or wetness, and irregularities in and below the surface like swelling. In the muscles I might find contraction, hardness, stringiness, ropiness."

It seems osteopathic physicians must have sensitive hands indeed. But it's not that hard to learn, Dr. Heilig says. Students are immersed in learning how to relate to the entire patient, not just blood counts, and the sense of touch is developed naturally along the way. "I ask the first-year students, 'Can you tell the difference between hot and cold?' and of course they can," he says. " 'And can you tell the difference between silk and wool?' And they can do that, too. The next step is to take those sensory abilities and learn to concentrate and focus them."

Manipulation to the Rescue

Once the doctor's suspicions have been raised by palpation, manipulation often follows if it's called for. But why manipulation, and how does the doctor decide?

Some osteopathic physicians think of manipulation as an adjunct treatment to mainstream therapies like medication. "But I think of medication for a symptom as the adjunct," Dr. Heilig says. "What is most important is to maintain the soundness of the body, its structural integrity, its good circulation. Manipulation can help the body fight infection and recover from the wounds of trauma and necessary surgery."

Static on the Line

Your nervous system is essential to blood circulation, and blood governs the care and feeding of every part of your body. Nerve fibers and blood vessels extend in an organized maze throughout your body. Any interference in the line can have repercussions both locally and far afield.

"Let's say someone has a bad spinal curvature," Dr. Stella says. "The areas where there is the greatest stretch and strain are areas that are in spasm. Any nerve going through this spasm area is going to have an impairment of the nerve impulse," and thus of the blood supply. It's as if you stopped feeding a plant, or began starving yourself.

Disease can be the result, although this conceptual model doesn't deny the germ theory. "When you have a prolonged irritation you may have a cutdown on the amount of blood supplied," Dr. Heilig says. "When you don't have nutrition supplied to that part, it doesn't have enough immune resistance. So if there's a bug around, it can get started."

The bottom line? "An organ that doesn't have the proper nerve impulse is not going to function as well as it should," Dr. Stella says. "It's basic physiology. But if you can do something to improve the texture of that spasmed or diseased muscle fiber, the reflexes from that area will return to normal. And that means the patient is going to get better sooner." Manipulation is what the doctor orders.

System Overload

The other side of the coin is called the reflex effect. "Suppose you put your finger in a vise and leave it there," Dr. Heilig says. "It's going to keep sending one nerve impulse after another, and those impulses are going to build up at the spinal cord and other parts of the nervous system, to a point where they spill over like water over a dam."

Or suppose there is a tightening in the back in the area that supplies the stomach with nerves. That nerve switching station could decide, "This means we should cut down on the blood supply to the stomach."

"It's not because you have a pinched nerve but because you've set up a noxious stimulus," explains Dr. Heilig. "Whether it's a vise, or a tight shoe, or a sprain or a strain or bursitis, impulses are pouring into the nervous system. The effect spills over and begins to mess things up. To the extent it's in the musculoskeletal system, we can do something about it with manipulation."

The Static-Overload Combo

Some nerves govern body secretions. "You may have a combination of impaired blood supply and excessive stimulation to nerves in charge of stomach acid," Dr. Heilig says. "The resistance of the stomach wall is down so there's less mucus secretion, more stomach acid secretion, and the next thing is that the stomach begins to digest itself."

The Non-Electric Short-Circuit

Structural problems in muscles and joints can also interfere with the nerve axon, Dr. Heilig says. The axon is a nerve fiber leading from one nerve cell to another. The nerve impulse, which is electrical, is passed down these fibers.

But inside the axon is what is called the axonal cytoplasmic flow. That's how neurotransmitters like norepenephrine (which constricts blood vessels and increases blood pressure and heart rate), proteins like ATP (which stores energy in all cells) and peptides (parts of proteins) get to where they're going.

"If an area is stressed or strained," Dr. Heilig says, "the normal healing processes, which can include swelling, could affect the flow through the axon." Once again, manipulation might be helpful.

The Treatment

So there you are in Dr. Luber's examining room. He's taken your medical history, listened to you tell where it hurts, and pushed and prodded his way around your body.

Now you lie faceup on the roller table, and he places the two electrified pads on your lower back. He fiddles with knobs, and you feel a slight tapping sensation on your back. Another knob fiddle, and the sensation turns to a tingling feeling that pulsates in waves. Still another fiddle, and the tingling becomes constant.

You know electricity is flowing into your back, and you gain new respect for Ben Franklin. But it doesn't hurt at all. In fact, Dr. Luber says, "the electric current is fatiguing your tightly spasmed back muscles. It helps me get through the spasm to the spinal joints." In that way, the electrical stimulator works like the roller table.

There may be any number of manipulative approaches, from "holding techniques" to gentle "thrusts," which can restore a joint, especially in the spine, to normal movement, reduce asymmetry and relieve tenderness.

Soft-Tissue Technique

This method is usually used on the muscles surrounding the spine. The doctor's hands rhythmically stretch and press the muscles. The main purposes are to relax the muscles and connecting tissue, and to allow the joint full motion.

Lymphatic Technique

The doctor applies pressure rhythmically and at varying rates to the upper chest. The changes in pressure enhance the lymphatic and venous flow throughout the body and affect the drainage of fluids and secretions in the chest. This is said to be helpful in upper respiratory infections.

Finding an Osteopathic Physician

Osteopathic physicians are listed in telephone directories under "Physicians and Surgeons." Look for the "D.O." after their names. Although the 25,000 American osteopathic physicians are found in every state, there are strong concentrations in Michigan, Pennsylvania, Ohio, New Jersey, Florida, Texas and Missouri. Write the American Osteopathic Association, 142 East Ontario Street, Chicago, IL 60611.

Muscle Energy Technique

If the doctor is working on your knee joint, for example, and the leg is tight and will not extend, you may be asked to raise the leg against resistance. This automatically relaxes the opposing muscles that may have kept the leg from extending.

Counterstrain Technique

Here the doctor moves your limb for you to the point of least discomfort. It is held there until the spastic muscle relaxes, then the limb is gently moved toward its normal position.

Functional Technique

Strain/counterstrain is one of several "functional techniques" that can be used. Usually this technique is used to gradually guide a joint to the point of maximum ease of motion.

THE HEALING POWER OF OSTEOPATHIC MANIPULATION

While manipulation is especially effective for musculoskeletal problems, osteopathic physicians say it is hard to conceive of any condition or illness in which careful, pertinent manipulation would not be of some benefit. After all, the point of manipulation is to restore nerve and circulatory functions and thus help the body heal itself. If an arthritic joint is acutely inflamed or extensively damaged, manipulation of *that* joint may not be the way to go. But if structural strain helped produce the arthritic joint, removing that strain may help the patient. Manipulation can also be used along with conventional treatments for just about anything else: in pneumonia to maintain unimpeded motion of the chest, which in turn helps blood and lymph flow; in viral and bacterial diseases to enhance the release of antibodies; in hypertension to release tension and lower blood pressure and in diabetes, not as a substitute for necessary insulin but to help the pancreas function better if its ability to produce insulin has not been totally lost.

The combination of modern medicine, manipulative therapy and a holistic outlook make a visit to an osteopathic physician a sort of one-stop shopping excursion for medical care.

Chapter 28

PET MASSAGE

"Hippocrates told his students to never give medicine without massage, and I've found that to be excellent veterinary advice as well," explains veterinarian Michael W. Fox. "A healing massage is an excellent complement to veterinary care. It gives sick and injured animals an extra little 'lift' that aids in their recovery.

"And I also believe that an animal that's massaged regularly is better able to resist illness and other problems to begin with," says the author of *The Healing Touch* (originally published as *Dr. Michael Fox's Massage Program for Dogs and Cats*).

"Dogs and cats that are 'gentled' regularly—especially early in life—are very relaxed. And it's well recognized that relaxed animals are better able to resist disease and stress as they age," he explains.

Dr. Fox should know what works to keep animals well. Trained as a veterinarian, an animal psychologist *and* a certified massage therapist, he is the director of the Center for Respect for Life and the Environment,

an affiliate of the Humane Society. He was formerly the society's scientific director.

Even with those kinds of credentials, he still has to put up with some ribbing from his scientific associates for having authored what is generally considered to be *the* how-to book on a far-out subject.

"Some people do shake their heads when they hear my name," he admits cheerfully, "but many veterinary professionals are very supportive of the concept. At the very least, they understand that people who massage their pets regularly are going to notice problems much faster than the ordinary pet owner. Early diagnosis is a benefit that goes hand in hand with pet massage."

Unleash the Healer Within

But the benefits of massage, Dr. Fox explains, go far beyond having a healthier pet. "Many pet owners have told me that using the techniques in

203

Dr. Winter's Five-Minute Massage

"You can give your pet a good healing massage in just five minutes," says Dr. William Winter. "Just touching those neck muscles deeply is almost instantly relaxing. It's an extremely powerful touch that can change a dog's or cat's attitude in moments.

"Start by holding your animal's head in your hands. Look right into his eyes and breathe with him. Synchronize your breathing and then 'lead' his breathing down to a slower level. This should take about a minute.

"Then move around to your animal's side and begin turning his head gently from side to side until you can touch his nose to his rib cage. This duplicates the natural neck movement that animals get in the wild while hunting. Go a little further each time you move the neck. Depending on your pet's patience, try to spend about two minutes on this.

"Now really *massage* the neck. Feel below the hair and skin until you find the lumps and bumps of the muscles. Use the same amount of pressure as you'd use to peel an orange and deeply penetrate with your fingers. Hold on until you can feel the area heat up; that's the way to tell that you've really opened up those blood vessels and improved the circulation.

"Don't just move the skin around —you've got to get down to those muscles! It's a skill that's asleep in most of us, and the only way to bring it out is to practice, practice, practice! Two minutes of this—not too soft and not too hard—and you're done.

"It's very easy to learn to do. A little patience is all you need to get great results. I've taught hundreds of people to do it, and it has brought me more joy than any other part of my job."

my book has helped them to discover their own healing powers. It's a feeling they might otherwise never have experienced because of a natural reluctance to massage people. But luckily, there aren't any cultural taboos against touching animals.

"Giving a massage to your pet allows you to experience something that therapists who massage humans have known for centuries—that locked up inside ourselves is a powerful ability to heal others with our hands."

Carvel Tiekert, D.V.M., agrees. Founder and president of the American Holistic Veterinary Association, Dr. Tiekert says that massage therapy produces "happier animals *and* happier owners—because the owners now have the ability to do something at home that can help their pets stay healthy.

"It's not a substitute for good veterinary care," he explains. "It's a great follow-up therapy—something you can do for your pet at home after a visit to the vet, or as part of a regular good-health program.

"I try to get the owners of all my 'patients' to massage their pets on a regular basis. 'Start out massaging your animal every day,' I tell them, 'especially if there's a problem you're hoping to correct. Then establish a pattern where you give your pet a good massage a couple of times a week. And don't worry about doing it too often. One medical benefit of massage is that it improves circulation. That's something you can't overdo.' "

Massage for Special Problems

Here are some massage techniques that may help your pet in specific situations.

Sprains, Arthritis and Dysplasia

Begin with five minutes each of relaxing massage and firmer strokes all over the animal's body, Dr. Michael Fox says. Follow with five minutes of deep massage and acupressure around the hips, thighs and lower back (in that order). Go lightly if there is pain and occasionally flex and extend the legs. (Only massage *after* initial pain and swelling have subsided.)

Large-Breed Pups

To help them grow without pain, give deep friction massage up and down all four limbs 10 to 15 minutes daily. Follow with 10 minutes of concentrated massage (mostly kneading) to the joints of the front and hind legs. Each limb should be flexed and extended 10 to 20 times.

Old Age

Massage the extremities with smooth strokes, beginning at the toes and working up to stimulate circulation. Softly stroke your pet for five minutes afterwards.

Serious Injury or Illness

When serious medical problems make other forms of massage impossible, Dr. Fox advocates the "healing hands" technique. Simply place your hands very lightly around your pet's ill or injured area and breathe in, imagining that you are drawing the pain and sickness out of that part of his body. Breathe out, and feel the healing energy flowing out of your hands and into your pet. Visualize the area—and your pet—returning to its natural, healthy state.

"Touch your pet knowingly," says Dr. Fox, "and your healing touch will be awakened."

William Winter, D.V.M., a doctor of (human) chiropractic with a holistic veterinary practice in Minneapolis, says there's an added bonus for owners who practice pet massage. "*Your* blood pressure will drop almost instantly when you begin the massage," he explains. "As your pet relaxes and begins to experience your healing powers, a wonderful feeling of calm will claim you as well."

One thing that all proponents of pet massage suggest is that pet owners receive a massage themselves before they attempt to work on their pets. "To learn to give one, first get one," advises Dr. Fox. "Feeling someone else's fingers beneficially manipulating your skin and muscles will make it easier for you to 'feel-see' with your fingers when you massage your animal companion. "The tonic effects of receiving a massage will also convince you of the benefits more than words ever could."

A Note of Caution

Never massage an animal that has a fever, is in shock, is extremely disabled or has heatstroke. If any of the following conditions are present, any hands-on treatment should be limited to *very* light (fingertip only) massage: recent fractures, sprains, torn muscles, ligaments and ruptured disks, acute inflammation due to a bite or infection, swelling caused by blood blisters, enlarged lymph glands, fresh cuts, bruises, abrasions or newly formed scar tissue, and any area that seems unusually tender. (With any of the above, see your vet as soon as possible.)

If your pet is ill or debilitated, make him as comfortable as possible before starting to massage. A soft blanket or foam rubber pad makes a good "massage table," and an electric heating pad will provide additional comfort (and relax tightened muscles) if the room is cold.

Dr. Fox urges that *your* comfort be assured as well. "Be sure to position yourself so that you don't have to reach out or bend too much to massage your pet," he warns. "It is important that you be as comfortable as your animal."

Digging Deeper

Everything you need to know about pet massage is in the book *The Healing Touch* (Newmarket Press).

The American Holistic Veterinary Association can direct you to practitioners in your area who include pet massage in their range of alternative therapies. For a list of the Association's members in your state, send a stamped, self-addressed envelope to the American Holistic Veterinary Association, 2214 Old Emmorton, Bel Air, MD 21014.

THE HEALING POWER OF PET MASSAGE

Dr. Fox first discovered *his* healing power while attempting to care for a wolf with distemper-caused inflammation of the brain. "In college we were taught to put such animals to sleep," he recalls, "but something in me refused to give up. Out of a combination of desperation, a hunch and the rewarding experiences I'd had with people, I decided to try to massage the ailing wolf.

"She seemed to enjoy being stroked and spoken to in a quiet, reassuring voice, so I began by lightly massaging the muscles around her neck and head. I massaged her limbs and applied deep pressure up and down along the sides of her spine. For five days and nights I continued to massage her for 15 minutes every two to three hours.

"She not only recovered, she lived for eight long active years afterwards. A few months after recovering from what is generally a fatal disease, she delivered a litter of healthy pups."

A New Zest for Life

King, a six-year-old golden retriever, lived as sedentary a life as his owner, and showed it. Obesity, lethargy and an overall loss of interest in life only added to the pain caused by his hip dysplasia, an inherited problem that greatly limits the activity of larger animals.

Dr. Fox prescribed a low-calorie diet, regular walks and daily grooming followed by a therapeutic massage. "It took a couple of weeks for King and his owner to develop a good massage relationship," notes Dr. Fox, "but soon the massage began to relieve some of the pain in King's hips.

"Within three months King was a new animal—active, happy and filled with a zest for life. His owner felt better as well, and the last time I saw him, he was teaching his friends how to massage *their* pets!"

Extremely large and small dogs have special problems that benefit greatly from massage, says Dr. Fox. "The normal size of a 'natural' dog is between 35 and 40 pounds," he explains, "and when they're bred to be much larger or smaller than that, the result is a lot of physical stress on their bodies. Massage can greatly ease the aches and pains that these abnormal body alignments can cause."

Pain and Stiffness

"If your animal has trouble coming down the stairs, it's probably due to neck pain," explains Dr. Tiekert. "Trouble going up steps is almost always caused by back or hip pain. Most vets treat such problems with steroids and muscle relaxants, but you can ease your pet's pain with massage.

"I tell people to follow the techniques in Dr. Fox's book, and they're amazed at the improvement they see. I've seen owners massage away the pain of arthritis in older dogs and greatly relieve the back and disk problems that trouble so many small dogs.

"People tell me that pets that were walking around stiffly now come running when they know they're going to get a massage. Pretty soon, even steps aren't a problem anymore!"

Behavior Problems

"We've used massage to end behavior problems as well as illness," reports Dr. Winter. "Dogs that are barking all the time, digging or chewing on furniture calm down greatly after just a few weeks of regular massage.

"Several people have told me that their dogs stopped being afraid of loud noises after they began massaging them. One dog in particular, who always seemed to be angry and who had a biting problem, became a happier, better-adjusted animal after regular massage.

"So many of these so-called behavior problems are actually the result of constant pain in the animal's back and neck. Once that pain is massaged away, the pet's behavior and personality return to normal. Massage is a great way to get cats to stop destructive behavior, like inappropriate urinating or clawing the furniture.

"Massaging an animal all over is fine, but if you want to get rid of neurotic behavior, like constant barking or overeating, spend 90 percent of your time massaging the muscles and bones of your pet's neck," Dr. Winter says, " 'Neck block' is responsible for most behavior problems in pets."

RELAXING RUBS FOR YOUR DOG OR CAT

Here are a few techniques from Dr. Michael Fox that you can try on your own pet. To prepare for the massage, he suggests you close your eyes and breathe slowly and deeply for a few moments to relax and energize yourself. Shake your arms and shoulders and rub your hands together to get your circulation going. Prepare your pet by gently stroking him with both palms—always in line with the lie of the fur—while talking in a gentle, reassuring voice.

28-1

Using light fingertip pressure, make small circular movements around the muscles that lie on each side of the spinal ridge—clockwise first, then counterclockwise. Gradually increase the pressure as much as the animal will permit. Don't lift your fingers from your pet while you're performing this technique. Repeat three or four times.

28-2

Press the ball of your thumb onto each acupressure point (see illustration 28-9) all the way down the back, beginning at the nape of the neck and moving down to the rump. Maintain pressure on each point for two or three seconds.

28-4

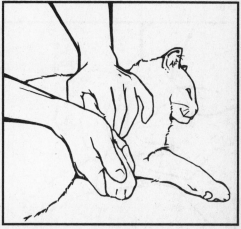

Hold the front leg and squeeze the muscles of the paw between your fingers and thumb for at least one minute. Take each digit and move it up and down with a gentle, vibratory movement.

28-3

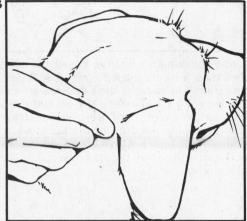

Use fingers and thumb to give a light, circular massage to the base of the skull. Gradually make deeper and smaller circles and follow the muscles forward as your pet relaxes. Continue under the neck, avoiding pressure on the windpipe, and work the muscles on each side of the throat, moving up to the base of each ear. Be very gentle just beneath the ear, where the lymph glands are located. (Swelling or pain in this area can be a sign of sickness.)

28-5

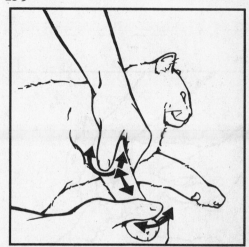

Knead across the tendons of the wrist and then hold the paw and flex it, extending and inwardly rotating it to help relax the tendons. Move up the foreleg, making circular, kneading motions along the muscles with your fingers and thumb.

(continued)

RELAXING RUBS FOR YOUR DOG OR CAT—*Continued*

28-6

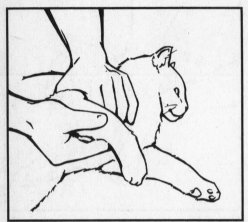

Work up to the elbow. Deeply stroke and squeeze the muscles around the elbow joint. Then push and pull to flex the limb at the elbow area.

28-8

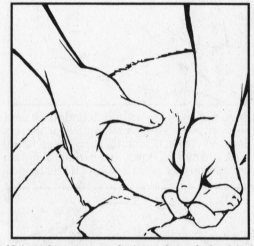

Using the same technique, knead the hind feet, then work up the leg slowly. Use fingers and thumb to massage the ligaments around the knee. Flex and extend the leg and use a circular motion of your fingertips to massage the hip. Apply pressure to the acupressure points of the hind leg, give a few light strokes to the area, then turn your pet over and do the other side.

28-7

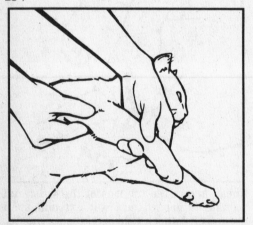

Move up to the shoulder, repeating slow, deep strokes over muscles and tendons. Turn your pet over and do the other side.

28-9

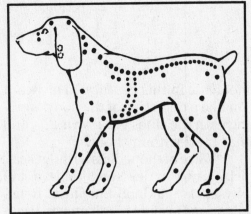

Location of major acupressure points in dogs. (Cats share similar points.) For any given point, apply direct pressure gently, then increase gradually and hold for up to 30 seconds as you breathe out.

28-10

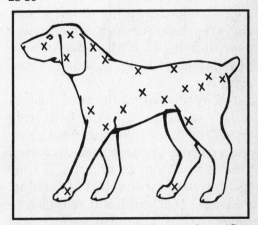

Location of diagnostic points in dogs. (Cats are similar.) Pay especially close attention to these areas as you massage your pet. Pain, heat, swelling, or shrinkage detected here may be early signs of illness or injury. If you discover a problem, stop the massage and call your vet immediately.

Chapter 29

PHYSIATRY

Would you take your bad back or sore shoulder to a doctor in a specialty that most Americans have never even heard of? If that doctor is a physiatrist, you might want to consider it.

Why physiatry? Because doctors in this small but growing field have broad and extensive training in physical medicine. They recognize that most pain is muscular in origin and they use physical means, like stretching, massage, heat, cold and exercise to relieve it. Physiatry also uses some of the newest diagnostic tools, like thermography and electromyography. But the physiatrist's chief tool is touch.

"Despite all the high-tech advances in diagnosis, soft tissue [muscle] injuries are still best found, and treated, by a hands-on approach," says Willibald Nagler, M.D., physiatrist-in-chief at New York Hospital–Cornell Medical Center in New York City. "Musculoskeletal problems are difficult to diagnose and do not always benefit from surgery or medication, which are the modalities which have dominated

medicine in this century. In my work I'm like a detective of the body, working with the clues you give me . . . and that I feel with my hands."

"We're orthopedists without scalpels," says Charles Norelli, M.D., a staff physiatrist at Good Shepherd Rehabilitation Hospital in Allentown, Pennsylvania. "A physiatrist who doesn't actually *feel* the cause of a patient's pain is negligent, in my opinion. Physiatrists have resurrected the art and science of touch."

That art and science is proving effective at handling one of humanity's most common—and vexing—pains. Arthur C. Klein and Dava Sobel, two health writers, discovered in a nationwide poll that back pain sufferers, many of whom hurt for years and vainly go from doctor to doctor, often get the best results when they finally find a physiatrist. For their book *Backache Relief* they interviewed nearly 500 hurting folks. Their conclusion? Physiatrists are "exceptional healers" who are "your best bet among all practitioners—medical and nonmedical—for

212

both acute and chronic back problems," Klein and Sobel write. Fully 86 percent of their respondents reported being successfully treated by physiatrists. That was a significantly higher rate than for other specialties most people in pain turn to, such as orthopedists or neurologists.

An Odyssey of Pain

Dave Freedman saw them all, in a quest for pain relief that began in 1973. At 6'3" and 215 pounds, he was getting ready to try out for a Big 10 football team. Then, one day in the gym, 275 bench presses proved to be a few too many. He tore seven muscles in his upper back. "I couldn't sit or walk without awful pain," he says. "I not only didn't make the team that year, I spent the season fogged out by painkillers. In two years I saw 15 doctors —neurologists, orthopedists, osteopathic physicians, surgeons—everybody had a different diagnosis. I had three operations, and none of them helped."

His dreams of an athletic career in ruins, Dave took on the grueling grind of medical school. Even immersed in medicine, however, he couldn't find relief from his continuous pain, and he took a leave of absence. Then he found Dr. John Mennell, a physiatrist and enthusiastic proponent of hands-on healing.

"It was beautiful," Dave remembers. "Dr. Mennell put his hands on my spine, and very gently pushed on the muscles. He felt each level, step by step, until he got the total muscle-ligament picture. It turned out that I had a torn ligament as well as torn muscles. Dr. Mennell prescribed massage, manipulation, exercises and even some self-hypnosis to help manage the pain."

For the first time in seven years, Dave was fairly pain free. But he still had some spine curvature, from the early hunchbacked days after his injury. Resuming medical school, he met physiatrist John E. Toerge, D.O., who was at that time a resident at the Rehabilitative Institute in Chicago. To Dave's massage and manipulation regimen, Dr. Toerge added a treatment physiatrists call "stretch and spray." The painful area is sprayed with a super-cool topical anesthetic, and then stretched to relax the knotted-up muscles. Dr. Toerge also discovered some trigger points at the base of Dave's neck, which he treated with injections.

"I still have some pain, because I had what Dr. Toerge calls a real 'train-wreck' injury. But I can work," says Dave, who is now an M.D. himself, working for a large pharmaceutical company. "And I can swim and lift weights."

The Secret of Their Success

What's the secret of physiatry's success? There is nothing magical or mysterious about it. "We're trained to look at, and listen to, the whole patient," says Dr. Nagler. "We're lifestyle doctors, and there's a lot of bad lifestyle out there.

Dr. Norelli agrees. "Pain is as individual as people's personalities. We try to draw on the body's ability to correct itself by prescribing individualized exercises and other forms of therapy. To do this properly requires extensive patient evaluation, which is one way we differ from the other disciplines: We take time to fully examine each patient."

Looking at the whole patient includes touching him, and not just where it hurts. "There is what I call 'the physiatrist's handshake,' " says Dr. Toerge, who is now the director of the spinal cord injury program at the National Rehabilitation Hospital. "When I shake a patient's hand, I put my other hand up on their shoulder. What I feel then can be a real indicator of their problem. Sometimes I feel tightness, or a postural change like one shoulder being drawn up higher than the other. It usually tells me how they are doing, too: If they are tense or relaxed, still hurting or feeling better. We have become a nontouch society, but I feel that touching is a great opportunity to learn about a person."

Physiatrists look at how the patient sits and stands, says Dr. Toerge. "We ask, 'Does your pain get worse after a commute in rush hour traffic, or when your teenager walks into the room? Is it better first thing in the morning, or after sitting for a while? When does it hurt? Where does it hurt? How does it hurt?' We tend to have the gift of the gab, but it's valuable."

A Sensitive Touch

What can you expect from a visit to a physiatrist? A fairly long session, especially the first one. There are the questions that Dr. Toerge mentioned, and a full medical history.

Some physiatrists use a pain questionnaire, which may include a diagram of the body. You're asked to mark the sites of pain, and describe how extensive or severe the pain is, as well as areas that are numb or less sensitive.

There may be range-of-motion tests, where the doctor asks you to move a certain way or to resist pressure he puts on your arm or leg or shoulder. Or he may palpate, feeling for trigger points of knotted muscle, or for muscles that are "guarding" or forming a stiff protective splint around an injured joint. He may feel for areas of referred pain, where injury in one part of the body makes another place hurt.

"A physiatrist uses the sensitivity of his fingertips the way a cardiologist uses his finely-tuned ears to listen to heart sounds through a stethoscope," says Dr. Nagler.

Andrew Fischer, M.D., Ph.D., chief of rehabilitative medicine at the Veterans Administration Hospital in the

Bronx, New York, describes the physiatrist's touch as a gentle, careful probing with the fingertips in the area that pains you. If he needs to exert greater pressure, the physiatrist brings his thumbs into play, or presses on the back of his palpating hand with his other hand.

It's that simple, but it's not a simple skill to learn, says Dr. Fischer. "The technique of palpation is really an art that can be learned only with extensive experience and most efficiently under direct supervision of an experienced teacher who shows the student where to palpate, what to feel for and what to concentrate on. Without this direct instruction, it is extremely difficult to learn to diagnose muscle spasm or some sensitive point. Palpation is the most sensitive method for pain diagnosis, and for the identification of its source."

Once the cause of your pain is established, the team goes into action. Physiatrists direct many specialists, who may include physical therapists, occupational therapists, masseurs and others. Depending on your needs, the physiatrist himself may perform some treatments, such as stretch and spray, or manipulation.

You may also be given an exercise program to do at home, and special instructions. "A big part of our treatment is rehabilitation. Not only exercise, but teaching people how to do everyday things, like getting out of bed, lifting, washing the dishes, get-

---

For More Information

Is there a physiatrist in your future? It's likely. Physiatry is a small specialty now—with about 2,000 practitioners nationwide—but it expects to grow rapidly into the twenty-first century.

For more information and the name of a physiatrist in your area, contact:

The American Academy of Physical Medicine and Rehabilitation
122 South Michigan Avenue, Suite 1300
Chicago, IL 60603-6107
(312) 922-9366

The Association of Academic Physiatrists
8000 Five Mile Road, Suite 340
Cincinnati, OH 45230
(513) 232-8833

The National Chronic Pain Outreach Association
4922 Hampden Lane
Bethesda, MD 20814
(301) 652-4948

---

ting in and out of the car," says Dr. Toerge. "We educate people how to live without causing or aggravating pain. That's what rehabilitation is—learning to live in a way that causes the least pain."

THE HEALING POWER OF PHYSIATRY

Physiatrists do more than just treat backaches and tennis elbows. Advances in medicine mean that many more people survive devastating illnesses like strokes and spinal injuries. Physiatrists can assist them, as well as people who have lost limbs and are learning to use artificial ones.

Arthritis can incapacitate people too, and keep them from doing the things they want and need to do. As the Baby Boomer generation ages, with no cure for arthritis in sight, physiatrists expect that their services will become increasingly in demand. "We can put years back in life, and life back in years," says Dr. Nagler.

One person who had her future restored by physiatry is Cynthia Rochen, a registered nurse in Maryland. There was a time she was afraid she would never be able to take care of herself, let alone any patients.

"I spent five years being jerked through the medical mill after being rear-ended in a car crash," she says. "They told me in the emergency room that it was just a severe neck sprain, and it would get better if I rested. But the pain just got worse. It got to where I couldn't turn right or left, and I couldn't take notes in class. I walked stiffly. I couldn't sleep very well. I couldn't even drink soda out of a can.

I saw a neurosurgeon. He ordered all sorts of tests, including a CAT scan and a myelogram [an X-ray of the spine done with a contrasting dye]. Because the tests found nothing he didn't want to operate. So I opted for medication and physical therapy. They didn't work.

"Getting through nursing school was like an endurance battle. I was very frustrated, and I was scared, because some of my nursing professors doubted that I would ever be able to do the heavy lifting and moving that a nurse has to do."

Then one day Cynthia felt a particularly bad flareup of her pain while she was blow-drying her hair. She went back to the doctors, who put her in a neck brace and prescribed more physical therapy, to no avail. Finally she reluctantly agreed with the hints that it might be all in her head, and saw a psychologist. He, however, was convinced Cynthia's problem was really physical, and sent her to another neurosurgeon. Two more myelograms showed nothing.

The surgeon decided she had a chronic cervical sprain, and told her she would just have to live with it. Then, through the National Chronic Pain Outreach Association, Cynthia found Dr. Toerge. "What a difference!" she says. "He took an extensive history, and for the first time I felt like I was being treated as a person, and not just another case. Then when he started the physical examination, he went right to the spot that hurt the most. He did some very gentle manipulation, moving my head, neck and back, to check my range of motion." Subsequent treatments brought considerable relief.

But Dr. Toerge established that a mechanical problem was preventing Cynthia's complete recovery. A diskogram revealed a herniated disk, and after surgery she continued to improve under Dr. Toerge's care. She is sure that his program of rehabilitative exercises and swimming made a big difference in her recovery. "His hands allowed me to work, and do what I wanted to do. I could finally ride a horse again, after five years! I went beyond pain relief to endurance, strength and mobility. I was on my way."

Chapter 30

PHYSICAL THERAPY

"The pain was so bad I wanted to die." You can tell by the sound of Mary Smith's voice that the sentiment being expressed was considered more as a real option than an idle threat. Because of degenerated disks in her spine, she was in a world of hurt.

"The pain never let up. Never. It felt like I had 20 charley horses in my back. You can't believe it. It hurt from my lower back all the way down to my toes . . . you just can't imagine."

But her physical therapist could imagine it. Pain is the physical therapist's nemesis. Every day he rolls up his sleeves and goes into hand-to-hand combat against it—using massage, exercise, electrical stimulation, ultrasound and other techniques. But his hands are his best weapons: "The mere act of touching, the mere fact that someone is putting his hands on you has a therapeutic effect," says Mary's physical therapist Ken Trzecki, P.T., a private practitioner in Buffalo, New York.

"Touching seems to trigger healing responses that are both physical and emotional," says Trzecki. "Clinically we see it happen over and over again." So do patients, including Mary Smith. "I had been out of work for seven weeks but physical therapy has really helped," she says. "I still have some pain, but it is much less; I can handle this pain, and now I can even go back to work." As rewarding as that must be, helping to relieve pain is just one aspect of a physical therapist's practice.

Masters of Motion

Most people do what moves them. Physical therapists, on the other hand, are concerned with what movement does to people. "Physical therapists are movement specialists," says Trzecki, who has been a P.T. since 1973. "We're trained to evaluate normal movement, and to recognize and correct abnormal movement. Our treat-

Let's Get Physical

What should you expect, in terms of both time and money, if a visit to a physical therapist is in your future? "There isn't a standard for how long a physical therapy treatment should be," says Ken Trzecki, P.T. "In general, average treatment time is about an hour. Often it depends on whether the patient needs to exercise while here. Some treatments require that the person be on a certain machine for 20 or 30 minutes.

"Also, when you get to the hands-on treatment, the special techniques for mobilizing the tissue in the joints, the neuromuscular techniques, that's where the time adds up."

Often, physical therapy treatments are scheduled at least three times a week, especially in the beginning of a program. It's all based on what ails the patient. "Some of the latest research is showing that for simple problems, once a week may be plenty," says Trzecki.

"How long you will need therapy varies with your condition also. For neurological problems, you could be in active physical therapy from a year to a year and a half. Common injuries and joint problems may only require six to eight weeks of treatment."

How much you pay for each treatment will depend on where you live. A typical session may run about $40 to $45, with some treatments going as high as $150. "If you live in New York City or Los Angeles, you'll pay more than if you live in Cleveland or Buffalo," says Trzecki. You'll also pay more to see a specialist than you would to see a general practitioner. Fortunately, most health insurance policies pick up part of the cost of physical therapy. But some may do so only if you are referred by a doctor, so it's a good idea to check beforehand.

---

ments are geared to restoring normal or at least functional movement."

That training is not something you pick up overnight. In fact, it takes four to five years of intensive hands-on experience in a physical therapy program at a university or college.

"Physical therapy students study a core of basic sciences—anatomy, physiology, bio-mechanics, exercise physiology and neuro-anatomy," explains Susan Roehrig, Ph.D., P.T., director of the physical therapy program at the State University of New York at Buffalo. "In addition they take courses in various physical therapy techniques such as rehabilitation, prosthetics and orthotics."

Upon graduation, students get their B.S. in physical therapy, but that

Help for What Ails You

"Physical therapists treat people from the nursery to the nursing home," says Susan Roehrig, Ph.D., P.T. "Sometimes we give short-term care. Seeing someone for two days to teach them how to use crutches is one example. And we also give long-term care. In the case of a serious head injury, for instance, we might work with a patient for years." A list of conditions that physical therapists care for—supplied by the American Physical Therapy Association—reads like a who's who of medical ailments.

• Musculoskeletal problems like rheumatoid arthritis and osteoarthritis.

• Fractures and dislocations of the hip, ankle, foot, wrist, shoulder and many more.

• Joint surgery involving the shoulder, elbow, hip, knee, ankle and wrist.

• Tears, sprains, bursitis, tendinitis. Often these conditions affect the shoulder, elbow, wrist, sacroiliac, hip, knee, ankle, back, or neck.

• Spinal disorders, including scoliosis and degenerative disk disease.

• Neurological problems such as stroke, transient ischemic attack, head injury, Parkinson's disease, multiple sclerosis, paraplegia, cerebral palsy and spina bifida.

• Peripheral neuropathy: conditions such as sciatica, Bell's palsy, carpal tunnel syndrome.

• Skin problems, including burns of the head, neck and extremities, skin ulcers and psoriasis.

• Cardiopulmonary diseases, such as coronary heart disease, chronic obstructive pulmonary disease, congestive heart failure, pneumonia, bronchitis, high blood pressure.

• Circulatory disorders, such as peripheral vascular disease, peripheral artery bypass, lymphedema.

• Systemic diseases, including diabetes, cancer, central nervous system problems, AIDS, osteoporosis and osteomyelitis.

---

still doesn't give them the right to use the initials P.T. after their name. "To practice on your own, you still have to pass a state licensing exam," she says.

Your First Visit

It's always the same music playing in the background. As you sit on one of the mauve and chrome chairs in the physical therapist's waiting room, your fingers tap out the rhythm to "Up, Up and Away." You look calm, reading the three-month-old copy of *Time*, but your mind is racing as you're about to face the music with the therapist. The only thing you're thinking is, "What is he going to do?"

"First you need to be evaluated," says Trzecki as he leads you into a small examining room. You sit up on the Naugahyde bench and nervously swing your feet. "I need to know what's bothering you. I need to get a per-

Finding a Physical Therapist

When choosing a therapist, Susan Roehrig, Ph.D., P.T., says it's important to look for one who is licensed because "the license assures you that your physical therapist meets certain minimal educational and practical standards."

Finding (and visiting) a physical therapist, though, might not be as easy as you think. It depends on where you live. Currently only one-third of the states allow you to find your own physical therapist directly through a system called "practice without referral."

In other words, in those states you can go to the physical therapist without seeing your doctor first, says Dr. Roehrig. "But if you live in the other two-thirds of the country, you'll need a physician's referral."

Let's say you live in a "without referral" state. How do you get started? Dr. Roehrig suggests that you let your fingers do the walking.

"Phone books in many areas only list *licensed* physical therapists," she says. "But check the directory heading carefully. If it says 'Physical Therapy Services,' the people listed there might not always be licensed."

Another approach is to call a hospital in your community that you trust, and have them recommend a physical therapist for you. Colleges and universities that have a physical therapy program—there are over 100 such programs nationwide—are also good sources for recommendations. The schools will sometimes give you the names of three or four physical therapists, which helps narrow the search.

Professional associations can also help. You might try contacting your state association of physical therapists. Or you can write or call the largest national association, The American Physical Therapy Association, 1111 N. Fairfax Street, Alexandria, VA 22314 (703) 684-2782.

Look to your own body for direction too. If you've hurt your arm pitching in the office softball game, for example, a physical therapist who specializes in sports physical therapy may be best. "What's important," says Dr. Roehrig, "is determining what type of physical therapy you need and then going to a facility that has the appropriate staff."

Currently the American Board of Physical Therapy Specialities recognizes six specialities: cardiopulmonary, electrophysiologic, neurologic, orthopedic, pediatric and sports physical therapy.

sonal history. How did the problem happen? When does it hurt? Does it hurt all the time? Does it hurt when I do *this*?"

Of course. That's why you try not to do that anymore. You think to yourself, "Hey, let's just forget this. I don't need that ankle anyway." But quickly and expertly, he takes your swollen foot into his hands, and gently begins flexing it.

"After the personal history, if the person has a joint problem, I focus in on that joint," he says. "I try to see if it is moving fully—not properly, but fully. Does it straighten out all the way and does it bend all the way? Is there a normal range of motion?" If not, the physical therapist can often devise a guided series of gentle exercises to increase mobility and lessen discomfort.

"People relate to being touched. People get better by being touched," Trzecki says. "The greatest thing physical therapists can offer people is that as practitioners we lay our hands on them, and we lay them on for an extended period of time."

"There are a variety of ways that physical therapists can help the people they see," adds Dr. Roehrig. "In some cases, they can do treatments that will cure the problem. In other cases where a cure is not available, they can help evaluate and control the pain, work to decrease muscle spasms and do other things that make living with pain easier."

THE HEALING POWER OF PHYSICAL THERAPY

Living with pain wasn't easy for 51-year-old Ethel Emmerson. She never really thought much about going up and down stairs till she developed leg problems. Then even a small riser seemed to loom ahead like Mt. Everest.

Ethel's problem was in her right knee. It felt like someone had glued sandpaper to the underside of her kneecap. "I was getting pain through the whole leg," she says. "I could hardly walk at all. I certainly couldn't walk up or down stairs normally."

She did manage to walk into Trzecki's physical therapy clinic. Stepping up to the examining table made her cringe in pain. But as the therapist sat on the stool in front of her and took her knee in his hand, she took the first step on the road to recovery.

"When we touch, we feel for a variety of things," Trzecki explains. "We check the contour—does the anatomy appear normal? We check the nervous system—is the patient able to feel and perceive? Is the texture of the skin and tissue normal? Are there lumps? Do the joints move as they should?"

Ethel's knee did, but it sure hurt. Every day the sandpaper under her kneecap got coarser. And that's where the problem was. She was diagnosed as having arthritis of the kneecap. Fortunately, arthritis is one of the problems that physical therapists can treat. "We work on treating the symptoms and trying to prevent further damage," says Dr. Roehrig. "For treating symptoms, we use heat or ice to decrease the pain. Then we show the person how to conserve energy by using larger joints instead of smaller joints whenever possible."

Twice a week Ethel came for physical therapy. The therapists used their hands, machines and education. "They taught me how to do special exercises," she says. "I work out at the clinic for about an hour and a half, and at home I lie down on a flat surface, put a coffee can under my knee and then raise my foot up and down."

The results? After three weeks of treatment, "the pain in my leg is completely gone. It really is. Just this morning I walked up the stairs normally with no problem."

Severe Back Pain

Walking up stairs was way out of Mary Smith's reach. Hers was a back pain very few know, and most would never want to know. The mere act of getting out of bed put her in agony. "When I got up in the morning it hurt real bad," she says. "My leg bothered me. My back tightened up. I couldn't even go to work for seven weeks."

Most days she couldn't even get out of bed. Shifting position on the pillow was all the pain she could bear. Finally, she put her back into the hands of a physical therapist. Three times a week for an hour and a half, "he massages my back, which feels great. It loosens up the muscles and it feels good."

The therapist also showed her some exercises she could do herself to help strengthen her back muscles. "I ride an exercise bike for eight minutes daily to help strengthen my lower back. At home I lay on the floor, straight out, and then I push up from my waist just using my hands. That also strengthens the lower part of my spine and helps me feel better."

Getting out of bed can still be a problem, but she says doing the exercises relieves the pain. And once up, she now has a place to go. "I'm going back to work. I can handle this pain now, and I can't wait to return."

Carpal Tunnel Syndrome

For some people, though, work *is* the problem. People who use their hands a lot at work—supermarket check-out personnel, for example—sometimes come down with a problem called carpal tunnel syndrome. The wrist is a boney area, densely packed with tendons, nerves and blood vessels. Space is at a premium, so it's easy to injure the structures in the wrist through oft-repeated motions.

In the early stages, you get a dull, achy feeling in your hand," says Susan Isernhagen, P.T., who specializes in occupational medicine and carpal tunnel syndrome. "As the problem progresses, you begin to get some numbness in the fingers. Your hand will ache at night even when you're not using it, and generally you will have a tingling feeling in it." Your hand may feel like it has gone to sleep, but it doesn't want to wake up.

"People whose occupation involves using their wrist a lot often get carpal tunnel syndrome," explains Isernhagen. "If you have to bend your wrist and twist it toward the little finger side often—using a screwdriver or typewriter or doing assembly work—you are compressing the carpal tunnel and making the tendons bend around a corner. After time inflammation may result."

The first thing a physical therapist will do is try to teach you other ways of moving your wrist. He may also show you an on-the-job exercise that will help relieve the symptoms. "You want to get the tension out of the muscles and restore the circulation," says Trzecki. "A slow, rhythmical, circular movement of the wrist will help the muscles relax. Relaxing your neck, shoulders and elbows may also help. But just doing the exercise for 30 seconds and then going right back to your original task won't help. Do it for a few minutes, or switch to some other task that doesn't require the same movement."

Tennis Elbow

As long as that task isn't playing a set of tennis. Then your problem may migrate up your arm and into your elbow. Your *tennis elbow*. But this inflammation of the extensor tendon in the elbow isn't just confined to tennis players.

"If the arm is used a lot, anyone can develop the problem," says Trzecki. "Bowlers get it. Secretaries get it. We even see it in kids who play lots of video games. It's basically an overuse syndrome."

If you've reached match point, and can't stand the pain anymore, you'll love the treatment you get from a physical therapist. "Generally we use thermal therapy, either hot or cold packs. Usually cold is applied in the acute stage," says Trzecki. You can also get a real charge out of other aspects of the treatment. "We use electrical stimulation to change the permeability of the cells and enhance blood circulation. It helps heal the inflammation more quickly," he says.

Knee Injury

Back, back, back, it's a long serve. You come up fast on the back line. You stop, pivot to set up your deadly forehand smash, and suddenly you crumble to the asphalt. Visions of yourself as Jimmy Connors quickly leave your head as you lie clutching your knee and screaming like John McEnroe.

Six weeks later the cast is off and you're back in your tennis shorts . . . mainly so that your physical therapist can see your knee better. Her grip on your knee shows more expertise than your grip on your tennis racket ever had.

"Oftentimes a therapist will use massage to break up adhesions around an injured joint," says Dr. Roehrig. "We use it to decrease muscle spasms. And we use our hands as a guide to show where we want the extremity to move. Through touch, we give input to the muscles, even showing the patient that this is the particular muscle we want to work, and helping him move it there."

Stroke Rehabilitation

Getting there, or anywhere can be a serious problem for someone who has suffered a stroke. Many times the victim is paralyzed on one side of the body. In other cases, movement is possible but the muscles are very weak.

Once the immediate crisis is over, one of the first people a stroke patient meets in the hospital is a physical therapist. "The sooner we can start working with someone who has had a stroke, the more likely we are to make a difference," says Pamela Duncan, P.T., assistant professor of physical therapy at Duke University School of Medicine and a hospital-based physical therapist.

"We teach the patient how to improve their activities of daily living. Wherever possible, we teach them to walk, to eat by themselves again, to dress themselves. And if the person has suffered just a mild stroke, we can help them get back to normal."

Each stroke patient is carefully evaluated and a specialized physical therapy program is designed. "Most of stroke rehabilitation involves a one-on-one hands-on approach," says Duncan. "We try to help them move when they may not be able to move for themselves. Many times telling a stroke victim to lift her arm may be asking her to do the impossible. So instead we try to assist the patient through the movement. We also do a series of muscle contractions. We structure the therapy so that in time they can start getting control of their extremities again. We guide them through movement patterns until they gain enough self control so that they can do it themselves."

Click.

The answering machine is turned on. The towels are folded and put away. The last patient walks out the door. Ken Trzecki walks up to the front window of his office and prepares to draw the curtains. He stops for a second to watch his last patient of the day—a knee patient—get into his small gray Toyota. Looking outside, staring through his reflection on the glass, he says, "You know, physical therapy teaches people to be independent, to find independence within their capabilities. Our goal is to see that the person can take care of himself—and no longer needs medical attention for his problem."

Using his once twisted leg, Trzecki's patient pushes the clutch in, puts the car in gear, and drives off into the rest of his life.

Chapter 31

POLARITY THERAPY

You can't see it. You can't feel it. But it's there—surrounding you, swirling through you as you laugh and dance and make out your grocery list. "It" is your life force, an invisible energy source that powers everything you think, feel and do, momentous or mundane. It is the inexplicable spark that makes you who you are.

At least that's what Randolph Stone, doctor of osteopathy, naturopathy and chiropractic, and developer of polarity therapy, believed. The late Dr. Stone based his system of healing upon numerous centuries-old writings about the nature of energy throughout the cosmos, and found some support in modern science as well. Everything in the universe, science says, consists of energy vibrating at varying speeds, from slowly vibrating rocks to incredibly quick-moving light rays. Somewhere between the two of these lies a particularly interesting energy form: human beings. Not only do you and your loved ones consist of vibrating energy but, polarity's theory continues, energy constantly flows around you and through you like a cascading waterfall.

Interesting, you may say, but big deal. Because what does all this talk of energy and vibrations have to do with treating sore muscles or leading a healthier, happier life? Plenty, say polarity therapists. Health and happiness, they believe, are directly linked to the smooth, vibrant and properly directed flow of your life energy. Pain and problems, in fact, are a sure sign of sluggish or obstructed energy flow. Clear up problems in your energy field, they say, and your body's natural healing powers automatically kick in to remedy your problems, whatever they may be.

"The better our energy currents flow, the better we're able to attract what we need to be healthy human beings," says Alan Siegel, a naturopathic physician (N.D.) who is director of the Polarity Therapy Center of San Francisco and vice-president of the American Polarity Therapy Association. "The body's ability to heal itself is very dramatic. I treat life energy, not disease. And it's life energy that heals, not me."

Go with the Flow

Energy flows in five currents through and around the body in certain predictable pathways, according to theories of polarity therapy. On the right side of the body, they move down the front of the body and up the back. On the left side, they are reversed. The head holds a positive charge and the feet a negative one.

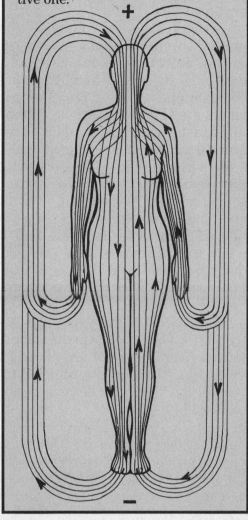

The Battery in Your Body

Energy flows along certain patterns in your body, Dr. Siegel explains, with specific areas holding positive or negative charges. Your head and the top parts of your body, for instance, are positive, while your feet and your lower body parts are negative. (See the box "Go With the Flow" for details.) To get obstructed energy released and properly balanced, polarity therapists involve their own energy—a powerful combination.

"It's like recharging a car battery," Dr. Siegel explains as you settle in for a test run of this unusual emergency roadside service. Stripped down to your underwear, you're lying faceup beneath a sheet on a padded table in his quiet office.

"I always use two hands. One of my hands is positive, the other is negative, like booster cables. Energy flows from my right hand to my left. When I place my hands on you, I am creating a current, stimulating *your* energy. I can place my hands on opposite polarity points anywhere on your body and create a current."

Sounds kind of dangerous, like being struck by lightning. You wonder if you're up for this, but too late. Dr. Siegel's booster cables—uh, hands —attach themselves to opposite sides of your neck. You brace for an electrifying shock, one that will really get your engine racing. But you feel . . . almost nothing.

"Yes, it's kind of subtle," one of

Dr. Siegel's clients will later tell you. To say the least. You feel a gentle touch but that's about it. He slides one hand under your neck, the other onto the center of your forehead and holds that position for a couple of minutes. He places one hand in the vicinity of your stomach, the other on your forehead, and pauses again. He moves to your feet, putting one hand on your ankle, the other on your toes. He gently tugs on each toe. Other than those tugs, you still feel not much of anything.

The bare-bones touch continues: One hand goes to the right side of your pelvis, the other to your left knee. One hand presses your shoulder while the other holds your finger. One hand grasps your wrist, the other painlessly tugs your fingers and they each make a popping sound—energy being released, Dr. Siegel explains. One hand squeezes your side just below your ribs, the other squeezes your lower arm. One thumb rests on the point between your eyes, the other presses into your belly button.

You turn onto your stomach. Dr. Siegel places one of his hands on the back of your neck and the other near the bottom of your spine and holds this position for a minute or two. He explains that he's balancing your chakras, five bundles of particularly intense energy along your spine which are said to govern specific organs of the body. One hand stays on your neck while he moves on one by one to the other chakras. At one point his hands begin to quiver slightly. It's your energy

vibrating, he tells you, not his hands moving. Good energy, he says. When he is finished, he brushes excess energy from your back in two or three long sweeps and wipes it off his hands in a basin in the corner. And you, who were unable to feel much of anything during the hour-long session, suddenly realize you're pleasantly wiped out, completely relaxed and quite uninterested in peeling yourself off the table anytime soon.

Others have been equally surprised. "I went with some skepticism at first," says Tony Pontin, vice president of a successful manufacturing company and one of Dr. Siegel's regular clients. "I lead a very busy, stressful life, which includes running every other day. To my amazement, after just a few visits I noticed I was running further and faster than I had done for some time. But beyond that, polarity gives me a remarkable sense of well-being. I'll have a session at the end of a day and go home to bed. The next day I feel more lively and energetic, more willing to face the world than I did the day before."

In some cases, the results of polarity sessions have been very dramatic. Regina Nash first tried one about 15 years ago. "That was a transformation for me," she says. "I made major changes in my life. Before, I was sort of a hippie, just bopping along. Suddenly, I gathered up my thoughts, opened up and changed my whole life." She goes in for a "tuneup" several times a year. "I have more direction in my life now and better relationships with people. And I'm more in tune with the world, less troubled by it."

Polarity therapy attempts to address the whole person—mind, body and spirit. As such, in addition to its hands-on aspects, it involves nutritional counseling (Dr. Stone encouraged a vegetarian diet), psychological counseling that emphasizes the power of positive thinking, and between-sessions exercises called polarity yoga. The degree of emphasis on any of these areas varies from practitioner to practitioner.

So does, as it turns out, the therapist's touch. Contrary to Dr. Siegel's gentle introduction, going to some polarity therapists might actually hurt. "There are people who think that in order to release energy blocks you have to put a stick of dynamite in the river," Dr. Siegel says.

Force or Finesse?

The gentle approach was perfected by the late Pierre Pannetier, N.D., student of Dr. Stone and Dr. Siegel's teacher and mentor. Dr. Pannetier, says Dr. Siegel, "worked with people he could hardly touch, people with burns and rheumatoid arthritis for whom the slightest touch was excruciating. He discovered that a person's life force could be released without using the kind of pressure Dr. Stone had used. I never use force. In fact, I could do a very effective session without touching the person at all. We are surrounded by energy. You don't need to touch the body to release it."

But other polarity therapists may apply a stimulating or deep touch, depending on their preference and what they sense is best for their client. "A treatment is based on the need of the client at the time," says Ray Castellino, D.C., a chiropractor and polarity therapist in Santa Barbara, California, who serves as president of the American Polarity Therapy Association. "The client's body constantly gives the therapist cues about what it needs. The skilled practitioner knows how to sense the client's pain threshold. In fact, pain serves a purpose. Sometimes it's good, even desirable. Deeper penetration of a muscle or a polarity point is sometimes needed. And this touch can bring the person to the other side of the pain."

"Polarity helped me learn to honor my pain, to grow through it," says client Celeste Wiedmann. Nearly paralyzed after being thrown from a horse, and retraumatized by an automobile accident following her partial recovery, Wiedmann came to see her pain as the source of important lessons about her life, lessons she grappled with during three years of polarity sessions with Dr. Castellino. Today, after being told by physicians that she would never walk again, Wiedmann is on her feet leading an active, painfree life.

"Deep work takes away a lot of the defensive 'armor' people wear," says Ayn Rose, a polarity therapist on the East Coast. "When people come to me and are very tight, I like to dig in. It's a relief for them."

One person who appreciates Rose's deeper work is Jeffrey Goldberg, owner of a chemical company in Boston. "It's not pleasant like massage," he says. "It's as if she is pushing buttons in me, pressing hard. Sometimes it is uncomfortable. Sometimes it hurts. But places she pushed hard three weeks ago—like my chronically tense and sore neck—you could push those spots today and the tension and pain are no longer there.

"And the results—they're incredible. My body and my mind both relax. After a session my wife says I'm nicer that day. I handle my work better. I seem to be able to handle crises in a more relaxed manner. My whole dis-position is less keyed-up. I try to go for a session every week, and I recommend it to others."

Finding a polarity therapist may take some searching. Dr. Castellino estimates there are somewhere between 400 and 500 practitioners with various degrees of training in the United States. Expect to pay between $25 and $100 for a one-hour session. The American Polarity Therapy Association (APTA) can help you find a practitioner through their national directory. You can, by the way, learn polarity on your own. "Anyone can do it," says Dr. Siegel, who wrote a book for this very purpose. (See the box "Polarity Resources" on this page for information on both the APTA and this book.)

Polarity Resources

The following books can provide additional insight into polarity therapy:

Health Building: The Conscious Art of Living Well by Randolph Stone (CRCS Publications).

Polarity Therapy: The Power That Heals by Alan Siegel (Prism Press).

For books, posters, video and audio tapes and information on polarity therapists in your area, contact the American Polarity Therapy Association, P.O. Box 44–154, Somerville MA 02144 (617) 776-6696.

THE HEALING POWER OF POLARITY THERAPY

Polarity therapy doesn't treat disease. It treats body energy. When body energy is balanced, pain and suffering may be alleviated.

All pain is blocked energy, says Dr. Siegel. Unblock the energy and the pain subsides. Polarity has proven beneficial for many types of pain, from the mild to the murderous.

Back and Neck Pain

"I've seen people suffering with such back pain that they could not walk and had to be carried in by friends," says Dr. Siegel. "After one treatment they got up and walked out the door." He concedes that not every person with back trouble responds so quickly. Sometimes it takes four or five sessions. "But once you get the life force unblocked, things can be very dramatic."

Tony Pontin, who originally came to Dr. Siegel for stress relief, has since discovered an additional benefit: relief from neck pain. "I have several impacted vertebrae in my neck from playing rugby rigorously for many years. This can get extremely painful," he says. Previously, he'd seen chiropractors and osteopathic physicians for manipulations, which helped. Then he told Dr. Siegel about the problem. "To my amazement, without any manipulations the same thing happens. I get up from his table and move my head and all the bones click and my neck is back in position. It's remarkable."

Cysts

Polarity therapist Ayn Rose says she's seen cysts disappear after a polarity session. "I treated a woman who had a cyst in her right hip, a few days before she was to go in for surgery to have it removed. Although she was pretty skeptical about polarity, she came in for a session, and when she went in for surgery, the cyst was already gone."

Menstrual Pain and Migraines

Menstrual cramps, too, can be alleviated with one treatment, says Dr. Siegel, as can bladder infections.

And migraine headaches, polarity therapists believe, are primarily digestive problems resulting from gas being trapped in blood vessels of the brain. This can also be connected to emotional problems. "When you get out of balance emotionally you don't digest your food as well," Dr. Siegel says. He treats migraines with a special release-of-gas treatment and reports a high success rate.

Emotional Problems

Practitioners say polarity can also help get at emotional problems, because balanced energy leads to balanced emotions. "Emotions are energy," says Dr. Siegel. "They have a higher vibration than the physical body, so are often the source of physical problems." One benefit is that "when people get their emotional energy unblocked, they express themselves more. They start telling the truth about how they feel," says therapist Ayn Rose. In addition to hands-on work, polarity therapy addresses emotions with its emphasis on positive thinking—teaching clients that, as Dr. Siegel puts it, "when you think more positively, when you're calm and relaxed in your thoughts, your body tends to move into that state of being."

Stress

Overall stress, both physical and emotional, is often relieved in the course of a polarity session. "The body becomes more flexible, supple and soft," says Ayn Rose. "The person gains more of a sense of himself, becomes more centered."

Aging

Some of the problems of aging, from arthritis to constipation, can be treated with polarity therapy. "As we grow older, the systems of our body just don't work as well," says Dr. Siegel. "Polarity can very gently help people fire up their energy." Energy problems can occur in infants as well, for whom pain or illness seems particularly disturbing. "You can put one hand on a baby's head and another on his feet and find he is balanced in a very short period of time," Dr. Siegel says.

Quick Recovery

Some people enjoy quick recovery from illness through polarity. Regina Nash checked in for a session with Dr. Siegel while suffering from a case of pneumonia. She could hardly lie down because of her coughing. Before the session's end she had stopped coughing, and her recovery overall was very rapid. Now she makes sure to get in for a session "if I feel I'm coming down with something. For instance, one day I had a fever, saw Dr. Seigel after work, and the next day woke up and was just fine."

Even pets can benefit from polarity therapy. Dr. Siegel says he used it to save the life of his cat, who was near death and diagnosed with leukemia. Polarity therapy sessions extended his feline's life by several years.

"Whatever the disorder, we're just treating the energy," Dr. Siegel notes. "If you get your life energy balanced, anything is possible."

ENERGIZING EFFECTS

Polarity therapists use a variety of techniques to boost energy and treat problem areas. Here are just a few examples. Feel free to practice with a friend. You might be surprised at the results.

31-3

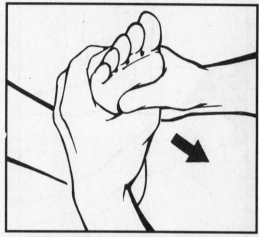

Leg pull. To free energy at the hip and lower back, stand at your partner's feet. Grasp the right foot with both your hands, palms overlapped at the instep, thumbs below the ball of the foot. Ask your partner to inhale. As she does, flex her foot as you bend it toward her head. Ask her to exhale. Just before she has exhaled all the air in her lungs, and with the foot still flexed, pull the entire leg toward you one inch in a short, quick pull. Hold this position for several seconds and release. Repeat on her left foot.

31-2

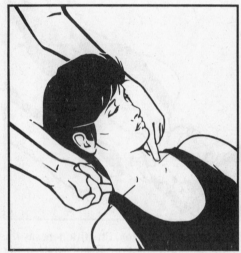

Releasing neck tension. With your partner lying on her back, sit behind her head. With the middle finger of your right hand reach as low down on the right side of her neck as you can, close to her spine. Gently press down. If the spot is sore, imagine a diagonal line running through the center of her neck from your finger to a spot on the front of her neck. Press this spot with the first finger of your left hand. That spot will probably be sore as well. Alternately stimulate both places very gently until the soreness disappears. Continue up the right side of her neck. When you reach the ridge of her skull, switch hands and repeat on the other side of her neck.

(continued)

ENERGIZING EFFECTS—*Continued*

31-4

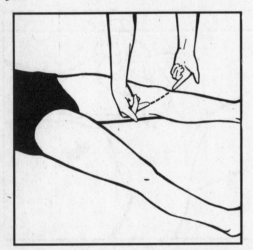

Knee pain treatment. To relieve pain caused by energy blocks in the knee. Sit beside your partner's knee. With the index finger of one hand, seek out sore spots on the top of the knee around the kneecap and around the inside and outside of the knee. When you find a sore spot, imagine a line through the center of the knee to the opposite side. With the middle finger of the other hand, find a sore spot in this area. Alternately stimulate each spot gently until the soreness disappears. Repeat on other sore spots. You may also use this treatment on elbows, wrists and other joints.

31-5

Lymphatic stimulation. Practitioners say this technique stimulates the lymph system, and may be beneficial for colds and swollen glands. Stand at your partner's right side while she lies on her back, her head turned to the left. Place your right thumb in her navel, pressing down in the direction of her right shoulder. At the same time, stimulate the top of her right shoulder by squeezing your fingers and the heel of your left hand together. Start at her neck and move down to her shoulder. Repeat five or six times while maintaining the navel contact. Then hold both contacts without stimulation for 30 seconds. Repeat these steps on her left side.

31-7

Front brushing. To balance the currents related to sensory functions of the body. Your partner should be seated with her hands on her thighs. Stand in front of her. Place your hands on her shoulders beside her neck. Brush your hands in one continuous motion out to her shoulders, down her arms and her legs. Repeat five to ten times. Do the last two or three brushes ½ inch from her body.

31-6

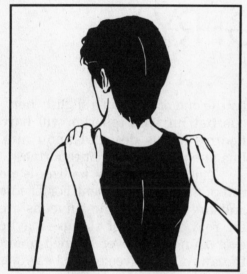

Back brushing. To balance the energy currents related to motor functions of the body. Your partner should be seated. Stand behind her and place your hands on her shoulders. Bring your hands toward one another and cross them at her spine and neck. Then brush the body down on either side of the spine to her buttocks. Uncross your hands and repeat five to ten times. Brush in a gentle, continuous movement. Try doing the last two or three brushes ½ inch from the body and see if you can feel her energy.

Chapter 32

PSYCHIC SURGERY

It is said that from the grassy hills of Luzon, the largest island in the Philippines, come men of unusual powers. Like birds that can fly without wings, these men are said to perform surgery without scalpels. They are said to enter the bodies of their patients using only their hands. They are called *psychic surgeons.*

Reverend Pedro Sanchos, commonly known as Brother Pedro or simply Pedro, is well known in the Philippines. He has followers in Japan, Korea, Mexico, Canada and the United States. (In a few of these countries, where his activities are illegal, Pedro would rather his name *not* be well known. So it has been changed for this story at his request.)

Many first- and second-hand accounts tell of his hands dipping into people's bodies, coming out bloody, clutching diseased tissues and organs.

By the end of this day, a slightly nervous but intrepid reporter will have Pedro's hands descend upon him. Imagine yourself as that reporter.

This, you quickly realize, is no run-of-the-mill assignment. For if Pedro and the other psychic surgeons are for real, then most things—maybe everything—you ever learned about the laws of the universe must be wrong. But of course, the world was once thought flat, so you try to remain open-minded.

What Pedro does is seemingly a form of faith healing, and even the medical establishment these days admits the importance of faith in healing. The problem is that it's generally the *patient's* faith that seems to matter, not the surgeon's. Psychic surgeons, however, appear to operate independently of their patients' beliefs. Besides, how do you explain the blood and guts?

Linda B____ serves as Pedro's assistant while he is in this country. She decides who will see Pedro and who won't. You contact Linda, but she is wary. Pedro awaits trial in California, where he is accused of practicing medicine without a license, and you could be a law enforcement officer. You assure her that you are not, that you only want to write a story. After numerous reassurances, she arranges a meeting.

An Investigation into Hands-*In* Healing

You pull up to an attractive home in suburban New Jersey. It's a nice Sunday afternoon, and there's a crowd out front. Cars with license plates from New York, Connecticut and Pennsylvania fill the street. You're told that about 150 people will be healed by Pedro by the end of his three-day stay.

In front of the house you meet Peter. He tells how Pedro once removed a tumor from his wife's breast. Now the couple has returned because they want a baby, and have had no luck. "I think he make my sperm stronger," says Peter, a recent Russian immigrant. How? "He go in me, he put his whole finger in, and he pull something out. Incredible."

Other people you meet on the front porch tell their stories. "I believe in Pedro more than 200 doctors," says one heavily accented man resting on a cane, who says he has seen Pedro several times in the past.

You enter the house. It smells of incense and coffee, but mostly eucalyptus. A tape player emits a mellow song—a Sanskrit mantra, you are told. A young woman in blue jeans collects money (suggested donation: $45), asks newcomers to sign a release, and hands out little numbered entrance tickets.

Pedro takes a break soon after you arrive. He is a small man with dark muscular arms extending out from his blue dress shirt, sleeves rolled up to the elbows. He smiles shyly and shakes your hand. His English is so-so. After an informal introduction and a pleasant lunch of Philippine chicken, you are invited to witness your first psychic surgery and are ushered into a small room. It reeks of eucalyptus.

An old refrigerator, two yellow chairs, dozens of plastic foam cups, oodles of cotton balls, piles of towels, a large green plastic trash bag and a table draped with a pink polka-dotted plastic sheet decorate the room. On the table lies Tom, a 25-year-old man complaining of pain in his lower spine.

Pedro gingerly strokes Tom from head to toe, in the same way you might pet a horse's nose. Nurse-aide Linda stands at Tom's head, cupping her hands over his scalp without touching it. After about a minute of this, Tom is asked to turn over onto his stomach. More stroking. The psychic surgeon's hands reach the lower spine, the trouble point.

Linda hands Pedro a foam cup. He pulls out what looks like a little white egg, or maybe a big round cotton ball. He places it on Tom's spine and a red fluid immediately oozes out. Pedro's hands dig deep. So do your eyes. Psychic surgeon hands and intrepid reporter eyes wrestle over the patient's spine for about 15 seconds. Pedro points out to you that his sleeves are rolled up. "No magic," he says.

Then he pulls out from Tom's spine—or *seemingly* pulls out from Tom's spine—a slug-sized red glob. What is it? "Something the body doesn't need," says Pedro, waving the little something for a moment in front of Tom's eyes, then tossing it into the cup. You ask again. "It's a physical manifestation of an ill spirit," says Linda.

Pedro and his assistant prepare for their next patient. The mysterious glob gets passed out the door to another assistant. She moves to scoop it into the kitchen garbage disposal. You ask if you can have it. She is reluctant, but gives it to you—with a warning: "It will probably disappear on you. It comes from another dimension, you know."

Still some time before *your* surgery. You pass the time with several other patients. "The first time Pedro worked on me, it was a miracle," says one 30-year-old woman wearing a large crystal pendant and a diamond nose ring. "I felt a tingling, a kind of high. It was unreal." Following that operation,

An Interview with Brother Pedro

What follows is a brief discussion with "Pedro Sanchos," who is a self-described psychic surgeon from the Philippines.

Question: Brother Pedro, how did you get into psychic surgery?
Pedro: My grandfather, my father, and many of my uncles are psychic surgeons. I started when I was five years old. People would pay me in marbles. Later, I tried to stop healing. I got very sick. A voice told me if I didn't go out and help as many people as I could then I would not get well.

Question: Can anyone learn to do what you do?
Pedro: It's like playing the piano. Anyone can learn, but some are born gifted. The gift runs in my family.

Question: What is it like operating with only your hands?
Pedro: When I operate, I feel electricity in my hands. Any negativity in the body will attract them like a magnet. When I find it, the negativity just pops up into my hands.

Question: This stuff that comes out of the body, what is it?
Pedro: Scientists back in Manila tried to analyze it. They said they could not tell what it was. Of course they could not. It comes from the body, but it is not of the body—it is of the spirit.

she says that her lost psychic powers returned.

Leka, a 28-year-old woman suffering from a recently diagnosed thyroid tumor, tells you she came because she's desperate. "I felt he really was psychic," she says of her encounter with Pedro. "I know a lot of these guys fake their effects using chicken gizzards, but I feel this guy is real. And even if there is a little showmanship," she adds, "is it such a sin to do something to augment someone's faith?"

Your turn. Pedro leans over you and starts to stroke. Other patients told you he can go right to your problem. With you, he misses. You help him out by telling him about your recent bouts of heartburn.

You are turned onto your back, and Pedro goes right for the tummy. He reaches for a cup. Since you've already witnessed what's going to come next at least ten times (and none varied very much from the first), you decide to close your tired intrepid reporter eyes and relax. Others today have told you about feelings of being "entered," and of "altered states of consciousness" on Pedro's table. You feel only a man's fingers pushing against your belly.

Regardless, Pedro finds something. "Want to look?" asks Linda. You pass.

A Messy Monday

Usually by 1:30 in the morning you've long since drifted off to blissful sleep. But this morning you're lying on a hotel bed somewhere outside of Hackensack, New Jersey, squeezing little packets of McDonald's fancy ketchup over your stomach. You're kneading it, pressing it, curling your fingers and pushing your knuckles hard into your tummy. You're playing to an imaginary audience, trying to make it think that you're piercing the skin with your hand.

The audience is unimpressed. No matter. The point of this exercise in condiment application is to determine if you need to call your eighth-grade science teacher, Mr. Meunkle, to tell him that everything he ever taught you was wrong.

According to two M.D.'s that Linda puts you in touch with later in the

Psychic Surgery Resources

Of all the techniques described in this book, psychic surgery is one of the most open to question. The practice is illegal in the United States, so we don't recommend that you seek out such a healer. The Philippine consulate in New York, however, does provide a directory of practicing psychic surgeons in that country to those seekers who are determined and willing to travel. It is said that Brazil also boasts a good number.

day, maybe you should call Mr. Meun-kle. Dr. Martin Dayton of Miami Beach and Dr. C. Norman Shealy of Spring-field, Missouri, say they've both wit-nessed psychic surgeons at work and are fairly certain there was no trickery.

But according to the chief of pa-thology at a large Pennsylvania medi-cal center, with whom you hook up later in the day, you needn't disturb Mr. Meunkle. The contents of your foam cup (which never did disappear into another dimension) have been analyzed. "It looks more animal than human," he says. "Probably chicken."

Linda is upset and angry when she learns that the glob was given to you instead of deposited into the gar-bage disposal as intended. "How could you do this? It's a very spiritual thing. It can't be analyzed in a laboratory. Pedro would never allow you to have a sample. You've got to judge him by the results he gets."

And you're forced to admit, judg-ing from the results of your own sur-gery, that there just may be something to Pedro's powers. For despite Linda's stern reprimands for taking the cup to the lab, you are experiencing no heartburn.

Chapter 33

REFLEXOLOGY

You say, "Ooooch! Ahhh!"

Reflexologist Ki Tomlinson says, "That's the adrenals. They have a lot to do with stress, and tenderness is common there."

You say, "Unnhhh! Ahhhh!"

Tomlinson says, "That's the right side of your neck. People develop a lot of tension from holding their heads wrong, clenching their jaws."

You say, "Ahhh!"

Tomlinson says, "Are you falling asleep? Go right ahead."

You say, "Oooh! Ahhh!"

Tomlinson says, "Been having a problem with the back of your head?"

You say, "Well, my little girl hit me there with her Chatty Kathy doll."

Treatment from the Bottom Up

Tomlinson is "working" your feet with reflexology. You're lying on her table, listening to restful music. She began the treatment by stretching and massaging your feet with a light cream, then powdered them to dry them off.

All you had to do was lie there, "take a deep breath through your nostrils, chest and abdomen, hold it as long as comfortably possible, then very slowly exhale. Let go of the day, all worries and concerns," Tomlinson commanded in a soft, even, calming voice. "Breathe deeply again, slowly exhale. And a third time. Empty your mind. Now visualize a time in your life in which you experienced your greatest health, well-being and happiness. Focus on that time for a few minutes."

A few minutes passed. "I'm still trying to find it," you murmured, struggling to remain awake. Several times Tomlinson pushed in on a point on the sole of your foot said to correspond to the solar plexus—"a key point for relaxation," she said. "It seems to slow the breathing down." You agreed,

241

but only to yourself. You couldn't seem to find the words.

Finally you remembered the period of your life when you felt your best. "Now bring your awareness back to the present," Tomlinson said, "and carry that peaceful feeling with you throughout the session."

And despite occasional twinges from the pressure, you find it remarkably easy indeed to retain that feeling, to the point of snoozedom. The hour drifts by, the session is over, you sit up refreshed. As you walk toward your car, you find yourself bouncing along the pavement, as if gravity had lost its grip.

These Feet Are Made for Talking

As you bounce, you find yourself marveling at how Tomlinson could tell where your body is stressed and strained. After all, she was pressing her thumbs (with their ironlike grip) into different parts—and finding all the sore points—of your *feet*. That's a long way from your head, neck or adrenals.

For every *-ology* there's a theory. Reflexology teaches that every part of the body has a direct line of communication to a reference point on the foot, hand and ear. In a nutshell, your feet may be far from the center of your being, but they have a loud, clear yodel. (The reference points of both

33-1

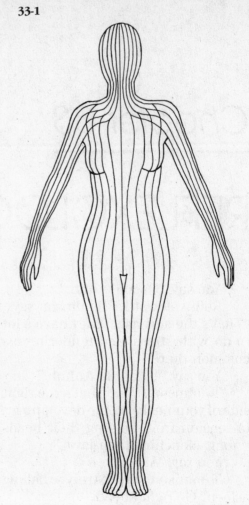

The theory of body zones is fundamental to reflexology. There are ten zones, each ending in one of your toes. Each part of your anatomy —from head to toe—is associated with a zone.

feet are mapped in the illustration on page 243.)

By massaging these reference points, reflexologists say they are helping the corresponding body parts heal themselves through improved circulation, elimination of toxic by-products

33-2

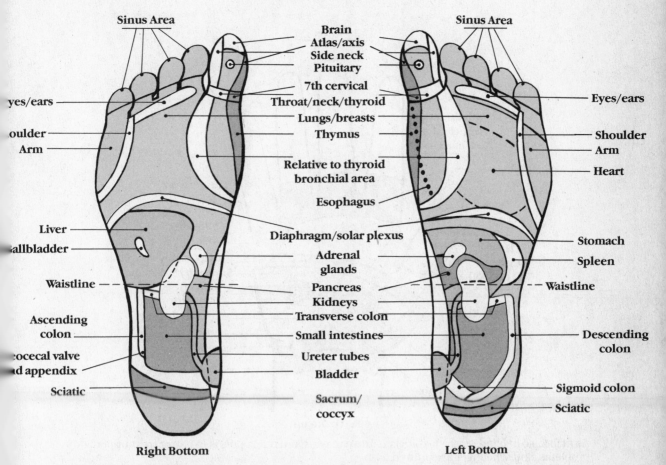

Sinus Area

Brain
Atlas/axis
Side neck
Pituitary
7th cervical
Throat/neck/thyroid
Lungs/breasts
Thymus

Relative to thyroid
bronchial area

Esophagus

Diaphragm/solar plexus
Adrenal
glands
Pancreas
Kidneys
Transverse colon
Small intestines
Ureter tubes
Bladder
Sacrum/
coccyx

Sinus Area

Eyes/ears
Shoulder
Arm
Heart

Stomach
Spleen
Waistline

Descending
colon

Sigmoid colon
Sciatic

yes/ears
oulder
Arm

Liver
allbladder

Waistline

Ascending
colon

cocecal valve
d appendix

Sciatic

Right Bottom **Left Bottom**

Each zone terminates in the foot, and each organ, gland, bone, or muscle found in a particular zone has its reflex point in the corresponding zone of the foot. The heart point is in the left foot, the gallbladder in the right foot.

and overall reduction of stress. Gratefully, your body responds with better functioning.

"It's just a gateway into the energy and organ systems of the body," says Ronald Hoffman, M.D., medical director

33-3

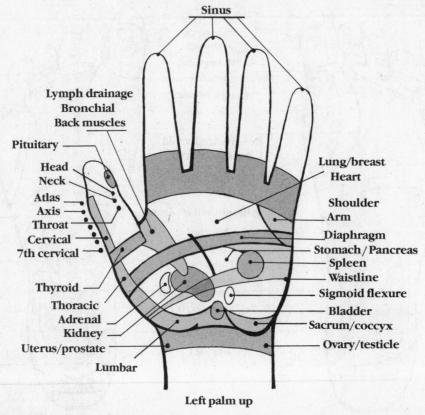

Left palm up

As in foot, so in hand, say reflexologists. You can use hand reflex points to better treat upper body problems, and when feet are injured.

of the Hoffman Center for Holistic Medicine in Manhattan. "The foot is a homunculus—a little human. So are the hand and the ear." (For complete maps of hand and ear reference points, see the illustrations above and on page 246.)

So reflexology is scientifically sound? "I think the scientific basis remains to be better established," Dr. Hoffman says. "But it's easier to establish the basis for a connection between the ear and the digestive system. There's definitely documentation which suggests that if you press certain points on the outer ear, you have a concrete effect on the vagus nerve regulating digestion, heartbeat and appetite. The sensation of pain to the ear can actually make you vomit. So I think reflexology has scientific validity that hasn't been discovered yet. It's an empirical science—it's been researched in the clinic, not the laboratory."

Dr. Hoffman describes himself as hard-nosed and scientific. "Once you're trained as a doctor, you tend to think like a doctor. But I've seen healing happen in patients I've turned over to Ki Tomlinson and others." He's seen sufficient results that "four or five times a week" he refers patients to Tomlinson or other reflexologists.

"If someone with syphilis comes into my office, I won't say, 'Well, why don't you try reflexology?' Instead, I'll treat them immediately with conventional therapy, which in this case is penicillin," Dr. Hoffman says.

"But if someone with a bizarre irritable bowel syndrome has undergone thousands of dollars in tests, and we've ruled out parasites and cancer and other things, and the person still has recurrent abdominal pain, and the next suggestion is to use medication, which may cause drowsiness or can potentially alter the body's mineral balance, then why not try reflexology?"

At that question, your feet jump to their ... uh ... feet. "Yeah, why not?" they clamor. "We don't get a lot of attention. But we sure do carry around a lot of weight in this gravity-intense, concrete-paved, shoe-encased world."

Dr. Hoffman agrees with your feet. "The feet are such an important part of the body," he says. "That's where we get our grounding impulses from, where the rubber meets the road. But so often our contact with the world through our feet is a harsh kind of painful and insulated contact. We've lost the really sensual aspect of touching the earth because of shoes and pavement. There's obviously a lot of energies to be delivered through the soles of the feet. Animals tune into earth energies through their feet, which have exquisitely sensitive pathways. So it stands to reason we could signal the body by pressing points down there."

Are Your Feet All in Your Mind?

Even without scientific evidence of pressure points in the feet linked to organs several feet up, there seem to be other reasons why reflexology might be your kind of hands-on healing.

There's the well-documented placebo effect—whereby our belief in the power of a treatment, *any* treatment, can sometimes bring results. "And there's the concern, the interpersonal contact, the tactile sensation, the relaxation created by the friendly ministrations of the therapist," says Dr. Hoffman. "That enables a lot of healing to occur in the body."

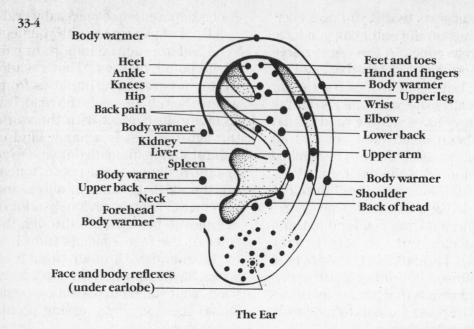

33-4

Body warmer
Heel
Ankle
Knees
Hip
Back pain
Body warmer
Kidney
Liver
Spleen
Body warmer
Upper back
Neck
Forehead
Body warmer
Face and body reflexes
(under earlobe)

Feet and toes
Hand and fingers
Body warmer
Upper leg
Wrist
Elbow
Lower back
Upper arm
Body warmer
Shoulder
Back of head

The Ear

The ear also contains reflex points for the entire body. Because of its small size, specific areas are harder to treat, but it's easier to treat the entire body simply by squeezing various warming points between thumb and index finger for several seconds.

Dr. Hoffman believes reflexology works for some people in part precisely because these people are able to accept the possibilities. "If a patient responds to this therapy involving hands being laid on with guidance and support and energy, many of these pain syndromes will respond," he says. "Hands-on healing is a much more healing ministration than just giving a patient a prescription. And reflexology in particular is a gentle, supportive, aesthetic kind of massage which is directed at supporting a certain part of the body."

In other words, let your body know you care, and your body will take it from there. Reflexologists believe your hands can speak a kind of sign language to your feet (or your hands or your ear). Your feet, in effect, become eyes and ears tuned into a healing message.

The message is the massage.

Healing or Helping?

Although Dr. Hoffman says he's seen reflexology cure people, reflexologists themselves do not make that claim. "We never claim to cure any condition. Only the body itself can do that," says Manhattan reflexologist Laura Norman, director of Laura Norman and Associates Feet First Reflexology Center.

Nor can reflexologists claim to diagnose illness. "But if there's some soreness in a reflex point it can indicate some sort of imbalance," Tomlinson says. "It doesn't have to be a chronic imbalance. It could be only temporary. Or it could be something serious. My sister is also a reflexologist, and while she was working on one man's foot the area corresponding to the pancreas was so tender she couldn't even touch it. She suggested he have his pancreas checked, which he did. The doctors discovered a tumor there. So if a point is extremely painful you might want to have the corresponding organ checked."

Look at reflexology as a way to help your body heal itself, says Norman, who is a licensed massage therapist and author of *Feet First: A Guide to Foot Reflexology,* a self-help book. "I never guarantee to cure anything, but I *can* guarantee to reduce stress and help people relax. Relaxation is the key to better health and well-being."

Healing is a step-by-step process. "When people relax," Norman says, "their circulation improves because relaxation reduces vascular constriction so blood can flow more freely. This helps to break up crystal deposits caused by excess uric acid. These deposits settle throughout the body, but especially in the feet, thanks to our old friend gravity. And because the feet are farthest from the heart, blood tends to stagnate there. Reflexing the feet helps improve circulation, and the direct pressure on the feet also helps to break up the calcium deposits."

Feet Are Steps Ahead

Circulation and crystals aside, are there any advantages to reflexology over other forms of massage? And why reflex your feet instead of hands or ears?

Norman believes there's no beating the feet. As a New York State-licensed massage therapist, she's tried shiatsu and many other touch therapies for her clients' conditions. "In most cases," she says, "I've found I've had the best, most powerful results with reflexology, working mainly the feet, and sometimes the hands."

A major advantage of foot reflexology, Norman says, "is that it's not stressful or intrusive. Intrusive is a very important word here. A lot of people are very self-conscious or uptight about their bodies. They don't feel as safe having to take off all their clothes as having to take off just their shoes and socks. They can relax more deeply, knowing I'm just at their feet and that I'm not going any further. In a full-body massage, a person might follow along with me, thinking, 'OK, now she's on my legs, next she'll be on my arms. Is she going to touch my breasts? Is she going to take the towel off my rear end? Are my thighs going to bounce?' "

Then there's the matter of time and mess. "In a massage, people are time-conscious about having to get undressed and oiled up and then having to shower off so they don't get their clothes oily," Norman says.

Reflexology is also an advantage when there's an injury to a part of the body. "Sometimes if someone has a problem in a particular area—like their back or shoulder—it could be painful working on that site directly as you would in a massage," she says. "Working directly on an inflamed area can aggravate it more. But it doesn't help the injury or soreness to completely ignore it either. With reflexology you can work on that part of the body indirectly through the feet. It's always safe, unless there's an injury to the feet."

Which brings us to the times when hands or ears have a reflexological (we made that word up) advantage over the feet. "When there's an injury to the foot, you don't want to work right on that injury," Norman says. "Since the hands and feet directly correspond—we call it referral—we can work the corresponding area in the hand and get the same benefit as if we were working the feet.

"Or if there's an upper body problem, affecting the head, neck or shoulders, the hand is more useful because it's closer to those areas. It doesn't mean you shouldn't work the foot as well as the hand, but you might want to combine working the hand and foot. And vice versa if the problem is in the lower part of the body."

Finally, the hands don't need to be reflexed as much as the feet for a simple reason. "We use our hands in our work and our daily activities," Nor-man says. "We even work out crystalline deposits when we pick up or grab things." Every day your hands are getting naturally reflexed.

Reflexing Yourself

"My vision is for everybody to be doing this on each other and themselves," Norman says. "I work on my own feet for five minutes every night."

All you have to do is sit comfortably in a quiet place, Norman advises. Apply a light, absorbent, greaseless lotion and massage your feet. Then apply powder and continue massaging until all the lotion is gone. (When you start reflexing, you don't want your hands to slide off.)

Grasp the ankle, heel or toes of one foot firmly in one hand, place the thumb of your other hand on the sole of your foot at the heel, and apply steady, even pressure with the edge of your whole thumb. Keep the thumb slightly bent at the joint and use a forward, caterpillar-like motion. This is called thumbwalking: Press one spot, move a little forward, press again, and so on.

When you reach the toes, start again at a new spot on the heel. Continue until the entire bottom of the foot has been worked. Then do the top of the foot, using your fingers to do fingerwalking.

Work the entire foot twice this way. Then return to sensitive areas

Reflexology Resources

You can probably find a reflexologist in your area through a physician who practices holistic medicine. Others likely to know of reflexologists are osteopathic physicians, chiropractors and massage therapists.

Another good source of information is the International Institute of Reflexology, which has trained about 50,000 reflexologists in the last 30 years. It presents seminars and workshops worldwide. Write the institute at P.O. Box 12642, St. Petersburg, FL 33733–2642.

Reflexologists have written several books describing their approach. They include:

Better Health With Foot Reflexology by Dwight C. Byers (available through the International Institute of Reflexology).

Body Reflexology: Healing at Your Fingertips, Helping Yourself with Foot Reflexology, and *Hand Reflexology: Key to Perfect Health,* all by Mildred Carter (Parker).

Feet First: A Guide to Foot Reflexology by Laura Norman (Simon & Schuster).

Hand and Foot Reflexology: A Self-Help Guide (Prentice-Hall), *The Complete Guide to Foot Reflexology* (Prentice-Hall) and *Hand Reflexology Workbook* (Simon & Schuster), all by Kevin and Barbara Kunz.

How to Heal Yourself Using Hand Acupressure (Hand Reflexology) by Michael Blate (Falkynor Books).

and gently work them. When working harder-to-reach spots, use the hook-and-back-up technique: You hook your thumb into a specific point and back it up towards your wrist. Don't slide the thumb on the skin—move only the underlying tissue.

Visiting a Reflexologist

"Except for injuries and serious illness, there are no contraindications for reflexology," Norman says. "People on medication who are going to have full sessions should take precautions and should get their doctor's approval first. And they should monitor their condition carefully, informing their doctor about how they're feeling so medication can be adjusted if necessary. And they must continue with regular reflexology sessions even when their condition is stabilized."

A session usually ranges from $25 to $100 per hour, Norman says. Often reflexologists will offer package deals —six sessions for the price of five, for instance.

Norman recommends regular sessions "in the interests of preventive health care. If there's a particular condition we're trying to help, anywhere from one to three sessions a week is advisable. If it's for relaxation and prevention, once every other week may be enough."

THE HEALING POWER OF REFLEXOLOGY

As many illnesses and conditions as there are, that's how many problems reflexologists claim to be able to help. That's because their hands-on healing art is designed to help the body do its own healing.

A complete list of disorders is too long to include here: A book by Dwight C. Byers of the International Institute of Reflexology in St. Petersburg, Florida, names problems beginning with acne, ending with wrist sprains or fractures, and including (among many others) alcoholism, bedwetting, constipation, diabetes, fatigue, high blood pressure, kidney stones, multiple sclerosis, pyorrhea, shingles, urinary trouble, and whiplash.

Norman, Tomlinson, and Dr. Hoffman are full of stories about how reflexology has proved useful in a wide range of problems.

Kidney Stone Relief

Television talk show host Regis Philbin became a client of Norman's when "he was in the hospital for kidney stones, and was scheduled for surgery the next morning," she recalls. "I visited him there and worked on him for about an hour, and he passed the stone within 12 hours. He didn't need surgery."

Sometime later Philbin invited Norman to appear on his show and treat him for a swollen salivary gland "that was popping out on his neck like a little golf ball," she says. "I worked on him right on the show for a few minutes, and gave him a full session after the show. By showtime the next day the swelling had disappeared."

Tomlinson tells the story of a ten-year-old girl "having migraine headaches about every two months. I treated her a couple of times, and the migraines decreased in frequency. I think if she had come in regularly, they might have disappeared completely."

The Case of the Irritable Bowel

Dr. Hoffman was treating a 40-year-old, hard-driving professional man, "very skeptical and rational," for irritable bowel syndrome. "It's a nonspecific intestinal problem that can be really debilitating," he says. "The man felt completely out of control and powerless in dealing with it. He'd already seen a gastroenterologist for tests. We assessed his digestion, tried digestive aids, even manipulated his diet and found he wasn't allergic to anything. We treated him for *Candida*, which often causes bloating and gas, and that didn't work. We worked on his style of eating. We tried stress reduction and relaxation, and that didn't take.

"Almost in desperation I said, 'Go to a reflexologist, and who knows? Maybe that'll work.' And somehow it did!"

A Burst of Creativity

Lacey Ann Brady (not her real name), a 31-year-old public relations worker in Philadelphia, turned to reflexology five years ago when she found herself emotionally stressed, overweight and "not too healthy. I'd heard of Laura Norman, so I went for a treatment. I loved it. I went to La-la Land right on the table."

Brady began getting weekly treatments. "I lost 30 pounds within six months," she says. "It just fell off. I can't swear that reflexology did it all, but I can tell you that my life became much easier. I was less stressed, and I had less reason to overeat."

As a writer, she often finds her creativity blocked. "So I go get a reflexology session," Brady says. "It opens me up. It's almost as if they go into your mind with a spoon and unclog the parts of your brain that aren't functioning 100 percent. The day after a session I'll bolt out of bed ready to go for hours and days. I've learned to get in touch with my body in a way I never had before. Reflexology gave me a whole new perspective. The sessions felt so good that I was motivated to improve my health and to take my life in hand."

Severe Back Pain

Manhattan businesswoman Alexis Chasman had been having severe lower back and sciatica-like pain. At one point she was bedridden for two months. "During my recovery exploration process," she says, "I went to orthopedists and osteopathic physicians, I had x-rays and CAT scans, and there never was a definitive diagnosis. It was painful and frightening."

Then Chasman visited a podiatrist who prescribed orthotic inserts for her shoes—"which helped a great deal"—and recommended she visit a reflexologist—Laura Norman. The first session gave her "the deepest form of relaxation I've ever experienced," she says. "It was also better for me at the time than direct hands-on bodywork that would have involved touching and moving inflamed areas. Norman worked with points on my feet that really seemed to correspond with my back, in a way that was painless and effortless for me—not like the physical therapy I was going through three or four times a week."

Chasman sees reflexology as "one of the integral parts in my recovery process." Even after she improved, she held onto reflexology as a way to relax and maintain her health.

REFLEX ACTION

For beginners as well as experienced practitioners, reflexology is a matter of learning where to press. Here are some of the basics.

33-5

Massage the feet to relax them and improve circulation before you begin reflexing. Use a light, absorbent cream. Rotate your thumbs over the entire foot as shown. Then firmly squeeze the whole foot from top and bottom, and from side to side.

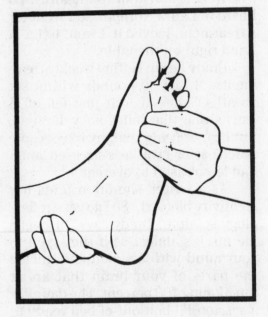

33-6

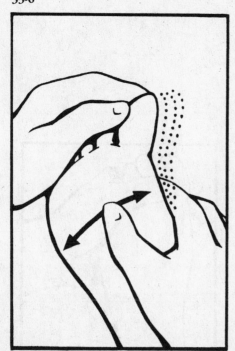

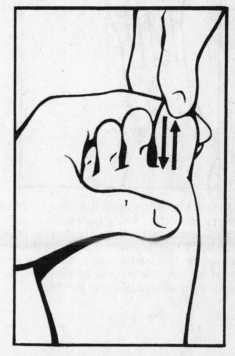

33-7

This technique is especially good for relaxation. Put your thumb on the diaphragm reflex point as shown, angling up under the metatarsal bones. Lift the foot by the toes with your other hand and pull the foot onto your thumb. Back off, then move your thumb a fraction of an inch toward the outside of the foot and again pull the foot onto your thumb. Repeat until you reach the outside. Change hands, put your thumb on the central reflex point, and repeat the motions, this time moving your thumb toward the inside of the foot.

To improve the functioning of eyes and ears, reflexologists suggest working the inside of the big toe of each foot from tip to base.

(continued)

REFLEX ACTION—*Continued*

33-8

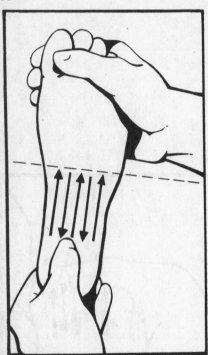

To relieve indigestion, work the intestinal reflex points. Hold the foot as shown, and "walk" your thumb from the lowest part of the reflex area up to the "waistline." Begin at the outside of the foot, and return to the base after you reach the waistline, repeating this motion until you reach the inside of the foot.

33-9

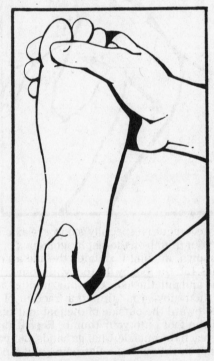

To ease sciatic pain in the lower back, hold the foot as shown; be sure to keep it straight up. Work the thumb along the reflex area from one side of the foot to the other.

Chapter 34

REICHIAN THERAPY

Laura broke down and cried. A big, sobbing, body-wracking cry unlike anything she'd had in years. And as she cried, great walls of emotional defenses built up over half a lifetime came tumbling down around her, and it felt good, so she cried some more.

The psychotherapist stopped kneading Laura's chest at that point, satisfied that the session had gone far enough today. Under her touch, Laura had been able to release a good deal of the chronic muscular tension—the "body armor"—that had gripped her chest and kept her from feeling anything inside for so long.

The therapist slowly removed her hands from Laura's body and sat back on the edge of the mattress. She talked to Laura in soothing tones, encouraging her to acknowledge the pain inside and let it go.

A Different Drummer

To those not acquainted with Reichian therapy, something must seem very wrong with the above scenario. After all, touching a patient's partially clothed body during a therapy session would be considered highly unethical in most forms of analysis. Psychotherapy has always been a hands-off medical discipline.

But to those who practice this body-oriented style of analysis, a different drummer beats and a different philosophy rules. To them, the mind cannot be divorced from the body, and emotional healing cannot be brought about by talk alone. The hands are needed.

Some consider that guiding philosophy as radical today as it was when psychiatrist Wilhelm Reich first advocated it more than 50 years ago. Reich was an Austrian-born protégé of the great Sigmund Freud.

But unlike Freud, who remained wedded to the Victorian idea of denying the body, Reich argued that we *are* our bodies. Whereas Freud didn't believe in looking at his clients—let alone touching them, Reich faced his

A Medical Maverick

Wilhelm Reich died in a federal prison here in the United States. He was a victim, some claim, of his own ideas and practices in a world that wasn't ready to hear what this influential man had to say.

What Reich had to say often centered around open sexuality, which he strongly advocated. At other times it centered around American medical practices, which he strongly condemned—going so far as to allege active collusion between drug companies and doctors. That charge did little to endear him to his professional peers, or to the Food and Drug Administration (FDA), which eventually won an injunction against his books.

In 1954 a federal court ordered his books burned, and Reich was sent to prison a short time later for selling "Orgone accumulators" to the public. Reich claimed his accumulators could increase energy flow in the human body, but the FDA cried fraud. It had him jailed when one was shipped across state lines in violation of a court order. He died in 1957 two days before his parole hearing.

clients and used his hands in an attempt to break down tense muscle tissue and free restricted emotions.

For Reich believed that the body's energy, which he called "orgone," can become trapped in chronic muscular contractions called "armor." Armor can trap emotion as well as energy, he said, and is a double-edged sword—serving a useful protective function in times of real stress or danger, but doing more long-term harm than good.

The body contracts to avoid pain, he observed, but in so doing cuts off pleasure as well. The aim of Reich's therapy was to relieve inhibition by ridding the body of chronic muscular armoring, thus permitting the release of deeply-repressed emotions and the reestablishment of a free flow of orgone. Once this was done, he said, the individual would be able to experience an "orgasm reflex," a spontaneous pulsation of the entire body at orgasm, permitting full energetic discharge. Reich viewed the orgasm reflex as the key indicator of emotional and physical health.

The Intensity of Orgonomy

Orgonomy is the most intensively hands-on of the present day Reich-based therapies. The following passage, from the 1971 book *Me and the Orgone*, vividly illustrates how a therapist uses his hands in combination with psychoanalysis to bring about an emotional response. The patient is actor Orson Bean:

"Turn over," he said, and I flopped over and he began prodding at my back, around my shoulder blades. He found a spot he liked and began to press it. He pressed it hard and I let out a howl. He squeezed it and he pinched at it and I lay there and screamed . . . . Suddenly he began gouging at that sore, knotted muscle again and he didn't stop, and then I really hit the bed . . . . I cried harder than I ever cried before . . . . Finally, I recovered and turned over on my back.

"How do you feel?" asked Baker.

"I feel fantastic relief," I answered.

"I think Bean pretty well described it," says Richard Blasband, M.D., president of the American College of Orgonomy in Princeton, New Jersey.

Though the above techniques may sound rather drastic, Dr. Blasband says they are based on Reich's teachings and have remained essentially unchanged. After all, Reich trained Bean's therapist, Dr. Elsworth Baker, who went on to found the American College of Orgonomy. Dr. Baker then trained Dr. Blasband and the other senior members of the college, who are dedicated to carrying on Reich's work in its original form.

"The goal is always to bring the patient into contact with himself and with his feelings," says Dr. Blasband, "and to get the blocked feelings expressed in the session." To do that requires a certain amount of intensity in each session, and a high degree of emotional stamina and professional training on the part of the therapist.

An orgonomist typically possesses a medical degree and has completed a residency in either psychiatry, internal medicine or both. There are only about two or three dozen qualified psychiatric orgone therapists in the entire United States. "The amount of training is something of a deterrent, of course," says Dr. Blasband. "But the real reason our numbers are small is that people aren't prepared to go into this work emotionally, even if they are trained psychiatrically or medically."

From Talk to Touch

In a typical session, Dr. Blasband says, the patient is asked to undress to his underwear and lie on a couch. That's followed by some beginning discussion about what's been going on in the patient's life during the past week or so. "If there's something that's bothering the patient and the therapist can pick up on it," Dr. Blasband explains, "then there will be a discussion of that. We feel it's very important to determine how people are living out in the world, not just in therapy."

Then the therapist might ask the patient to start breathing in a deep, relaxing way, encouraging him to give in to any feelings that may surface. "If some emotions do come up, as they often will, then the therapist just lets that continue," Dr. Blasband says. "If not, then the therapist has to dig for the emotions he thinks may be blocked by the patient's character resistances and inhibitions. In that case he may have to analyze those obstructing attitudes, or work on those muscle groups wherein he thinks the inhibitions are being held."

That could mean some deep tissue work on the muscles of the eyes, neck, throat, chest and so on, following a basic, head-to-pelvis, armor-busting pattern outlined by Reich decades ago.

Dr. Blasband says the length of therapy depends on what a patient wants from analysis. "If you simply want relief of a symptom such as depression, sometimes that can be obtained in months. If you want a thorough analysis designed to help you reach genitality, which is the true goal of the therapy, that can take 250 or more therapy sessions." He defines genitality as "the ability to be what you would have been if the world hadn't interfered with your natural development." It typically means a total change in character for the patients who seek it, he says.

Each orgonomist sets his own fee scale. "For the person who can afford it," says Dr. Blasband, "we charge the same as the standard going rate for psychoanalysis in the community." Expect to pay anywhere from $50 to $115, depending on your location.

Are more mental health professionals beginning to take an interest in orgonomy? "Yes," Dr. Blasband replies. "There are new therapists coming into the field all the time—not in droves, by any means, but a few every year."

All things considered, that's probably just how Wilhelm Reich would have wanted it to be.

The Bioenergetic Approach— A Reichian Offspring

If the number of practicing orgonomists has remained relatively small over the years, the number of *bioenergetics* practitioners has only grown.

From a few dozen therapists ten years ago, the number of bioenergetics practitioners worldwide has skyrocketed during the 1980s, now numbering 1,500. Most were trained through a network of some 50 bioenergetics societies in the United States, South America and Europe.

Overseeing the entire operation is the New York City-based International Institute for Bioenergetic Analysis, which also publishes a journal and books, coordinates conferences and hosts professional workshops throughout the year. In short, bio-energetics is well organized, well accepted and growing stronger all the time.

All things considered, that's probably just how Alexander Lowen wants it to be. The most widely known of all neo-Reichian therapists, Dr. Lowen studied under Reich for several years and also underwent therapy with him. He's been busy popularizing his mentor's principles since the late 1950s. Today, in his 70s, Lowen has written ten books and still leads bioenergetics exercise classes that reportedly leave therapists half his age gasping for air.

Thanks to Lowen's tireless efforts, bioenergetics practitioners are now visited by "a very broad spectrum of clients," says Jodi Schneider, certified bioenergetic therapist and codirector of the New York Society for Bioenergetic Analysis. "We see a lot of people coming in who feel disconnected from their bodies, or disconnected from their emotions. They feel a lack of integration between mind and body."

Some of these are people who have typically tried other types of therapies and haven't gotten anywhere, she says. "They come to us with this feeling of wanting to work more with the body and more with their energy systems and emotions. They don't want to talk about feelings—they want to have experiences."

Bioenergetics seems able to deliver on that count. Many bioenergetic exercise classes begin with yogic stretching and may progress sometime later to clients throwing temper tantrums on the floor.

Those who have gone through such "experiences" report feelings of great power afterward, however. And those who undergo individual analysis sometimes report dramatic changes in their self-image in short periods of time, even though serious therapy can last for years.

"It generally takes three to four months to deal with the 'presenting issue,'" notes Robert Glazer, Ph.D., director of the Florida Society for Bioenergetic Analysis in Gainesville, Florida. "That's the depression, anxiety and night terrors or other problems that brought the person in. Once they get through that, I give my clients the option of going for broke—of going for 'character analysis,' which can last two or more years."

Shedding the Armor

Dr. Glazer defines character analysis as a "complete personality overhaul." Says he: "It's going back, regressing, into the foundation of the personality. You slowly peel away the layers, build new strengths and give the person more options."

The bioenergetics practitioner uses direct dissolution of body armor along with various postures, expressions and exercises to help clients regain body awareness and release repressed emotions. Though the hands are often used, Schneider says that massage doesn't accurately describe what bioenergetics therapists do. "Neither does manipulation," she says. "Breathing and exercise are a part of the process, though, and there might be pressure placed on a person's jaw or work done around the eyes."

Some sessions have no contact at all, she adds. "There might be physical work by the client, but no physical contact with the therapist." When there is direct contact, pressure may be applied to some point on the body, as opposed to deep massage.

Dr. Glazer says a typical session might begin with the client relating something of importance that's going on in her life—be it anxiety and depression, or happiness and well-being. Particularly, if it's negative, the therapist tries to discern how that emotion is being manifested in the body.

"I want to get a feeling of where the energy is blocked," Dr. Glazer says. "What areas are very still? Is it around the belly, the pelvis, the eyes?"

Once the block is located, the next step may involve either stretching, expressive exercises or breathing work. "The very first thing we do with depressed patients is try to get them breathing stronger," Dr. Glazer says. "The more they breathe the more we can stoke their internal fires and give them the energy they need to cope with life. And at the same time, the unconscious factors that interfered with their natural breathing—the emotions and feelings—start to come up again."

That's where the analytic part of bioenergetics comes into play. "You have to get to the fear or emotional pain that's keeping the body in its frozen pattern," Dr. Glazer says. "Then, as you release the energy, you can release the psychological component that put the body in that pattern to begin with."

Three Release Mechanisms

Bringing about that release can take several forms. "If someone is angry, I'll hand them a tennis racket and have them beat the mattress in my office," says Dr. Glazer.

Another releasing movement mimics the type of childhood hitting, kicking and yelling widely known as a temper tantrum. "A person will start to lose control and start to cry," says Dr. Glazer. "When they do that, they learn that it's safe to let these feelings out."

A third release mechanism is the "breathing stool," which is actually a 24-inch-tall wooden kitchen stool with two blankets rolled together and strapped to it. The client stretches out over the stool faceup, with the blankets on the stool pressing squarely in the center of the back, directly behind the heart. "When they stretch like that, it opens up breathing constrictions," says Dr. Glazer. "If someone is tight around the throat, the chest or the diaphragm, this slowly but methodically stretches the body."

Reichian Resources

These books can help you learn more about Reichian therapy:

Bioenergetics by Alexander Lowen, M.D. (Penguin).

Man in the Trap by Elsworth Baker, M.D. (Macmillan).

Me and the Orgone by Orson Bean (St. Martin's Press).

To find out more about specific types of Reichian therapy, or to find practitioners in your area, contact:

The American College of Orgonomy
P.O. Box 490
Princeton, NJ 08542
(201) 821-1144

The International Institute for Bioenergetic Analysis
144 E. 36th Street
New York, NY 10016
(212) 532-7742

Bioenergetics and orgonomy differ in some important ways. An orgonomist, for example, emphasizes the orgasm reflex and working with body armoring.

"With bioenergetics," Dr. Glazer says, "the important thing is a person's self possession, his sense of self, and awareness of his body and inner world—in relation to his sexuality and life function."

Bioenergetics also tends to be less structured than orgonomy, and less hands-on intensive. "Generally," says Dr. Glazer, "Orgonomists work on you and keep working on you. In bioenergetics, the hands-on work is often used to activate the body, to get it moving on its own."

Bioenergetic therapists undergo a four-year training course that consists of 140 hours of training therapy, 20 days of training workshops per year, and another 50 hours of personal supervision under a qualified bioenergetic trainer. Would-be practitioners need to possess or be working on a graduate degree in the helping professions, in order to be accepted for training.

Prices for therapy vary widely, depending on location. Dr. Glazer, a certified bioenergetic therapist whose graduate training is in clinical psychology, charges $70 an hour. Many practitioners in the Northeast and major metropolitan areas may charge close to $100. Psychotherapy treatment is covered by most major medical health insurance policies.

Worth it? "To really work with the foundation of the personality you go to the body," says Dr. Glazer. "The way in which a person's deeper emotional issues are locked in the body is the route to making that person feel better."

Chapter 35

ROLFING

Tell someone that you're going to get Rolfed and they'll invariably respond by mentioning the word "pain" or "hurt." Sometimes both.

"I hear that really hurts," they'll say, or they'll ask, "Isn't there a lot of pain involved in that?"

Well, yes, it does hurt and there is some pain. But anyone who says the pain is unbearable or that the hurt lasts for more than a few seconds has probably never been Rolfed.

It's really not that bad.

Rolfing is much like the late Dr. Ida P. Rolf herself, the woman who developed the form of deep tissue massage that now bears her name. That is, it's blunt, it's to the point, and it doesn't seem to care much if you like it or not. But for many people, it works.

Dr. Rolf was convinced that the key to health depended on placing the body in balance with one of the strongest forces in our environment— gravity. To that end, she developed a manipulative technique based on three simple ideas about human structure: (1) Most of us are out of alignment with gravity; (2) we would function much better if we were aligned with gravity; and (3) our bodies are so plastic that we can be brought back into alignment with gravity at any time.

If we didn't spend so much of our energy fighting gravity, Dr. Rolf reasoned, we would have more than enough energy available to live in good health. "This is the gospel of Rolfing," she wrote. "When the body gets working appropriately, the force of gravity can flow through. Then, spontaneously, the body heals itself."

The Big "G"

While osteopathic physicians emphasize the importance of bones and other massage techniques concentrate on muscles, Rolfing focuses on the network of connective tissue that contains the muscles and links them to the bones.

A Healer Who Was After Bigger Game

Dr. Rolf, who earned her Ph.D. in biochemistry in 1920, originally used yoga to help bring pain relief to a small circle of acquaintances. Trial and error, combined with tons of practice, led to the development of the craft that eventually became her legacy.

She was acquainted with yoga from an early age, but believed it fell short in its ability to stretch and strengthen the body. She was also familiar with osteopathy and homeopathy.

Dr. Rolf was interested in all these things as a way to improve her family's health problems and correct her own spinal curvature. Though such disciplines helped guide her thinking, no single modality or combination of existing therapies seemed to provide the holistic answer she was seeking—until she perfected Rolfing.

As biographer Rosemary Feitis puts it: "She was after bigger game. She wanted nothing less than to create new, better human beings. The ills would cure themselves; the symptoms would melt as the organisms became balanced."

Dr. Rolf died in 1979 at age 84. Fourteen years earlier she had predicted that Rolfing would die with her, a prediction that, happily, has proven wrong.

When this connective tissue covers and envelops the muscles, we call it fascia. When it thickens into straps and binds muscle to bone, we call it a tendon. When it joins bone to bone, we call it a ligament. Whenever it fails to do its job, we call it a pain.

We call it a pain quite often, Dr. Rolf realized, and she believed she knew why: Connective tissue is pliable enough to hold whatever patterns of movement or posture the body adopts, good or bad, and gravity is strong enough to keep it that way.

When the body is in balance, gravity supports and holds connective tissue in place, like a stack of blocks neatly placed one on top of the other. But if the body adopts an unbalanced posture, gravity goes to work on the connective tissue and molds it into an unnatural shape. Picture an old house where misaligned beams have settled and where it's hard to close the doors or keep things from rolling off countertops any more.

Our bodies develop unbalanced postures quite easily, Rolfers point out. Remember that fall from the bicycle when you were eight? Okay, maybe not—but your body has never forgotten it. Your knee was banged up pretty badly, which caused you to limp for a week or so. To compensate, you shifted your weight to the other leg. In so doing, you also shifted muscular effort through your pelvis, up your spine and eventually throughout your body. Although the limp disappeared soon enough, that system of compensations left its imprint in a broad, complex pattern of shortened fascia from head to toe.

By itself, that pattern of shortened fascia would do you little harm. But, thanks to gravity, patterns of imbalance tend to reinforce themselves over time. They also deepen by repetition, and the body's weight begins to center progressively farther from its natural vertical axis. Gravity becomes an increasingly destructive force.

Back to the Blueprints

To a Rolfer's trained eye, most people have slipped out of their vertical axis. They typically let their head slump forward too far and carry their buttocks too far back and too high. They also let one shoulder or one hip lead the other slightly when they walk, and they let the knees track out or in just a bit. The ankles, following the knees, tend to throw the weight to the outside of the feet, where one foot always seems to be carrying a bit more weight than the other.

This imbalanced posture causes the muscles of the neck and shoulders to tighten as they fight to keep the 12-pound head erect. Likewise, some of the back muscles will tighten to support the curved spine, while others will not be used at all. Joints in the lower leg won't align as they should, resulting in a painful knee or a jerky, "disjointed" movement while walking. Circulation will be restricted as the fascial network tightens to counter the downward pull of gravity. Headaches, fatigue and pain result.

The Rolfer's goal is to put the body back in line with its original blueprint specifications—to get it working along a single vertical plane extending from the head to the shoulders through the thorax to the pelvis and down to the legs. This is done in ten sessions.

The Rolfer works deep into the body, following Dr. Rolf's belief that connective tissue is plastic enough that it can be worked back into its proper, original shape if enough "energy" is applied to it.

In Rolfing, that energy takes the form of hand and arm pressure designed to reach and stimulate the collagen base of the connective tissue. Rolfers attempt to change the characteristics of the collagen itself, moving it from a solid "gel" state to a more fluid "sol" phase. As the collagen moves to the sol state, the body loses its stiffness, moves more freely and aligns itself properly at the joints.

Rolfers say the benefits of proper alignment are many: Muscles brought nearer to their optimal location require less energy to perform. The head and chest go up and the trunk lengthens. The pelvis begins moving in a horizontal plane, bringing the abdomen and buttocks in. The knees begin tracking forward and the soles of the feet meet the ground more squarely. Connective tissue lifts the body's weight as it was meant to and we appear more at ease.

Best of all, Rolfers say, once the body gets aligned, gravity will keep it that way.

Finding a Rolfer

Finding a Rolfer is relatively easy to do. Rolfing is probably one of the best organized of all the hands-on therapies, thanks in large part to the efforts of The Rolf Institute, headquartered in Boulder, Colorado. The institute has been turning out a steady stream of Rolfers since 1972, and there are now more than 600 practicing their trade in virtually every state in the nation, as well as in 23 foreign countries.

Despite those large numbers, becoming a certified Rolfer is no easy task. "We are highly selective," says Sue Melchior, the institute's school administrator.

Thousands of inquiries are received each year, but only a handful are ever accepted. "We have certain prerequisites that must be met in order to make an application to our school," she notes. "Those include courses in human anatomy, physiology, kinesiology, massage training and experience."

Formal courses in psychology are also required, as well as proof that Rolfing has had an effect on your life. "You have to show us that it's touched you in your life and that you're working with those principles and those theories already," Melchior says.

Actual training takes place in two nine-week classes. Students enter the first class as auditors, observing and learning principles and theory. They are given an interview at the end of the first nine weeks to assess progress and determine their ability to continue. Students enter the second phase of classes as "practitioner students" and begin doing actual hands-on work under the supervision of the instructors. If all goes well, they will graduate and be awarded certification by the Rolf Institute—though their training is far from over.

"Then they need to take continuing education classes for three to five years after certification," Melchior says, "and then take our advanced training." Finally, four to five years after enrollment, a Rolfer's training is complete.

The institute provides a complete listing of its graduates, including their addresses and phone numbers. A quick glance through the Rolf Institute directory shows Rolfers located from Belfast, Maine, to Cazadero, California, and virtually all points in between. "We can recommend the people in our directory to anyone in the world," Melchior says. "We know they are qualified."

Getting Rolfed

Monday morning finds you limping around the house with another backache. You've heard enough about the "pain" of Rolfing that the thought of going to see a Rolfer makes you nervous. But that pain can't be as bad as this pain, so you decide to try one session.

An ad in the Yellow Pages shows there's a Rolfer located in an office building within a few miles of home. The office is nice, but spartan. She shares the place with three other hands-on practitioners who offer a variety of techniques ranging from sports massage to something called jin shin jitsu. Each one has her own therapy room. You follow your Rolfer into the room on the left and notice how small she is and how good that makes you feel. How can it possibly hurt?

You fill out a short health questionnaire and discuss with her what you hope to get out of Rolfing. She is friendly and open, but very direct. Your back hurts almost every morning, you tell her. The knees have been feeling a little stiff, too. You want the pain to stop. She nods. "Strip down to your underwear," she says. "Then stand up against that wall." Part of your mind wants to resist this command—after all, she's not a doctor. But she says it with such nonchalant force that before you know it your clothes are folded on the floor and you're standing at the wall, ramrod straight.

She pulls out a Polaroid camera and takes a picture of your front, your sides, your back. Your posture has always been good, you think, so you're not really sure what this is going to prove.

She asks you to lay down on a low, padded table in the center of the room. You lay on your back and try to relax. She moves to the side of the table and starts working on your rib cage, probing between the ribs. The feeling is not pleasant. Her fingers work down deep and move things around that have never been moved before. She talks to you and helps keep your mind off what she's doing. The pain lasts only a second, you notice, and it's never more than you can stand.

She works down to your diaphragm and begins kneading the area where it joins your ribs. This will help your breathing, she says. You hope so, you reply through gritted teeth. Whatever she's doing down there sure doesn't tickle. She tells you she was a ballerina and that Rolfing improved her dancing tremendously. After she hung up her toe shoes she decided to become a Rolfer.

The conversation flows back and forth. She's used to talking and listening, and she seems to do both equally well. You begin to relax as she moves away from your chest and down to your hips, then to the back of the thighs. None of her deep, kneading movements tickle, but your thighs feel longer and stronger when she's done.

Next you sit on the floor and she begins working on your back, standing above you for added leverage. Although she's working very deeply, there is little pain here. In fact, the deeper she works, the better it feels. She asks you to stand and you spring effortlessly to your feet.

You're surprised by how quickly you popped off the floor. Your head feels light and dizzy. You feel somehow taller. She asks you to walk back over to the wall and you simply glide there. Every joint feels smooth and ready for motion.

She takes more pictures. This was just the "get acquainted" session, she says. The second session focuses on the legs and feet, while the third session concentrates on working the shoulder, ribs and pelvis into an even stack. The fourth session gets deep into the body's core, working from the inside of the ankles to the pelvic floor, followed by work on the hamstrings and on the back and neck. The fifth session works the deep muscles of the stomach, while the sixth focuses on the pelvis. The seventh concentrates on balancing the neck and head on the spine, and the eighth, ninth and tenth tie the rest together.

She asks if you're going to come back for all of them now that you've had the first. You nod noncommittally and turn your attention to the pictures she's arranged in front of you. They are the before and after pictures from your first session. You hold them side-by-side and witness a remarkable, physical change in your appearance. She wants to point out some things, but your eyes are faster than her hands. It's apparent that your right shoulder is higher and farther back than the left shoulder in all the "before" pictures. You'd never noticed it before. The shoulders have evened out considerably in the "after" shots.

You pick up the next set and notice that your back looks more symmetrical as well. The "lat" muscles on either side of your spine travel evenly from waist to armpit now. In the "before" pictures, the right muscle looks nar-

Rolfing Resources

The Rolf Institute, P.O. Box 1868, Boulder, CO 80306, is a one-stop source for information on Rolfing. The institute's free directory provides a complete list of every certified Rolfer practicing today. A free pamphlet also lists the books, pamphlets, videotapes and audio-visual information currently available about Rolfing. Highly recommended: *Ida Rolf Talks about Rolfing and Physical Reality.* Those in a hurry can call the institute at (303) 449-5903.

rower than the left. Your head now seems to be sitting on your shoulders a bit straighter, too, and your feet are together and directly under your pelvis. You pick up the first shots and notice that you had been standing with them shoulder-width apart, the way you had always stood, the way that made you feel balanced before.

"Yes," you reply. "I think I will be back. It didn't hurt that much." She smiles and nods her head. "No," she says, "it never does." You feel so energetic the rest of the day that you can't get to sleep until after midnight. Even so, you wake up the next morning feeling great and the pain in your back is gone. You place a call to your sister. "I just got Rolfed," you say. "You must be crazy," she replies, "I hear that really hurts."

THE HEALING POWER OF ROLFING

It sometimes seems that, for one reason or another, people will try many forms of treatment for chronic pain before seeking out the assistance of a Rolfer. Usually they wish they'd seen the Rolfer first and saved themselves a lot of time, trouble and money. Such was the case for Leslie Dannin.

Dannin injured her back at age 16 during high school cheerleading tryouts. She sought out the services of a chiropractor and stayed with him for years, even though the treatments brought only limited, temporary relief.

"My back kept getting continually worse," she says, "until the point where, in graduate school some years later, I tried to open a window and pinched a nerve in the middle of my back."

The pain from the pinched nerve practically paralyzed the left side of her body, Dannin says. When driving, she was able to steer with only her right hand, finding it far too painful to lift her left arm to the wheel. After graduation, she spent the next year and a half sleeping on the floor. Nothing less than a flat, hard surface would let her get more than a few minutes rest at night.

"I really didn't know where to turn," she recalls. She felt fairly certain that a traditional physician would do nothing but prescribe medication or surgery, and she wanted neither.

But she'd been unable to find relief with either chiropractic or oriental massage, so she made up her mind to simply live with the pain.

"Then one day this friend of mine noticed that I was unable to get comfortable when sitting," she says. That friend turned out to be Bill Harvey, a Philadelphia Rolfer who thought he might have the answer to Dannin's problem.

"I had never heard of Rolfing and don't remember how we started talking about it," she says, "but he suggested I try it." Dannin was fresh out of options, so she agreed to see Harvey as a client.

"In the very first session he corrected the pinched nerve that had been troubling me for three years," she says. "The next day I felt so good I was jumping around. You couldn't get me to hold still. That night I slept in a bed for the first time in years. It was just incredible; I slept the whole night."

In subsequent sessions, Harvey went on to correct a chronic temporomandibular joint (TMJ) problem that had also been nagging Dannin for years. He also worked on her knees and ankles, lining her up from head to toe. "Now my posture just naturally relaxes into place," she says.

Dannin doesn't remember experiencing any pain with her initial Rolfing sessions: "Whatever he did to my back when I first saw him was nothing compared to the pain I was suffering. Absolutely nothing." Dannin finished her tenth session more than a yéar ago and has had no recurring back problems since then.

Help for Hip Problems

Bobbie Ball was involved in an automobile accident three years ago. "I didn't think it amounted to that much at the time," she says. "But I had had a previous hip injury, and the accident just aggravated it to the point where I couldn't get comfortable any more."

Like Dannin, Ball also sought the services of a chiropractor for relief. When that failed to produce results, she tried an orthopedic surgeon and received therapy through his clinic, but that failed too.

"Someone suggested Rolfing," she recalls, which resulted in a visit to Elizabeth Swenson, a Ft. Collins, Colorado, practitioner. "It did the trick," Ball says. "I was very impressed."

Though parts of the Rolfing proved "very painful," Ball notes that both of her hip sockets felt like they were jammed. "And," she says, "Rolfing was the only thing that, somehow or another, seemed to lengthen the muscles and get the joints to relax."

Ball says that a combination of Rolfing, chiropractic and massage, along with a regular program of walking and swimming, has helped keep the pain from recurring.

Rolfing's results do seem to be fairly long-lasting. Psychiatrist Debra London was first Rolfed almost ten years ago. "It wasn't that painful," she says, "and it resulted in some fairly permanent improvements in the hip problems I was having then."

So, following recent breast-reduction surgery, Dr. London went back. "I felt as though my body was still carrying those heavy breasts," she says. "And I felt that if I was Rolfed again, it would help me change the old patterns."

Because Dr. London had been Rolfed before, she received advanced Rolfing sessions that concentrate on solving specific complaints, instead of following the ten-session routine adhered to in basic rolfing.

"It has helped. I'm definitely standing differently now," she says. "My weight has shifted and I'm walking differently. I'm aware of having choices, of not being locked into old patterns of movement."

Boosting Performance

Though Rolfing speaks most eloquently when someone suffering chronic pain finds sudden relief through the hands of a skilled practitioner, many others use it to simply help improve athletic performance. Such is the case with martial artist Eben Pyle.

"I can't recall when or how I heard about Rolfing, but I was basically looking for something that would help with my general health," he says. "And I thought it would be interesting to see if Rolfing could also improve my performance in the martial arts.

"In the long run I would have to say it has helped," notes Pyle. "I have better use of my body. I've become more limber and I'm able to do movements that would have been harder had I not been Rolfed."

Pyle says that for him, Rolfing has never been painful. "I fall asleep sometimes during a session, and I know this might sound a little crazy, but sometimes I laugh."

Paul Oertel says that sometimes he cries. Like many others, he has experienced the emotional release that occasionally occurs with deep tissue massage.

"I use Rolfing as an adjunct to my performing, acting as well as dancing," he says. "When I come back from touring I'll tell my Rolfer that my ankle wouldn't work on a certain move, or I couldn't express this emotion or I couldn't reach that note."

Through Rolfing, Oertel has been able to improve and maintain his performance level for the past 13 years. "It's simply fantastic," he says.

Chapter 36

SPORTS MASSAGE

Richard Smith slings sheaves. And it hurts. "For the sheaf toss you have to take a burlap bag stuffed with hay—it weighs 16 pounds—and throw it over a high crossbar using a pitchfork. It tends to put a strain on your muscles," he says as he rubs his forearm.

Smith is not a farmer who has eschewed the modern methods of getting hay up into the hayloft. He is a weekend warrior, and his personal battle is called Scottish Games. Every weekend during the summer months he drives up and down the East Coast just to toss things around with a few friends.

"When you participate in Scottish Games you have to do a caber and stone throw," he adds. (You thought bags of hay were bad, imagine trying to do this.) "The caber is an 18- to 20-foot log that weighs as much as 140 pounds." And Smith spends his weekends seeing how far he can throw it. But that's not all.

"The stone toss is much like the shot put, but the stones weigh 16 to 20 pounds." In any language, this is not what you call your normal weekend workout.

Richard Smith throws things when he works out; Keith Van Horne, on the other hand, ends up being the throwee. As an offensive tackle for the NFL's Chicago Bears, Van Horne spends his weekends getting tossed around by the opposing team's linebackers. This guy knows personally how that sack of hay feels.

Off their respective fields of battle, Van Horne and Smith have two things in common. One, come Monday they hurt with major league muscle pain. And two, both turn to sports massage for relief.

"In sports massage, the athlete is treated by a massage therapist who has a background in anatomy, physiology and kinesiology [movement]," says Karen Lessman, director of the

National Sports Massage Team for the American Massage Therapy Association.

"The athlete and the massage therapist are working together to achieve a certain goal," says Bruce Stephens, former coordinator of the sports massage program at the Massage Training Institute in California. Often that goal is enhanced performance.

"Sports massage is used by the athlete who's pushing to the limit, and wants to stay as finely trained as possible without going over the edge," says Lessman.

Pushing the limits helped Van Horn and his teammates win the Super Bowl in 1985. He prepared for that game as he had for all the games in the previous five years: by getting sports massage. "Before games, it helps you get ready," he says. "Sometimes when my hamstrings are tight, massage really loosens things up and gets blood flowing into the area. It's like doing warm-ups, but you never leave the table. It makes you feel good."

Russian Roots

Many sports massage techniques developed in Eastern bloc countries as a way for athletes to block out the pain of physical competition. "The Soviets perfected sports massage about 15 years ago," says Michael Yessis, Ph.D., editor of *Soviet Sports Review Journal.*

"Their athletes were working hard with double and triple training sessions per day, but research told them they had to do even more to be successful. They started looking for ways to help the body recuperate faster, and that search brought them to sports massage." Every Soviet team now has a sports massage therapist assigned to it, and the therapist travels with the team to every competition.

Word of this new massage technique soon emigrated westward, and researchers in Sweden decided to test its effectiveness. At the Karolinska Institute in Stockholm, competitive cyclists pedaled until they were exhausted.

Then they either rested for ten minutes or had a ten-minute massage. Finally, they were asked to do 50 knee extensions on an exercise machine that tested their leg strength. The researchers found that the cyclists' quadriceps muscles were 11 percent stronger after the massage compared to after the ten-minute rest.

West Meets East

Strength is a valuable commodity in the NFL. To have it is to be a champion. To find it, most coaches search America's college ranks. But not Johnny Parker, strength coach of the New York Giants. He did his looking in the USSR.

Two trips to the USSR to study strength conditioning made Parker a believer in sports massage. "One Soviet weightlifter told me, for example, that during portions of the year when he

The Games People Play

Whatever your sport may be, maybe what you need is a good massage. "Sports massage is good for any kind of activity that requires you to use the same group of muscles over and over again," says Karen Lessman, of the National Sports Massage Team.

Here's a listing of sport-specific strokes that Lessman says may help keep you on top of your game.

Baseball

Don't balk about getting sports massage for this game, especially if your shoulders or back hurt. "Do direct pressure and cross fiber friction of your back and shoulder muscles during the week and use compression, combined with range of motion and stretching exercises before you take the field."

Cycling

Here you get strain in your quadriceps, gluteal muscles, lower back, and neck and shoulder area. "Before you bike, do a compression stroke by sitting down on the floor with your leg out straight. Take the palm of your hand and press straight into your quadricep muscle on the upper leg so that it doesn't roll on the bone. Press in and out for a few minutes, as if you were doing a gentle CPR stroke, but to your leg, not your chest."

Golf

Here low back and shoulder strain is about par. Before you pick up your clubs and take some practice swings, you should get a grip on yourself. "Use your fingers to massage your lower back area. With your fingertips, do a circling motion on both sides of your spine and right across the tops of your hips."

Rowing

Man must have been meant to sail, because rowing causes problems with your arms and back. And while it's one sport where you needn't keep your eye on a ball, it does help to keep a ball on your back. "Get an old tennis ball, one that has lost that initial hardness, and put it on the floor," says Lessman. "Then lay down on it so that it's in the spot that hurts. Relax your weight down onto it, and that way you'll be able to work those pressure points you can't normally reach—especially up between your shoulders."

Skiing

Cross-country skiing can make you sore, especially in your calves and quadriceps. "Use an effleurage technique to get the blood flowing through your leg muscles, then a compression technique on your calf. Just sit on the floor and cross your ankle over your opposite leg. Then compress into your calf toward the bone. That will help to loosen up the muscle."

The Winning Team

Presently there are about 230 certified sports massage therapists throughout the country. They are certified by the American Massage Therapy Association, which is the only national professional organization that certifies sports massage therapists.

To be certified, the therapists need to have 28 hours of intense training in sports massage, plus at least 10 hours experience working with an athlete. They must also document that they've participated in at least two athletic events providing pre- or post-event massage. After all of that, they must pass a written and hands-on exam.

Once they get their hands on you, expect the session to run anywhere from 20 minutes to an hour depending on whether you are having maintenance or therapeutic treatment.

Costs nationwide range from $30 to $70 an hour. Shorter treatments should cost less.

For more information on where to find a certified sports massage therapist, write to The American Massage Therapy Association, Department of Information, 1130 West North Shore Avenue, Chicago, IL 60626, or call (312) 761-2682.

worked out three times a day, he'd get a two-hour sports massage between each workout. It made him stronger."

So the New York Giants players began to get sports massage therapy after every game. "The year we went to the Super Bowl, and won, was the year we started to use it," says Parker.

The players told their strength coach that after a tough game or workout sports massage made them come back harder and stronger the next day. And as Parker soon found out, it helped the team in other ways, too. "Massage is a tremendous recuperative, or restorative measure for athletes. It really helps to heal them up and bring them back after a game."

Leaving a Mark

Boom. The ground shakes when the 140-pound log hits. As it rolls to the side, you can see a two-inch-deep hole in the ground. Richard Smith has left his mark on another Scottish Games field.

Sports massage has also left its mark on Richard. "As competition gets more intense, even in weekend amateur events, you need to train harder than ever before," he says. "The problem is that if you overtrain, your body starts to break down. Sports massage helps to avoid that."

Smith bends over, picks up a four stone, and heaves it into the sun.

THE HEALING POWER OF SPORTS MASSAGE

"When you exercise, you create microtrauma in your muscles," says Bruce Stephens. "There is a bit of swelling of the muscle tissue, and massage helps reduce it. Massage also enhances circulation, which aids in the healing process."

Sports massage can be done either pre-event (before you compete or work out) or postevent. Those who get pre-event massage say it helps them avoid injury. "I tend to get muscle spasms in my neck during bike races," says Todd Stern, a Tampa, Florida, amateur athlete who spends his weekends competing in triathlons. Some of the bike races that he rides as part of the event are 56 miles long, and those neck problems used to cramp his style. But not anymore. "The times that I've gotten a pre-event sports massage on my neck, I've had no symptoms during the race," he says.

Therapists say a pre-event massage can also help avoid serious injuries. "We use the time to work on tendons and ligaments, warming and stretching them. Connective tissue doesn't have its own blood supply, so it tends to warm up more slowly," says Stephens. "Connective tissue that's not warmed up is more likely to be torn or overstretched. So by massaging these tissues before exercising or training, they are much less likely to be injured." Postevent massage, on the other hand, "helps reduce soreness, maintains flexibility and reduces cramping," according to Lessman.

Here are some additional tips from the sports massage pros on how to handle that aching body from the ground up.

Tender Feet

"Most people who begin fitness walking experience foot pain," says Lessman. "To treat it, massage your feet after walking. Use lotion or talcum powder, and massage it in all over. Use your thumb to massage the bottom of your feet where it hurts the most. Press in with your thumb around the ball of your foot and work your way outward to the side of your foot. Do each foot for five minutes."

And if you're lucky enough to have a Jacuzzi, "Put your foot up tight against the jets. That will make your foot feel great, too."

Sore Shins

"Sometimes the muscles in the back of your leg get strong, but the muscles in the front are not strong enough. This causes your shins to hurt," says Lessman.

"You can make the front muscles stronger by doing exercises that put resistance on the top side of your toes. Use a big elastic band, hook it around something stationary, sit down, and then hook it over your toes. In a controlled motion, pull your toes up and back toward your body against the resistance and then release."

Aching Knees

"Exercise can make the area just under your knee cap painful, and you can develop patella tendinitis," says Stephens. "If that happens, sit with your leg straight out in front of you. Using the webbing of your hand between your thumb and index finger, press down on the knee cap. The patella will pop up slightly. Then take your other hand and apply friction massage underneath the bottom edge of the patella. That will help ease the pain of tendinitis."

Pain in the Butt

"Very often if you overexert yourself, you get sore in your gluteus medius," says Stephens. If this is the seat of *your* trouble, Stephens has a treatment that's a ball to do. "Take a softball, lie on your side and roll the ball around on your gluteal muscle. When you find a spot that hurts, press the ball down on it for a few seconds, then move on to the next sore spot. This will help loosen up any problems."

THE TRIPLE PLAY OF SPORTS MASSAGE

Sports massage therapists believe that different folks need different strokes. "We use some specific techniques that a regular massage therapist may not use. Our three basic strokes are compression, direct pressure and cross fiber friction," says Karen Lessman, of the American Massage Therapy Association.

Here's a Lessman lesson on these special hands-on healing strokes.

36-1

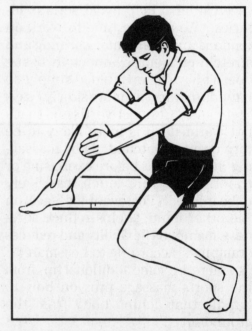

Compression. Basically this stroke compresses the muscle toward the underlying bone. It spreads the muscle fiber and increases circulation. It's done in the belly of the muscle—the wide central part. You can do it on nearly any muscle both before and after an event or workout.

To do compression on the muscle just outside the shin bone, press and release with the palm of your hand. Don't press on the shinbone itself, but work each area of the muscle belly from just below the knee to just above the ankle.

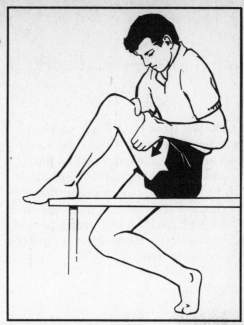

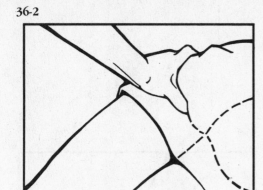

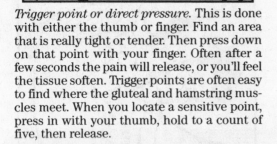

36-2

36-3

Trigger point or direct pressure. This is done with either the thumb or finger. Find an area that is really tight or tender. Then press down on that point with your finger. Often after a few seconds the pain will release, or you'll feel the tissue soften. Trigger points are often easy to find where the gluteal and hamstring muscles meet. When you locate a sensitive point, press in with your thumb, hold to a count of five, then release.

Cross-fiber friction. This stroke is applied perpendicularly to the direction of the muscle fibers. In the top of the leg, for example, the muscle fibers of the quadriceps basically run from the hip to the knee. So you should massage your leg sideways across the grain. Do this stroke so the finger moves with the skin. Do it on tight tissue near the ends of the muscle—either near the hip or the knee.

SOOTHING A SORE SHOULDER

You can get shoulder pain from any one of a number of sports such as tennis, softball, or golf. But you can also paint yourself into a painful situation without even leaving your house. "Some people get sore shoulders painting their kitchens," says Bruce McAllister, director of the athletic training curriculum at Northern Illinois University.

"For eight hours on a Saturday, they do the same kind of stroke with a paintbrush that they would be using if they were playing tennis or racquetball. Weekend warriors can get hurt on or off the court."

If you've been courting shoulder pain, McAllister may have the massage treatment for you. "If your pain has been diagnosed by a physician as tendinitis, this technique may help," he says. "I normally get about a 92 percent success rate."

James Councilman, M.D., head coach of the Indiana University men's swim team, says McAllister's technique put him back into the swim of things.

Shoulder problems were making it hard for Dr. Councilman to train for his goal of swimming across the Catalina Channel. "The sports massage therapy

(continued)

I received from McAllister worked wonders," he says. "I can now swim two or three miles and feel no pain."

The treatment can be self-administered, but McAllister recommends having a trained sports massage therapist perform it on you over a period of several days. Here the main points are summarized.

36-5

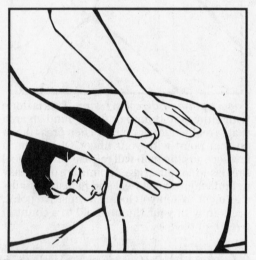

Before the massage begins, warm the shoulder for 15 minutes with a warm towel or heating pad. This not only increases the temperature in the shoulder area, but it also helps relax the subject.

36-4

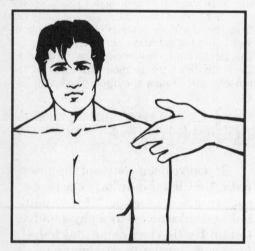

First you need to find out exactly where it hurts. You can do this by pressing lightly on the shoulder with your finger. The spots where it is sensitive are where the work needs to be done.

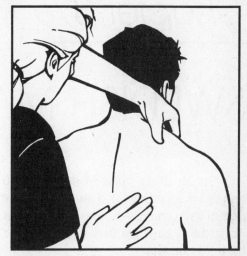

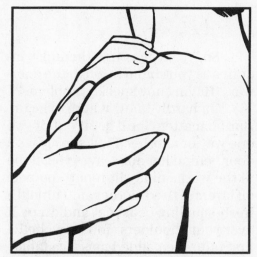

If it's the trapezius muscle (the large, flat triangular muscle found on each side of the back) that hurts, it can be worked by grasping it between the thumb and the other fingers. Work in a gentle rolling motion down its length.

36-8

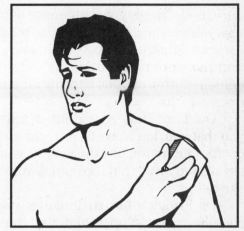

Now the massage begins. The finger of the person giving the treatment and the subject's shoulder skin should move as one. The important thing here is friction, *not* pressure. So rub the fingers across the fibers of the tendon, ligament, or muscle; never straight up and down. Placing the middle finger on top of the index finger will help give added support.

After the massage, the shoulder should be stretched through its whole range of motion. Once stretching is completed, a 20-minute ice massage of the area should be done to help cool the joint and the surrounding tissue.

Chapter 37

SWEDISH MASSAGE

On Monday, your boss says you can start looking for a new job if he doesn't see that 200-page sales report on gadgets and gizmos in his in-box by 5:00 P.M. sharp.

On Tuesday, you drag yourself through the day with a fever and a throat so raw you could swear an army of marauding microbes marched through it with sandpaper stuck to their soles.

On Wednesday, your teenage son tells you he somehow managed to total his driving instructor's car—not to mention the state police barracks—while demonstrating parallel parking for his license exam.

On Thursday, your dentist tells you that you don't have to worry about cavities anymore, but the sooner you get started on all that root canal work, the better.

On Friday, after battling evening rush-hour traffic on a highway that seems to be under construction only when traffic is already bumper-to-bumper, you pull in just in time for your appointment.

"So," your massage therapist inquires as you slump through the doorway, "Having any special problems?"

You hardly know where to begin. But no matter. She'll get it out of you one way or another. First she closes a door behind her and leaves you alone in the warm, dimly lit room. You peel off layers of tired clothes. You unfold a fresh-smelling bedsheet and drape it over your shoulders. You crawl belly-first onto the padded massage table.

"Ready?" she asks from the other side of the door.

"Umhum," you grunt, your face buried in the table's soft headrest.

You hear the door open, then close. Footsteps pad softly around you. You know you should clear your mind, but you're still thinking about your job, about your boss with the bottomless in-box. A button clicks and music begins to play—a piano. The sheet is drawn slowly down your back and tucked in at your waist. You know you should calm down, but you're still thinking about your son, the car, the police. Somewhere near your feet, liq-

280

uid gurgles from a plastic bottle. Moistened hands briskly rub together. You know you should relax, but you're still thinking about the dentist, about his perfect white teeth getting bigger and bigger as he leans toward you and tells you to say,

"Ahhhhhhhhhhhhhhhhhhhhhh!"

Two warm, strong hands smooth sweet-smelling oil onto your back in long, gentle strokes. The palms move along the flat, sore muscles on either side of your spine, starting near your hips, sweeping up your back, curving around your shoulders, teasing your neck, then sliding down and doing it all over again, each time with a bit more pressure. Now they're on the right side of your back, the hands pulling at skin and the muscles beneath in a gentle, kneading motion, and now they're on your left side. It feels good. Oh, yes, it feels so very good.

Now the fingers get into the act. Firm fingertips explore the channels along your spine. They travel slowly, cautiously, on a search and destroy mission for knots and kinks and tangles. You're starting to tingle. The fingers and hands—and elbows and forearms—work your stiff shoulders now, your tight neck. Oh, it hurts, but it's a *good* hurt, one that means everything will feel extraordinarily better when it stops. Your forehead is getting damp. You're forgetting about all the things you thought you could never forget about. You're aware of music playing—violins—but you're losing track of time, of the seconds and minutes that will

When Not to Massage

As therapeutic as massage can be, experts warn that in a few situations it should be avoided or done only with special care lest you risk endangering a person's health. Among them:

• Do not massage a person with high fever, cancer, tuberculosis or other infectious or malignant conditions which might be further spread throughout the body.

• Avoid massaging the abdomen of a person with high blood pressure or gastric or duodenal ulcers.

• Do not massage the legs of someone with varicose veins, diabetes, phlebitis or other blood vessel problems. Massage could further stress the vessels or even dislodge a blood clot, which could lead to an aneurysm or stroke.

• Massage no closer than six inches on either side of bruises, cysts, breaks in the skin and broken bones. Never massage them directly.

• A person whose body is swollen with "pitting" edema (when you press the skin of such a person with your fingertip, the mark stays depressed) should not be massaged. Gentle massage of a person with nonpitting edema is acceptable.

• You may massage people with swollen limbs, but do so very gently and only above the swelling and in the direction of the heart.

make up this long and delightful hour.

The strong hands squeeze your arms. Pummel your thighs. Slither down your calves. You feel tension seeping out through your skin—here, there, everywhere. The gentle hands stretch your ankles. Knead your toes. Rub your abdomen. You feel limp. Your breath is slow and deep. The warm hands caress your face. Run through your scalp. Cup over your eyes. And then, suddenly, finally, they stop. They go away. The door opens and closes. You can't be sure of it, but you think you might be floating. You can't open your eyes. You can't lift a finger. All you can do is lie there in exquisite detachment while the music—a harp now—plays on and you wonder: Could this be heaven?

Massage for Millions

If you don't consider such a massage session one of the high points of your week—or of your life—it's probably because you just haven't tried one yet. But more and more people are.

"More than a million Americans receive a massage each year," says Robert Calvert, editor and publisher of *Massage Magazine*. You'll find massage therapists plying their trade in an intriguing variety of settings, he says, from homes and health clubs to medical offices and corporate offices. Many professionals have even set up

shop at airports and shopping centers. What's more, as our understanding and appreciation of the benefits of massage grows, many of us are taking matters into our own hands on an amateur basis—learning the basic techniques and offering this special gift to friends and loved ones.

When most people talk about massage, they are usually talking about classic Swedish massage, the most commonly practiced form in Western countries. Massage as an approach to health care actually dates back as far as 2700 B.C. in China. But about 150 years ago, Peter Ling of Sweden developed a systematic form of massage that integrated ancient oriental techniques with more modern principles of anatomy and physiology. The system was introduced in this country by Dr. S. W. Mitchell in the late 19th century.

Originally developed primarily as a medical treatment, Swedish massage emphasizes several basic strokes applied to the soft tissue of the body, often quite vigorously. A number of additional styles have since emerged from the original form. Shifting the focus from the purely physical, these more "holistic" practitioners often endeavor to treat the mind and spirit as well as the body in their work. Even among therapists trained in the traditional form, Calvert notes, a great many of them ultimately develop a more eclectic approach.

"My working definition of massage is 'structured touching,'" says

Everything You Wanted to Know about Massage but Were Afraid to Ask

Is massage sexy? The subject is a touchy one for professionals. They have, after all, worked very hard to let the public know that massage as they practice it is worlds away from the services generally offered at sleazy massage parlors downtown.

"I think we've been in a cultural bind where touching has been associated with sexuality. That precludes a lot of the healing, therapeutic benefits of touch," says Paul Davenport, director of the Florida School of Massage. "Fortunately, in the last 10 years we've gotten more into touching for touching's sake."

Nevertheless, massage does have its intimate, sensual aspects, which can be pretty frightening to some. "We're inviting people to do something really different—to allow themselves to be touched—and that's scary," says Ron Clark, director of the Austin School of Massage Therapy. "I've had clients who were ready to bolt for the door. I tell them, 'If you want to be massaged in a wetsuit and a trenchcoat, that's okay with me. Whatever it takes, make yourself comfortable.' "

And although massage may not be a direct turn-on, it can actually aid some people in overcoming sexual dysfunctions.

"Sexuality is often associated with performance and self-concept, which can cause a lot of anxiety," says Davenport. "Learning to touch and be touched in a way that's *not* oriented toward a goal can help people stop worrying."

Some people with sex problems may enjoy touching their partners but have difficulty being touched themselves. "I occasionally refer my sex therapy clients to a massage therapist so they'll learn to be less tense while they're being touched," says clinical psychologist Robert Mark, Ph.D. "I suggest that they concentrate on how it feels and encourage them to ask the massage therapist what he's doing. I think that for them, learning some of the principles of massage can help."

David Palmer, director of the Amma Institute, a massage school in San Francisco. Beyond that, he says, the actual intention behind massage can vary considerably, "from making someone feel better, to correcting body alignment, to transforming someone's life."

Good Medicine

"Massage has very powerful phys-iological effects," says Robert King, president of the American Massage Therapy Association (AMTA) and co-director of the Chicago School of Mas-sage Therapy. "It tracks down distor-tions throughout the body, corrects them and creates a condition we call 'muscular equilibrium.' In this state, the body becomes a really good envi-ronment for wellness to occur."

"I used to have almost constant backaches from a pinched nerve in my neck," says Jim Colucci, a printing company salesman whose doctor gave him a prescription to visit the Swedish Institute's P. H. Ling Clinic in New York City. Now he makes sure he gets in for a session every week, because, "the pain is definitely relieved by massage."

Bob Kiss is another massage con-vert. "I tend to be skeptical, even cynical," he says, "but there's nothing more convincing than the way you feel." For him, finding relief from an old athletic injury was all the con-vincing he needed.

Kiss's injury occurred during a high school basketball game. "I caught the ball in the rim of the basket and twisted my back very badly," he recalls. "Doctors couldn't correctly diagnose it. They told me it was psychosomatic, all in my mind. So for a decade I just lived with the pain. I had to sleep with my knees held up to my chest.

Finally, a chiropractor sent me for my first massage. It's helped a lot."

Kiss also credits massage for reg-ular relief from a chronic occupational hazard. "I'm six-foot-four and a pro-fessional photographer," he explains. "That means I spend all day hunching over a little camera. I end up with an enormous neck and shoulder ache. Massage relieves the tension and helps me stand up straighter. It also leaves me feeling completely relaxed and able to deal with things much better."

But backaches are just one slen-der sliver of the full range of physical ills amenable to massage. Practitio-ners count on their handiwork to treat everything from bronchial asthma to broken bones, from indigestion to insomnia. (See "The Healing Power of Swedish Massage" for details on spe-cific conditions.)

"At first, doctors were reluctant to give their patients prescriptions for our clinic. But now that they've seen results, they make referrals frequently and with much greater confidence," says Jean Eckardt, assistant director of the Swedish Institute, the only school in the country that teaches med-ical massage.

"I've referred patients to massage therapists for a variety of problems, from back spasms to sleep disorders, and I don't generally see them very much after that," says Tessa Fischer, M.D., a family practitioner at the An-chor Medical Center in Chicago. "I could prescribe sedatives, but I don't like to. I consider massage a very beneficial alternative."

How It Works

What's the secret of this feel-good medicine? Practitioners say that massage imparts a major physiological change: It helps improve circulation by encouraging the movement of blood through the veins back toward the heart. That in turn enables fresh blood to pour through the arteries. Efficient blood flow is important to every system of the body, but taut, tense muscles often interfere.

"Problems in our muscular system are an often overlooked culprit in a wide variety of disorders," says Robert King. Healthy circulation means that oxygen and other nourishing materials are reaching cells throughout your entire body, helping you to think more clearly, metabolize your food more efficiently and possibly even resist disease more easily. Good circulation also means that poisonous waste materials—like the lactic acid that stores up painfully in tired muscles—are being swept away.

By triggering the release of the body's natural painkillers—hormones called endorphins—massage also has a tranquilizing effect on the central nervous system. No wonder a good rubdown can leave you with a sense of euphoria.

"Massage is actually a form of hypnotic trance and as such, it can be deeply relaxing," says psychotherapist Mark Maginn, who often sends his own clients for massages to work out the physical kinks that result from mental stress.

"The primary benefit of massage is relaxation," agrees Swami Kriyananda, director of the International School of Massage Therapy in San Francisco. "Massage can help you become aware of where tension is in your body, how you can release it and how you can prevent it."

For Diana Schuback, an artist in her late sixties, tension release is definitely the goal when she checks in for her weekly massage. "I'm generally an intense person, even a little hyper," she says. "I have a hard time relaxing. Massage gives me an opportunity to do that. It calms me down. It gives me an incredible feeling of well-being."

Deidre Yunginger had ideas other than relaxation when she went for a massage for the first time. "I needed relief from some problems I was developing in my knees and feet from playing rugby," says the young marketing consultant. "But after a couple of visits, I realized how great massage is for relieving stress. I don't play rugby anymore, but I still go in for my massage every two or three weeks. I don't even have to look at a calendar to know when it's time for another session. I can *feel* it."

Although every patient at the Swedish Institute's Ling Clinic has been dispatched there by a doctor who has made a specific medical diagnosis, most of the conditions treated can actually be linked to stress, says clinic supervisor Alexis Phillips. Excess stress has numerous effects, from high blood pressure to headaches.

"Most people experience a great deal of stress, whether they work as executives or secretaries, whether they live in the city or the suburbs," she says. "Massage is one of the very few times when a person will have 30 minutes or an hour absolutely focused on herself. This really has a calming effect."

Visiting a massage therapist can not only help you relieve tension. It can also help you uncover its source. Psychotherapist Maginn often finds massage helpful for clients who have difficulty expressing emotions.

"Emotions are based in the body," he says. "Frequently massage can loosen up some of the emotional stuff that's going on, and that helps a person work things through in therapy."

One emotion that poses a problem for many people is anger. "People express anger physically. It's not just something that happens in your head," says Margaret Avery, a licensed massage therapist and director of the Desert Institute for the Healing Arts in Tucson. "When you get angry on your job, or things in your life just aren't going right, you get tight. You clench your fists even if you're not actually shaking them at somebody. You move awkwardly and hold tension throughout your whole body.

"There's nothing worse for your body. Your muscles are very live, supple tissues. When contracted like this for a long period of time, they are actually being damaged. As a result, your body starts to lose its efficiency overall."

But as relaxing as massage is, it can also be stimulating. Classic Swedish massage strokes applied rapidly with deep pressure, as opposed to slowly and gently, can be invigorating. And for some people, even a relaxing massage can result in a welcome burst of energy.

"I've gone for a massage on a summer day when I was just dragging, when I'd had a tough day and was tired and beat," says Jim Colucci. "I came out of there feeling like I just had eight hours sleep. It's rejuvenating."

Finding a Pro

If you haven't already experienced massage, now's a good time to make an appointment with a pro. There are about 15,000 professionally trained massage therapists in this country, estimates *Massage Magazine*'s Robert Calvert, and their legions are growing.

A massage therapist may have 100 hours of training or 1,000—training varies from state to state, as do licensing laws. "What's most important is that you find a therapist who's 'on the legit,'" says Calvert. "Steer clear of massage parlors, which generally are a cover for prostitution and usually have nothing to do with therapeutic massage."

Massage for an Easier Pregnancy

If you're pregnant, you may be excitedly anticipating the joys of motherhood. But you may *not* be expecting the sundry aches and pains that often accompany this major body stressor. Massage can relieve some of that discomfort and possibly even make labor easier.

"A lot of pregnant women develop lower back pain and problems in their hips," says Mimi Moreno, codirector of the Center for Therapeutic Massage in Gainesville, Florida, where she teaches massage to moms-to-be and their partners. "They retain fluid and become swollen. They get neck problems because they have to sleep on their sides so much. These can all be treated with massage."

The sooner a pregnant woman starts getting massaged—ideally, once or twice a week, Moreno says—the better. Some women begin the process in the very early stages to loosen up muscles in their backs and to get their bodies into proper alignment to better handle the burden of childbearing.

Massage for the pregnant woman differs from ordinary massage. For one thing, any abdominal stroking should be limited to self-massage. For another, many of the strokes are applied while she lies on her side, propped up with pillows. And she isn't confined to a small room or expected to sit still. "If she's uncomfortable, her circulation can get blocked. She needs a lot of space so she can get up and move around. She might even need to get up a couple of times during the session to go to the bathroom," says Moreno.

The unfortunate mother-to-be who is stuck in bed for any extended period will especially appreciate the circulation-promoting aspects of massage. "Massage is like your best friend when you're in bed all the time," says Moreno. And for the many women who work throughout their pregnancies, massage can be rejuvenating after a long day on the job.

Massage can help prepare a woman for labor by showing her what it feels like to truly relax, says Moreno. This is important because "birthing is a process of letting go." And when labor begins, brief massages given during the long pauses between contractions can encourage her to go on with this demanding process.

After birth, the mother's belly can finally be massaged, says Moreno, which helps get it back into shape and tones her uterus. Massage can also relieve pain in body parts she might have strained during labor.

But there's yet another benefit, says Moreno, that's psychological rather than physical. "Too often, pregnant women think they're fat and ugly. I think massage shatters those stereotypes by helping a woman and her partner accept her body. They come to see that she's really very beautiful."

The best way to find a legitimate professional is through the grapevine, says AMTA president Robert King. "If a friend has had a massage with satisfactory results, that's a good start. Second, make sure the therapist is certified."

Business cards and flyers may also lead you to the man, or woman (whichever you'd be more comfortable with) you're looking for. So may your local telephone directory. "Look for several things in an ad, such as the words 'nonsexual' or 'therapeutic.' License numbers and affiliation with professional organizations may also be listed," says Calvert.

Take note of a few things at your first appointment. The practitioner should always respect your modesty by properly draping you with a sheet or towel throughout the session. Also, while he may very likely ask about your medical history to see if there are any conditions he should know about before your massage, he should not be diagnosing you. Finally, rapport is very important. If you can feel that the person laying his hands on you is trustworthy, you're probably in the right place.

Expect to pay anywhere from $25 to $90 for an hour-long, full-body massage. If you shop around, you might find someone less expensive. House calls are more expensive, because you're paying the person's travel time to and from your home. (For more help in finding a pro, see the box "Massage Resources" on page 292.)

Do-It-Yourself Massage

But it's not necessary to see a professional to enjoy the benefits of massage. In fact, you and a companion may prefer to experiment with basic massage techniques on your own. Nonprofessionals are certainly advised not to use massage to attempt to treat serious medical problems. But the relaxing, rejuvenating benefits of massage are available to anyone willing to learn. (See the box, "Swedish Strokes—Mastering the Basics" on page 299 for an introduction to the most commonly used techniques.)

"I think that anyone who is willing to be sensitive, present and available for another human being is able to give an effective massage," says Paul Davenport, director of the Florida School of Massage in Gainesville. "Massage therapists don't actually *heal* anyone. Rather, we provide the context in which a person can begin to heal himself."

Massaging a mate or friend can be one of the most caring things you do. "Massage is really important to me and my wife," says Eric Kaufman, a lawyer in his late twenties. "Often, say if I fall asleep on the couch after work, I'll wake up and she'll be massaging my hands. Or if she has had a rough day, I feel sympathy and want to help her feel better.

"I like touching her a lot. Somewhere I read that you should hug some-

Keeping the Calm

It's all over. For an exquisite hour you've been stroked, kneaded, squeezed and pummeled—turned upside down and inside out. But now you're just lying there in the quiet, wondering how and when you'll ever manage to peel yourself up off the mat. And why. Because maybe, just maybe, if you don't move a muscle, this feeling, this exquisite post-massage calm, will last forever.

"The wonderful feeling you get from massage results from the release of natural painkillers called endorphins," explains Margaret Avery, director of the Desert Institute for the Healing Arts. "They create a type of natural euphoria. Unfortunately, you can't quite duplicate that once they start to subside."

But you might be able to forestall the feeling's departure. "It's best if you can just lounge around after a massage," says Alexis Phillips of the Swedish Institute. "Take a nice, long soak in a hot bathtub." Then crawl under the covers and drift off to sleep.

Many massage therapists urge their clients to take up stretching, yoga, meditation or biofeedback between sessions to help keep tension at bay.

"I think a physical discipline like exercise is important for everyone," adds Swami Kriyananda, director of the International School of Massage Therapy. "We all have these animal bodies, and the kind of physical activity most of us are involved with on a day-to-day basis isn't enough. We need regular, adequate exercise to feel vitality, to have some sense of control over our bodies, and to maintain our natural grace."

body at least once a day. So I like to make a point of touching, and massage is one way to do that."

Kevin Starbard, a political activist who is studying massage, likes to give massages to friends. "I consider massage a great gift. I have this skill that I like to use without expecting anything in return. My friends will usually make a request for a massage in a coy way, saying something like, 'Oh, my shoulder hurts here.' And I'll oblige. I like making people happy."

How do you go about learning the techniques? You might consider getting at least one massage from a professional, under whose trained hands you can probably soak up a lot about what feels good and how it's done. You can also read books about massage. Or you can even take a class taught by a professional therapist like Mara Nesbitt of Portland, Oregon.

"I teach a lot of couples who just want to be able to help each other," Nesbitt says. "A woman will say, 'My husband comes home from work, his shoulder hurts and this is what I do. Am I doing it right?' Or she comes home and her feet are killing her. How can he help her? They already like to touch each other, but they want to be able to do it in a more educated way."

Keep in mind, too, that *giving* a massage can be as satisfying as receiving one. "I always tell my students that as much as giving massage is about nurturing and support and healing another, first off, you're doing it for yourself," says Paul Davenport. "Our basic human need for touch is satisfied whether you are the person being touched or the one doing the touching."

Not a few massage professionals entered the field after a fulfilling experience of seeing the difference touch made to a loved one. "I used to massage my father's feet after work. He was a cab driver in New York," recalls Kriyananda. "I liked helping him. I saw the benefit to him. I saw the difference when he was able to release tension."

The very act of involvement in moving through a massage leads to personal satisfaction, too. "I always feel when I finish giving a massage that I've gotten a massage myself," says Alexis Phillips.

Tips for Beginners

Despite the old image of Olga and Heinrich, the stereotypically hefty, solid masseuse and masseur, you don't have to be particularly big to give a great massage. You don't even have to be strong. But there are some guidelines you should follow.

Use Your Body

"It's not important whether you have small hands or large hands, whether you weigh 100 pounds or 300 pounds. These things have nothing to do with being able to give a good massage," says Phillips. "A small person can give a deep massage without straining herself by learning to use her body effectively."

The trick is to learn to bend your knees, breathe rhythmically and use what body weight you do have to your benefit. Once you establish that balance —through practice, practice and more practice—you will be able to work without tiring quickly or hurting yourself.

Study the Charts

Although it's not absolutely necessary, it's very helpful to learn something about the human body—where the bones and muscles and organs are—before you start massaging someone. Why? Because you want to make sure you're massaging muscles and other soft tissues rather than putting pressure on bones or delicate internal organs. Dig out that old high school biology textbook or buy yourself an inexpensive anatomical chart for easy reference.

Relax

"Massage is not just the physical act of manipulating someone's body," Kriyananda notes. "It involves energy, *your* energy. In order to get somebody else relaxed, you have to be relaxed yourself." To that end, he always does a meditation or yoga exercise before a massage session. Find your own form of relaxation and practice it before you inadvertently transmit your tension to somebody else.

Communicate

"I make it a point to always talk to a new client before a session, to find out who they really are," says Kriyananda. "This breaks the ice."

Although you and your massage partner may already know each other quite well, massage is an extremely intimate act; you may still feel somewhat tense about it. Talking for a while beforehand might help.

And be sure to keep the lines of communication open during the actual massage. (This is true when you're visiting a professional therapist, too.) Not that you want to engage in nonstop conversation, but it's especially important that the person receiving the massage feel free to speak up. "If any area is painful or tender, don't be shy about saying, 'That hurts there,' or, 'I would feel better if you pressed a little softer there,'" says Mara Nesbitt. "Or if anything feels particularly good, go ahead and say so. Getting feedback is very gratifying to the person giving massage."

But not all communication is verbal. Watch for nonverbal signals by listening "through your hands."

"You can tell a lot about what's going on with a person in the first few strokes, when you first apply oil and begin to touch him on his back," says Alexis Phillips. "You're going to be able to feel a lot about the other person's body. You can tell if it's tense, if it's being treated well, if it can handle deep work or whether you'll need to work lightly."

You may notice your partner stiffening up under a particular stroke. Try a different one in the same place, or move to another area and come back to this one later. Watch your partner's face for signals. "You may be working on a painful area and not realize it until you notice your partner biting his lip or see a tear coming down his cheek," says Paul Davenport.

And pay attention to his breathing. If the person you are massaging is in pain, he may hold his breath. Remember too, that breathing is an interaction. If you remember to inhale deeply and evenly, your partner will generally follow suit.

Time It Right

Most people can't afford more than one massage a week from a professional, but there's generally no harm

Massage Resources

The following organizations can direct you to a professional massage therapist:

Alliance of Massage Therapists, Inc.
c/o Swedish Institute, Inc.
226 West 26th Street
New York NY 10001
(212) 736-1100

American Massage Therapy Association (AMTA)
1130 West North Shore Avenue
Chicago IL 60626
(312) 761-AMTA

Associated Professional Massage Therapists and Allied Health Practitioners International
1746 Cole Boulevard
Golden CO 80401
(303) 526-1740

The following books have been recommended by professionals for further information on massage techniques:

The Art of Sensual Massage by Gordon Inkeles (Simon & Schuster).

The Art of Swedish Massage by Bertild Ravald (E. P. Dutton).

The Book of Massage by Lucinda Lidell, Sara Thomas, Carola Beresford Cooke and Anthony Porter (Simon & Schuster).

The Complete Book of Swedish Massage by Armand Maanum and Herb Montgomery (Harper & Row).

Healing Massage Techniques, by Frances M. Tappan (Appleton and Lange).

The Massage Book by George Downing (Random House).

You can keep up to date on Swedish massage and a variety of other hands-on styles with *Massage Magazine*. For subscription information, write to *Massage Magazine*, P.O. Box 1389, Dept. PM, Kailua-Kona, HI 96745 or call (808) 329-2433.

done in getting a relaxing massage more often than that at home. When's the best time for a massage? "There's no simple answer to that," says Davenport. "It's highly individual. Some people relax better in the morning, some in the afternoon, and others do better at night." Some people are energized by massage and enjoy an early session to get them going before a busy day. These same people often don't do well with massage at night, since it tends to relax them initially and then leave them wide awake. For others, a nighttime massage is the perfect precursor to drifting off to sleep. You and your partner will need to discover for yourselves your own best time.

As terrific as massage feels, it's best not to have one that's longer than an hour or so. Lying flat on your back or on your stomach for too long can actually leave you feeling worse than you did before the massage, warns

Alexis Phillips, especially if you have lower back problems or knee problems. And if you're trading massages with a partner, let at least a day pass before the person who received the massage gives one in return.

Go with the Flow

"Giving a massage is like watching a wonderful ballet or listening to an incredible symphony in your mind," says Phillips. "Your movements should like that flow. Once you learn that flow, the massage will be much more relaxing for both of you."

THE HEALING POWER OF SWEDISH MASSAGE

Practitioners say Swedish massage, and the variations that have grown out of it, can be beneficial in treating a wide range of physical and psychological conditions.

Arthritis

The circulation-boosting aspects of massage can sometimes help to relieve the pain of arthritis, says Margaret Avery, director of the Desert School for the Healing Arts.

In osteoarthritis, a vicious cycle takes hold when you would like to exercise but can't do so because of the pain. "Not moving is very harmful," says Avery. "You need to move, to exercise, in order to have good circu-

lation. The health of one's joints, the site of arthritic symptoms, depends in large part upon the flow of blood."

Massage can be a form of "artificial exercise" that helps blood flow, increases the range of motion of limbs, and helps maintain the suppleness of your body's soft tissues—which all add up to keeping your joints moving to the best of their ability.

The painful inflammation of rheumatoid arthritis sufferers can also be lessened, Avery says. "Massage is especially useful after surgery to joints in the feet, hands or elsewhere. It helps people rehabilitate themselves."

A full-body massage, paying a little extra attention in the area around arthritic joints, is generally an effective treatment, she says. "The time of day is also important. A person with arthritis usually wakes up stiff. To start the morning with a massage could be really beneficial."

Back and Neck Pain

The majority of people who come in to the Swedish Institute's Ling Clinic have neck or back problems," says supervisor Phillips. Pain in the neck, shoulders and back can result from stress, poor posture, even job-related functions such as working for long periods of time hunched over a computer terminal.

Massage should be focused not only on the sore spots but on the muscles attached to them, says Ron Clark, director of the Austin School of Massage Therapy. "Often one pain is a symptom of a particular dysfunction somewhere else. We treat the pain but also try to figure out where it came from."

Emotional sources are also examined. "A pain in the neck can literally be caused by dealing with somebody who's a pain in the neck," he says. "I can work the physical pain out with massage, but the person also needs to acknowledge that this difficult relationship can be affecting him."

Broken Bones

It's one of life's miracles that a broken bone, put in a cast and given time, can heal itself. Massage assists the process by bringing fresh blood to the injured area, which helps to heal the break and flush away debris.

Massage, which is never done on the break itself but in surrounding areas, can also help prevent nearby muscles from losing strength completely. If you have a broken ankle in a cast, for instance, your entire leg is limited in its motion. Also, your arms and shoulders can become overtaxed from walking on crutches. Massage relieves tightness in all affected areas and may help you regain your original strength and flexibility more easily when the cast is removed.

Bronchial Asthma

Massage is used to help clear out the phlegm and mucus that collect in the bronchial tubes of a person suffering from this disorder, says Alexis Phillips. "Lying flat on a table, head lower than the feet, the person is massaged in the area over the lungs with a stroke called cupping. This produces a vacuum that loosens the material up." The effleurage stroke is then used to help move the phlegm out of the chest area.

Heart Disease

Here the effects are largely indirect. Heart disease is a stress-related disorder, and massage helps lower stress. It also helps circulation, and that takes some of the work off the heart, says Janine Kramer, director of the Swedish Institute's Ling Clinic. "I can't say much about the physiological effects of massage in the recovery of people with heart disease, but they *are* going to feel better. And if they feel any stress about the fact that they had a heart attack, massage can help to relieve that. It can provide great comfort."

Habit Reform

One powerful benefit of massage, say many practitioners, is the heightened "sense of self" it can induce. Becoming more aware of your body and its relationship to your thoughts, feelings and actions can give you a new sense of power over your destiny.

"People who have massages often change. They look different, stand up straighter. They might start losing weight," says Jean Eckardt, assistant director of the Swedish Institute. "They focus on feeling good about their bodies and they start to take better care of themselves."

Massage may give you the helping boost you need to quit or cut back on smoking and other unhealthy habits. "The process of massage helps people accept themselves," says Margaret Avery. "This is the first step toward changing unhealthy habits. First you admit that it's okay that you've been doing all these terrible things. After that, you are able to make decisions about changing that prove to be much more successful."

Indigestion and Constipation

Massage can sometimes relieve digestive problems caused by poor muscle tone or a sedentary or bedridden situation, says Avery. Loss of muscle tone impedes digestion. Furthermore, "the stomach is an area that collects tension, even in the person who might not have digestive problems yet," she says. Gentle massage increases circulation to the area assisting digestion. Massage done to the colon—always applied clockwise, the same direction as the process of elimination—can help relieve constipation, she says.

Neuromuscular Disorders

People suffering from multiple sclerosis, spastic paralysis, flaccid paralysis or other neuromuscular disorders may find some relief in massage. "We can't cure a person, but massage can often relieve a great deal of the tension and strain and discomfort," says Alexis Phillips.

Spasms are relieved primarily by the application of the massage technique called tapotement, a vigorous pounding. When used for 20 to 60 seconds on a particular muscle, the muscle becomes exhausted and spastic contractions cease, she says. "Charleyhorse" muscle cramps can be often be relieved in the same manner.

Problems of the Elderly

Elderly people can sometimes find tremendous relief through massage from problems that commonly accompany the aging process. One common symptom is edema or swelling, often in the legs or ankles. Oftentimes this results from lack of movement. "If you're not using the muscles, the circulation moving up the limbs is going to be sluggish," says Janine Kramer. So fluids tend to pool in the extremities.

"The problem is really very simple to deal with. Just elevate the legs and do very gentle massage above the swelling and up toward the heart to help the blood pour back into the torso."

Massage is also a powerful aid to the older person who feels isolated and in need of a friendly touch. "A lot of our clinic patients are elderly women who have lost friends and relatives through death and are lonely," says Kramer. "Massage helps fill that gap. They have our attention for a half-hour or hour. They can talk to us or just let us work on them. And they come out feeling good."

Emotional Problems

Massage can assist people in working through emotional disturbances.

"A lot of people who are carrying around tremendous tension will never go to a counselor, but they will go to a massage therapist to get a relaxing massage," says Paul Davenport, director of the Florida School of Massage Therapy. "Oftentimes, massage is a door into a place where they discover that they can actually do something about the way they feel. The massage therapist can then possibly refer them to a counselor."

Psychotherapists, on the other hand, sometimes refer *their* clients for massage to assist the therapeutic process. "Massage is almost a 'professional caress' with the hands," says psychiatrist Glenn Miller, M.D. "One of the taboos of traditional psychotherapy is touching. Not that you can't shake a person's hand or put your arm around his shoulder, but real hands-on physical contact is considered a no-no. This way, however, while the psychotherapist is touching deep levels in the mind, the massage therapist is touching deep levels in the body."

People who have experienced significant losses can work through the grief process more quickly if they visit a massage therapist, clinical psychologist Robert Mark, Ph.D., believes. "Because of the stress, their adrenal glands work more, secreting hormones that wake them up at night and make them pretty tense," he says. "If they can be physically soothed, these hormones will clear out more quickly and allow them to get on with healing emotionally."

Massage also benefits that breed of person who has a hard time treating himself well. "I like to refer people who don't have much experience being nice to themselves," says psychotherapist Mark Maginn. "Once they experience massage, they get hooked. It feels great, it's relaxing and it reduces stress."

What's more, massage is a chance for a hard-working psychotherapist to relax. "I like to go for massage myself, to lie there on a table and not have to listen to anybody," says Maginn.

Recovery from Surgery

Surgery is traumatic for your body. But, therapists say, massage can aid recovery in a number of ways.

Undergoing anesthesia can be very disorienting, says Margaret Avery. "We do massage to help a person regain homeostasis [internal balance], to reunite them with their sense of touch and body awareness."

After surgery, problems can occur with scars. "While scars are healing, they sometimes adhere to the tissue underneath," says Janine Kramer. "If you've ever seen a scar that looks like it's sucked in, it's because it has adhered." Massage on either side of the scar, however, can help prevent adhesion.

After the surgical insertion of an artificial hip, knee or other joint, "you need to exercise to strengthen the muscle around the joint," says Margaret Avery. "However, such exercise irritates the nerves and creates waste products in the muscles. Massage therapy will help clear out these waste products. With the pain thus alleviated, you can continue exercising. As the muscles become more flexible, you get faster and better recovery."

Massage can also be crucial if the person recovering from surgery is bedridden for long periods. Immobility can be dangerously debilitating. Janine Kramer helped one such patient, who had had a cancerous lung removed, applying very gentle massage over a period of several weeks to stimulate his circulation. "Just getting that blood moving is very important, because otherwise when you're finally ready to get out of bed, you won't have the strength or energy to move," she says.

Sleep Disorders

Tossing and turning at night? "A lot of the problem may be tension," says Swami Kriyananda, director of the International School of Massage Therapy in San Francisco. "Some people get so wired. They function on abnormally high levels of adrenalin and are hooked on things like caffeine. But massage can definitely provide some release."

If, on the other hand, your problem is that you sleep *too* much or feel tired throughout the day, a massage that emphasizes vigorous strokes may stimulate your system and give you more energy and stamina.

Sprains

Limping around—or not moving at all—with a sprained ankle? "There's a lot that massage can do to help," says Janine Kramer. Getting massages at different stages of such an injury can help you regain movement more quickly, she says.

In the initial inflammatory stage, when the ankle swells, massage can help drain fluid from the area. The recommended treatment is to elevate the injured area and put ice on it to counteract the heat from the inflammation. Massage is then done above the injury in the direction of the heart to help drain debris that tends to settle and adhere to the joint. This accomplished, the joint will not stiffen as much as it otherwise might, says Kramer.

But some stiffness will almost always occur. Massage can help at that point, too. First, long, smooth massage strokes can bring fresh blood to the area and help to lengthen tissue. Second, the massage stroke called friction can break down stiffening adhesions and warm up the areas around the joints, which makes movement easier. ———

Temporomandibular Joint (TMJ) Syndrome

Getting lots of dental work or oral surgery done can leave you with a jaw painfully out of joint. "Sitting for long periods with your mouth open and head back while a dentist pushes down on your jaw can cause temporomandibular joint (TMJ) syndrome," says Kramer, who treats many patients referred by their dentists. Tension, tooth grinding or a faulty bite are other common culprits. The painful consequences include migraine headaches, facial pain, and severe neck spasms, all of which can often be alleviated with massage, she says.

AIDS Patient Support

"Massage therapists are introducing the concept of positive, nurturing touch to people who are catastrophically ill," says Robert King of the American Massage Therapy Association. That association operates a clinic for people suffering from acquired immune deficiency syndrome (AIDS), at which slow, gentle massage is done and taught to family and friends. "We know we aren't curing AIDS, but we are adding to the quality of life of people with a terminal illness," he says.

Cases of Physical Abuse

People who have been physically or sexually abused are often very mistrusting of others. Massage may help to overcome that fear.

"I often recommend massage for people to whom human contact is a problem," says psychiatrist Glenn Miller, M.D. "Massage is a nurturing form of nonsexual touch. If a person can learn to be comfortable with the touch of a single individual, that's a good step in learning to trust people."

SWEDISH STROKES—MASTERING THE BASICS

Want to make friends and influence people? Familiarize yourself with these basic strokes of Swedish massage, and they'll be putty in your hands.

You generally begin a massage by working on a person's back. The first stroke is always effleurage, which is followed by other strokes as you feel they are appropriate. Apply greater pressure when stroking in the direction of the heart to encourage blood flow through the veins. Complete your work in the area with more effleurage, then move on to another part of the body, beginning again with that same stroke.

Apply all strokes to muscles and soft tissues only. Do not massage bones or sensitive organs.

37-1

Effleurage (ef-flur-ahj), or stroking. A French word meaning touching lightly, effleurage gently acquaints your subject's body to the feeling of being touched and warms it up for later strokes. This is a long, gliding stroke. Run your hands along the length of the torso from the neck to the base of the spine, for example, or from the shoulder all the way down to the hand and fingertips.

This stroke can be done with the palms of one or two hands, your knuckles, fingertips or the ball of your thumb. Practitioners say it increases circulation, helps the sweat glands function and nourishes and rejuvenates the skin.

(continued)

SWEDISH STROKES—MASTERING THE BASICS—*Continued*

37-3

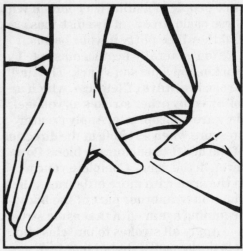

37-2

Petrissage (pet-ris-ahj). With one or two hands, with two thumbs or with your thumb and finger, carefully "pick up" muscles and lift them away from the bones, then roll, wring and squeeze them. Perform petrissage with your knuckles on people who have very thick, well-developed muscle.

Massage experts say this stroke increases circulation, clears out toxins like lactic acid and stimulates the passage of nutrients to the cells, which can contribute to increased muscle size and strength.

Friction. Using your thumb or fingertips, apply this deep, circular movement near joints and other bony areas such as the sides of the spine. Also use it in the "belly" of a muscle. Always make sure you've applied plenty of effleurage and petrissage first to warm up your subject's body.

Friction breaks down adhesions, which are knots that result when muscle fibers bind together. It contributes to more flexible joints, tendons and muscles and helps reduce swelling. Follow it immediately with effleurage.

37-4

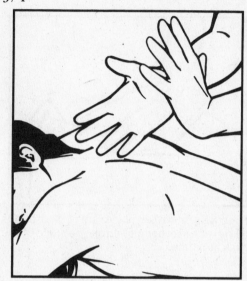

37-5

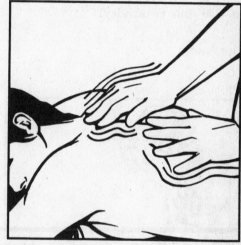

Tapotement (tap-ot-mon). A short chopping stroke that comes in many forms. *Chop* or *hack* with the edge of your hand. *Tap* with your fingertips. *Clap* with your palms or the flat surface of your hands and fingers. *Beat* with the edge of your closed fist.

Applied for a few seconds, this stroke can be very stimulating. Done for ten seconds or more, tapotement will begin to exhaust the muscle, making this a very effective treatment for muscles that are strained, cramped or suffering any type of spasms.

Vibration, or shaking. Spread hands or fingers on your subject's back or limbs, press down firmly and rapidly shake for a few seconds with a trembling sort of motion. Therapists say this stroke stimulates the nervous system and increases the power of muscles to contract. It also boosts circulation and increases the activity of the glands.

A STEP-BY-STEP FULL-BODY MASSAGE

We've illustrated a typical sequence of strokes in a full-body massage. Each may be repeated several times and embellished as you see fit. Or you may skip certain strokes (except for effleurage) altogether. No two massages are ever alike, nor should they be. Use your creativity!

The Back

37-6

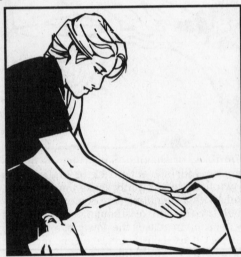

Your first strokes will usually be to your partner's back. Warm a small amount of oil on your palms. In a kneeling position, apply effleurage in long, gliding strokes. Start at the neck, slide down the back and up again. Repeat several times. Be sure to lean into the stroke to minimize strain to your own back.

37-7

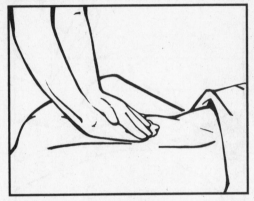

For a deeper stroke, place one of your hands on top of the other and stroke one side of the back at a time.

37-8

Effleurage can also be applied with your forearm. Kneel beside your subject while you lean into a long back and forth stroke.

37-9

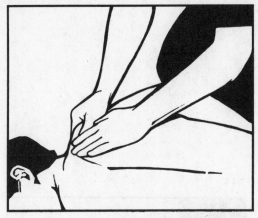

You may now move into deeper petrissage strokes. With your thumb and fingers, "pick up" the muscle all along the back and shoulders and gently knead it.

37-11

Petrissage in the lower back can help ease stiffness and pain. To relieve strain on your own back at the same time, sit beside your partner with your legs straight in front of you. Lean away slightly while kneading the muscles just below the waist.

37-10

For another approach to petrissage, roll your knuckles down the muscles along the spine. Be careful not to apply massage strokes on the spine itself.

37-12

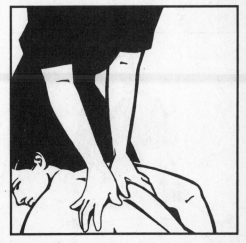

Apply friction by inserting your thumbs in the indentations along the vertebrae and pressing away from the spine.

(continued)

A STEP-BY-STEP FULL-BODY MASSAGE—*Continued*

The Back—*continued*

37-13

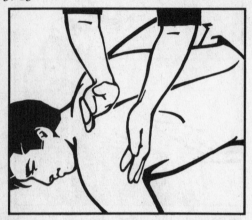

Apply stimulating tapotement by forming your hands in a C-shape. With their sides, strike the muscles up and down the back with a chopping motion for several seconds.

37-15

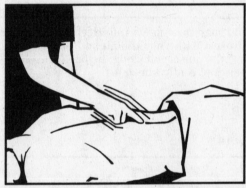

Follow with vibration. Place your fingers at the sides of the spine and press down while vibrating rapidly. You may also perform this with your palms, separately or one on top of the other.

37-14

You may also perform tapotement with your fingers, knuckles, fists or the flat of your hands.

The Back of the Leg

37-16

If your subject is draped, pull back the sheet or towel to expose one leg and a portion of the buttocks. Kneel at his side, apply oil with your hands in a long effleurage stroke that begins at the feet, then moves up the leg to the buttocks and back down again. Remember to move up on your knees and then down again with each stroke.

37-18

Put your partner's foot over your shoulder and apply deep petrissage with your knuckles in long upward strokes.

37-17

Gently bend the knee and pull the toe back for a relaxing stretch.

37-19

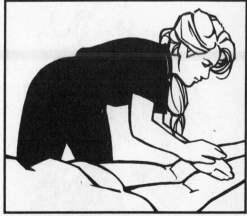

Apply tapotement up and down the leg. Complete work on the leg with effleurage.

(continued)

A STEP-BY-STEP FULL-BODY MASSAGE—*Continued*

The Foot

37-20

Place your partner's foot on your lap and pull back on the heel.

37-21

Apply effleurage with your forearm.

37-22

With your knuckles moving along the middle of the foot, apply a deep petrissage.

37-23

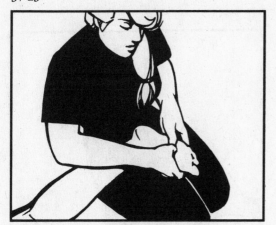

Firmly press into the center of the foot with a series of friction strokes.

37-24

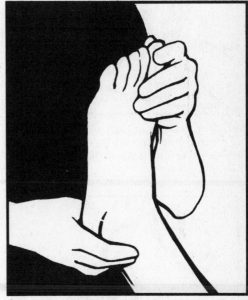

Complete your work on the foot by squeezing each toe and the spaces between them. Switch to the opposite leg and foot and repeat all the previous strokes.

(continued)

A STEP-BY-STEP FULL-BODY MASSAGE—*Continued*

The Front of the Leg

37-25

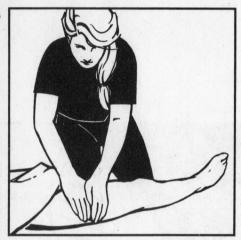

Ask your partner to turn over. Apply oil to your hands and smooth them up and down the leg in an effleurage stroke. You may also use your forearms.

37-27

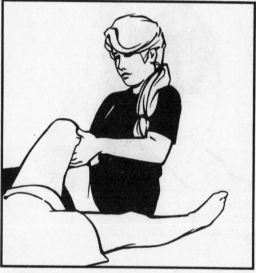

Apply a kneading petrissage stroke to the back of the calf while you lean back.

37-26

Bend your partner's knee and sit on his toes. Apply oil to your hands and smooth it over the calf muscles. Then work the back and front of the upper leg with an effleurage stroke.

37-28

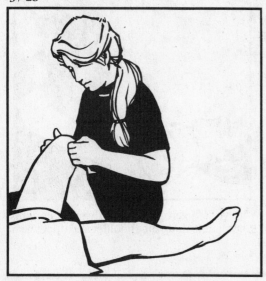

Place your fingers on the soft tissue around the kneecap and apply friction. Never massage directly on the knee—you could dislocate it.

37-29

Apply vibration to the thigh muscles for a few seconds using your fingertips or the flat of your hand. Complete work on the leg with effleurage and then repeat the previous strokes on the opposite leg.

(continued)

A STEP-BY-STEP FULL-BODY MASSAGE—*Continued*

The Arm

37-30

Raise your partner's arm and tuck his wrist under your arm. With oiled hands, apply a sweeping effleurage stroke up and down his arm from his shoulder to the tip of his fingers.

37-32

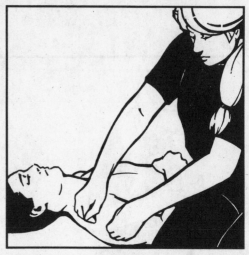

With your fingertips held tightly together, apply tapotement along the shoulder and upper arm.

37-31

Apply a kneading petrissage stroke.

37-33

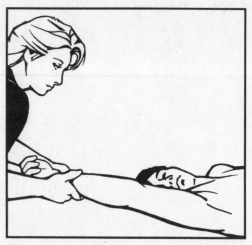

Gently lift the arm and pull it back for a nice stretch.

The Wrist and Hand

37-34

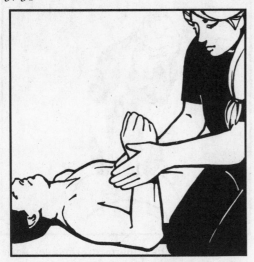

Place your palms on both sides of the wrist and gently roll them back and forth.

37-35

Use the same rolling motion on each individual finger.

37-36

Lean back and gently squeeze the fingers and stretch them toward you.

(continued)

The Neck

37-38

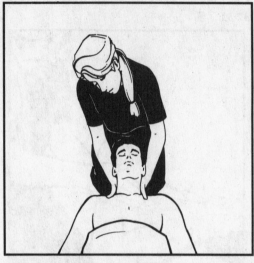

Place both hands underneath the neck with wrists flat on the mat, and apply kneading strokes with the fingertips.

The Shoulders and Chest

37-37

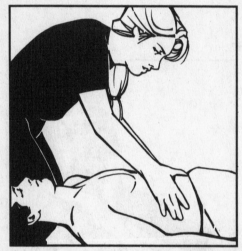

With oil on your hands, apply effleurage starting at the shoulders, moving down to the navel (on a woman, massage just to the top of the breasts) and up the back of the neck. Do not massage the front of the neck.

37-39

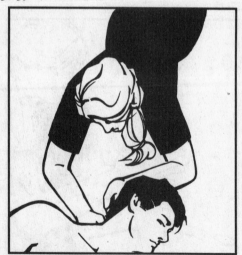

Ask your partner to turn his head to the side. Firmly stroke the back of his neck and shoulders with your knuckles. Complete work in this area with effleurage.

The Face

37-40

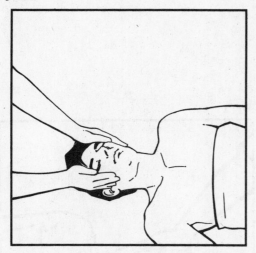

With a small amount of oil on your hands, apply gentle effleurage strokes from the neck and along the sides of the face. Do all face strokes in an upward motion and from the nose out toward the ears.

37-41

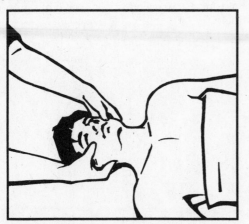

With your thumbs or index fingers, gently follow the shape of the cheekbone up toward the temples.

37-42

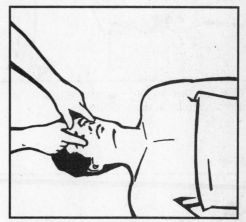

With your index finger, do a series of small circular strokes beneath the eyes, up to the top of the head and sliding down the bridge of the nose.

(continued)

A STEP-BY-STEP FULL-BODY MASSAGE—*Continued*

The Face—*continued*

37-43

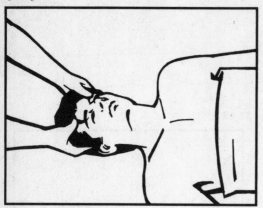

With the fingers and thumbs, apply a light friction stroke to the temples.

37-44

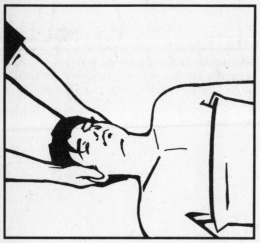

Wiggle, squeeze and slightly stretch the ears.

37-45

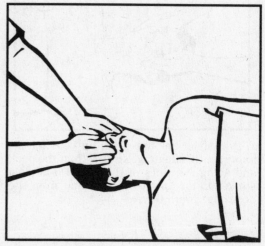

Warm your hands by rubbing your palms briskly together. Then place them over the eyes and hold for a few seconds for a relaxing grand finale.

Chapter 38

THERAPEUTIC TOUCH

Cathleen Fanslow stands behind you, centering herself with a short prayer. You sit sideways in an armless chair in her New York apartment. This traditionally trained registered nurse practices therapeutic touch and is preparing to assess and treat your bioenergetic field. Your *what?*

It's all Einstein's fault. He said, "$E = mc^2$" and threw science into a tizzy. He meant there's no difference between matter and energy. Both are made up of all kinds of particles. If the particles stick together, that's matter. If they don't, that's energy. One is always becoming the other.

These matter-energy particles make up what physicists and therapeutic touch practitioners call fields. You are an amalgamation of complex fields of life energy that are coextensive with the universe, they say. Or as therapeutic touch practitioner Janet Macrae, R.N., Ph.D., says in her book *Therapeutic Touch: A Practical Guide*, "We swim in a sea of living energy that interpenetrates and activates all our systems." Your bioenergetic field, your life energy, extends beyond the visual boundary of your body. A person not only is more than a body, but actually *is* the energy being used and received during therapeutic touch.

As physicists regard the universe as a whole, therapeutic touch practitioners view and treat the body and its field as a whole, not just connected parts. The verb "heal" comes from the Anglo-Saxon word *haelan*, meaning "to make whole." This understanding is crucial to the concept of therapeutic touch, which is concerned with the whole person, not just the physical body.

Disease is "disorder, dysrythmia and disharmony" in your bioenergetic field, Fanslow says. Therapeutic touch "assesses" where your field is weak or congested, and then directs energy into your field to balance it. This helps your system heal itself.

And you thought your body stopped at your skin. Thank you, Dr. Einstein.

Step-by-Step

Therapeutic touch is certainly esoteric as far as mainstream medicine goes, but it is being taught in leading university nursing/medical schools across the country. Its origins are in the ancient religious practice of laying on of hands, but Dolores Krieger, Ph.D., professor of nursing at New York University, and others have tested its effects and shown them to be real. Dr. Krieger is most responsible for defining and popularizing therapeutic touch, and has devised a method for learning and using it. Every day in hospitals around the world, nurses are relieving pain, reducing swelling, helping bones to knit, and ushering sleepless patients into slumber with therapeutic touch.

They do it in a standard five-step process. It can be learned from books, says Judith Smith, R.N., Ph.D., director of long-term care and health promotion at Johns Hopkins University School of Nursing, "but it's one of those methods where practice under supervision helps a lot. You have a tendency to discount a lot of the sensations you perceive when you practice therapeutic touch without feedback." Each person perceives the field in his or her own way.

Centering

"Holy Spirit of God take me as thy disciple." Eyes closed, breathing deeply and regularly, Fanslow intones to herself the short Catholic prayer she learned in childhood. This is the first step in therapeutic touch, called centering. It opens the conduit between the practitioner and her source of healing life energy.

"This solidifies your bond with the source of the energy," Fanslow says, whatever you conceive this source to be. "I image a golden light coming in the top of my head and encircling my heart. I need to be still so my chattering mind doesn't interfere."

Centering establishes your intent, essential to therapeutic touch. Intent and compassion to help or heal "is what actually initiates the healing process," Fanslow says. "You have to see the person as whole and well and image them in that way before and during the act of therapeutic touch. This helps the absorption of energy at a deep level."

You have to intend to become "a calm, focused conduit for the universal life energy and to direct the energy to the patient," Dr. Macrae says. Studies have shown that nurses who centered themselves before treating patients got much better results than nurses who merely went through the motions of therapeutic touch without centering.

Assessment

Following her prayer, Fanslow spends no more than a minute assessing your field. As you sit sideways on the chair so your back is exposed, she stands and then kneels alongside. She holds her hands with palms toward you about one to three inches from your body. One hand is in front, the other in back. She passes her hands smoothly down along the field from head to toe. Then she kneels in front of you and passes both hands down the front of the field with a gentle, rhythmic motion, synchronizing her field to yours. Finally, she kneels behind you and repeats this motion.

The sensations she is noting are subtle, but with practice anyone can recognize them (although, Fanslow cautions, "some people have more potential than others"). Some people sense it as warmth; Fanslow feels a vibratory rhythm. "It's changes in the rhythm in different areas of the body that have certain meaning to me," she says. "A very rapid vibration might indicate an infection or headache. A slower vibration might be something like a chronic back syndrome, some long-established arthritis, or a wound that has healed."

The field of a healthy person will feel whole and evenly distributed. The field of an unhealthy person will give off what Dr. Macrae labels "cues."

- Loose congestion—a cloud or a wave of heat, thickness, pressure, or heaviness.
- Tight congestion—a blockage in the flow of energy, marked by a sensation of coldness, emptiness or lack of movement.
- Deficit—a sensation that the field is pulling or drawing in, or that it has a hollowed-out area. A deficit is almost always found beneath blocked areas.
- Imbalance—the energy in one area isn't flowing with the whole, as if it were rapids or a sluggish part of a stream. Imbalance may produce a needles-and-pins or static electricity effect.

You haven't given Fanslow any clues about what's bothering you. So you're impressed when she announces her verdict. Without touching your physical body, she's found every sore point: Your neck, your lower back, your knees, every place you ache part or all of the time. But she doesn't stop there. "There's an emptiness, a sadness, in your heart, as if you've been hurt," she says. Neck, back, knees, heart—very common places for people to hurt. She could be guessing, but if so, she's guessed right.

Clearing Congestion

Now begins the treatment. Fanslow holds her hands over your tightly-congested neck and makes repeated sweeping movements downward. At the end of each stroke she literally shakes the energy off her hands like water. She duplicates the sweeping over your back and knees.

Fanslow's method often includes physical laying on of hands instead of keeping them several inches away. Now you feel a strong warmth penetrating your body—she has one hand over your heart, one hand opposing it on your back. She says she's trying to melt the crystalline shell enclosing your heart, and let the light inside where it's still all soft and responsive.

Filling the Holes

Adding energy where there's little or none is simple. The patient's bioenergetic field naturally sucks up the energy like a milkshake through a straw, and stops when it gets enough. It doesn't burp.

Therapeutic Touch Resources

Dolores Krieger has written *The Therapeutic Touch: How to Use Your Hands to Help or to Heal* (Prentice-Hall) and *Living the Therapeutic Touch: Healing as a Lifestyle* (Mead). Janet Macrae is author of *Therapeutic Touch: A Practical Guide* (Alfred A. Knopf).

To find a practitioner or classes, write the Nurse Healers and Professional Associates Cooperative, Inc., 175 Fifth Avenue, Suite 3399, New York, NY 10010.

Balancing the Field

Actually, this is what's being done in the above steps, since an obstruction or deficit unbalances the entire field. Dr. Krieger calls this step "unruffling" the field. Sweeping down the field, you're filling in the holes, making the crooked straight and the rough places smooth.

THE HEALING POWER OF THERAPEUTIC TOUCH

The power of therapeutic touch, like any healing power, is much more noticeable in the very sick than in the healthy or slightly ill. Two of the primary benefits of therapeutic touch are "a rather profound, generalized relaxation response" and pain relief, Fanslow says.

Fanslow has seen this happen in comatose patients. "Very often they're on life support systems, in coronary care or intensive care units," she says. "You can see the heart rate and respiratory rate decrease on the machines."

People with heart disease respond especially quickly, she says. Besides the decreased heart and respiratory rate, their skin flushes, showing blood flow to the smaller vessels as their "aged, arteriosclerotic vessels are relaxed."

Arthritis Relief

Using therapeutic touch as the primary therapy, Fanslow treated four arthritic patients for a year. "Pain, inflammation and joint swelling decreased," she says, and continuing therapeutic touch kept those symptoms at bay. The beginning treatments were given two to three times a week for 30 to 45 minutes each. Later they were reduced to weekly sessions.

People with edema—accumulation of fluid—in the lungs, around the heart or at the site of an injury, find decreased swelling after therapeutic touch, Fanslow says.

As a rehabilitation nurse, Fanslow worked with amputees, stroke patients, paraplegics and quadraplegics. A tough row to hoe for patient and nurse, but she found therapeutic touch helped immensely. The stroke patients had the most noticeable response. "Spasticity was markedly reduced and pain dramatically lessened," she says. "They began to talk or gesture about feeling a sensation of flow in the affected extremities. It greatly lessened their fear. But what greatly impressed me was the change in how they saw themselves. The energy made available to them seemed to help the disequilibrium and body distortion they felt. Despite their crippling strokes, they were able to see themselves as two-sided again, increasing their sense of wholeness."

Fanslow also found that Parkinson's disease patients had a gradual decrease in tremors and were able to walk better while on a therapeutic touch regimen.

Help for Headaches

A University of Missouri-Columbia study found that therapeutic touch reduced headache pain by up to 70 percent in most of the subjects tested. In the four hours following the session, pain lessened even further.

Pain is closely related to anxiety, and therapeutic touch is an extremely potent reducer of anxiety, according to several studies.

A chronic condition is harder to treat than an acute one, Fanslow notes. A disease that's held on for months or years has become ingrained in the person's energy flow, and more time is needed to "retrain" the bioenergetic field. Dr. Macrae reports that a woman with a 20-year case of severe emphysema improved only gradually at first, but after eight months of weekly treatments experienced a dramatic change.

Comfort at Life's End

Fanslow's work now is exclusively with the dying and cancer patients. "Therapeutic touch facilitates the dying process," she says. "One of the things we see very graphically in the dying is the bioenergetic field beginning to separate from the physical body.

As we die that field becomes much more open and fragile. And that is what we call dying.

"Therapeutic touch on dying persons is done very frequently for short periods of time. Just as the field is very open for energy to leave, it's also very open for energy to go in, although it's easily dissipated. You can strengthen the field for a short time. The beauty of this touch-centered approach is that the energy goes right to where it's needed, and that is at the heart level. You're giving them the energy and strength they need to let go of life, of family, of relationships. It takes a tremendous amount of energy to let go. Therapeutic touch eases the difficulties of resolving the life-death conflict within all of us."

You can also use therapeutic touch on yourself for whatever ails you, Fanslow says. First center yourself, then visualize the energy coming down from above and flowing through your body. Place your hands over the area you want to treat and visualize the energy flowing out of your hands into the affected area.

GETTING IN TOUCH

Although the best way to learn therapeutic touch is in a class, these illustrations give an idea of what's involved. The technique is simple and straightforward, and as with anything else, practice makes perfect.

38-2

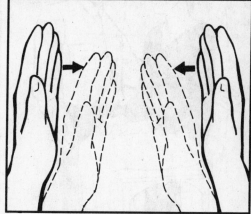

The last time, as you return to the original close-in position, test the field between your hands every two inches for a sense of bounciness, resistance or elasticity. Note other sensations as well, like heat, cold, tingling or pulsations.

38-1

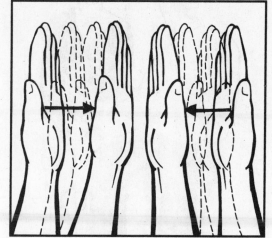

This exercise will help you to sense the bioenergetic field. While sitting comfortably with both feet on the ground, bring your palms together until they're about a ¼ inch apart. Then draw them back until two inches separate them, slowly bring them back together to the first position, and again separate them until they're four inches apart. Repeat the process, increasing the separation to six inches, then eight inches.

(continued)

GETTING IN TOUCH—*Continued*

38-3

To assess another's bioenergetic field, have the person sit comfortably on a stool or sideways on an armless chair. After you center yourself, sit or kneel beside the chair. Beginning at the top of the head, with your hands three to five inches from the body (the extent of the field), bring your hands smoothly down the front and back of the person's body. The hand in back stops at the hips while the front hand continues to the toes.

38-4

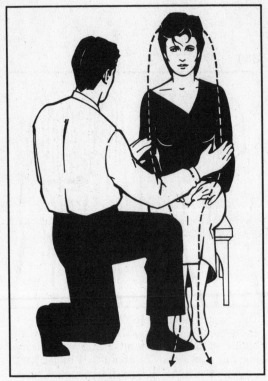

Then kneel in front of the person and move both hands smoothly and gently through the field from the top of the head to the bottom of the feet.

38-5

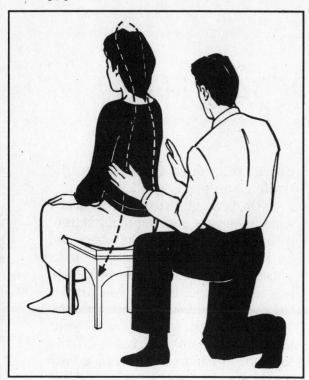

Repeat for the back, down to the hips. Each time, notice sensations of blocked or absent energy that can be treated.

38-6

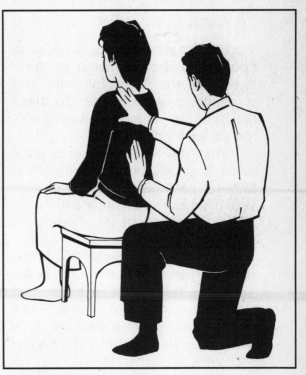

A typical treatment. If the field is deficient or feels cold or hollow along the spine, for instance, place your hands over or directly on the area. For congestion sweep your hands downward until you notice a smoothness in the field. For a deficit, allow energy to flow into the "hole" until it feels filled and balanced.

Chapter 39

TRAGER APPROACH

Receive your first Trager® session from Sheila Merle Johnson, program director of the Trager Institute, and you might be surprised by the lively conversation—especially since *you're* not saying a word.

First, she closes her eyes for a moment and takes a deep breath. When her eyes pop open she starts moving your head and neck gently and rhythmically. "Hello, little guys!" she says cheerily.

Little guys? As far as you know, there are just two of you here. There's you, lying face-up under a sheet on the bodywork table. And there's her, perched behind you on the edge of the table while she cups your chronically sore neck in her hands.

"So," she continues, gently rocking your head from side to side, "How are we all doing today?" After a couple of minutes, she slides down from the table, places her hands under your chin and—uh-oh—starts giving your head a long, firm pull. You brace for a strain, a pain, a bone-clicking crack.

But there's none of it. Actually, the stretch feels pretty good.

"Oh, yeah, guys, that's good. Really good," she says, resuming her skillful head-tossing. Your head flops back and forth in a steady rhythm. The tight muscles of your neck are becoming less and less so. In fact, you realize, they've lost most of their tension. That's when it dawns on you: It's your *muscles* Johnson has been talking to—and they have been doing a very good job of listening.

Communication is the key to the Trager Approach—though verbal conversation actually only supplements the real work going on. The factor that supposedly makes all the difference, the factor that distinguishes Trager from other forms of bodywork, is mind-to-muscle contact between a Trager practitioner and his or her client. Using a series of always-gentle, never-painful movements that include shaking, rocking, and leading body parts through their range of motion—movements not at all like traditional massage strokes

324

—the Trager practitioner is able, it is said, to convey the feeling of vibrant health directly to the client's tissues.

"What could be softer? What could be freer?" Johnson silently muses in the tradition of Trager while lightly moving on to your taut shoulder. If her mind and your muscles are in sync, the gentle stretch she intuitively applies may furnish both of you with the answer. And should your shoulder, not to mention the rest of your body, go with the flow of that and other movements applied in the course of a full-body session, your reward could be heaven on earth—a state of relaxation like no other. Best of all, the change will be long-lasting, because your unconscious mind with its elephantine memory won't want to forget the feeling.

Sounds too good to be true, but is it? Ask Shirley A. Tabackman, who suffers from a condition called chronic costochondritis, an arthritic type of inflammation along her ribs that is aggravated by changes in the weather. Over the years, Tabackman has been treated with painkilling medications, cortisone injections, osteopathic manipulations, acupuncture and finally, Trager sessions.

"I find it to be absolutely therapeutic," she says. "At the end of the first session, I was totally loose."

She felt vastly improved in just four weekly sessions, and she continues to go every three weeks or so. "Today, I can tell when the weather is changing because I have little twinges.

But little twinges are a lot different than feeling like railroad spikes are being driven through you with a 20-pound sledgehammer."

What's more, she says, "I can be hugged now. Before, hugging hurt too much. The Trager work has made a tremendous difference in my life. My body does not feel the same. I have more energy and move around more easily."

Terrific Touch

From whence came Trager? From Milton Trager, M.D., who continues to practice and refine his trademarked work well into his 80s. Trager was an aspiring professional boxer in his teens when he discovered he had an unusual talent for touch. His trainer, who gave him a daily massage after a workout in the ring, traded places with him on the table one day. "After a few minutes," recalls Dr. Trager, "he rolled over and said, 'Where'd you learn to do that, kid? You got hands.'"

Since then, Dr. Trager has worked on thousands of patients with problems ranging from bad backs to muscular dystrophy. And he has trained more than a thousand others in his approach—people whose effectiveness in the work, he says, is in direct proportion not to their technical skills but to their personal development.

That development is dependent upon "hook-up," the state of meditation in which Dr. Trager and his students

A Conversation with Milton Trager

In the interview that follows, the originator of the Trager Approach explains his philosophy.

Question: How is the Trager Approach different from massage?
Dr. Trager: With traditional massage, you might take a kink out, you might stop a spasm, but it will come back because of your unconscious pattern. I'm after the mind, not just the body.

Question: How did you discover the connection between the body and the mind?
Dr. Trager: I would do something to the person in the first session, and then and there the problem was corrected. I knew I hadn't done much with my hands. There were just two other things in the room that could have made it happen: That person's mind and my mind. After several years of this I concluded it *must* be the mind.

Question: Why is it important that you reach the mind?
Dr. Trager: The whole problem is in a person's mind, patterns in the mind. You're blocked by your patterns. Your body is locked up until they are released.

Question: What is your experience while you're working on a person?
Dr. Trager: I can feel restricted areas of the body. And I ask myself, how should things actually be? I don't have a preconceived notion. I step out of the picture at that moment. My hands take over and automatically convey to that person's mind how it should be.

Question: And the feeling you're trying to convey has to do with being lighter, more relaxed?
Dr. Trager: Definitely lighter, but I don't aim toward feeling lighter. Nothing is really aimed. Nothing is directed. It's a happening. It's a natural, healthy state to be in for anybody who's lucky enough to get it.

Question: Many people tend to believe that being too relaxed and light and free could actually be counterproductive.
Dr. Trager: Because they're in the habit of driving to accomplish. That's what's wearing them out. But you could accomplish the same things without it.

Question: So a person who has released those old patterns is released from physical discomfort and actual diseases?
Dr. Trager: This will improve all systems of the body.

Question: Does your work help people think more clearly?
Dr. Trager: I believe that if a person does not have tension, he can be open to thinking more clearly.

Question: Is your method effective for emotional problems?

Dr. Trager: I see lots of people with emotional problems. Sometimes during one of my classes a student will break down, cry and scream as pent-up emotions are finally released. A psychiatrist who witnessed this said, "Milton, it would take a psychiatrist two years twice a week to do what you did in 20 minutes." But I'm just bringing people into the state of being where they belong instead of having a bunch of junk running them. No junk, no problem.

Question: Do you ever go into deep muscle work?

Dr. Trager: No, I see no reason for that. It just makes people tighter. In fact, my work is getting lighter every year.

Question: What do you consider your biggest successes?

Dr. Trager: I get a big thrill when a limb that wasn't moving moves, when a person who couldn't walk is now walking without a problem. But the main reason I'm doing this work is for my self-development. I'm a better person for having done this work on someone else. My work is really a philosophy, not bodywork or massage. Its goal is to bring people into a state of hook-up, feeling connected to a vibratory force, without which you're no place. If we all had hook-up, there would be no wars.

all conduct their hands-on business. Hook-up, as Dr. Trager defines it, is "becoming one with the energy force that surrounds all living things." When your Trager practitioner closes her eyes at the start of a session, she is momentarily leaving you only to reach out to you from a higher plane. And if things go well between you, you might be joining her there in the course of your session.

So the theory goes, it is while your practitioner is in this state—and hopefully you with her—that Trager work can reach your unconscious mind, repository of all experiences, pleasurable and painful. "Old painful patterns in our unconscious control us," says Johnson. "The patterns that say your right shoulder is higher than your left. Or that your jaw is clenched most of the time. Or that you respond with a certain pattern of tension to situations in your everyday life."

The only solution, Dr. Trager believes, is to convey new patterns to the unconscious mind, which in turn sends the message to muscles. "The movements of Trager work give you a sensory experience, just as hiking gives you a sensory experience, or swimming, or being rocked," says Johnson. "Throughout our lives, our self-awareness is shaped primarily through sensory experiences. Dr. Trager's theory is that if you input a positive experience into the sensory system, it will naturally replace the negative one."

Painful mental and emotional patterns are also subject to revision, Dr. Trager says. Pent-up feelings can emerge. Thinking can become clear. Problems can be solved.

"The Trager person I went to see had a really loving presence about her," says Caitland O'Malley. "I've never felt like I felt when I got off that massage table. I felt very young. So my body felt good—but my mind felt *great*. I was in the process of trying to make a very difficult decision in my life. After I got off that table, I was pretty clear as to the best thing to do."

Positive benefits can come quickly. "Some people come in for one Trager session and that's all they need, physically and attitudinally. Others come in for a series of sessions," says Johnson. "It's like a discovery, a different way of

perceiving life. If the body ceases to struggle and feels lighter and more graceful and daily motion is easier, another change often comes along with that: You start viewing life as easier. You don't have to make such a big deal out of everything."

THE HEALING POWER OF THE TRAGER APPROACH

Although Trager work primarily aims to educate people in body awareness, practitioners have noted beneficial effects in treating numerous conditions, a few of which are described below. (Many people also benefit by practicing Mentastics[SM]—or mental gymnastics—which are do-it-yourself movement exercises developed by Dr. Trager in conjunction with the bodywork. See the box "Trager Resources.")

Musculoskeletal Problems

From the start, Dr. Trager has applied his approach to the treatment of serious neuromuscular disorders such as polio, muscular dystrophy and multiple sclerosis, as well as less serious musculoskeletal problems. While he doesn't claim to cure those diseases, some clients have regained movement in limbs that were previously paralyzed. This results, Dr. Trager believes, when the body begins to put to use muscle and nerve pathways that have not been damaged by disease.

Trager Resources

Trager practitioners, many of whom have backgrounds in other forms of massage or bodywork, undergo six months to a year of specialized training in this approach, and there are ongoing educational requirements. You can expect to pay $25 to $60 for a typical 90-minute session.

For help in finding a practitioner in your area, contact the Trager Institute, 10 Mill Street, Mill Valley, CA 94941-1891 (415) 388-2688.

For more on the Trager philosophy plus do-it-yourself movements, read *Trager Mentastics* by Milton Trager, M.D., and Cathy Guadagno, Ph.D. (Station Hill Press).

Emphysema

Emphysema sufferers have also reported improvement. "I remember one woman who could hardly walk to my office," recalls Dr. Trager. "She was in the pattern of not being able to take a deep breath. After the session she waltzed right out of here and all the way home."

Back Problems

Bad backs are a Trager specialty. He and his students have worked on thousands of them. A great many of them, he says, showed remarkable improvement after just one session. Some sufferers have even managed to avoid back surgery as a result.

Athletic Performance

Athletic performance is said to reach new heights with Trager work. The movements help athletes peel away unnecessary tension and allow their muscles to function at top efficiency. A tennis pro attributes his light movement on the court and lack of leg cramps to Trager sessions. A triathlete says the sessions gave her new feelings of power and strength. Coaches report fewer injuries and quicker recovery from those that do occur.

Emotional Benefits

And people who have learned what it's like to unwind in the hands of a Trager practitioner can reap many emotional benefits. "Most of us tend to react to emotional situations with far greater force than we need to," says Johnson. "We grit our teeth, tighten our chest, screw up our digestion." Through Trager sessions, or even by mentally recalling one, "a person with the most Type-A aggressive personality can develop an ease and grace that makes life much more pleasurable," she says.

GYMNASTICS FOR YOUR MIND

Want to sample the benefits of the Trager Approach? Try a daily dose of Trager Mentastics, gentle "mental gymnastics" which promise to bring you into the same relaxed and physically graceful state as an actual hands-on session—though not as quickly. Making use of your body's own weight and the effects of gravity to open and move each part, the movements "create wavelike shimmerings that resonate through the body and have a loosening and lightening effect on both the body and mind," says Cathy Guadagno, Ph.D., a Trager practitioner and coauthor with Milton Trager, M.D., of *Trager Mentastics*. (You can also try them in group classes. For information, call the Trager Institute.) Here are just a few examples.

(continued)

GYMNASTICS FOR YOUR MIND—*Continued*

39-1

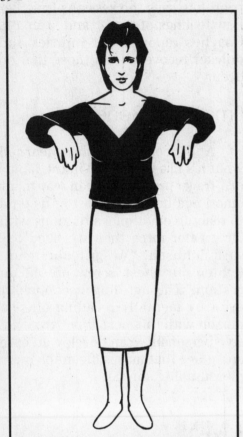

39-2

Slowly raise your arms, palm down, to chest height in front of you. Elbows and wrists should be relaxed and slightly bent. Feel the weight of your arms. Then allow the weight and heaviness to drop your arms so that they swing down by your sides. Repeat. Feel the effortless bounce at the bottom of the drop. Done with a soft, focused awareness, practitioners say this may bring you into the state of hook-up.

Choose the arm that feels freest and allow it to loosely hang down from your shoulder close to your leg. Gently move your hand and fingers as if you are strumming a guitar or shaking drops of water off in a continuous motion. Ask yourself, "What could be freer?" Feel the shimmering move up the muscles of your elbow, arm and shoulder. Repeat with the other arm.

39-3

39-4

Alternating from leg to leg, kick to each side with the subtle feeling that your leg is falling down and out of the hip socket. Your foot should stay fairly close to the floor. Feel the bounce in your thighs, calves and ankles as the foot drops. This movement can create a jiggle in the lower back which is said to help relieve tensions in that area.

Continue to kick while walking forward, as if you are kicking a tin can. Take small steps without sustaining the kick. Do not kick hard or in a deliberate manner. Softly put your hands on your hips to feel the bounce. Be aware of how you feel. With practice, you will develop a feeling of softness which may deepen your feeling of hook-up.

Part III

HANDS-ON
PAIN RELIEF

Chapter 40

HEADACHE AND JAW PAIN

When you're in pain, few things are quite as soothing and uplifting as the touch of another human being. How much better for your tense, aching muscles if that person is wise in the ways of massage. And, how much better for your own human need to give if you know your hands can also help others.

In this and the five chapters that follow, we've outlined and illustrated some basic massage techniques that professional therapists recommend for those times when you or someone you care about needs fast relief from pain, and when seeing a professional therapist just isn't appropriate.

Learning and applying these techniques won't make you an LMT (licensed massage therapist). But they could help bring relief from pain and stress when you need it and that's what really counts.

We've started with tension headaches and jaw pain. From there we'll be working our way down to the neck, the shoulders, the back, the legs and feet.

The decision to start with headaches and work down was an easy one. There are few pains more torturous than the brain-mashing throb of a headache (though some backache sufferers may disagree), and few pains more common.

A nationwide study conducted by Louis Harris & Associates for the Bristol-Myers Co. found that 73 percent of all adults—that's 127 million of us—have one or more headaches during the year. About 15 million live with the threat of migraine attacks.

Productivity lost as a result of severe headache pain costs our nation an estimated $6.2 billion annually. Unfortunately, headache sufferers more than offset that lost production by spending some $8.4 billion a year searching for relief.

"About 70 percent of my clients complain of head pain, or pain in the neck and head, or pain in the neck, shoulders and head," says Jeanne Aland, lead instructor at the Atlanta School of Massage, and a private practitioner specializing in hands-on pain relief.

Most suffer tension-related headaches, she says, and not migraines. Migraines, which result from the dilation of blood vessels in the head, are not terribly responsive to massage, though Aland believes that massage between attacks "assists the body in healing itself and so, in a nondirect way, would be helpful."

Adela Basayne-Smith, a licensed massage therapist and massage instructor at East-West College in Portland, Oregon, agrees. "Mostly I see tension headaches in my private practice. Sometimes I see migraine sufferers, after the headache's been raging for several days, but they usually don't want to be touched in the beginning."

Tension headaches, on the other hand, seem to respond quite well to massage techniques—many of which are surprisingly quick and easy to do. Aland says there are two distinct types of tension headaches. "The simple tension headache typically starts in the back of the head and moves around to the front," she says. "It's caused by tense muscles in the neck and head."

The other type of tension-related headache is what both Aland and Basayne-Smith refer to as a digestive headache. "If someone has digestive problems, that will sometimes show up as a headache," Basayne-Smith explains.

"This headache occurs behind the eyes and is fairly intense," notes Aland. "The cause is usually somewhere down in the belly or intestines." Both simple and digestive headaches respond well to massage, she says, though each should be treated in a different way.

FIVE-MINUTE FIXER

Here's a fast simple-tension-headache reliever, courtesy of Jeanne Aland.

40-1

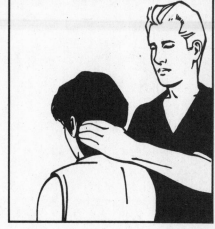

With the recipient seated in a chair, stand to the rear and slightly to her side. Form your hand into a "C" with the thumb and fingers. Place the web of the hand under the skull where it joins the neck—thumb under the bone behind the ear on one side, index finger under the bone on the other side.

(continued)

FIVE-MINUTE FIXER—*Continued*

40-2

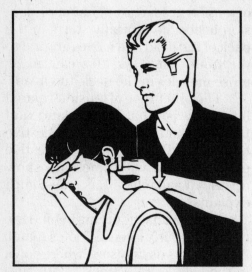

40-3

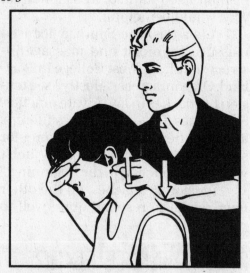

Put your other hand on the person's forehead, just below the hairline. Encourage her to relax her head forward into your hand. You may need to nudge the head forward with the rearward hand until the head is completely relaxed. Tell the recipient to breathe in deeply and exhale. As exhalation begins, squeeze the thumb and fingers of your rear hand together, then lift them by lowering your wrist. Hold that position and instruct the person to again breathe in deeply and exhale.

As exhalation begins, continue the squeezing and lifting motion, applying a bit more pressure and lifting a bit higher than before. Hold that position and then repeat the breathing, squeezing and lifting procedure one final time.

DIGESTIVE HEADACHE HELPER

Aland says this one provides simple, quick relief for digestive headaches—the kind that settle in right behind the eyes. You can try it on yourself or someone else.

40-5

Tell the recipient to breathe in deeply and exhale. As exhalation begins, gently squeeze the tender spot. Hold and instruct the recipient to breathe in and exhale again. Apply slightly more pressure during this exhalation. Hold and repeat the procedure one final time. The headache should be gone. If it lingers, repeat the procedure one or two more times.

40-4

With the recipient seated in a chair, take up a position on her right side. Take her right hand and find the sensitive spot located in the webbing between the thumb and index finger. Pressure on this spot should produce a sharp twinge.

THE PRESSURE STRETCHER

"The best thing for tension headaches is a combination of pressure
points and stretching," says Adela
Basayne-Smith. Here's a technique
she recommends that can be performed
on yourself or someone else.

40-6

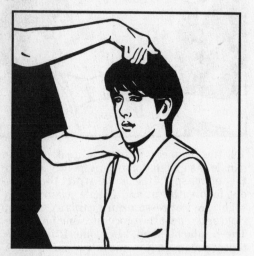

Trace the centerline of the skull from front to
back. Starting at the hairline in front, apply
moderate pressure with the thumb along this
bone searching for sensitive, slightly painful
spots. When one is found, increase the pressure slightly and hold for about one minute.
Release slowly. Work toward the back of the
skull.

40-7

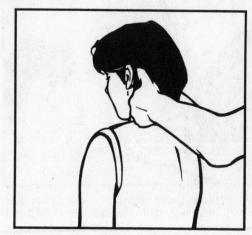

From the back of the skull, work around the
sides toward the temple, applying pressure to
sensitive areas where found.

40-9

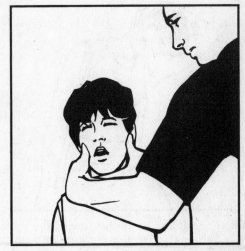

With the jaw muscles relaxed until the mouth is slightly open, lace your fingers together and press the thumbs against the muscles covering the jaw bone. Hold with moderate to firm pressure for about one minute.

40-8

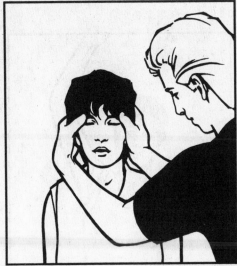

Move to the face and begin working the area around the eyes, starting at the bridge of the nose and moving outward underneath the brow bone and around the bottom of the eyes, pushing down on the lip of the bone.

(continued)

THE PRESSURE STRETCHER—*Continued*

40-10

Reach up and over the head with the right hand, placing it on the left ear. Pull the head to the right with the hand and arm, allowing the weight of the head to assist in this move until the entire torso is slowly stretched to the right.

40-11

Relax and allow the right arm to drop. Next, extend the left arm to the ceiling. Then, as if there was a hook extended from the ceiling, pull the torso back to center with the left arm. Keep the pace slow and deliberate. Repeat on opposite side.

QUICK-FIX TENSION HEADACHE MASSAGE

This easy-to-follow technique can help break up a tension headache after a long, stressful day. A light massage oil or cream will help reduce friction on the face and help your fingers move easily over the skin. Remember to use only light to moderate pressure with these moves.

40-13

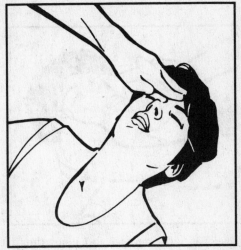

Use the pads of the first two fingers of one hand and stroke from the bridge of the nose to the top of the forehead.

40-12

With the recipient faceup on a bed or padded floor, start in the center of the forehead with the pads of your thumbs and iron out lines to the edge of the hairline. Then work in vertical rows from just above the eyebrows to the top of the forehead.

40-14

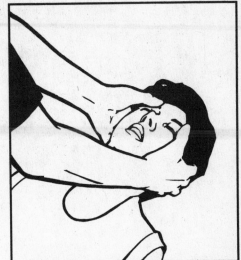

With the index fingers or thumbs, stroke from the bridge of the nose along the upper eye socket ridge to the outside corners of the eyes, then stroke along the lower eye socket ridge to the corners. Do this very slowly.

(continued)

QUICK-FIX TENSION HEADACHE MASSAGE—*Continued*

40-15

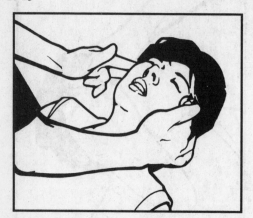

Move over to the temples and, using the first two fingers of both hands, make tiny circles all around the temples, reversing circle direction several times.

40-16

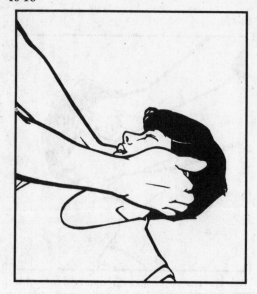

Reach back to the bone behind the ears and, using the first two or three fingers of each hand, rub small circles from the top to the bottom of that bone and back up again. You can alternate this with simple stroking motions up and down the bone. Use medium to firm pressure for this move.

PAIN-POINT RUB

This technique, developed by Ronald M. Lawrence, M.D., consists of rubbing small circles over a bony point nearest the site of pain at a rate of two to three cycles per second. It's very important to direct the pressure against the *bony point only* (see illustrations for guidance). If the bony surface is large, start the circles from the middle of the bone and work out. You can use either the finger or thumb.

Treatments can be given two or three times a day, but it's a good idea to limit sessions to once daily when you first start. Begin with light pressure. Keep the circles going for about two minutes, but always listen to the person you are rubbing and stop if they say stop.

40-18

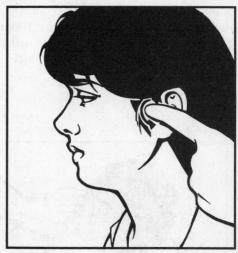

Rub this point for TMJ (temporomandibular joint) pain relief. You can feel the joint when the person opens or closes her jaw. Look for it immediately in front of the ear.

40-17

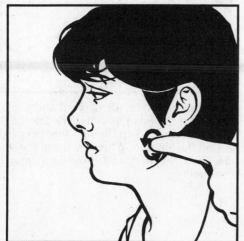

Rub this point for temporary relief from toothache in the lower jaw.

40-19

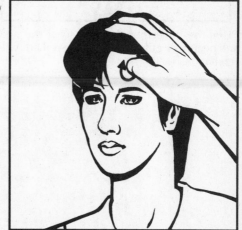

Rub this point for relief from frontal sinus pain and simple tension headaches. Either the thumb or index finger can be used for these techniques. See which works best for you.

VIBRATING MASSAGE

Here's a tried-and-true headache relief technique that massage therapists have counted on for years. Have the recipient lie face downward on floor or bed, while you take a position directly over the head.

40-20

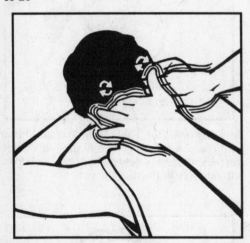

Place the fingertips at the base of the neck and begin a circular vibrating movement with the hands.

40-21

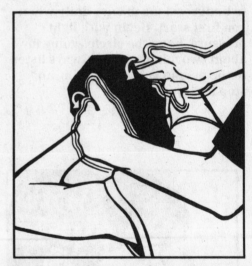

Slowly move the hands upward and around the side of the head as you work toward the top of the skull. Keep the pressure very light around the temples. When the top of the skull has been reached, the movement can be repeated.

DEEP-STROKE HEADACHE HELPER

The experts say this one can help clear up those pounding frontal headaches.

40-22

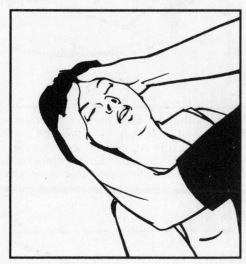

Grasp the forehead with the palms the same way you would a basketball, placing the thumbs together at the hairline.

40-23

Using firm (but not excessive) pressure, stroke laterally toward the edge of the forehead. Try to stretch the skin so that the person's eyes must close. Stroke in one direction only. When you reach the edge of the forehead, return to the original position and repeat two or three more times.

SINUS BUSTER

Therapists say sinus headaches, eyestrain and general tension in the area around the eyes and nose can be relieved by deep stroking. Here's a technique the pros use for dealing with this nagging problem.

40-25

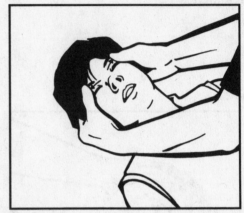

When the thumbs reach the valleys between the eyes and nose, stop kneading and make deep strokes upward over the eyebrows and out toward the temples. Return thumbs to starting position and repeat four or five times.

40-24

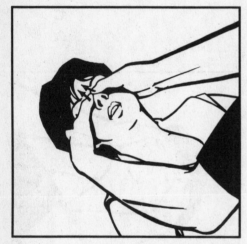

Place the thumbs together at the tip of the nose with the fingers at the temples. Begin kneading up toward the bridge of the nose.

40-26

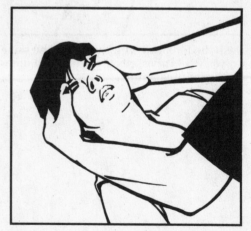

Place the fingers on the temples and the thumbs in the hollows of the eyes. Stroke over the ridge above the eyes to the tips of the eyebrows. Repeat four or five times.

40-27

Now place the thumbs over the bridge of the nose and knead upward in small circles to the hairline.

40-28

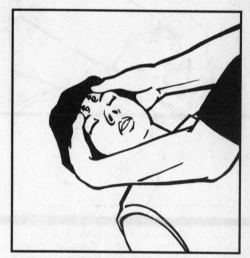

Return to a slightly different position at the lower border of the eyebrows and repeat the movement, going upward and then returning to a different spot until the entire forehead has been covered.

THE RESISTER

This technique is highly recommended by Basayne-Smith for either headaches or neckaches that leave their victims unable to move the head without pain. The following moves force the muscle on the opposite side from the pain to contract, causing the painfully tense muscle to relax.

40-30

Instruct her to turn her face away from you and, as she does, resist this movement with firm pressure, making her work to turn her head against your hands.

40-29

Have the recipient lie faceup on a firm surface. Take a position near the head on the side *opposite the greatest pain*. Place the thumbs and index fingers together forming a triangle. Place the center of the triangle over the recipient's far ear and turn her face toward you.

40-31

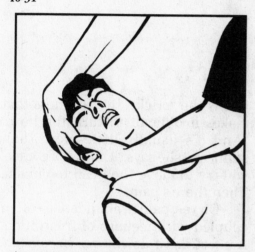

Allow the recipient to continue turning her head against your hands until she reaches a point where the discomfort peaks. Instruct the recipient to continue turning the head, but resist it with enough force to prevent the head from turning any farther. Hold this resistance for several seconds as she slowly exhales. Allow the recipient to relax.

40-32

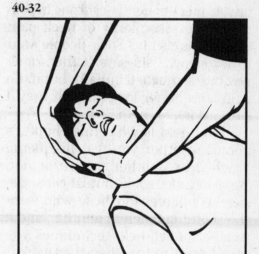

Continue this hold-relax procedure throughout as much range as the recipient can tolerate. Repeat on opposite side, if needed.

Chapter 41

NECK PAIN

"People have different responses to neck pain," says massage instructor Adela Basayne-Smith. As a licensed private practitioner specializing in pain relief, she sees plenty of neck pain sufferers as clients: "Some people want to be touched," she says. "Others don't want to be touched initially, but if the pain goes on for long enough they'll start asking for help."

And help is what this chapter's about, whether you feel like being touched by another person or not. We've included some mutual-care massage techniques for those who want the soothing touch of another, and a number of self-help techniques you might want to try when that neck is so tender you don't want anyone else to touch it.

Thankfully, when it comes to neck pain, most cases are tension-related. So the calming touch of massage can often help.

"Probably 90 percent of the clients I see ask for some type of massage to their necks," says massage practitioner Jeanne Aland. She says the most common type of neck pain she encoun-ters is the "crick," that stiffness that makes it difficult to turn the head. "And it's usually little more than stiffness," she says. "Unless, of course, you try to move the head too much. Then there's pain."

Oh yes, pain in abundance—often coupled with feelings of frustration. A short drive downtown becomes a harrowing, torso-twisting ordeal. The sound of your name shouted behind you produces a reflex turn of the head, followed by instant pain. Neck pain has a knack for making you feel awkward as well as uncomfortable.

But there are a number of things you can do to help get relief. Whenever the neck is just too tender for massage, Basayne-Smith suggests trying hot and cold presses. "In the first 24 hours of pain, I would recommend applying just ice," she says. "And a bag of frozen peas works great. Apply it for 20 minutes every hour."

After that, she recommends alternating the ice pack with a heating pad in five-minute intervals. "The idea is to set up a vascular pump," she explains. "You want to get those blood vessels constricting, then dilating, constricting, then dilating—pumping that blood into the muscle."

Keep at it for as long as it takes to bring some relief, Basayne-Smith advises. "Maybe even three-minute or two-minute intervals of hot then cold. Whatever you're comfortable with."

THE PULLER

Massage therapists say this move is good for bringing blood back into stiff neck muscles without placing too much strain on the recipient.

41-2

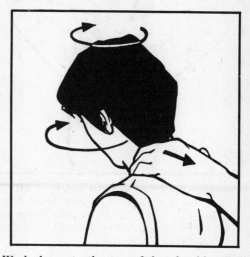

Work down to the top of the shoulder. Pull back on the muscles along the ridge of the left shoulder as the recipient turns her head to the right. Then pull back on the ridge muscles of the right shoulder as she turns her head to the left. Repeat the above procedure two or three times to alleviate stiffness.

41-1

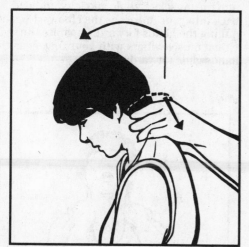

Have the person sit in a chair while you take a standing position behind her. Start at the top of the neck just below the skull. Gently pull down on the neck muscles bordering the spine as the recipient slowly puts her chin to her chest.

SELF-HELP TENSION TAMER

Here's one you can do to yourself for relief from tension and pains that gather in the neck.

41-3

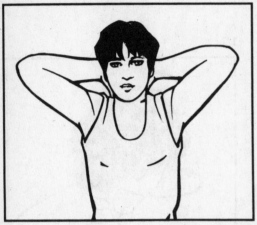

Place the fingertips of both hands on either side of the spine just under your head. Keep the fingers straight and point the elbows up, applying pressure to the neck muscles through the balls of the fingertips.

41-4

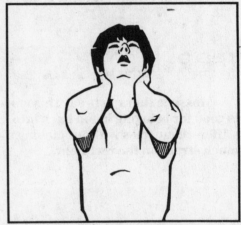

Stroke forward with the pressure going deep into the muscle. Exhale and let your head fall back into your fingers as the elbows descend, pulling the hands forward. Separate the individual muscle fibers with your fingers as the hands glide forward.

41-5

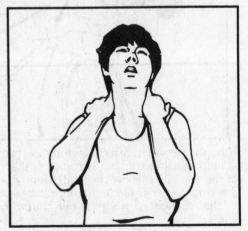

Travel the length of the neck all the way down and out along the top border of the shoulder blade. Repeat as needed.

THE PUSHROLLER

Here's a self-help technique the pros say they count on to help stimulate circulation in the neck and relieve stiffness.

41-6

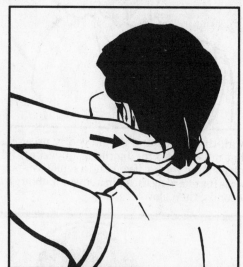

Start at the base of the skull with one hand on each side of the spine. Let the head relax and fall back into the fingers. Using the first three fingers of each hand, push one side of the neck and then the other toward the center of the spinal column.

41-7

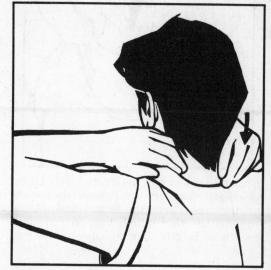

Alternate hands in a rhythmic motion working down the neck as far as you can reach. Use moderately deep pressure and repeat five times.

PRESSURE-POINT NECK RELIEF

This do-it-yourself technique is a solid helper for relieving stiff necks, according to professional massage therapists.

41-9

41-8

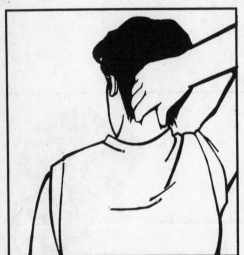

Grab the back of your neck with one hand by placing the fingers on one side and the thumb on the other. Draw the fingers and thumb toward each other until they are an inch apart on either side of the spine with muscle between them.

Work the fingers and thumb gently up along that muscle into the hairline, squeezing and releasing as you go. If you find a sensitive spot, press it as hard as the pain allows for about 10 seconds, then slowly release.

41-10

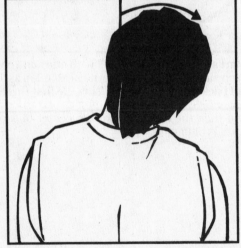

Next, stretch that muscle by bending your head forward, then to the right, then to the left. Repeat the above steps until you've located and pressed all the sensitive spots you can find. Repeat this treatment every two hours or so until you feel fully relaxed.

SELF-HELP SCM SQUEEZER

Jeanne Aland instructs her neck-pain clients to try this one at home. SCM stands for sternocleidomastoid muscle, for those who like to know such things.

41-12

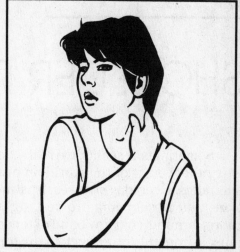

Reach across the front of your throat with the right hand, placing it on the left SCM muscle. Wrap the fingers entirely around the muscle, keeping the thumb to the front.

41-11

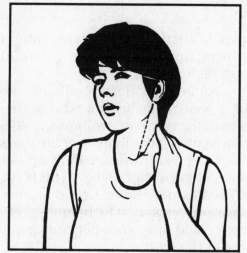

Use a mirror to locate the large SCM muscles located on either side of your throat.

41-13

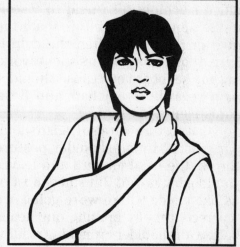

Turn your head to the left in order to relax the muscle into your hands. Starting at the bottom of the neck, work this muscle with a slow, kneading motion, moving the thumb and fingers in opposite directions. Rub the entire muscle from bottom to top. Repeat on opposite side.

Chapter 42

SHOULDER PAIN

Sometimes, it seems, we really do carry the weight of the world on our shoulders. Everyday stresses, frustrations and upsets come to rest right there, forming a narrow band of tense muscle from the lower neck to the top of the arms.

Those of us who spend long hours working at typewriters, computers, word processors and other assorted office machines also tend to take it in the shoulders. Furniture that's too high or too low is often the culprit here, though long hours spent working at a keyboard can cause shoulder pain regardless of chair and desk adjustments.

Bad posture can also lead to shoulder pain. A round-shoulder posture throws the head forward and leaves you looking down. But since most of us like to see where we're going, we "correct" this by arching our heads back with shoulder-crunching results. "Holding your head in that forward-jutting position puts a tremendous amount of strain on the muscles in the back of the neck and upper shoulders," says Susan Fish, a New York City physical therapist. "And a

muscle that's in a constant state of contraction can become a painful muscle."

Author Jack Hofer recalls the case of a woman in Kansas who underwent surgery to remove fibrous, gristle-like tissue that built up over the years from her habit of hunching up her shoulders during the day. In his book, *Mini-Massage*, Hofer says that massage and relaxation techniques probably could have kept her from going under the knife.

Perhaps. After all, the shoulders do seem naturally well-placed and well-suited for the soothing, healing touch of massage. The fingers and thumb naturally fit along the top ridge of the shoulders, while the palm nicely covers that ball of muscle covering the shoulder joint.

And this holds true whether we reach back and massage the shoulders with our own hands, or seek out the touch of someone else. For that reason, we've included a number of self-help techniques in this chapter— quick fixes that can be performed periodically throughout the day any time you feel tension settling in. We've included a number of mutual-care techniques, too, so you or someone special can have something soothing to look forward to at the end of a long, hard day.

"Remember, the primary area of pain is going to be along the upper ridge of the shoulder running from the neck to the shoulder joint," says massage instructor Adela Basayne-Smith. "This is typically a tension-related pain—what we used to call 'Manhattan Shoulder' when I lived in New York."

But, she says, be it Manhattan or Muskogee: "It's going to be a combination of pressure points, stroking and stretching that brings relief in this area."

PRESSURE-POINT RELIEVER

There are usually two "incredibly sensitive" pressure points about midway out toward the shoulder joint, says Adela Basayne-Smith, and moderate to firm pressure on these can help bring fast relief to tense, stiff shoulders.

42-2

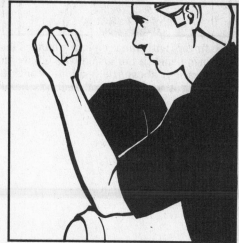

Once located, use the elbow, thumb or fist to apply firm pressure. Hold for several seconds and slowly release. Do both sides.

42-1

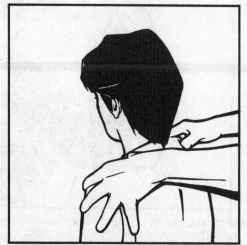

Place the recipient in a chair with the head and shoulders relaxed. Use the thumb or index finger to probe along the top of the shoulder for pressure points.

(continued)

PRESSURE-POINT RELIEVER—*Continued*

42-3

Lace fingers with the recipient's hand. Place your arm beneath her arm at the elbow and slowly raise it above the head and continue stretching it up for several seconds before releasing.

42-4

As an alternative treatment, Jeanne Aland recommends placing the elbows on the shoulder ridge in the hollow just above the collar bone. Protectively encircle the person's head with your arms.

42-5

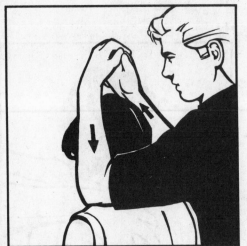

Alternately press on the shoulders, using first the left and then the right elbow. Pick up a slow, rhythmic pace and gently increase the pressure until you're working at the recipient's limit of tolerance. Continue for two to three minutes before stopping.

GUNILLA'S ROTATOR

Gunilla Knutson, former Miss Sweden and author of *Gunilla Knutson's Book of Massage,* says this is the *only* massage movement devoted purely to relieving pain in the shoulders. That may or may not be so, but this technique seems effective—though it requires strength to give and endurance to receive.

42-6

Have the recipient lie facedown. Take a position above the middle back and grasp both shoulders, lifting them together. Rotate the shoulders in a wide circular pattern, as wide as the recipient can comfortably tolerate. First rotate them back to front six times, then change direction, rotating them front to back.

42-7

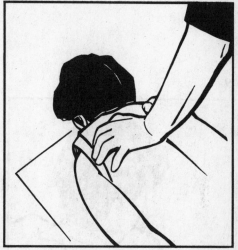

Release the shoulders and apply pressure to the sides of the spine, stopping the movement immediately if the recipient reports pain. Repeat the rotation and pressure until the shoulders relax and become easy to move.

42-8

Next, stroke the entire shoulder area from the base of the neck and the collarbone right down to the shoulder muscles at the top of the arms, exerting firm pressure.

UPPER-RIDGE RELAXER

Here's a quick-fix massage to relax tense shoulders.

42-9

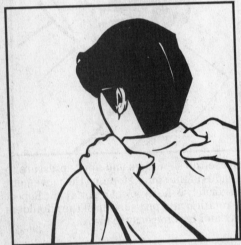

With the recipient sitting in a straight chair, place one hand over the top of each shoulder, thumbs to the back and fingertips to the front. Work back and forth from the end of the shoulder to the base of the neck with a gripping or clasping motion.

42-10

As you move back and forth, vary the position of your thumbs to cover as much of the upper back as possible, using firm pressure.

42-11

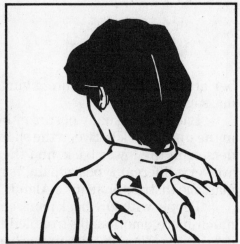

Use two or three fingers of each hand to make circular or stroking movements in the area between the spine and the shoulder blades, from the bottom point of the shoulder blade to the base of the neck.

42-12

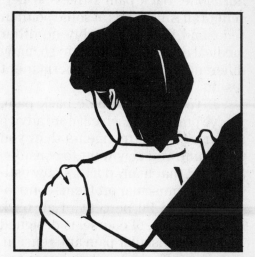

To finish up, place both hands over the round part of the shoulder and upper arm. Use a firm gripping pressure to massage the muscles over the shoulder joint.

Chapter 43

BACK PAIN

It may be small consolation for you to know this, but if you're suffering from back pain right now, you're not alone. Back pain strikes 90 percent of all Americans at some point in time, and there's probably no other medical condition treated in so many different ways with so few permanent results.

If you suffer chronic back pain, you've probably received more advice and tried more treatments than you can count. You may want to consider, however, that many doctors now estimate that muscular problems contribute to 80 to 90 percent of all back pain. Massage, of course, is designed to relieve muscular pain and tension. So it may offer hope where more traditional remedies have failed.

Many people who suffer acute, short-term back pain—the type caused by overexertion—seem to know instinctively that either a hot bath, a good rubdown or both is just what's needed to ease those aches and pains.

There are, however, a few things the experts would like you to remember about back pain before giving a massage:

"Back pain usually occurs either in the upper back between the shoulders or in the lower back, and these are very different types of pain," says massage instructor Jeanne Aland.

"People with low-back pain seem much more emotionally troubled by it," she says. "People with upper-back pain recognize that it's typically stress and their hard-charging, nose-to-the-grindstone attitude that's causing the problem. With low-back pain, however, people tend to feel more like innocent victims."

Wallets carried in rear pants pockets in men and high heels on women are two common causes of lower-back pain, she says. A bulky wallet may constantly torque the spine while sitting and change the tone of the lower-back muscles, leading to pain.

"With women," Aland notes, "there's a tendency to engage in unconscious posturing when wearing heels that also torques the pelvis and causes the same problems for them that carrying a wallet causes in men. In both cases we're talking about tightening up muscles that can't loosen up later."

Massage instructor Adela Basayne-Smith says there's a common pattern of pressure points associated with lower back pain. Knowing where to locate those points can make you very popular with someone suffering from low-back pain.

"These pressure points usually run across the top of the iliac crest (top of the hip bone) and down the buttocks in what's called the 'jeans-pocket pattern,' similar to the outline you'd find on the seat of a pair of blue jeans," she says. "Simply trace out a pattern like that on the recipient, and apply pressure for a few seconds to any painful spots."

THE TINGLER

Here's a quick, refreshing technique for relieving fatigue and that "tired back" feeling.

43-1

Place both hands on one side of the back, fingers about ½ inch out from the spine.

43-2

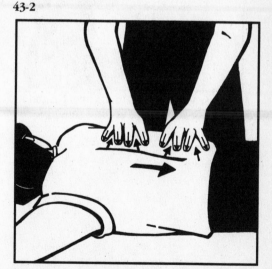

Push down with firm pressure while pulling toward you in a kneading motion, working slowly from the upper back to the tailbone and back again. Do the other side.

THE POCKET PRESS

Here's one massage therapists recommend for the lower back, based on the theory that most lumbar region pain is actually caused by tense muscles located further down on the body.

43-3

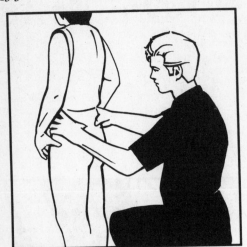

With the recipient standing, kneel behind her and anchor the fingers around the hips.

43-4

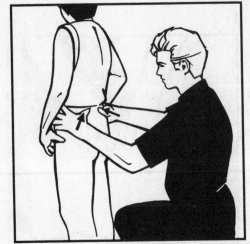

Work the upper buttocks with the thumbs, reaching in and up as far as you can until the entire area is covered. Use firm pressure.

THE ENERGIZER

Massage pros use this to get energy flowing along the pathways on either side of the spine, and to help relieve tension and rebalance the muscles.

43-5

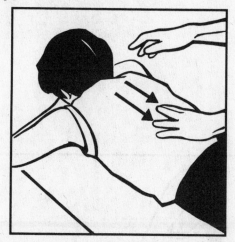

Place two fingers of one hand on either side of the spine between the shoulder blades. Drag the hand down the back along the spine until it reaches the tailbone.

43-6

As the first hand reaches the tailbone the other should be starting between the shoulder blades. Continue this movement as rapidly as you can for up to one minute.

43-7

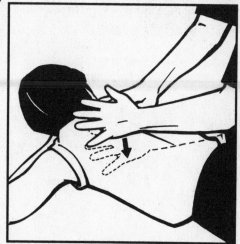

To finish, use the flat surfaces of the hands and fingers to briskly slap from the upper back to the tailbone.

LOWER-BACK DO-IT-YOURSELF

This one helps relieve pain and tension as far up the spinal column as you can comfortably reach.

43-8

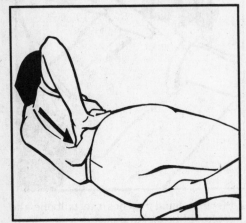

Lie on your side on the floor with knees bent and posture relaxed. Use the flat of the thumb to stroke down along the sides of the spinal column from as far up as you can reach down to the tailbone. Repeat several times.

43-9

Next, stroke with the thumb beginning at the spinal border and flaring outward, following the line of the ribs. Return to the spinal border, place thumb slightly below previous position and do again. Repeat this motion several times. Turn over and repeat on opposite side.

Chapter 44

LEG PAIN

It's a hard world we live in—just ask your legs.

Miles of concrete assault our legs in office buildings, shopping malls and airport terminals. We pound our limbs against it almost every day, then go home to hit the fitness trail, where we often walk, run or dance our way across some more. Too often the result is pain.

Consider that more than $2 billion is spent annually on "sports medicine." That money isn't being spent just by athletes, but by average people who sought fitness on legs that were ill-prepared for the tasks they were being asked to perform. And whether it's a runner's knee or a shopper's cramp, leg pain can and does work its way into other parts of the body, including the back.

Sports-massage therapists say the problems they most often see are cramps in the back of the leg, shin splints, "trick" or runner's knee, swollen ankles, fatigue, feelings of pins and needles, numbness, sciatica, heel spurs and sore bones.

But take heart. Some experts believe that many of the above complaints can be traced to muscle spasm, which means they respond favorably to massage. But first some cautions:

"With leg pain," says Susan Koenig, academic director of the National Holistic Institute, a massage school in Emeryville, California, "I always recommend searching for swelling, especially if it's a pain from overdoing. If there is some general swelling, it's very helpful to lie down and put the leg up high so that gravity can take circulation back to the heart."

For those times when trauma isn't involved—when your legs are simply tired after a long day of standing or stiff after a brisk weekend workout—the soothing touch of massage seems particularly well suited. Because the legs are within easy reach for most of us, we've included a number of self-help techniques in this chapter, as well as some relaxing mutual-massage movements.

"When it comes to my own legs," Koenig says, "I do what I call intuitive massage. I just search along and feel for trigger points or tight spots, applying pressure to them as I go. When I find one I simply press on it, holding for three to 10 seconds."

For calf cramps that wake you up in the middle of the night, Koenig offers this tip: Fill your bathtub with an inch or two of cold water and walk around in it barefoot for a few minutes before going to bed. No more cramps, she claims.

REAL RESISTANCE

"I really like resistance massage work," says massage instructor Susan Koenig. **"It's a very safe way to work on sore muscles without doing any further damage."** Resistance works by forcing blood and fluid through the muscles, she says. Here's one variation you can have done by someone else, or do to yourself.

44-1

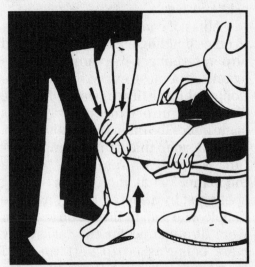

Have the recipient sit in a chair. Place your hand on the knee, applying moderate pressure. Ask the recipient to lift her leg as you apply resistance. Allow the foot to slowly lift an inch or so from the ground for a count of five seconds. Relax the leg. Alternate from leg to leg and repeat several times.

THE SHAKER

Stiffness in the thighs is sometimes responsive to shaking, as in this simple technique.

44-2

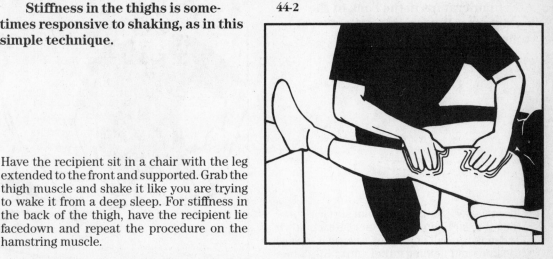

Have the recipient sit in a chair with the leg extended to the front and supported. Grab the thigh muscle and shake it like you are trying to wake it from a deep sleep. For stiffness in the back of the thigh, have the recipient lie facedown and repeat the procedure on the hamstring muscle.

THE CRAMP ENDER

For those all-too-common cramps in the back of the calves, here's a quick-relief technique.

44-4

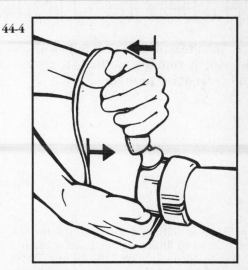

44-3

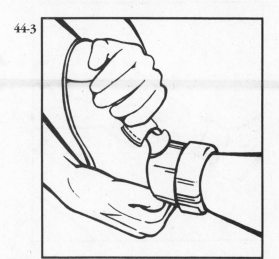

Have the recipient sit in a chair facing you. Place her heel on top of your knee and brace it with your hand. Place the other hand over the top of the foot.

Instruct the recipient to flex the foot backward against your hand. Let the foot move slowly back while placing firm resistance against it. At the point when the cramp pain sharpens, resist the foot completely and hold in that position for several seconds. Continue this procedure throughout the entire range of motion.

HAMSTRING HELPER

For cramps in the back of the thigh, try this speedy first-aid treatment.

44-5

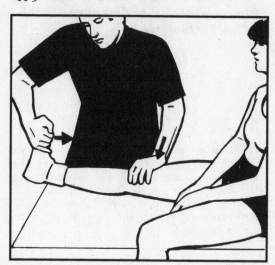

Place the recipient's leg on a flat surface. Force the leg to straighten at the knee. Reach down and grab the ball of the foot, pulling it toward the knee and holding it there until the cramp ceases.

SELF-HELP TECHNIQUES

The illustrations that follow show three do-it-yourself methods to treat and prevent leg problems.

44-6

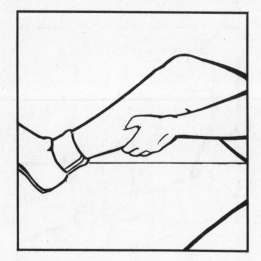

The Pincher. To relieve tight leg muscles, use the palms and fingers or the thumbs and fingers to gently hold and pull the muscle. Travel up and down the leg, holding and releasing front, back, inside and outside of thigh and calf muscles.

44-7

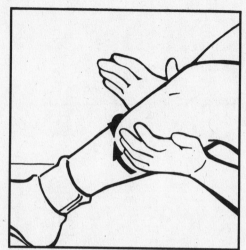

The Roller. To help relieve leg cramps, place your palms on either side of the calf muscle, straddling the bone. Roll the muscle body back and forth around the bone, working up and down the calf in a rolling, rhythmic motion. This technique can also be applied to the thighs. Roll for three to five minutes per leg.

44-8

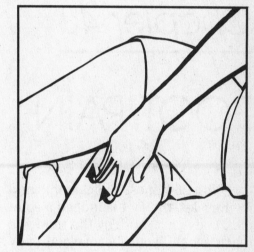

The Circle Rub. To improve circulation, lie on your side and bring both knees toward your chest, bending the bottom leg more than the top. With the balls of the fingertips, make small circular movements to the inside of the bottom leg and the outside of the other. Move along the muscle body, separating the fibers as you work up and down the leg. Use the heel of the hand for larger circles or greater pressure. Roll to other side and repeat.

Chapter 45

FOOT PAIN

With 26 bones, 56 ligaments and 38 muscles, the foot is indeed a complex body part. And, by the time you reach age 35, your feet have already carried you about 45,000 miles.

Small wonder that so many of us suffer from aching feet at one time or another. There's just so much to go wrong.

Thankfully, those overworked and often-neglected ligaments and muscles respond well to massage. There's only one thing to remember—press *hard*.

"Don't be afraid to pour it on," advises massage instructor Jeanne Aland. "If you really want to have an impact and produce a lasting effect, you have to be willing to use some pressure."

Aland believes in using "a lot of thumb pressure, right into the sole of the foot. Especially right behind the toes and all around the heel." Thumb pressure and friction in the hollow place on top of the foot right where it joins the ankle also feels good, she says.

Just remember to work hard. Notes Aland: "If you're working with people who have foot pain, they are hurting already and they want relief. They'll put up with the pain during the massage to get that relief."

DEEP TREAT

This massage is designed to work deep and help revive sore muscles in tired, aching feet.

45-1

Cushion the sole of the foot in the palm of one hand and stroke down from the ankle to the toes with the other, using firm pressure. Follow a straight path over the instep to the toes and repeat on either side of the instep, covering the entire foot twice.

45-2

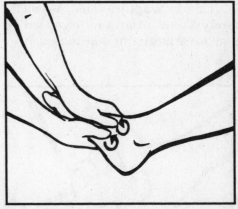

Grasp the sole with the palms and place the thumbs under the anklebone on the inside of the foot. Knead in small circular movements over the ankle to the metatarsal joints on the bottom side of the foot, then stroke back with the thumbs to the original position. Press firmly, rolling the muscles underneath your thumbs. Repeat once.

45-3

Grasp the toes with the left hand. Cup the right hand slightly and place the side of it at the base of the toes. Exerting deep pressure, stroke down the sole toward the heel, turning the hand so that it ends the movement with the palm flat on the table. Repeat this movement several times.

FEELS SOLE GOOD

This one's aptly named, as you'll surely discover the minute you get or give this stimulating sole massage.

45-4

Place the thumb pads of both hands on one sole with your fingers laced around the top of the foot. Using firm to heavy pressure, work from the base of the toes to the bottom of the heel several times with a kneading or pulsing motion. Dig into the tissue to stimulate the entire sole of the foot. Work from front to back and reverse.

45-5

Make a tight fist and work with a twisting motion into the sole of the foot from toes to heel. Brace the foot with your other hand to keep the recipient from having to push against your pressure. Work each foot from front to back and reverse several times.

Part IV

MASSAGE: A USER'S GUIDE

Chapter 46

THE MASSAGE SETTING

Dreaming of heading to the coast for one of those California earthquakes of a massage? You know—the crumbling, tumbling, humbling kind that promises to loosen ancient knots, release limitless creativity and restore your faith in all members of the animal, vegetable and mineral kingdoms. Or is it to other points on the globe that you're drawn? Banishing your tensions to another time zone sounds like a fine idea, but consider this before you start packing: You don't need to go any farther than your own home to experience the far-away feelings and relaxing benefits of a great massage.

A spare room or even a corner of your bedroom can be a quite suitable place for you and a close friend to explore the unique geography of the human body through massage. In private and familiar surroundings, you can practice—at your own pace and at little or no expense—many of the massage techniques described in this book.

Creating an environment conducive to a truly relaxing massage can be simple and even fun. The following guidelines will help you arrange for a terrific hands-on experience at home.

A Room of One's Own

"A separate room for massage is best," says massage therapist Marilyn McAfee, who massages clients in a workspace in her home when she isn't on the road massaging Olympic athletes or runners in the Boston Marathon. "The whole point of massage is to relax completely. You need a space that's free of everyday distractions and feels completely your own."

This should pose no problem if yours is a huge house in which extra rooms go begging. Most of us live a bit more simply, but still you might manage to set aside a separate space with a bit of rearranging. How about that room down at the end of the hall, for instance, the one carpeted with wall-to-wall junk you've been forever meaning to throw out? Now's a good time to do it.

You might be able to create a room where one doesn't even exist right now. McAfee sectioned off a corner of the heated basement of her Pennsylvania house, put up a couple of walls and a door and—voilà!—instant workspace.

How big should your room be? "What is most important is that the room feel comfortable," says Kathryn Hansman-Spice, director of the Potomac Massage Training Institute in Washington, D.C. "It's a matter of personal preference. You don't want to feel cramped, but some people actually prefer smaller spaces to larger ones. They feel safer. Remember that you're trying to establish an intimate setting."

If you decide to invest in a massage table (we'll get to that later), your space should be big enough that the person giving the massage can move around it comfortably. Allow at least two feet on all sides, says Hansman-Spice, in order to properly position yourself to give an effective massage. If you're planning to give massage on a mat on the floor, you'll need enough space to perform maneuvers like crawling, sitting, kneeling and stretching.

A separate room for massage isn't absolutely necessary, though. The main point is to be someplace where you can completely let go. You may find an uncluttered corner of your bedroom or family room relaxing. If you have a fireplace, a massage on the rug in front of the glowing embers can be exquisite. Be sure to find a place that's very quiet, outside hearing range of chit-chatting family members, roaring traffic, blaring television sets, agitating washing machines and ringing telephones. Massage is a process of entering a peaceful place within oneself. For many people, making that transition is difficult enough without having to fend off high-decibel distractions.

For a change of pace, consider, too, the potential pleasures of a peaceful outdoor setting when the weather is right. (See the box "Massage Alfresco" on page 378.)

Your special space selected, you're now ready to make a few additional preparations.

Keep It Warm

Ever try to relax when you're shivering with cold? It's not easy. So keep the room you do massage in nice and toasty—at least 70 to 75°F. This may seem too warm, but massage oil on the skin tends to make a person colder. In climates where winter roars in like a lion, keeping the room temperature up in the 80s can be delightfully cozy. By the way, you needn't blast up the heat in the whole house if your massage room is on the cool side. Try a space heater instead.

Massage Alfresco

"The best massage that I ever received," recalls Kathryn Hansman-Spice, "was outdoors in a gazebo in Hawaii. The warm, tropical breezes were flowing through. I could hear the fronds of palm trees waving in the wind. It was wonderful."

A massage outdoors can be paradise if the circumstances and climate are right. For massage therapist Jan Benlein, who works in California and Hawaii, giving massages outdoors comes naturally.

"In Hawaii, I have an open lanai [patio] surrounded by wild gardenias, hibiscus flowers and exotic vines with huge leaves shaped like hearts. The foliage, the birds, the warm weather—they're all absolutely lovely," she says.

Benlein's California clients, ensconced on a patio surrounded by a tall fence, often partake of a form of skin-bracing massage that involves a thorough dousing in cool water from her garden hose!

Fresh air, sunshine, warm breezes and the ministrations of great massage—the mere thought probably has you heading for the door with a mat and a bottle of oil. Just remember to find someplace relatively quiet. And stay out of direct sunlight if you or your partner is fair-skinned and prone to sunburn. Finally, make sure the coast is clear of mosquitoes, a definite deterrent to relaxation.

Go find yourself a warm-weather friend and share a sensational experience.

Keep the Lights Low

Bright overhead lights are great for performing surgery, but they're a glaring eyesore during massage. Soft, indirect lighting emanating from a floor or table lamp is best. Or turn the lights off altogether and do your massage by the light of a few flickering candles. But a pitch-black room won't do, since it leaves you in the dark as to where you are with the massage.

Keep It Pleasant

Decorate your room with pretty paintings or photographs of natural scenery. Add plants, seashells or other items you find aesthetically pleasing. Clear out anything that's distracting. Books on a shelf, for instance, tend to draw your attention to their titles and away from your massage.

Getting Equipped

Some leisure-time activities require a lot of special equipment. Massage, fortunately, is not one of them. Aside from your empathetic hands, the most important tool is a comfortable surface for your partner to lie on while you work your magic.

Your bed is *not* a good surface for massage, says McAfee, though it may seem the perfect place. In the same way that you sink into the mattress at bedtime, your partner will sink down and away from the strokes of your massage. And you will end up with an aching back from the strain.

At some point you might want to invest in a massage table, but it's not absolutely necessary. The floor is suitable, especially while you're still learning the techniques. The drawback with floor massage is that it can be hard on your back. (Floor massage techniques described in chapter 37 can help prevent back attacks.)

If your floor isn't already carpeted with a thick rug, spread out a sleeping bag or several blankets covered with a bedsheet, suggests Alexis Phillips, an instructor and clinical supervisor at the Swedish Institute of Massage in New York. An exercise mat or a six-foot by three-foot piece of good quality foam rubber padding about two or three inches thick can be quite comfortable. Again, cover them with a sheet. You'll also need several pillows to sit and kneel on while giving a massage.

If you do eventually opt for a massage table, you will be getting two major benefits—improved leverage and lessened backstrain for the person who is giving the massage. What you will pay for a table depends on its features. For $200 or $300 you can get a basic padded table that folds up for storage. For $450 you can get a very nice adjustable model. For a few thousand dollars, you can buy one with a height-adjusting hydraulic lift and even built-in music. (See the box "Home Massage Resources" on page 381 or contact a local massage school for additional information.)

But before you go out and spend big bucks for a ready-made table, consider making your own. You can build a perfectly sufficient massage table for less than $100, says Hansman-Spice, who has helped many a fledgling practitioner hammer away at inexpensive alternatives. For starters, keep in mind that a standard massage table is 28 to 30 inches wide, 72 inches long, and wrist-high. (That is, when your arms are hanging down at your sides, your flattened palms should rest comfortably on the tabletop.) Then try one of the following designs for size.

Buy two wooden sawhorses or a pair of metal folding picnic table legs. Nail or screw a wooden board or door on top. Add a two-inch thick foam mat covered by a bedsheet.

Another option is to buy a used, six-foot long conference table (preferably one with folding legs for easy storage) from an office furniture store. You might need to alter the height and add stability by adding wooden braces at strategic places. Add a foam mat and sheet.

Your massage partner may appreciate a small, soft pillow under his head and another under his knees to relieve strain while he's lying on his back. A bedsheet or several towels to "drape"—as the pros put it—your partner during massage may be important both for purposes of modesty and warmth.

"I won't ever leave the person I'm massaging exposed," says Hansman-

Music to Massage By

Your body will relax more quickly during massage if you tune into certain types of music, says Steven Halpern, Ph.D., a well-known composer of New Age music and researcher into the physiological and psychological effects of music.

The right kind of music can actually make your breathing deeper and more regular. It can slow your heartbeat, too. Relaxing music sets up "a physiological rapport that leaves you more open to receive the energy of the massage," Dr. Halpern says. "It also makes *giving* the massage easier."

Your muscles and skin actually resonate to good music, Dr. Halpern claims. "The surface of the skin is literally a gigantic ear. We have sound receptors all over our bodies which, when caressed by a warm sound, open up and receive. You can actually feel your muscles and skin getting softer." Music can also help balance the right and left hemispheres of your brain, he says, thereby reducing feelings of stress.

Although classical music or light rock may seem relaxing, their rhythms, lyrics and melodic tensions may make them anything but. Try something specifically composed to encourage calm, such as Dr. Halpern's "Enhancing Massage," or pieces by Kitaro, Georgia Kelly and other New Age musicians. Those played on electric piano, flute, harp, and standard piano are especially effective. Nature sounds also work—but be sure to visit the bathroom before listening to a babbling brook, or your bladder's automatic release response may require that you excuse yourself in the middle of your massage.

Not every piece of relaxing music works for everyone, Dr. Halpern says, so pay attention to your unique responses. Notice your heartbeat and breathing. If you develop tension in your chest or tightness in your neck, turn the music off. But if it feels good, keep listening.

Spice. "You can work on only one part of the body at a time. Meanwhile, keep the rest of the body covered. When you get ready to work on a certain area—the right leg, for instance—lift the sheet from that leg and tuck it under the left leg."

Marilyn McAfee prefers to drape several warm, bulky towels over different sections of her subject's body. "That way I can take off a towel in one section instead of having to continually rearrange an entire sheet." She also keeps a blanket on hand in the event that her subject gets really cold.

Oils and lotions to enhance your

Home Massage Resources

Interested in buying a massage table? These companies, among others, are interested in selling you one. Call or write for catalogs and information.

Colorado Healing Arts Products
P.O. Box 2247
Boulder, CO 80306
(303) 449-2425

Golden Ratio Woodworks
P.O. Box 297
Emigrant, MT 59027
(800) 345-1129
In Montana: (406) 333-4346

Living Earth Crafts
600 East Todd Road
Santa Rosa, CA 95407
(707) 584-4443
(800) 358-8292
In California: (800) 336-4114

Oakworks, Inc.
427 South Main Street
Shrewsbury, PA 17361
(800) 558-8850
In Pennsylvania: (717) 235-6807

Stronglite Massage Table Kits (sells do-it-yourself kits)
425 South 41st Street
Boulder, CO 80303
(800) 289-5487

TouchAmerica, Inc.
P.O. Box 1304
Hillsborough, NC 27278
(800) 982-9296
In North Carolina: (919) 732-6116

massage will probably also be of interest to you. (See chapter 47.) Finally, a selection of relaxing music tapes, preferably long-playing ones that you don't have to change mid-massage, can help get the process flowing.

"Use sounds that will help you ease your mind," says Hansman-Spice. "For some people, that's New Age music. For others, it's nature sounds—birds chirping or waves rolling in."

"The environment you create should be totally conducive to relaxation," she says. "It should feel safe, comfortable, uncluttered and supportive. You should be walking into a world that says, 'This is your place, your time to let go of all the cares of the world.'"

Chapter 47

MASSAGE OILS

A great calm descends as you prepare for your massage. You and your partner retreat to the cozy corner you've set up for this purpose. The lighting is muted, the temperature soothingly warm. Your partner—who without much persuasion has agreed to go first—lies on his stomach beneath a freshly laundered sheet. Relaxing music plays softly. You are ready to begin. Gently lifting the sheet from your partner's shoulders, you draw it down his back and fold it across his waist. You briskly rub your palms together to warm them. You lean forward, reaching toward the smooth planes of your partner's shoulder blades.

Wait just one minute.

You've forgotten the massage oil. Without it, touching is apt to be tough —not at all the relaxing experience you hoped for.

"You need oil to be able to glide your hands smoothly over the surface of the skin," explains Paul Davenport, director of the Florida School of Massage in Gainesville. Using massage oil or a similar lubricating substance can enhance your partner's enjoyment of the experience and make the going a lot smoother for you.

Your choice of a lubricant is a matter of personal preference. A few professional practitioners use bath or baby powder, but others say it doesn't shake out as a great glide. Lotions get votes pro and con, too. For one thing, they're not as messy as oil and lotions are ideal, some say, for deep-muscle massage, which requires a lubricant that thickens slightly while it is worked into the skin. But lotions get soaked up very quickly and hence require constant reapplication. Cocoa butter, thicker than oil but not quickly absorbed like lotion, is another alternative for deep-muscle work.

By far, oils are the skin-smoothers of choice for four out of five professionals, says Robert Calvert, professional massage practitioner and publisher of *Massage Magazine*.

A World of Choice

How many types of massage oils are there to choose from? It depends on what part of the world you're asking about.

"In India, where massage is an ancient art, there are hundreds," says Calvert. "In Europe, where lotions and creams are favored, there aren't as many. Here in the United States, the selection falls somewhere in between."

Available at many health food stores, cosmetics counters and through the mail, massage oils come with a variety of ingredients. Some are unscented, some give your nose an altogether new experience. Some are called "natural," while others try to be slick and sophisticated. And the promised benefits—from the simple to the sublime—offer something for just about everybody.

The Basics

These uncomplicated oils contain relatively familiar oils such as almond, avocado, olive, coconut, apricot and peanut. "Our Therapeutic Massage oil and Revitalizing Massage oil are formulated to be very light, contributing to a nice, smooth massage," says Biotone's Jean Shea, who created the formulas. Most professionals today prefer such lighter oils, she says.

Basic oils are generally either very mildly scented or simply unscented. "Many people don't want to go away from a massage smelling like a flower," Shea says. Even if you and your massage partner both enjoy scents, the one *you'd* like to smooth on may be one *he'd* rather you didn't.

Some other brand names to look for among the basics include Elan, Original Swiss Aromatics, Rainbow Research, Soothing Touch and Jason Natural Cosmetics. How big is the market for basic oils? "I wouldn't even want to try to estimate," says Shea. "All I know is that it's growing all the time."

Healing Herbs

Certain types of oils are absorbed by the skin during massage, many practitioners say. Adding substances like herbs to the oil, they believe, can further a massage's therapeutic effects.

Mara Nesbitt, a massage therapist in Portland, Oregon, prepares an oil containing calendula, lemon balm, lavender and other herbs she says she has chosen for their abilities to help relieve inflammation, muscle pain and bruising.

You can also purchase a prepackaged product called Mean Bombay Green (Myostal), produced by a pharmaceutical firm in India. The oil "contains more than 40 herbs that traditionally have been used to relax tight muscles and pacify the nervous system," claims Ray Rosenthal, distributor of Indian Herbal products.

Essential Oils

Extracted from flowers, herbs, roots, leaves, barks and woods, essential oils deeply penetrate the skin and have powerful medicinal and psychological effects, say their producers. These often-expensive oils are not massage oils *per se*. But they can be purchased, like the perfumes and colognes they resemble, in small quantities and then added to basic oils to create especially aromatic—and supposedly healing—massage oils.

The Aroma Vera company, for example, features some 60 types of essential oils plus another 11 blends —or "synergies"—said to increase circulation, relieve pain and bring about a sense of calm, among other things.

"Most essential oils, which have been studied in prestigious medical universities in Europe, have an antiseptic effect," claims Marcel Lavabre, of Aroma Vera. "They protect you against infection and they stimulate cell regeneration, especially in the skin." Essential oils are used in aromatherapy, a popular part of massage in Europe.

The Madini family of Morocco has been producing essential oils for a very long time—for 14 generations, to be exact. The oils are not simply powerful, says Stephanie Marco of Talisman, a store in Woodstock, New York, that distributes the oils. "They are charged with energy," she claims, "prepared in an alchemical fashion and prayed over in the Islamic tradition. They are therapeutic emotionally and spiritually."

Essences of Gems

As if massage oils containing spiritually charged plant oils weren't exotic enough, you can even find oils containing essences of semi-precious stones such as lapis lazuli, says Mary Stout, training director for the staff of massage therapists at the Kripalu Center for Yoga and Health in Lenox, Massachusetts. "But the effects were very subtle," she says of her brief experiments in giving gem-laden massages.

Choosing an oil suitable for your purposes can be fun, but it might get expensive, too. You can spend $10 for an eight-ounce bottle of basic massage oil or almost $300 for one-third ounce of a rare essential rose oil from Turkey. (For help in making your selection, see the box "Choosing the Right Oil" on page 385.)

Making Your Own

An alternative to purchasing premixed massage oils is making your own, as many professional practitioners do.

Almond oil, sesame oil, peanut oil and other vegetable oils make perfectly sufficient massage oils without adding anything else, says *Massage Magazine*'s Robert Calvert.

Almond oil is perfect for the beginner, he says. "It lasts for a long time, it's not too thick, not too thin and not too greasy."

One oil *not* to use is mineral oil, he adds. Its large molecules can clog up your skin pores. (Baby oil, too, contains mineral oil.)

Choosing the Right Oil

What qualities are important in selecting a massage oil? Follow the guidelines of *Massage Magazine*'s Robert Calvert, who oversaw his publication's review of more than 30 oils:

Cap Device

As inconsequential as it may seem, the cap on the massage oil bottle is important as an aid to controlling the amount of oil dispensed. (The bottle itself, by the way, should be breakproof plastic.) A standard twist-off cap is the worst kind, Calvert says. When you remove it and set the bottle down, an oil spill is just waiting to happen, and you can't easily control the amount of oil you pour out. Choose a product with a cap that flips open or stays open, much like a squeezable ketchup bottle, dispensing only a small amount of oil at a time.

Scent

In rating the odors of oils, the comments of Calvert and his reviewers ranged from "mild" to "yuk!" Try to get a good whiff of the massage oil you're thinking of buying. An unpleasant scent can undo an otherwise pleasant massage.

Slipperiness/Greasiness

See if you can get a handful or small sample of the oil you're interested in so you can do actual hands-on tests of its slipperiness and other characteristics. Slipperiness and greasiness are related to the kind of massage you're planning to give, Calvert says. If you're planning to use techniques that move deep into muscle tissues, you want an oil that's *not* slippery and greasy. If you're doing a general massage, such as Swedish massage, a slippery and somewhat greasy oil is just right, because it is not easily absorbed.

Viscosity

The thickness of an oil makes a difference when it comes to what's called "drag." Olive oil, which is very thick, increases drag, allowing you to do long, slow strokes, Calvert says. Lighter oils, or a mixture of thick and light oils, are best for moderately or fast-paced strokes.

Workability

Ask yourself how you like the oil overall. Does it feel good on your hands? How does the person receiving the massage like it? Your answers will be very subjective, but no matter; the point of all of this is to choose an oil that you enjoy and can count on for many a pleasurable massage.

How to Apply Oil

There is a wrong way and a right way to apply oil during a massage. Slathering it all over your partner so that he feels like a basted turkey headed for the roaster—that's the wrong way. The right way is to apply oil to one area at a time, with sensitivity and subtlety, creating a trusting connection between you and your partner from the very first touch.

Always warm the oil first in your hand, says Florida Massage School director Paul Davenport. (Proper storage of oil requires that you keep it in the refrigerator, so a dose straight from the bottle to your partner's skin could be quite a shock.) View the application of oil "as part of the massage itself," he says. "Apply it to your own hands first. Then you can apply it to your partner's body."

The quantity of oil will vary depending on the type of massage you're doing. You'll need more oil for long, flowing strokes than for deep, stationary ones. It also depends on how dry your partner's skin is—and how hairy.

What's a good rule of thumb? "If I'm working on the leg—you work only on one section of the body at a time—I need enough to apply it in smooth, gliding strokes all the way from the foot to the hip and back again," says Davenport. "I put only enough oil in the palm of one hand that if I held my hand out flat, it wouldn't drip off, but the little cup-like depression in the middle of my palm would be filled.

Then I put my palms together and smooth the oil over both hands. That gives me just enough lubrication to move over the skin."

For an arm or other smaller sections of the body, a little less oil is required. "The important thing is to have enough oil so that you can glide over the surface of the skin, but not so much that it becomes an oily mess," Davenport says.

Leave the oil bottle sitting on or near the massage table or mat so you can reach it and apply more as you go along. Some practitioners believe it is important to maintain body contact with your subject throughout the entire massage, even when reaching for and applying additional oil. "For someone just learning, having continual contact is a good idea," says Davenport. "What you want to build in your massage is continuity, a sense of flow. If your hands come off and then go back on abruptly, that can be startling."

To maintain contact while adding oil, rest your upturned hand on your partner's body at the same time that you pour oil into your palm. But don't be compulsive about keeping in touch, Davenport says. That can be just as unsettling as an abrupt move. Mary Stout of the Kripalu Center expresses similar sentiments. "I prefer to focus on an in-depth energy contact. If I'm really with the person in my thoughts and in my heart, the physical contact doesn't have to be constant."

Finally, remember that oil on a

Homemade Healing

Try creating your own healing oils, using a base of vegetable oil and adding herbs or essential oils according to these recipes.

Herb Oil

This recipe was suggested by Mara Nesbitt, massage therapist: Gather or buy comfrey root, sage, St.-John's-wort, calendula, lemon balm, rosemary, lavender and angelica and combine them with sweet almond oil in a gallon jar. Place in the sun to infuse the oil with the herbal properties. Shake the bottle every few days. After several weeks, strain the oil through cheesecloth twice and through muslin once to filter out fine particles. Refrigerate, decanting just enough for a week's use at a time.

This oil is effective, Nesbitt says, for relieving inflammation, muscle pain, bruising and nervousness.

Essential Oils

This recipe was suggested by Marcel Lavabre of Aroma Vera: To four ounces of apricot kernel, sweet almond, grapeseed or other lightly scented vegetable oil, add 60 to 150 drops of essential oils. Makes enough for 10 to 12 full-body massages.

Lavabre recommends the following variations for specific healing qualities.

Calming. Add chamomile, fir, lavender, marjoram and orange essential oils to induce deep relaxation and to establish a balance of energy.

Tonic. Add lemon, nutmeg, peppermint, spearmint, sage and thyme essential oils. Use with an energetic, stimulating massage.

Pain reliever. Add birch, clove, ginger, juniper and marjoram essential oils for "rheumatic crisis," neuralgia and muscular pain.

Circulation. Add cypress, geranium, grapefruit, lemon and thyme essential oils to stimulate blood and lymph flow.

person's skin tends to have a chilling effect. Be sure to ask your partner from time to time if he's warm enough. And be prepared to cover him with another sheet or even a blanket.

Enjoy trying new oils and practicing the art of applying them, but remember that the real magic of a massage doesn't come in a bottle of sweet-smelling oil.

"Certainly people should feel free to experiment, but I don't believe they will find the perfect healing oil," says Robert Calvert. "My philosophy about touch therapies is that true healing takes place not because of a specific healing oil, but because of the quality of the relationship you are creating."

Chapter 48

MASSAGE TOOLS

Vrooom vroom. Click clack. Bzzzzzzzzz ... What are these people doing? Mike's got something that looks like an electric sander that he's running over his thigh. Alice is digging a little wooden "mushroom" into her shoulder. Jan looks like she's strapped into a parachute or something—is she *vibrating?*

Everyone is smiling.

We pulled this cast of characters together to try out a wide assortment of massage tools and gadgets currently being marketed in all sizes, shapes and price ranges, and to pick some winners. Here they are:

The Backstroke is a smooth, efficient little massage aid that is hard not to like. In fact, every one of our testers thought it was just great. Your partner grasps the wooden stem and runs the two attached racquetball-sized rotating spheres over either side of your spine. (Many of the ancient

Robert Walsh

oriental pressure points are found along this path.) One tester reported a nice tingly sensation radiating across his back. Another simply said "aaaah." Still another tried the Backstroke on his puppy and got a big wag in response. From Noriki, a division of Matrix International, Inc. Approximate price: $9.

The Backnobber, an S-shaped metal rod with wooden balls at either end, is designed to reach around and work the muscles of your back and shoulders as if you were standing behind yourself. The tool's action is designed to simulate the hands-on techniques of pain-control therapists

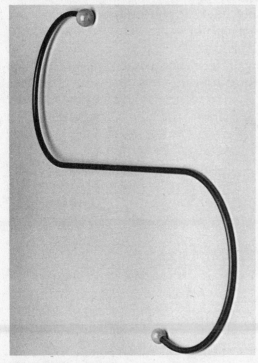

Robert Walsh

who practice trigger-point myotherapy and acupressure. It's so simple a concept, you'll be amazed no one thought of it sooner. You may also be amazed at how easily you can take a kink out of your own back. It sells for about $20, from The Pressure Positive Company.

The Conair Body Tone has 12 little rubber fingers that rotate once you plug it in. Of all the massage tools we looked at, this one most closely

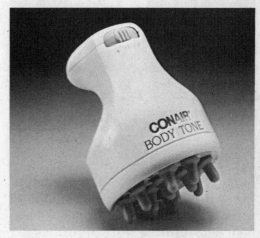

Courtesy of Hammacher Schlemmer & Company

approximates the feel of the human hand. That created a problem for a few of our reviewers, however, some of whom complained of "heebie jeebies." Others found the slow, natural movement more pleasing than the vibrations of most other electric massage tools. The Body Tone has two speeds, but not too much power—press it hard and it starts to groan. Be careful that those rubber fingers don't snatch your hair—they grab. Sells for around $45.

The Master Massager is the Mack truck of massage tools. It is heavy and powerful enough to give even a novice the massage power of Bruno at the health spa. A thick Naugahyde pad on this sturdy metal machine that oscil-

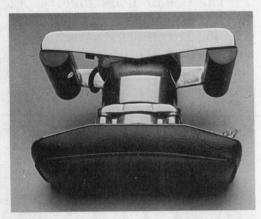

Robert Walsh

into your back muscles "like the thumbs of a masseur," as it says on the box. You may find at first that this particular masseur has Godzilla thumbs: that is, the thing hurts. But experienced Ma-Rollers say this pain is only a manifestation of your tension, and it will soon pass. One satisfied user says the $25 tool takes all the knots out of his back at the end of the day and leaves him feeling deeply relaxed. From Noriki.

Here's proof that a really good massage tool needn't cost a lot. Deemed good to wonderful by members of our panel were the following small, simple,

lates at up to 4,600 rotations per minute will shake, rattle and roll your muscle. This $115 mechanical masseur got nothing but "More! more!" from those receiving massages. From those *giving* the massages, however, we heard complaints about tired arms and itchy hands. From the Morton Company.

The Ma-Roller is a classic in the field. Lie down on the hard wood and allow its smooth, round bumps to press

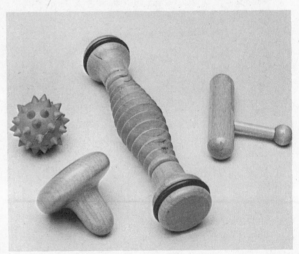

Robert Walsh

durable, and very inexpensive (under $10) items: **The Foot Flex** (center in photo above) from Noriki is a gracefully carved oblong wooden tool that can gently massage your stockingless feet. The pointed rubber **Sat-A-Lite Pain Eraser** (upper left) is for rolling over tense muscles or swirling under-

Robert Walsh

foot. The wooden **Knobble** from Knobble Associates (lower left) looks like a big mushroom; it really digs into those sore areas. The trigger-shaped metal and wood **Index Knobber** (right) from The Pressure Positive Company gives a quick at-home deep-pressure massage.

Long day on your feet? Slip 'em into a pair of **Foot Chargers.** They're soft and plush and go *v-r-m-m-m-m,*

Courtesy of Hammacher Schlemmer & Company

gently vibrating your soles back to their mellow old selves. They are well worth the $60 investment according to one tester who slipped her tired feet into the humming slippers after ten hours and countless miles with her four-year-old daughter at an amusement park. Another tester said they relaxed not only her feet but her entire body. Foot Chargers have a heating element to keep your feet toasty warm as they're getting massaged. These remarkable slippers can fit up to a men's size 13. From Clairol.

Bongers, alas, deliver a bit less than promised. Our reviewers found that these $12 rubberized meat ten-

Robert Walsh

derizers neither "smash evil cellulite," nor "give your body paroxysms of unbridled ecstasy." But they are loads of fun. Bong yourself or bong your partner or buy two pairs and bong each other. These rubber balls on springy metal handles offer an effortless way to give an energizing massage. From the Bongers Company of Los Angeles.

The Foot Spa from Clairol Research vibrates your feet and allows them to soak in warm water at the same time, meaning double relaxation for those tired footsies. It sells for about $55, is convenient to use, easily portable, fairly quiet and—above all—makes you feel like you're standing at ebb tide in some tropical sea. A four-way control dial allows you to adjust

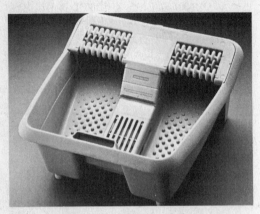

Courtesy of Hammacher Schlemmer & Company

foots in our testing team compared their first jump into the sandals to walking on—ouch—rocks. But after an initial period of discomfort comes the reward: One long-term user assures us that after several wears, the $25 sandals offer only revitalizing sensations to tired feet. From Maseur Products.

Now you can turn your own bathtub into a bubbly hot tub with the aid of the **HydroAir Spa,** from the Mitchell

both the heat and the vibrations. The Abacus-like rods of plastic discs are fun to roll your feet over while they dry.

Next time you're feeling down down under, walk off into the sunset in your Australian **Maseur Sandals.** Hundreds of rubber fingers are designed to gently massage the bottom of your feet as you walk. Some tender-

Courtesy of Hammacher Schlemmer & Company

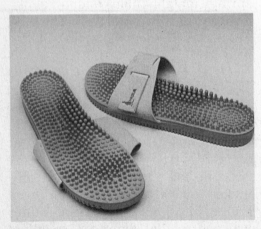

Robert Walsh

Corporation. Warm air is forced out of little holes along the length of a hose that rests snugly on the bottom of your tub. The Spa is quick to set up and dismantle and offers a lot of bubbles for $325. Its only drawback is the noise, roughly equivalent to that of an old-fashioned vacuum cleaner. If that doesn't bother you, the foaming warm water can be profoundly relaxing.

The **Acu-Massage Table,** at $1,900, is for those who are really serious about massage. In fact, short of hiring your own masseur, this is about as serious as you can get. This table heats up and sends eight rollers sliding underneath you, massaging 44 acupressure points on your neck, shoulders, back, thighs and calves. Just like a hands-on massage, most of what you'll experience on the Acu-Massage Table will be very pleasant, but there may be moments (such as when the larger roller is pushing against those tight back muscles) when you'll wince slightly. From HWE Products.

COPYRIGHT THE SHARPER IMAGE

Thump, thump, thump, here comes the **Thumper.** Massage experts call the action of this power tool *tapotement*, a steady percussive beat that loosens muscles the way karate chops do. This black belt of a machine (encased in jet-black plastic) sells for $300, so you'd expect to get a lot of chop. You do. The Thumper delivers 28 thumps per second. It's perfect for large muscles on large people. By HWE Products. Available only from the Sharper Image catalog.

The Acu-Vibe **Sports Massager** is slim and sleek, and for about $70 gives you enough vibrations to put any muscle to ease. Easy to hold and compact enough to slip into your gym bag, the sports massager is a nice alternative to some of the heavier-duty electric massage tools on the market. The rubber floating head is designed to direct its vibrations deep into your muscles.

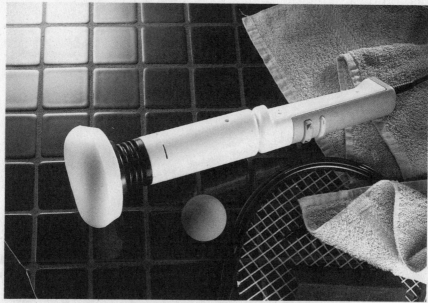

COPYRIGHT THE SHARPER IMAGE

Massage by Mail

Massage tools can be found in many department stores and specialty shops. Your best bet, however, may be through the mail: That's where most of the tools reviewed here were found. Below are a few places to start your shopping.

The Sharper Image has stores in many larger cities, or you can shop by mail. To order a catalog or find the location closest to you, dial (800) 344-5555.

Hammacher Schlemmer has stores in New York, Chicago and Beverly Hills. If you live elsewhere, they'll be happy to send you a catalog. Call (800) 233-4800.

Awareness & Health Unlimited in Columbus, Ohio, offers dozens of massage tools by mail. Call (800) 533-7087.

The Pressure Positive Company sells the Backnobber and other unique pain-relief tools. For a catalog, write to R.D. 2, Gilbertsville, PA 19525. Or call (215) 754-6204.

Slip yourself into the **Get-A-Way Chair,** and you won't want to get up for hours, maybe days—it's utterly luxurious. Rollers behind you smoothly glide up and down the entire length of your gently vibrating body, as soft music fills your head from the chair's built-in speakers. The attractive $1,900 chair (available in gray or beige) reclines almost to a horizontal position, has various settings to adjust vibration levels, and can also be programmed to concentrate on one particular part of your body at a time. From HWE Products.

COPYRIGHT THE SHARPER IMAGE

Chapter 49

TAPES THAT TEACH

Has every masseur and masseuse out there made an instructional videotape, or does it just seem that way? There's certainly a bewildering array of tapes available for purchase, all with the explicit purpose of trying to teach you the art of massage. But how much can you really learn using your VCR?

To find out, we put one of these tapes (*Massage Your Mate*) to an informal test. We loaned it to someone whose only qualification was that she had a "mate," her husband. She had never given a massage. Her only instructions were, "Watch this."

And she did. She popped the tape into the VCR, asked her husband to lie down on the floor in front of the TV, and then she just followed along.

Within two minutes she was giving a massage. "The tape was easy to follow," she says, "and my husband really enjoyed the experience. The tape gave me confidence. With another practice session or two, I know I could give a *really* effective massage!"

One word of caution: Most massage videotapes go into great detail when they massage the left leg, for example, but then they whiz through massaging the right leg. Our intrepid masseuse-in-training found that aspect to be confusing. "They assume beginners will remember the previous instructions, but you don't," she says.

One way around that is to keep your VCR remote control handy. In fact, it should be as much a part of the massage as the massage oil is. You can use it to pause the tape on a certain stroke to closely study the technique. Or you can rewind the tape and play a section over again just as you would reread a complex paragraph in a book when you don't quite understand the meaning.

But to get the full magic of these how-to videos don't just sit back and be a passive viewer. Get involved. That's how you will really learn.

To help you get started, we've reviewed and listed here several of the massage videotapes currently on the market. Enjoy.

Massage Your Mate
Running Time: 92 minutes
Format: VHS, Beta
Special considerations: hi-fi stereo
Suggested price: $39.95
Produced by Ozman Video Productions
Distributed by V.I.E.W., Inc.
34 East 23rd Street
New York, NY 10010
(212) 674-5550

The instruction on this video is presented by on-camera host Rebecca Klinger, a New York State–licensed massage therapist. The tape is broken up into what Klinger calls "chapters" dealing with both Swedish and oriental massage. Techniques concentrate on the abdomen, chest, back, neck, scalp, face, hands, arms and legs. Each section ends with a short review. During the review you get to see the strokes again, but this time in slow motion.

Another nice feature of this video is that while Klinger is explaining the strokes to you, one part of the TV screen shows her demonstrating them while a tiny window appears with an anatomical drawing of the body part in question. This way you actually get to see how the muscles run.

There's no background music on this video, and that's especially apparent at the end when Klinger suggests

that you conclude the massage "by cupping [your] hands over your partner's ears, then over the eyes." This sensory deprivation, she explains, will help your partner fully feel the effects of the massage.

Tips from the tape: In the back section, Klinger says it's good to begin the massage with a shiatsu warm-up. "Take your thumbs and press down on the side of the spine, never directly on the spine. Push the muscle across toward the outside of the body, not downward."

In the leg section, she advises the at-home viewer to use "no pressure at all on the back of the knee, especially if the kneecap is resting on the floor." With a determined look on her face she also adds, "Use lots of oil if the leg is hairy," and "When in doubt, effleurage."

Massage for Health
Running time: 65 minutes
Format: VHS, Beta
Special considerations: 40-page massage handbook included
Suggested price: $24.95
Produced by Steve Adams
Distributed by Healing Arts Home Video
1229 Third Street, Suite C
Santa Monica, CA 90401
(213) 458-9795

This is the *Gone with the Wind* of massage videotapes. It is a beautifully shot, big-budget production with Shari Belafonte-Harper as the host and sometime massage-ee.

It begins with a skit starring Shari and John Moschitta, the fast-talking actor featured in many commercials. Once Moschitta gets going it may be hard to understand what he's saying, but once the massage part of the video gets going, it is straightforward and easy to comprehend.

Two people do the massaging on the tape. Mirka Knaster is a massage therapist, contributing editor to *East-West Journal* and a former columnist for *Massage Magazine*. James Heartland was a sports-massage therapist at the 1984 Olympics and the Los Angeles Triathlon.

The video, which features Swedish massage, covers the whole body and is quite thorough. Almost nine minutes are devoted just to the front of the legs, for example. A soft musical score plays throughout the video, which ends with a 12-minute segment featuring Belfonte-Harper showing you what she calls "stress breakers." Those are stretching and self-massage techniques that she says are supposed to "release tension and act as quick pick-me-ups."

Tip from the tape: Before massaging the front of the legs, "check the lower back for a curve [between the back and table or floor surface]. If it's there, that indicates tension. So place a pillow under the leg not being massaged and that will lower the arch of the back."

Massage . . . The Touch of Love
Running time: 28 minutes
Format: VHS, Beta

Special considerations: for adults (nudity)
Suggested price: $39.95
Produced by Bruce Seth Green
Distributed by MCA Distributing Corp.
MCA Home Video
11312 Penrose Street
Sun Valley, CA 91352
(818) 768-3520

"Massage is an elegant testimony of friendship and affection and is a thoroughly sensual experience between two people . . . communicating love through touch." That's the opening line of this tape and while the off-screen female announcer doesn't emphasize the word "sensual," the video surely does.

This video has a rich visual quality, but if you don't have a taste for nudity, it might not be the one for you. From the first frame to the last you watch men and women massage each other from head to toe in front of a roaring fireplace.

But don't hit the eject button. There is no sex on this tape, but there are plenty of useful massage tips.

Swedish massage techniques are featured, with segments ranging from a high of about three and a half minutes for the back, to just over two minutes for the feet. Other segments cover the head and face, chest and stomach, arms and hands, legs and buttocks.

Whenever the announcer is giving you tips, the camera zooms in close so that you can see clearly how it is done. A celestial musical score plays softly in the background.

Tips from the tape: "When you are being massaged, never anticipate. Your partner needs no help. Just relax and enjoy." During the leg segment you learn that, "bending the knee is a good time to massage the calf because when the knee is bent the calf muscle is relaxed." In the same segment you are also told "that when you massage the lower leg, mentally divide the calf (vertically) into strips, then glide your fingertips from the ankle to just short of the knee."

Personal Massage for Health and Relaxation

Running time: 45 minutes
Format: VHS, Beta
Suggested price: $29.95
Produced by Herbert Shapiro,
  Registered Massage Therapist
Distributed by Superb Productions
1333 West Loop South, Suite 740
Houston, TX 77027
(713) 622-0880

According to Herbert Shapiro, the on-camera host, this videotape is "a step-by-step program of personal massage techniques that you can adapt and expand to your own personal needs."

Leading a group of people sitting on a living room floor, Shapiro goes through a series of Swedish and acupressure self-help massage techniques that range from a six-and-a-half-minute segment focusing on the legs and hips, to just under three minutes for the fingers and hands. Other segments include arms and shoulders, chest and neck, head and face, toes and feet, and the tape concludes with the back and neck.

This is not a big-budget production, some scenes are washed out, and there's a technical glitch where the audio does not quite match the speaker's lips in some parts.

While the title mentions health, there isn't any time devoted to the specific health aspects of massage. What *is* provided is lots of information on self-help techniques that can aid relaxation, and maybe relieve sore, aching muscles.

Tips from the tape: "Massage the neck while lying down so the muscles that hold the neck up while standing will be at ease." Regardless of the area that you are massaging, Shapiro gives tips on how to make self-help techniques easy: "The hand and arm doing the work—try to keep as close as possible to the side of your body with your shoulder down and relaxed. The part that is being massaged—try to rest it on something whenever possible."

Massage for Relaxation

Running time: 45 minutes
Format: VHS, Beta
Suggested price: $38.88
Produced by Cleo Mooney
Distributed by New & Unique Videos
2336 Sumac Drive
San Diego, CA 92105
(619) 282-6126

Massage for Relaxation is not just an instructional tape on massage. It is a philosophy of love. Massage is a way of loving, devoting time to the body and preparing it for the pleasures of life," so says Cleo Mooney at the beginning of this tape.

This low-budget production is broken up into two sections. The first segment—25 minutes worth—shows how to give a Swedish massage to someone else. The second part consists of various self-massage techniques for the face, neck, feet, and other areas. The tape ends in the shower, with Mooney showing you "the grand finishing treat . . . a salt rub." (Don't worry about adjusting your set's color. It's the videotape production that wasn't color-balanced correctly in spots. Just remember: It's them, not you.)

Tips from the tape: "People with glasses really enjoy it when you massage their outer ear." When giving a massage to someone else, Mooney advises that you "develop a rhythm like a dancer. Use your whole body to do the massage, not just your arms."

Don Wright's Basic Massage
Running time: 60 minutes
Format: VHS, Beta
Special considerations: some nudity
Suggested price: $19.95
Produced by Resolution, Inc.
Distributed by Academy Home
    Entertainment
1 Pine Haven Shore Road
Shelburne, VT 05482
(800) 972-0001

This is a no-nonsense approach to the genre that is loaded with information. Don Wright covers massage from head to foot with the emphasis on Swedish techniques. Everything is very carefully explained and demonstrated—Wright's lesson on the percussion stroke using the side of the hand is especially informative.

Music plays throughout the tape, but the natural sounds, of skin rubbing on skin, can also be heard, giving the soundtrack a more realistic, immediate feeling. This is not a big budget production, but when it comes to basic massage techniques, it's hard to beat.

Tips from the tape: To effectively massage the head and neck, "place your thumb and forefinger around the ear so you can hold the head easily in your hand." "And remember you're moving the skin, not just gliding over it."

Massage-Simple
Running time: 50 minutes
Format: VHS
Suggested price: $19.95
Produced by Rollin Swan
Distributed by Pooka Productions
12021 Wilshire Boulevard
Suite 383
Los Angeles, CA 90025
(213) 820-8253

There aren't any "experts" used on this tape, only beautiful models. But nonetheless, the information and tips provided are quite helpful.

This is virtually a head-to-toe Swedish massage, although the producers skip over the stomach area. They do focus for almost six minutes on the upper back, and the section on facial massage is unusually detailed.

At the end of each section the camera pans to the head of the model, who then looks up directly into the lens with a sexy stare. After a while, that started to rub us the wrong way.

Tips from the tape: "There's a [pressure] point between the thumb and index finger that is fantastic for reducing headaches. It's called 'The Great Eliminator' and it's in the middle of the 'meaty' area there. Apply pressure and hold for five seconds."

When massaging the front of the leg, "use the U shape between your thumb and finger to massage the calf, slowly working your way up to the knee. Use your fingertips to gently tap around the kneecap, like raindrops on a lawn."

During foot massage, "if your partner is ticklish, *increase* the pressure." Trust the experience of someone whose partner giggles while just putting on her socks, this works.

The Massage—Instruction for Beginners
Running time: 91 minutes
Format: VHS, Beta
Special considerations: stereo, some nudity
Suggested price: $39.95
Produced by Stephen J. Abraham
Distributed by The Bodymind Approach
5550 Mason Street
Omaha, Nebraska 68106

Illustrations take a straight twist in this video. Instead of just showing anatomical drawings from some medical textbook, massage therapist and host Stephen J. Abraham uses the human body as his canvas. You see the muscles in the jaw actually painted on the jaw. And the abdominal muscles are mapped out in a kind of massage-by-numbers approach. All in all, it's a very pleasant and effective way to learn. A light musical score plays throughout the video, which ends with Abraham giving pointers on how to kneel comfortably if you have to give someone a massage on the floor.

Tips from the tape: "Spread the oil on as if you're painting the leg with it. Cover every inch." When Abraham massages the back, he stresses that you should "massage the sides. Many times the sides of the back and armpits are overlooked." While massaging the front of the legs, he suggests that "after a friction rub . . . , feather [your fingers] down lightly on the leg to take off the friction charge." Whatever that friction charge is, the technique itself looks like it would feel mighty nice.

Feeling Good through Massage— The Edgar Cayce Way
Running time: 55 minutes
Format: VHS
Suggested price: $39.95
Produced and distributed by Association for Research and Enlightenment Press
215 67th Street
Virginia Beach, VA 23451
(804) 428-3588

"Realize that you are a channel of healing energy, and try and hold this attitude throughout the entire massage." In case you forget those words of advice, Analea McGarey, a registered physical therapist and host of the tape, will remind you of them often.

This presentation mixes massage with the spiritual teachings of Edgar Cayce, the early 20th century psychic healer. The techniques shown (basically Swedish) are clear and straightforward, but there's also something extra.

McGarey finishes the demonstration massage with a technique she calls the "Helmet of Gold." "Place your hands gently around [your partner's] head with your thumbs in the center of their forehead between the eyebrows. This area is known as the 'third eye.' Edgar Cayce indicated it is the center of spiritual sight. Through your hands focus the golden light, filling the body with the loving healing radiance."

From there the video goes into a nine-minute self-massage section with McGarey showing some additional hands-on techniques that you can use on yourself. A celestial musical score plays throughout the video.

Tip from the tape: "Focus the energy in your hands on the spine and slowly move them up.... There is energy in the spine that fills the entire body with vitality, and this movement will focus the body forces and draw them up the spine—balancing and clarifying the energy. Pause at the top of the spine to focus and visualize perfect health filling this body."

The Relaxing Touch: The Healing Art of Massage Therapy

Running time: 60 minutes
Format: VHS, Beta
Special considerations: won the Film Advisory Board's Award of Excellence, hi-fi
Suggested price: $29.95
Produced by Gary McKenna
Distributed by New Star Video
260 South Beverly Drive
Suite 200
Beverly Hills, CA 90212
(213) 205-0666

"Massage therapy is a scientific technique producing relaxation and stimulation," explains massage therapist William Ford, in a short introduction to this video. "It can ease mental and physical tension, and also help to alleviate aches, pains, and muscle spasms.

"These positive effects are due to the improvement of circulation throughout the body. Massage helps the body restore itself to a more comfortable feeling."

The masseur is Michael Levi, Ph.D., a visiting assistant professor in nutritional medicine at UCLA and former vice president of the California State Board of Massage Therapists. Throughout the tape, Dr. Levi talks more about the broad aspects of how massage can benefit your health. But he doesn't zero in on anything too specific.

This video is nicely shot, with pleasant music throughout. Time spent on each body area varies from over 13 minutes for the legs, to just over two minutes on the arms. And there's a particularly well-detailed segment on foot massage.

Tips from the tape: This video begins with one of the best and easi- est tips to remember when you are about to give a massage to someone. "It's important to think . . . smooth and soothe." Short and simple, it should be your motto.

Chapter 50

THE SPA EXPERIENCE

At 6:00 A.M., still crumpled like the bed you fell out of moments ago, you're storming up the side of a mountain. No slight incline or rolling hill, but a real mountain with green brush and red rock rising faster than your heart rate into the cool air over Vista, California. The long legs of the group leader disappear over a slope in the distance. Your chest pounds, and your face grows slick with sweat as you huff and puff after her. Just once you pause to admire the pretty view of strawberry fields stretching in every direction around the tile rooftops of Cal-A-Vie, exclusive spa and your almost-private paradise for one glorious week.

At 7:30 A.M. you're back at ground level, your stomach grumbling for breakfast in unison with those of your 17 fellow guests. At tables set with crisp linen and fresh flowers you enjoy something suitably healthy and low-calorie—a tiny bowl of delicious mixed-grain cereal adorned with five thin banana slices one day, fresh fruit cocktail and a thin slice of bran bread another.

With the last sip of your breakfast tea, you're off and running—and jumping and twisting and kicking—in a sun-dappled exercise room. To a steady Top 40 beat, you fight your way toward fitness through tendon-aching stretches, disco-dancing aerobics, weight-lifting, trampoline-bouncing, treadmill-walking, sit-ups, push-ups and pull-ups and anything else that might boost up your strength and stamina.

It seems to go on for hours. It does go on for hours. And just when you've had quite enough, when you couldn't possibly do another jumping jack, the music stops. You are finished, absolutely. You collapse in a tired heap, laughing weakly at your pain, belting down mineral water, knowing that soon—right after lunch, in fact—agony takes a hike to make way for ecstasy: A long, lingering afternoon of soothing, smoothing, tantalizing "treatments" given by the massage pros on Cal-A-Vie's extensive staff. For seven days, you are coddled and swaddled head to toe in every treatment offered, many of them more than once.

You have a traditional Swedish massage. Lying in a cozy yet airy room shuttered against outside light and sound, listening to relaxing flute music, you surrender to a soft-spoken massage therapist who brushes your skin with a light coat of nutty-smelling massage oil. For a long hour, she strokes, kneads and unknots every muscle in your body.

Then there are the "body glow" treatments, followed by aromatherapy. First, the therapist applies a slightly coarse cream of apricots and cornmeal to your skin, one small section at a time. Next, she gently wipes off the cream with a warm, rolled-up towel, removing along with it a layer of dry skin cells—the better to allow the pores of your skin to breathe, she says. Then she strokes your skin with a dry natural-bristle brush, bringing your blood rushing to the surface.

The aromas of aromatherapy change from day to day. Lavender, geranium, jasmine, rosewood, orange blossom, cypress, juniper, lemon grass —the essential oils of plants and flowers are absorbed through your skin, the therapist explains, with numerous therapeutic effects. The scent lingers in the air like a cool, fragrant fog. Your therapist's long, rhythmic massage strokes roll over you in slow waves. You flit back and forth between a light sleep and trancelike wakefulness.

You experience some types of massage you'd heard about but never tried. Shiatsu, for instance, the balance of yin and yang. Reflexology, seeking to soothe the pathways of pain in the arch of a foot, the tip of a toe.

Then there's thalassotherapy, turning you temporarily green with a coat of seaweed said to purge your body of toxins. And hydrotherapy, an underwater massage in a warm bath of sea salts and fragrant plant extracts, water jets rhythmically pulsating all around you.

You have scalp massages during hair conditioning treatments, hand and foot massages during manicures and pedicures, facial massages during beauty treatments. By week's end, you feel like a new person, like the person you know in your heart you're supposed to be—serene, happy, whole. You're ready to take on the world. You're ready to start planning your next visit to a spa.

A Vacation Whose Time Has Come

A million Americans go to spas every year, according to Jeffrey Joseph, president of Spa-Finders, a New York City travel agency that specializes in this unique vacation alternative.

"Spas are the Club Med of the 1980s," Joseph says. "In the past several years, their popularity as vacation spots has grown tremendously."

"In 1983 there were fewer than three dozen spas in the United States," notes another spa specialist, Naomi Wagman, president of Custom Spas Worldwide. "Today, there are nearly 300, not to mention several terrific ones just an hour's drive over the border in Mexico."

For some people, the term spa conjures images of crowds in Europe taking a therapeutic holiday submerged in baths of steaming mineral waters. Early spas in this country followed this traditional format, their guests "taking the waters" at hotspots like Saratoga Springs that promised relief from assorted aches and pains.

Today, spas encompass a vast range of styles and services and are located from one end of the country to the other (and throughout the world). Most American spas haven't a drop to do with healing waters, but they have a lot to do with self-improvement, from losing weight to reducing stress. Goals like those, and a structured program in which they can be accomplished, are the very essence of today's spas, says Joseph.

Who visits spas? "Most first-time spa-goers are undergoing some sort of change in their lives—a change of job, the last child leaving home, a stressful situation," says Joseph, "and they see a spa as a place where they can pull themselves together in a supportive atmosphere. It's their chance to change their lifestyle in a very positive way."

A great many people are attracted to spas' fitness programs, says Wagman. "Young people and older people alike go to spas," she says, "the young because they've grown up with the idea that they need to be healthy, and older people because they want to be fit, too. They realize there's no reason to age any more than they have to."

Fitness spas are in fact the most popular, says Joseph, combining challenging exercise programs with a variety of massage services. Spas that emphasize extensive pampering—massage, facials and assorted beauty treatments—are also well-attended. Unusual yet growing in popularity are holistic spas, where body, mind and spirit are addressed in environments that may feature everything from vegetarian cooking to meditation and yoga classes, often along with many unique types of massage.

Many spas combine a number of programs. Cal-a-Vie, for instance, encompasses the best of all worlds with its combination of high-powered fitness, gourmet diet and exquisite pampering programs. Great if you can afford it—at about $3,000 a week, this program is up there with the crème de la crème of American spas.

But you don't have to be rich to go to a spa. "In the old days, only the very wealthy could afford it," says Wagman. "The average working person wouldn't dream of it. But today, there are places where you can go for an entire week for as little as $500." Many spas also help you cut costs by offering weekend programs.

To find a spa that suits your specifications, talk to people who have gone to spas, or get in touch with a travel agent who knows the spa scene. Jeffrey Joseph's *Spa Finder* guide can give you an excellent overview with its up-to-date descriptions of more than 200 spas. (See the box "Your Spa Connection," above.)

Spas That Specialize

Going to a spa can certainly be a great way to experience first-hand many of the types of massage you've been reading about in this book. In fact, you may find it far easier and less expensive to go to a spa with an ambitious massage program than to seek out such services separately on your own—and you will enjoy the spa's added benefits while you're at it. To help you get started, we've compiled a sampling of spas that offer extensive massage programs.

Among the many factors you'll want to consider when selecting a spa is its cost. While $1,000 or more per week (per person, not including transportation or extra charges) seems to be typical for a week's stay, you'll certainly pay more at the most exclusive spas. You can also find out-of-the-way places that charge a lot less. We've indicated the relative cost—from ($$$) for the most expensive, to ($) for the least expensive—but be sure to check with individual spas or a travel agent for exact prices.

So go ahead—spoil yourself. You deserve it. Happy hands-on!

The Argyle
294 Country Club Road
Argyle, TX 77226
(800) 458-SPAS
Setting: Easy access to the Denton Country Club
Cost: $$
Emphasis: European-style luxury treatment, fitness
Action: Tennis, golf, horseback riding
Hands-on: From "the famed Kneipp system of hydrotherapy" to haysack wraps, this spa offers a

Texas-size treatment package. Includes Swedish massage, reflexology, salt glow, wet sheet wraps, and baths in mud, herbs, and botanic oils.

Baden-Baden Health Resort
611 El Camino Real
Carlsbad, CA 92009
(619) 931-1411
Setting: In a small villa-style hotel near San Diego
Cost: $$
Emphasis: Pampering, revitalization
Action: Aqua aerobics, martial arts, oceanfront walks
Hands-on: For something different, try the leg massage done with compressed air. The program also features underwater massage, paraffin and volcanic ash heat wraps and Swedish and deep-tissue massage.

Bluegrass Spa & Resort
901 Galloway Road
Stamping Ground, KY 40379
(502) 535-6261
Setting: 19th-century mansion in bluegrass country
Cost: $$$
Emphasis: Holistic fitness
Action: Stretching, aerobics, yoga, tai-chi
Hands-on: New Age program includes Swedish Esalen massage, Trager, polarity, shiatsu, reflexology, aromatherapy, salt glow and Dead Sea mud treatments.

Cal-A-Vie
2249 Somerset Road
Vista, CA 92084
(619) 945-2055
Setting: Peaceful, secluded valley north of San Diego
Cost: $$$
Emphasis: Stress relief, fitness and pampering
Action: Aerobics, hiking, yoga, pro tennis, golf
Hands-on: More than 20 therapists report every afternoon for hours of Swedish massage, shiatsu, reflexology, "body glow," aromatherapy, hydrotherapy, thalassotherapy, hand, foot and scalp massages plus numerous skin treatments.

Canyon Ranch
8600 East Rockcliff Road
Tucson, AZ 85715
(800) 742-9000
In Canada: (800) 327-9090
Setting: At the base of the Santa Catalina mountain range
Cost: $$$
Emphasis: Fitness
Action: Aerobics, court sports, mountain biking, life enhancement counseling, cooking classes
Hands-on: Offers bodywork not found at many spas, including Jin Shin Jyutsu, reiki, Trager, lymphatic massage, polarity and cranial system therapy, shiatsu and reflexology plus basic Swedish massage.

The Cliff Spa at Snowbird
Snowbird, UT 84092
(801) 742-2222
Setting: The ski slopes of Utah
Cost: $$
Emphasis: Fitness, weight reduction
Action: Skiing and other seasonal
    sports, state-of-the-art exercise
    equipment
Hands-on: End a day on the slopes
    with Parafango, a muscle-
    relaxing paraffin and volcanic
    ash heat wrap. Also offers a
    Swedish-style massage that incor-
    porates aspects of acupressure
    and shiatsu, plus hydrotherapy
    and herbal wraps.

Deerfield Manor
R.D. #1 (Route 402)
East Stroudsburg, PA 18301
(717) 223-0160
Setting: Country house in the Pocono
    mountains
Cost: $
Emphasis: Weight reduction, fitness,
    stress release
Action: Stretching, tennis, walks,
    yoga, aqua-aerobics
Hands-on: With a view of massage as
    good preventive medicine, the
    program includes Swedish medi-
    cal massage, deep-tissue and
    sports massage, shiatsu and
    reflexology.

Dr. Deal's Hawaiian Fitness Holiday
P.O. Box 279
Koloa'Kauai, HI 96756
(808) 332-9244
Setting: Tropical paradise
Cost: $$
Emphasis: Holistic health, weight re-
    duction, healthful gourmet cuisine
Action: Soft-impact aerobics to snor-
    keling, hiking
Hands-on: On the island that served
    as the location for the movie
    South Pacific, you'll find a
    varied program that includes
    Swedish massage, reflexology,
    shiatsu, polarity therapy,
    kinesiology, and deep tissue
    massage. Chiropractic adjustment
    and craniosacral therapy also
    available.

The Expanding Light
14618 Tyler Foote Road, Suite 25
Nevada City, CA 95959
(916) 292-3494
Setting: Foothills of the Sierra Nevada
    mountains
Cost: $
Emphasis: Spiritual reflection and
    rejuvenation
Action: Holistic medical treatments,
    retreats
Hands-on: Aspects of yoga are incor-
    porated into a program that
    includes shiatsu, acupressure,
    reiki, reflexology, and Swedish
    massage. A chiropractor is also
    available.

Feathered Pipe Ranch
P.O. Box 1682
Helena, MT 59624
(406) 442-8196
Setting: Big Sky Country in the Rocky
  Mountains
Cost: $
Emphasis: Holistic health
Action: Yoga, astrology, swimming,
  sunning, hiking
Hands-on: Muscle-sculpting massage,
  shiatsu and Swedish and deep-
  tissue massage are available during week-long personal growth
  retreats. Or learn to be a pro in a
  120-hour (2½-week) massage
  training program.

Harbin Hot Springs
P.O. Box 782
Middletown, CA 95461
(707) 987-0379
Setting: 1,500 acres north of the Bay
  Area
Cost: $
Emphasis: Holistic health, mineral
  pool bathing
Action: Swimming (swimsuits op-
  tional), sweat lodges, exploring
  nearby woods, streams and
  meadows
Hands-on: Specializes in watsu, a
  form of shiatsu performed in a
  whirlpool. Also offers Trager, reiki,
  reflexology, sports, deep-tissue,
  Esalen and Swedish massage.

Kripalu Center for Yoga and Health
Box 793
Lenox, MA 01240
(413) 637-3280
Setting: 350-acre estate in the
  Berkshire mountains
Cost: $
Emphasis: Holistic retreat
Action: Hiking, yoga, personal growth
  workshops, meditation
Hands-on: Therapists available 10
  hours a day, 7 days a week to
  perform a special Kripalu mas-
  sage, yoga therapy, polarity,
  shiatsu, reflexology, and an "out-
  rageous" 1¾-hour facial.

Le Pli Health Spa and Salon at the
  Charles Hotel
Charles Square
Cambridge, MA 02138
(617) 868-8087
Setting: In a hotel in the heart of
  Harvard Square
Cost: $$
Emphasis: Personalized nutritional
  consultation
Action: Low impact hydro-aerobics,
  indoor swimming overlooking
  the Charles River
Hands-on: Brings Russian massage
  to America, plus shiatsu, cross-
  fiber acupressure, polarity,
  Swedish and sports massage,
  herbal wraps and Italian mud
  treatments.

Murietta Hot Springs Resort & Health
    Spa
39405 Murietta Hot Springs Road
Murietta, CA 92362
(714) 677-7451
Setting: 46 acres of California coun-
    tryside
Cost: $$
Emphasis: European-style family spa
Action: Soaking in mineral pools,
    tennis, aerobics
Hands-on: Features a special "energy
    massage" that combines polarity
    therapy, acupressure, reflexology
    and craniosacral techniques to
    relieve tension. Also lymphatic
    massage, aromatic wraps, and
    the famous therapeutic Murietta
    mud baths.

New Age Health Spa
Neversink, NY 12765
(914) 985-7601 (800) NU-AGE-4-U
Setting: Colonial resort in the Cats-
    kill mountains
Cost: $$$
Emphasis: Holistic rejuvenation,
    fasting, fitness
Action: Cross-country hiking, skiing
    and snowshoeing, Zen meditation,
    tai chi, astrological consultations
Hands-on: Slow down during your
    juice fast with aromatherapy,
    shiatsu, reflexology, acupressure,
    Swedish and sports massage and
    Dead Sea mud wraps.

The Norwich Inn & Spa
Route 32
Norwich, CT 06360
(203) 886-2401 (800) 892-5692
Setting: In a country inn near scenic
    small towns
Cost: $$
Emphasis: Fitness, diet and pampering
Action: Swimming, jogging, tennis,
    golf
Hands-on: Program includes neck
    and shoulder massage, foot mas-
    sage and everything in between:
    full-body massage, body scrubs,
    aromatherapy, hydrotherapy and
    the house specialty, thalasso-
    therapy.

Rocky Mountain Wellness Spa and
    Institute
Box 777
Steamboat Springs, CO 80477
(800) 345-7770;
In Colorado (800) 345-7771
Setting: At the base of ski area in
    rugged mountain country
Cost: $$
Emphasis: Fitness, stress-reduction
Action: Cross-country and downhill
    skiing, swimming in natural min-
    eral springs, hiking, exercise
    classes
Hands-on: Improve your well-being
with a "body contour" herbal cream
treatment, lymphatic massage, reflexology, polarity, deep-tissue, sports
and Swedish massage.

Safety Harbor Spa and Fitness Center
105 North Bayshore Drive
Safety Harbor, FL 34695
(800) 237-0155 (813) 726-1161
Setting: Homey ambience in old
    Tampa Bay area.
Cost: $$
Emphasis: Exercise, nutrition and
    pampering
Action: Swimming in natural springs,
    weight training, stress manage-
    ment
Hands-on: Loofa scrubs, herb wraps,
    mineral baths and a variety of
    massage styles are offered by a
    staff of 30 massage therapists.

Sharon Springs Health Spa
P.O. Box 288-A Chestnut Street
Sharon Springs, NY 13459
(518) 284-2885
Setting: Victorian house in the country
Cost: $
Emphasis: Detoxification, weight
    reduction
Action: Yoga, dance, breath training
    and walking
Hands-on: Drive body toxins out
    with salt scrubs, herbal wraps,
    Dead Sea salt and mud wraps,
    aromatherapy, shiatsu, reflex-
    ology, Swedish massage and
    plenty of soaking, steaming and
    soothing in natural sulfur min-
    eral waters.

The Spa at Stowe
P.O. Box 1198
Stowe, Vermont 05672
(802) 253-9954
Setting: 200-year-old Vermont inn
Cost: $$
Emphasis: Fitness, nutrition
Action: Skiing, aerobics, squash and
    racquetball
Hands-on: Get Rolfed by appointment.
    Program also features reflexology,
    sports, deep-tissue and Swedish
    massage.

Sunrise Springs Resort
Route 14, Box 203
La Cienega, NM 87505
(800) 772-0500
Setting: Old Spanish community south
    of Santa Fe
Cost: $$
Emphasis: Holistic retreat, healthful
    gourmet food
Action: Hot tubs, sweat lodge,
    rollerskating, hiking
Hands-on: Wide-ranging program
    includes Trager, reiki, myotherapy,
    aromatherapy, Rolfing, deep-
    tissue and Swedish massage,
    reflexology, polarity therapy, and
    more. Acupuncture and chiro-
    practic services also available.

Index

Note: Page references in *italic* indicate illustrations.